Behavioral Response to Intervention

Creating a Continuum of Problem-Solving and Support

Randy Sprick, Ph.D.
Mike Booher, M.Ed.
Mickey Garrison, Ph.D.

with contributions by
Eleazar Ramirez, Ph.D., Vittorio T. Puente, Ph.D. & Alfonso Herrera

Published in the United States by
Pacific Northwest Publishing
2451 Willamette St.
Eugene, Oregon 97405
www.PacificNWPublish.com

11 10 9 8 7   6 5 4 3 2

ISBN: 978-1-59909-028-3

Cover design: Hannah Bontrager
Interior design: Natalie Conaway
Indexing: Potomac Indexing, LLC

TABLE OF CONTENTS

Chapter 1

Thinking Big *A Full Continuum of Problem-Solving and Support* 1

Chapter 2

Universal Prevention *The Role of the Leadership Team* 15

Chapter 3

The Framework *Building a Behavioral Response to Intervention* 53

Chapter 11

Chapter 12

THE AUTHORS

Randy Sprick, Ph.D., has worked as a paraprofessional, teacher, and teacher trainer at the elementary and secondary levels. Author of a number of widely read books on behavior and classroom management, Dr. Sprick is director of *Safe & Civil Schools*, a consulting company that provides inservice programs throughout the country. Each year, he conducts workshops for more than 20,000 teachers and administrators. As director of *Safe & Civil Schools*, he and his trainers work with numerous large and small school districts on longitudinal projects to improve student behavior and motivation. Dr. Sprick was the recipient of the 2007 Council for Exceptional Children (CEC) Wallin Lifetime Achievement Award.

Mike Booher, M. Ed., has worked as a school psychologist, lead school psychologist, and supervisor of psychological services for Guilford County Schools. He has developed school intervention and assistance teams, crisis intervention services, professional development activities for teachers and parents, and ADHD interventions. He also coordinated the Responsible Discipline Program (RDP), a schoolwide discipline and classroom management program based on *Foundations* and *CHAMPs*. For much of his career, Booher worked with school crisis and suicide intervention teams. He served as a co-trainer for the district's suicide intervention training and as a co-leader of one of the district's two crisis teams. In addition, Booher has taught at several universities and served as a clinical instructor for the School Psychological Program at the University of North Carolina at Chapel Hill.

Mickey Garrison, Ph.D., has been a teacher, administrator, and consultant. As a principal, her school was awarded national recognition and received attention from the George Lucas Foundation, which created a documentary about the school's accomplishments in mathematics (see www.glef.org/magic-of-math). She is currently the school improvement director for a joint venture among the Oregon Department of Education, Oregon's Education Service Districts, Oregon's K–12 system, and higher education. Under Dr. Garrison's leadership, districts are advancing school improvement from being an event to becoming an integral part of how their schools operate. As a consultant, Dr. Garrison specializes in training school teams to increase student achievement and improve behavior. She has coordinated numerous statewide and school district change initiatives. Dr. Garrison is currently developing training materials that support difficult-to-reach students in grades K–10.

ACKNOWLEDGMENTS

THE AUTHORS would like to acknowledge the following people who provided valuable input:

L.J. Sellers
Billie Jo Rodriguez
Jessica Sprick
Paula Rich
Bob McLaughlin
Lana Fry
Jim Whitaker
Laura Hamilton
Jane Harris
Sara Ferris
Natalie Conaway
Hannah Bontrager
Caroline DeVorss

TESTIMONIALS

"Educators charged with implementing an RTI framework in their school need very practical, hands-on guidelines and tools for making this new model of school improvement work. Of all the things written on RTI, there is nothing that approaches this book in terms of clarity and practicality. This book will be a goldmine for teachers and administrators who want to make dramatic improvements in student outcomes. This book is brilliantly conceptualized and written. It provides both a sound blueprint for guiding school improvement and a broad array of exceedingly practical, evidence-based practices that will transform how educators think about and design instructional conditions that foster hard work and productivity by all students. Without a doubt, this book will become one of the most frequently used resources for educators who want to make RTI work in their schools."

— Donald D. Deshler
Gene A. Budig Professor of Special Education; Director,
Center for Research on Learning, University of Kansas

"Response to Intervention (RTI), or more accurately multi-tiered coordinated early intervening services, is now at the forefront of every educator's agenda as our nation devotes its efforts to improving outcomes for all children using evidence-based practices. This volume, *Behavioral Response to Intervention*, is the first book I've seen that puts the science and practice of behavior support into a cohesive framework aligned with the big ideas of RTI. It provides proven practices from a team of authors without parallel in terms of their national impact in creating safe climates conducive to learning."

—Mark R. Shinn, Ph.D.
Director and Professor, National Louis School Psychology Program;
Projector Director, Northern IL Region of IASPIRE, a USDE/OSEP/ISBE Personnel
Preparation Project Supporting Implementation of RTI

"Randy Sprick's new book is a comprehensive and practical overview of the behavioral aspects of RTI. This isn't just about what Behavioral RTI should be—this book tells you exactly how to do it. If you're interested in this topic, you'll find an awful lot of valuable information here."

—Jim Knight, Ph.D.
*Research Associate, University of Kansas Center
for Research on Learning, Director of Pathways to Success*

"*Behavioral Response To Intervention: Creating A Continuum Of Problem Solving and Support* by Randy Sprick and his co-authors is a book that should be in the hands of any educator who works with the PBS and RTI models. Randy has a long history of writing and developing evidence-based interventions for implementation in the schools. This book provides a blueprint to answer many day-to-day questions that are often left unanswered in the PBS and RTI models. This resource book focuses on the "big picture" in developing a continuum of problem-solving that involves creating leadership teams, developing a culture of data collection, and identifying available resources down to such practical aspects as bullying prevention programs, social skills training classes, and homework rooms. The struggling student is the winner through this book's positive and practical approaches to prevention and intervention. It is a must for administrators, counselors, school psychologist, behavior specialists, behavior management team members, special education teachers, and any educator who wants practical and evidence-based answers to PBS and RTI's many questions."

—William R. Jenson, Ph.D.
*Professor, Department of Educational Psychology, University of Utah;
Author of the Tough Kid Book series*

"Randy Sprick and his colleagues have produced a truly seminal resource focusing on the behavioral side of the RTI model. This book explicates the RTI model for effective application in schools and classrooms in all the key areas of concern to educators and parents. The book is a roadmap to the successful implementation of RTI in the behavioral domain. It's indeed rare to see such a thoughtful, valuable resource that addresses so thoroughly all the critical issues and challenges involved in making the RTI model work as we think it should. There are very few, if any, RTI nitty-gritties of problem solving and implementation left untouched by this remarkable book. This is a book I wish I'd written. I congratulate the authors on this product, and I recommend it unconditionally."

—Hill Walker, Ph.D.
Co-Director, Institute on Violence and Destructive Behavior, University of Oregon

"Another incredible resource by Randy Sprick et al. It is research based, practical, and systemic in its approach to behavior RTI. This book will not sit on a shelf!"

—Judy Elliott, Ph.D.
Chief Academic Officer, Los Angeles Unified School District; Former Assistant Superintendent, School Support Services, Long Beach Unified School District

"Randy Sprick and his colleagues deliver yet another new fantastic resource that helps teachers spend less time working with resistance and disruption, and more time teaching. This book will help school personnel deliver effective services that include problem-solving, efficient use of personnel, and practical design/implementation of behavioral interventions. This is an excellent companion resource to Sprick's *Interventions: Evidence-based Behavioral Strategies for Individual Students.* While *Interventions* addressed the what, this book defines the who, when, why, and how of designing efficient and effective interventions. A 'must have' resource."

—Jim Ysseldyke, Ph.D.
Birkmaier Professor of Educational Leadership, University of Minnesota

"*Behavior Response to Intervention* (B-RTI) builds on the growing recognition that effective school interventions (academic or behavioral) should be
  (a) linked to school-wide systems,
  (b) based on regular data use, and
  (c) evidence-based.
The book provides accessible and proven strategies for schoolwide organization, classroom management, and individual student behavior support. Teachers will find specific intervention ideas with clear guidance on how to implement those ideas within a schoolwide system. School psychologists and behavior specialists will find that Response to Intervention themes familiar to academic support are extended to behavior supports:
  (a) invest first in prevention,
  (b) use data to identify and assess points of intervention, and
  (c) build a multi-tiered program of support with progressive increases in
      support intensity.
Administrators will find guidance for team composition, management and assessment that will assist in accurate use of recommended strategies throughout their school."

—Rob Horner
Alumni-Knight Professor, Department of Special Education and Clinical Sciences, University of Oregon

SAFE & CIVIL SCHOOLS

THE *SAFE & CIVIL SCHOOLS* SERIES is a comprehensive, integrated set of resources designed to help educators improve student behavior and school climate at every level—districtwide, schoolwide, within the classroom, and at the individual intervention level. The findings of decades of research literature have been refined into step-by-step actions that teachers and staff can take to help all students behave responsibly and respectfully.

The difference of the *Safe & Civil Schools* model is its emphasis on proactive, positive, and instructional behavior management—addressing behavior before it necessitates correction, collecting data before embarking on interventions, implementing simple corrections before moving to progressively more intensive and time-intrusive ones, and setting a climate of respect for all. As a practical matter, tending to schoolwide and classwide policies, procedures, and interventions is far easier than resorting to more costly, time-intrusive, and individualized approaches.

Resources in the series do not take a punitive approach to discipline. Instead, *Safe & Civil Schools* addresses the sources of teachers' greatest power to motivate: through structuring for student success, teaching expectations, observing and monitoring student behavior, and, above all, interacting positively. Because experience directly affects behavior, it makes little sense to pursue only the undesired behavior (by relying on reprimands, for example) and not the conditions (in behavioral theory, the antecedent) that precipitate experience and subsequent behavior.

Safe & Civil Schools acknowledges the real power teachers have—not in controlling students, but in affecting every aspect of the students' experience while they are in the classroom: the physical layout, the way time is structured, arrivals and departures, and the quality of time spent in the intervening interval.

 PORTIONS OF THIS WORK were originally published in 1993 under the title *Interventions: Collaborative Planning for Students At Risk*. Since that time, research continues to confirm that the proactive, positive, and instructional approaches suggested in the original edition are far more effective in managing and motivating students than traditional, authoritarian, and punitive approaches. From the literature on schoolwide behavioral support, classroom management, and interventions with individual students, we know, at a minimum, that students are most likely to thrive with educators who:

- Maintain and communicate high expectations for student success

- Build positive relationships with students

- Create consistent, predictable classroom and schoolwide routines

- Teach students how to behave successfully

- Provide consistent monitoring and supervision

- Provide frequent positive feedback

- Correct misbehavior in a calm, consistent, and logical manner

This book is designed to translate those broad ideas into specific actions you can take to improve the behavior of individual students. The previous edition included a procedural manual that delineated how to provide schoolwide coordination for service delivery and offered 16 specific interventions. Those interventions were combined, revised, and expanded—bringing the total to 19—in a new companion book titled *Interventions: Evidence-Based Behavioral Strategies for Individual Students*. The procedural portion of the first edition was expanded and updated to create this new text, *Behavioral Response to Intervention (B-RTI): Creating a Continuum of Problem-Solving and Support*. Our goal is to help school personnel organize the service delivery of behavioral support and intervention so that it fits a response-to-intervention (RTI) format.

Behavioral Response to Intervention gives administrators, school psychologists, school counselors, and behavior specialists information about how to organize the resources within a school to ensure that no students fall through the cracks and that students and teachers receive the support they need for students to be successful. This book can be viewed as a companion to *Interventions*—this book defines the who, when, why, and how of designing efficient and effective interventions, while *Interventions* addresses the what.

Behavioral Response to Intervention is part of a continuum of behavioral support products in the *Safe & Civil School Series*. This series is designed to help school personnel make all settings physically and emotionally safe for all students. In implementation projects throughout the country, my colleagues and I have learned that when expectations are clear and directly taught to students, much as you would teach a writing skill or a problem-solving process, the vast majority of students will strive to be cooperative and to meet those expectations. By implementing the preventive aspects of the series, teachers can spend less time dealing with disruption and resistance and more time teaching.

However, there will always be students who need more. Sometimes a student will need to work one-to-one with an adult to implement a behavioral intervention plan targeted at his or her individual needs. Sometimes a student will need multiple adults and agencies (the proverbial village) involved in designing and implementing behavior support that will help him or her function successfully in school and in the community. This book is about organizing services and problem-solving formats so that you design and implement the easiest and most efficient intervention first, then move to a more difficult and costly intervention only if the student does not respond to the easier and cheaper methodology.

INTRODUCTION

THIS BOOK is designed for school personnel who have some level of responsibility for ensuring that students' needs for behavioral (social/emotional) support are met. These personnel include building-based administrators, counselors, psychologists, problem-solving team members, special education teachers, and behavior specialists. District personnel such as special education directors/coordinators, directors of school psychology, and supervisors of school counselors are also included.

One major purpose of the book is to present a proposed model—a blueprint for how services can be organized. The primary objective of this service delivery structure should be to meet students' behavioral needs. Secondarily, the structure should ensure that intervention design and implementation occurs in the most time-, personnel-, and cost-effective manner possible—while still meeting students' needs. Without a sound structure (such as the blueprint this book suggests), there is a significant risk that one or more of the following will occur:

- Many students will drop out of school or be expelled. In recent years, graduation rates have hovered between 70% and 80% (depending on how the data is collected and analyzed). That means 20–30% of students are falling through the cracks, or more appropriately, falling into gaping canyons. When dropouts are asked why they quit, only 35% report academic failure as the primary reason, leaving 65% who drop out for other reasons that are likely social, emotional, or behavioral in nature (Bridgeland, DiIulio, & Morrison, 2006).

- School psychologists, behavior analysts, behavior specialists, and school counselors will have long waiting lists of students who need evaluations and services.

- So many students will be on individualized plans that general education teachers will be overwhelmed by point cards, checklists, and rating scales.

- A growing number of students will be referred for special education services.

- A disproportionate number of ethnic students will be referred for special education services for behavior/emotional problems.

TERMINOLOGY

This book addresses all of these issues by laying out a framework of prevention and intervention. This framework is based on the following theoretical assumptions and vocabulary:

Behavior support. Positive Behavior Support (PBS) is a long-term, long-view process. Its research-based strategies combine applied behavior analysis and biomedical science with person-centered values and systems change to increase quality of life and decrease problem behaviors.

Functional behavior assessment (FBA). Any misbehavior that occurs repeatedly is serving some function for the individual exhibiting it. The student may be trying to get something, such as attention from teachers or peers, or to avoid something, such as an embarrassing or stressful situation. Assuming that the student has a healthy and stable mind, the repetitive behavior can be viewed as a smart or logical choice for that individual at that point in time given his or her past experiences and perceptions. If a behavior (or set of behaviors) interferes with a student's success in school, an intervention may be needed. Interventions address the function of the misbehavior. For example, with a student who seeks attention, the intervention should try to reduce the amount and intensity of attention the student receives for disruptive behavior while increasing the amount and intensity of attention the student receives for productive academic behavior. In this text, references to *function-based interventions* simply mean that the intervention should be designed to help the student fulfill his or her needs by exhibiting responsible and appropriate behavior rather than by misbehaving.

Behavior Improvement Plan (BIP). Within the legal requirements specified for children with emotional/behavioral disabilities is a specification that after an FBA is completed, a BIP will be developed and implemented. A BIP is a set of strategies to support children with inappropriate classroom behaviors and is designed to support the child to learn new acceptable behaviors and to abstain from using inappropriate behaviors. Throughout this book we will refer to the "intervention plan," or in many cases simply "intervention," although these terms encompass the requirements of the

BIP. We choose these more generic terms because the BIP may refer to a legal require-ment for students with disabilities, whereas the term "intervention plan" includes any plan that is developed to help the child improve behavior, whether that child is receiv-ing special education services or not. Thus, if a BIP is required by law, an intervention that stems from the processes described in this book would be the student's BIP.

Behavioral response to intervention (B-RTI). School personnel should first try the easiest, cheapest, and least time-consuming intervention that has a reasonable chance of success. The only way to know that a simple intervention will not work is to try it. If a problem is resistant to a simple intervention, progressively more-detailed interventions should be planned and implemented though a collaborative effort be-tween the classroom teacher and support personnel.

Three-tiered model. This B-RTI model views Tier 1 universal prevention that en-compasses simple school and districtwide practices that apply to all students and are well known to all teachers. At the next level are Tier 2 targeted interventions—col-laborative, function-based interventions tailored to individual students. Tier 3 inten-sive interventions involve a full FBA conducted by the most highly trained personnel in your school or district. Although *intensive* often refers to special education, our model does *not* include or recommend any specific procedures for referring students to special education because most districts have this structure in place.

Evidence-based interventions. Function-based interventions should be selected from a menu of interventions with a proven track record of success—that is, evidence in the research literature shows they have been effective in a variety of settings with a variety of student populations. *Interventions: Evidence-Based Behavioral Strategies for Individual Students* has one such set, but any intervention that has multiple stud-ies demonstrating efficacy with a given population can be considered when matching student needs to a school-based intervention.

Interventionist. We use this as an encompassing term to describe any staff member who has responsibility for working with teachers and students to design an interven-tion plan. This term includes school psychologists, school counselors, lead teachers, department chairs, building administrators, behavior specialists, problem-solving teams, and multidisciplinary teams. Interventionists must be skilled in working with teachers, parents, students, and administrators to get everyone on the same page in helping the student learn to function successfully in school.

Case manager. The term *case manager* refers to the professional who has responsi-bility to ensure that a student's needs are met and that he and his family are not lost in cracks of the system, such as between two layers of problem-solving. As soon as a student's situation is considered a Tier 2 issue—that is, the professionals within the system are now working collaboratively because a teacher's individual efforts have not solved the problem—a case manager is assigned. From this point forward, this profes-sional will work to move problem-solving and intervention design along in efficient, effective, and humane ways. In many cases, the interventionist and the case manager may be the same, but some complex situations may require the case manager to enlist other personnel to serve as the current interventionist.

Early intervention. Student misbehavior is one of the leading frustrations for educators. Any major misbehavior chronically engaged in—insubordination, disruptions, disrespect, or refusal to do work—can make even highly skilled teachers feel helpless, frustrated, and angry. Often, by the time a teacher has asked for assistance, the only help he or she wants is alternative placement for the student—not so much for the needs of the student but to "get the student gone from my class." This book emphasizes the importance of creating a culture of early intervention and positive support so that teachers rarely reach this stage of frustration with students.

DESCRIPTION OF CHAPTERS

Each of the book's twelve chapters describes in detail one portion of the service delivery structure. These chapters can be used to construct a districtwide approach to B-RTI. Following is a description of each chapter:

Chapter 1: Thinking Big—A Full Continuum of Problem-Solving and Support. The first chapter lays out the big picture. Extending the architectural metaphor, in essence it allows you to see the whole structure—the view from the outside and the use of floor space on the inside. This view allows you to determine if the structure we advocate makes sense for your building or district. If it does, you can determine from this chapter whether you need to moderately remodel your existing service delivery structure (e.g., changing the way students at risk of failure are identified as needing assistance), more extensively remodel that structure (e.g., adding a problem-solving team if you don't have one), or completely remodel by adding major wings to the structure while changing the interior of existing structural elements. This chapter delineates the importance of behavioral support procedures throughout all levels of the school: schoolwide policies and procedures, effective classroom management, and multiple tiers of problem analysis and intervention design for individual students.

Chapter 2: Universal Prevention—The Role of the Leadership Team. In this chapter, we describe how a site-based team needs to choose the design and manage the remodel of the B-RTI structures in the building. This team also has to manage the maintenance of these structures and to teach the users (all staff) how to take care of and get full benefit from the new structures. This chapter provides information about who should be on the team, how the team should function, and what the team needs to do to create a full continuum of behavior support services within the school. It also includes checklists and forms that can assist the team in determining if the schoolwide discipline and classroom management practices are maximally effective. If they're not, suggestions are provided for how to work on these universal preventive practices while also developing the B-RTI structures.

Chapter 3: The Framework—Building a Behavioral Response to Intervention. This section shows the school-based leadership team how to involve school and district personnel in planning how the B-RTI process actually works. This chapter lays out two major considerations for a model of behavioral intervention: 1) problem-solving processes, and 2) a protocol of interventions. B-RTI suggests that the intensity of problem-solving and the interventions being implemented match the intensity of the problem. This chapter suggests a continuum of these two categories. This in essence is the basic blueprint for problem-solving and service delivery of individualized interventions.

Chapter 4: Develop a Process—Linking Needs to Available Resources. This chapter provides a more detailed blueprint for problem-solving structures within the school. This blueprint is analogous to electrical, plumbing, and HVAC drawings—or how things function in the framework that has been constructed. This includes suggestions for how student needs can be red-flagged so that those needs are identified early and the B-RTI process of problem analysis and intervention design can begin. There are additional suggestions for how to involve parents/guardians and how to ensure that teacher requests for assistance are handled promptly and in a manner viewed as helpful.

Chapter 5: Data-Driven Decisions—Create a Culture and Process of Data Collection. Here we provide information about how to train the staff (users of the B-RTI structure) to collect and use data for meeting students' needs. A central tenet of B-RTI is that objective data is the only legitimate way to determine if a given intervention is effective. Therefore, everybody in the system—teachers, administrators, and interventionists—needs to become skilled in the collection and analysis of data and in using that analysis to make decisions about modifying, maintaining, and fading interventions.

Chapter 6: The Interventionist—A Summary of Skills and Responsibilities. This section provides information about how to skillfully work with teachers, students, and parents. The interventionist needs to know how to guide intervention processes efficiently, how to design and implement interventions, how to monitor fidelity of implementation, and how to make data-driven decisions about modifying and fading interventions across time. Also included are suggestions for marketing intervention services to help foster a culture of collaboration within the school and to encourage teachers to ask for help in the earliest stages of a problem.

Chapter 7: Teacher Interview—Using an Intervention Decision Guide. This chapter gives detailed instruction on how to use the IDG tool to conduct a teacher interview that is designed to collect the maximum amount of information about the student's situation in the least amount of time. Then, using this information, the teacher and the interventionist develop a hypothesis about the function of the misbehavior and design an intervention that fits the nature of the problem. The rationale behind use of this tool is that the teacher has the most information about both the student and the context of the problem, so in early stages, why not base the problem analysis and the intervention design on the teacher's perceptions? In most cases, the teacher will have to carry out much of the intervention, so involving the teacher as the lead player increases the chances of his or her buy-in to the intervention.

Chapter 8: The 25-Minute Planning Process—The Role of an Intervention Planning Team. This chapter is designed to help any team charged with designing and implementing individualized interventions. In most cases, this will be a different team than the leadership team. This group does not design and maintain the overall structure but manages a particularly important room within that structure. This group meets to analyze the situation and data of an individual student and quickly develop a function-based intervention plan. This group should respond to both teacher requests and to students who have been red-flagged as needing assistance. A sample agenda for running efficient and effective meetings is provided, along with suggestions and tools for evaluating the effectiveness of the team.

Chapter 9: Multidisciplinary Team Approach—Using the Intervention Decision Guide. In this section, we provide step-by-step guidance in how to conduct a more extensive functional analysis of the problem. This includes reviewing and revising the teacher interview data and collecting other information through:

- Analyzing previous interventions and data collected

- Conducting a thorough records review

- Interviewing other school personnel who know the student

- Conducting student and parent interviews

- Observing the student in a variety of settings

This additional data will be used to design a more comprehensive intervention than has been implemented to date. This chapter also provides information about how the multidisciplinary team must monitor fidelity of implementation: Is the intervention actually being implemented consistently as it was designed?

Chapter 10: Connections—A Schoolwide Check-and-Connect Plan. This chapter describes a schoolwide structure that can be put in place as an early-stage intervention for any student for whom the Tier 1 universal interventions are not successful. In this system, a student has a carry card that staff use to monitor certain behaviors or traits on a period-by-period basis. The student checks in daily with the Connections coordinator (behavior specialist, school counselor, highly skilled paraprofessional), who debriefs with the student, charts data, and meets periodically with the student's teachers and parents to discuss progress. Once this structure is in place and the staff is trained, many students can be placed in the Connections program as an early-stage behavior intervention.

Chapter 11: Other Targeted Interventions—Mentoring and Other Ready-to-Implement Programs. Included in this chapter are descriptions of programs that can be put in place within the school as a buffet of procedures. When a student is flagged as needing assistance or a teacher refers a student, the teacher, problem-solving team, or interventionist can analyze the student's needs and see if something from the buffet of schoolwide services might help. Programs described include mentoring, meaningful work, First Step to Success, structured recess/structured lunch, social skills instruction, students targeted for special attention, bullying prevention/intervention, and homework help room.

Chapter 12: Gang Prevention and Intervention—A B-RTI Approach to Youth Gang Issues. This section describes the effect of youth gangs in society and the corresponding effect on school grounds—from a safety and civility perspective as well as from a financial point of view. The components of B-RTI can be effective strategies to address gang issues in school settings, and we focus on the importance of a district-level effort (as compared with campus-level) to organize district and community resources to address this complex issue. Using a model developed by the Dallas Independent School District Gang Program, the chapter describes the components of B-RTI that relate to gang issues and how they align with the recommendations from the Office of Juvenile Justice and Delinquency Prevention. Suggestions are provided for creating and maintaining a multi-agency gang task force.

> **Note:** Throughout this book (and throughout the entire *Safe & Civil Schools* library of products), the only absolute rule about behavior management is that belittling students has no place in any educational setting—all behavioral interventions must treat children with dignity and respect. To have a positive and lasting effect, interventions must build up student strengths and expand skills for replacing problem behavior, rather than trying to simply squelch or contain problem behavior.

HOW TO USE THIS BOOK

Chapters 1–4 are useful for decision makers—school-based leadership teams and building- and district-level administrators who can make policy decisions about problem-solving processes and coordination of different roles (who does what: school counselor, school psychologist, problem-solving teams, etc.). Chapter 12 on gang issues will also be of use to urban educators who make district-level policy decisions. A building-based or district-level task force can use these five chapters to identify strengths of current policies and practices and to develop proposed policies and procedures for addressing weaknesses in the current systems of problem-solving and intervention design.

Chapters 5–11 will be useful to anyone who sometimes works collaboratively with teachers to design behavioral interventions (problem-solving team members, school counselors, school psychologists, social workers, special education teachers/supervisors, and administrators.) An individual interventionist can use these chapters to reflect on current skill levels and set up an individual plan for expanding skills and strategies. A problem-solving team can use these chapters to conduct a book study to expand the skills of all team members.

REPRODUCIBLE FORMS

Blank versions of all forms that appear in this book are available on the accompanying CD. Note that some forms on the CD are not shown in the book. At the end of each chapter is a list of all related materials that appear on the CD.

Permission is given to administrators and educators who purchase the book to reproduce any form labeled "Reproducible Form" solely for the purpose of assisting school personnel with classroom management and intervention design and implementation.

The CD forms are provided in PDF format. They can be printed and filled out by hand. They are also enabled so they can be filled out and saved electronically when opened in Adobe Reader version 6 or above. See the Readme file on the CD for more detailed instructions on how to fill out forms using Adobe Reader.

CHAPTER 1

Thinking Big

A Full Continuum of Problem-Solving and Support

At its core, Behavioral Response to Intervention (B-RTI) is a problem-solving process. To be effective, it must be part of broader efforts to implement schoolwide behavioral support. Positive Behavior Support (PBS), the new popular term for behavior management, warrants some clarification.

Warger (1999) defines PBS as a long-term, long-view process: "Unlike traditional behavioral management, which views the individual as the problem and seeks to *fix* him or her by quickly eliminating the challenging behavior, Positive Behavioral Support and functional analysis view systems, settings, and lack of skill as parts of the problem and work to change those. As such, these approaches are characterized as long-term strategies to reduce inappropriate behavior, teach more-appropriate behavior, and provide contextual supports necessary for successful outcomes."

So PBS is a broad generic term for any set of procedures or techniques designed to enhance quality of life and minimize problem behaviors (Carr et al., 2002; Horner et al., 1990; Koegel, Koegel, & Dunlap, 1996; Sprick & Booher, 2006). PBS integrates applied behavior analysis, person-centered values, and comprehensive assessment linked to multicomponent interventions (Horner, Sugai, Todd, & Lewis-Palmer, 1990).

This chapter delineates the importance of behavior support procedures throughout all levels of the school: schoolwide policies and procedures, effective classroom management, and multiple tiers of problem analysis and interventions designed for individual students.

> PBS is a broad generic term for any set of procedures or techniques designed to enhance quality of life and minimize problem behaviors.

This chapter also presents a vision—the big picture—of how B-RTI works and how it fits into the broader PBS concept. It will allow you to assess your own PBS system and determine:

- Do we need to lightly remodel our service delivery structure—for example, by changing the way students at risk of failure are identified as needing assistance?

- Do we need to extensively remodel our structure by adding a problem-solving team to our school?

- Are we due for a massive remodel, such as adding major wings to the structure while changing the interior of existing structural elements?

WHY WE NEED A NEW MODEL

In simplest terms, *behavioral support* means changing the system to meet the needs of the student while also helping the student fit successfully into the system (Carr et al., 2002; Sprick, Garrison, & Howard, 2002). As is often the case when considering a system to support positive behavior, there is good news and bad news.

Good news. The principles underlying PBS are simple and based on common sense and a sound theoretical/research base. They boil down to this: Keep adjusting the variables in a student's situation until something starts to work. The best behavior managers in schools aren't necessarily those who know the most, but rather those who don't give up—the staff members who are relentless in their quest to get the best from their students. These teachers say, "I am going to keep manipulating your environment until I find a way to help you unlock your success."

Bad news. Although the principles are simple, most schools and teachers are not applying them. Why? The reason is just as simple. Student behavior problems drive teachers crazy. A lot of emotional baggage comes into play with many teacher-student interactions. Teachers are under tremendous pressure; they are held accountable for their students' academic success or failure. When a student is disruptive, noncompliant, passive, resistant, or exhibiting any other of the myriad of potential behavior problems, the student poses a direct and immediate threat to the teacher's authority.

In addition, many, if not most, schools operate under a culture of control. It is all too easy for teachers to get into a power struggle with a misbehaving student by trying to *make* the student behave appropriately. It's the human reaction to threatening situations: fight or flight. Teachers can't run screaming from the classroom (as much as they might like to sometimes), so the fight reaction kicks in. If this pattern continues, by the time the teacher asks for assistance or the student's behavioral needs rise to the attention of the administrator, school counselor, school psychologist, or other problem-solving professional, the teacher does not want help for the student; the teacher wants someone else to manage the student (think about repeated referrals to the office) or wants the student placed in a different setting. Problem-solving professionals, a role we call *interventionists*, commonly hear, "I have tried everything for this student. He needs to be placed in a special education setting."

Administrators, school psychologists, school social workers, and school counselors (when in the role of interventionists) must take this pressure into account when they try to create better behavioral practices in schools (Sprick, Howard, Wise, Marcum, & Haykin, 1998). It's not just a matter of sharing all the right information with the staff—you have to proactively change teachers' mindsets about student behavioral problems and, in turn, change their behavior by getting them to implement evidence-based PBS practices, thus reducing the frequency of power struggles, negativity, and frustration.

Simply handing the problem off to a different adult or moving the student to a different setting is no longer a viable option; too many students need help. Every adult in the school must become part of the solution. To bring about this cultural change, administrators must infuse the idea of PBS in adults at every level—general education teachers, special education teachers, and interventionists—and develop a common language of prevention and intervention that all school personnel can use to ensure that all students' behavioral and academic needs are met (Ervin, Schaughency, Goodman, McGlinchey, & Matthews, 2006; Sugai & Horner, 2002).

MANIPULATE VARIABLES

The first step for teachers in embracing PBS is to learn to manipulate the variables they can control. Thirty years of behavior management research and analysis have led us to believe that five variables have a promising, sound background for behavioral change: Structure, Teach, Observe, Interact positively, Correct fluently (Sprick, Knight, Reinke, & McKale, 2007). Those readers trained in the science of behavior analysis may notice that STOIC is a "what-the-teacher-can-do" version of ABC: Antecedent, Behavior, and Consequence, a model you're likely familiar with. See Table 1.1 for a comparison of the analytic ABC model and how it corresponds to prevention and intervention variables that can be manipulated in the STOIC framework.

STOIC

According to the dictionary, a *stoic* is someone who shows patience and endurance in the face of adversity. This perfectly describes the STOIC model and the teachers and administrators mentioned earlier who are relentless in their efforts to help students succeed. Following is a more detailed introduction to STOIC as a framework for guiding behavior support efforts.

> Thirty years of behavior management research and analysis have led us to believe that five variables have a promising, sound background for behavioral change: Structure, Teach, Observe, Interactive positively, Correct fluently.

Table 1.1

ABC versus STOIC

ABC Model Describes Student's Behavior	STOIC Model Describes Actions Adults Can Take
*A*ntecedent: What occurs before the behavior?	*S*tructure: Settings can be organized or disorganized, and this will have a major effect on whether the student behaves appropriate or inappropriately. *T*each: Directly teaching all students how to behave appropriately increases the chances that students will choose to behave that way.
*B*ehavior: What is the student's behavior in the presence of particular antecedents?	*O*bserve: Adults must actively monitor student behavior to determine whether to encourage responsible behavior or discourage irresponsible behavior.
*C*onsequence: What stimuli occur after the behavior? Reinforcing consequences increase the future occurrence of behavior, while punishing consequences decrease the future occurrence of behavior.	*I*nteract Positively: When the student is observed engaging in appropriate behavior, adults should provide age-appropriate attention and positive feedback in an attempt to reinforce the student's appropriate behavior. *C*orrect Fluently: When the student exhibits misbehavior, adults should correct the misbehavior in a manner that: • does not interrupt the flow of instruction. • does not serve to reinforce the student's misbehavior (as is often the case in power struggles). • does correct the misbehavior in a manner that reduces future occurrences of the behavior.

*S*tructure. The way any particular environment is structured has a huge effect on the way people behave and on their attitude within that environment (Luiselli & Cameron, 1998). Structural changes can be applied to a district environment, a school or building environment, a classroom, or even a student's virtual environment, meaning his mental and emotional surroundings. Although a student's environment outside school, such as her home situation, can be taken into consideration, the STOIC model depends on being able to adjust variables. While working with parents as partners, it may be presumptuous or inappropriate for school personnel to attempt to adjust variables related to a student's home life.

Throughout all aspects of behavioral problem-solving and intervention design and implementation, parents should be viewed and honored as active participants in the process. They should be informed about behavioral concerns at the earliest onset of problems and continually invited to be active partners with school personnel in helping the student learn to be successful in school. We make the assumption throughout this book that both parents and the student are active participants in B-RTI processes.

Structure within the school is the first and often the easiest variable to adjust in behavior support, largely because it's the one a staff that works as a team will usually have the most control over. In addition, thinking about structure is vital because a poorly structured setting can inadvertently set students up to exhibit problem behavior (Mayer, 1995). For example, the length of time students stand in a cafeteria line waiting for lunch can affect the cultural tone of the entire school. Let's consider two schools that have identical numbers of students enrolled. In School A, students stand in line for two to three minutes at most for lunch, and it's a nonevent. In School B, students wait in line for twenty minutes. Everyone is hungry, bored, and impatient. Getting to the front of the line becomes an aggressive event. Students who are prone to behavior problems soak up this negative energy and tension and carry it around all day. Then later that tension comes out in a classroom—for example, when a teacher inquires about homework assignments that have not been completed and the student reacts in a belligerent manner. School A experiences far fewer behavior problems overall.

*T***each.** The T in the STOIC acronym refers not to classroom academic instruction but to the teaching of behavioral expectations. Teaching expectations often works in tandem with establishing or modifying environmental structures, but it is an important variable on its own. Teachers and administrators must overtly and purposefully teach students all the details of functioning within the school and within the classroom. For example, it is not sufficient to tell students what we want them to do during instructional activities in the classroom. We must also include instruction in expected behavior that spans the entire school day and all relevant school settings—e.g., playground, cafeteria, hallway, and bus (Sprick, Garrison, et al., 2002; Sprick, Swartz, & Glang, 2005, 2007).

Teaching is more than telling. Similar to the way an athletic coach trains her team, communicating behavioral expectations means breaking the information down into manageable steps and practicing the steps—again and again, if necessary. The effective coach teaches not only specific behavioral expectations such as plays, patterns, and the rules of the game, but also broader expectations about sportsmanship, teamwork, and the benefits of hard work. School personnel must emulate effective coaches because success in school is certainly no less complicated than being a successful part of a basketball team. If you're used to thinking about variables according to the ABC model, these first two—structure and teach—fall into the antecedent group. They happen before the behavior and, if done well, are preventive in nature. If implemented poorly, they can set conditions that prompt misbehavior.

*O*bserve. This variable is both simple and effective. First, as any lead-footed driver will tell you, monitoring affects behavior. If a police cruiser is present, everybody goes the speed limit. If an adult is in the hallway, students behave in a more orderly way. Direct observation of behavior parallels the behavior component in the ABC model.

Observing students also gives them the incentive and opportunity to demonstrate that they are meeting your expectations. If the teacher is not watching, the student may think, "Why should I do what he asks if he's not going to see it?" Remember, this is a variable you can adjust, so if students are not aware that they are being observed, you must be more overt in the way you observe or in the amount of time you spend doing so. This helps ensure that students meet the expectations they have been taught within the structure the staff has created.

*I*nteract positively. This variable is considered a positive consequence of behavior. Teachers and administrators (in fact, all school staff) can and should interact positively with students—say hello, show an interest in them, give them meaningful, age-appropriate positive feedback. Even something as simple as greeting students when they enter the school or classroom can be enough to make them feel that the staff is present and attentive, and problem situations may be resolved when you approach students with a positive attitude.

*C*orrect fluently. The final variable is the corrective response to inappropriate behavior. When you observe behavior that is outside the boundaries of your expectations, you must correct it calmly, consistently, immediately, briefly, and relentlessly—in other words, seamlessly and fluently. The least positive thing educators can do is to let a student get away with misbehavior, because getting away with it can be partially reinforcing in and of itself. However, care must be taken to ensure that pre-established consequences for misbehavior are not so harsh that staff members hesitate to employ them for relatively minor infractions. What is important is that a staff member responds in some manner to each instance of student misbehavior. Remember, it doesn't have to be a firing squad—it can often just be a parking ticket.

Students not only need to know that educators are observing them, but also need to be certain that the staff will consistently enforce their standards and expectations. If you teach expected behavior without assigning any consequences when students

> The least positive thing educators can do is to let a student get away with misbehavior, because getting away with it can be partially reinforcing in and of itself.

misbehave, students will have no reason to behave as they've been taught. It is important to react quickly and correct immediately, but never in anger. These two variables—Interact and Correct—are consequences (positive and negative), thus fitting the third category in the ABC model.

Keep in mind, however, that correction is the weakest link. Some students will not respond to any punitive consequence, no matter how severe or repetitious. Even if a student does respond to a punitive consequence, we cannot expect that the student will then engage in the desired behavior without strategies in place to teach and reinforce the expected behaviors (Crosbie, 1998; Horner, 2002; Lerman & Vorndran, 2002). Therefore, the majority of energy and focus should be on Structure, Teach, Observe, and Interact.

CHANGE THE SYSTEM

As stated earlier, *behavior support* means changing the system to help meet the needs of the student while also helping the student fit successfully into the system. The first part of this statement focuses on making districts, schools, and classrooms the best places for all students. In the adult world, this is analogous to:

1. Public health care for all: vaccinations, prenatal care, and annual physicals

2. Public safety: traffic laws and consumer protections

3. Citizenship rights and responsibilities: basic freedoms, national defense, and taxes

CLIMATE CHANGE

At the broadest level, this means that schools need to become places where students want to be. So creating a safe, positive, and inviting school climate is an important part of PBS (Carr et al., 2002; Sprick, Howard, et al., 1998; Sugai & Horner, 2006). Schools need to think about students and parents as clients or customers, not as captives or laborers. Following are some of the objectives of a comprehensive and positive approach to changing the system:

- Increase academic engagement and use of class time (reduce tardiness, disruptions, and other misbehaviors).

- Ensure physical safety of students and staff (reduce fighting, eliminate assault and physical threats, reduce physical hazards— e.g., on playgrounds).

- Ensure emotional safety of students and staff (reduce disrespect, bullying, and harassment).

- Create an inviting climate and caring, supportive relationships between students and staff and between staff and parents.

- Build *connectedness* between students and the school (e.g., school pride, extracurricular activities, rituals, parent involvement, and traditions).

- Inspire high levels of motivation (reduce boredom and "doing just enough to get by").

- Create policies, expectations, lessons, routines, and rituals to facilitate all of the above.

- Ensure that no students fall through the cracks—that is, if these structural changes are not working for a particular student, experiment with individual interventions until the student responds successfully.

SERVICE DELIVERY

Most educators are familiar with the triangle used by public health (Commission on Chronic Illness, 1957) that has universal prevention and intervention at the bottom (with 85–90% of the population falling into this category), selected or targeted services in the middle (7–10%), and intensive services at the top (3–5%). (See Figure 1.1.)

Figure 1.1
Public Health Triangle

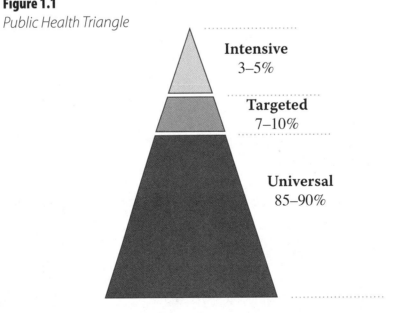

The problem with using this model for schools is that it assumes that 85–90% of the population is getting along fine with a minimum level of universal services. With graduation rates indicating that only slightly more than 70% of students nationwide achieve a high school diploma (Bridgeland et al., 2006), we cannot assume that our universal practices are sufficient for 85–90% of students.

So the B-RTI model of service delivery turns that triangle upside down (see Figure 1.2). In our model, universal services move to the top to represent the broadest level of services for the broadest group of students. The purpose behind inverting the triangle is to highlight the importance of spending the most time, energy, and money on Tier 1 interventions—those services applied by all staff members and directed at all students. Tier 2 interventions, or targeted services, are at the next level. They are for those students whose needs aren't adequately met and who fall through cracks of the universal prevention efforts. These services are collaborative—they involve more than one staff member, often an interventionist and/or problem-solving team. Students whose needs are not met by the wide net cast at the top of the triangle fall into the safety net of the next tier of targeted interventions. In essence, the B-RTI model functions like a sifting process. Only the 10–15% of students who don't benefit from Tier 1 interventions/universal services (creating a supportive structure/system and teaching behavioral expectations for that system) need services at the next level—Tier 2, targeted individual support.

Figure 1.2
B-RTI Service Delivery

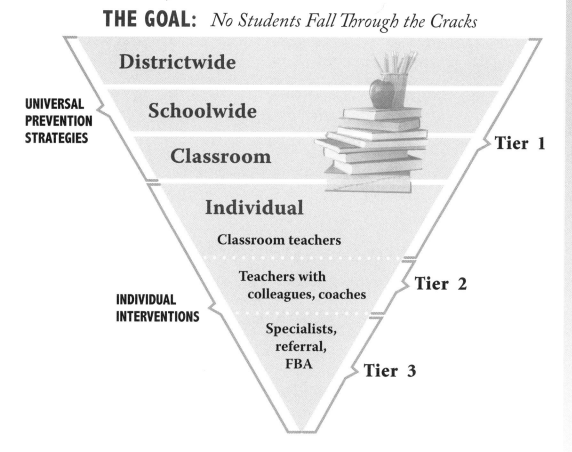

THE GOAL: *No Students Fall Through the Cracks*

UNIVERSAL PREVENTION STRATEGIES

Districtwide
Schoolwide
Classroom

Tier 1

Individual

Classroom teachers

INDIVIDUAL INTERVENTIONS

Teachers with colleagues, coaches

Tier 2

Specialists, referral, FBA

Tier 3

Intensive Tier 3 interventions are reserved for the small group of students who don't respond to Tier 1 and Tier 2 services and need specialized support. This service level involves a full functional behavior assessment (FBA) and a corresponding individualized support plan created by the most highly skilled personnel in the district. These interventions are beyond the scope of this book.

The language we use here to describe a three-tier model may not fit the language in your state or district. If, for example, your use of the three-tier model is mainly related to identification of students for special education services, change the wording of our suggestions within this book. We are mainly advocating a form of service delivery—that is, how the adults and systems in the school work together to ensure that all students' behavioral and emotional needs are met. The most energy goes into universal prevention, but there are services that meet individual student needs in a manner that matches the intensity of resources to the intensity of student needs.

LEADERSHIP TEAM

Constructing and maintaining PBS requires a site-based leadership team that consists of staff members who are highly respected by the entire staff. These influential people unify the staff to efficiently and skillfully design, create, and maintain all aspects of PBS and the organizational structure for B-RTI. All of the major models of school-wide discipline suggest the need for a leadership team to guide and unify the entire staff in Positive Behavior Support efforts (Knoff, 1996; Sprague & Golly, 2004; Sprick, Sprick, & Garrison, 1992; Sprick, Garrison, & Howard, 2002; Sugai & Horner, 2002, 2006; Sugai, Horner, & McIntosh, 2008). Chapter 2, "Universal Prevention—The Role of the Leadership Team," provides more-detailed information about the configuration and operation of this team and describes the content or outcomes of a problem-solving framework.

EFFICIENTLY SOLVE STUDENT PROBLEMS

The second part of the PBS framework definition is about helping individual students fit successfully—thrive both behaviorally and academically—into the system. The primary goal of B-RTI is to humanely help every student learn to function successfully in school in a manner that maximizes his or her ability to learn.

A secondary purpose of B-RTI is to accomplish this success in the most efficient manner possible. In other words, try the easiest thing first—it just might work. And if it is effective, you've spent very few of your school's precious, limited resources. If schools had unlimited resources, you could assign a highly skilled teacher and fully trained school psychologist to every student having any level of difficulty. But that would be like sending everyone with a headache to a neurosurgeon—an absurd waste of precious medical resources.

TIER 1

So problem-solving at the individual level should start simply, with interventions that are easy, unobtrusive, and able to be implemented in general education and special education classrooms. In this framework, all teachers should be familiar with Tier 1 interventions, those simple yet promising interventions that require a minimum of paperwork and administration and should always be tried first. The advantage of B-RTI is that for most students, it can solve early-stage problems in the early stages. To follow the medical analogy, it's similar to a standard action when you first get a headache—taking a couple of aspirin. For most students, the early intervention will do the job.

If you treat all students with highly structured multipersonnel problem analysis and intervention, there will most likely be an implementation delay, and resources that could have been used on a more necessary case will have been wasted (Crone & Horner, 2000; Walker & Shinn, 2002). What's more, as we will see in later chapters, a system that does not try simple, easy-to-implement analysis and intervention first may actually compound a problem and make things worse.

For example, if waiting lists for students to get assistance from a school psychologist are long, a minor, easily treated problem may go on for so long it becomes resistant to a simple intervention. In addition, a student who has deep-seated problems is on the same waiting list. His or her access to a multifaceted analysis and intervention may be delayed as the school psychologist spends time on problems that never needed help from someone with her skill and training.

TIER 2

For the individual students whose problems are more significant than a simple headache—those who slip through the net of Tier 1 interventions—the next step in the treatment protocol is Tier 2. The key word at this level of response is *collaborative*. The idea is that two heads are better than one, so it's important to get other professionals in addition to the teacher involved.

The other person who becomes involved is often referred to as an *interventionist*. An interventionist can be another teacher, a school counselor, a school psychologist, a school social worker, an assistant principal, or a highly trained behavior specialist. With or without specialized training, an interventionist is a third party to the teacher-student relationship. They fit into the B-RTI service delivery model as collaborative providers of targeted interventions. In the health model, the interventionist is parallel to the general practitioners, nurses, and nutritionists a headache patient might see before being referred to a neurosurgeon. Chapter 6, "The Interventionist," discusses the specific skills needed to function effectively in this role.

Tier 2 interventions also entail three planning structures. The first structure, brief team planning, is discussed in Chapter 8, "The 25-Minute Planning Process." This planning structure is meant to be quick and efficient, getting several professionals together to get a plan into action.

The second planning structure is a step-by-step protocol to follow when conducting a teacher interview. Outlined in Chapter 7, "Teacher Interview," the teacher interview is intended for interventionists, case managers, and school psychologists—anyone who is charged with designing behavioral interventions.

If the first two planning structures are ineffective, the third level involves a multidisciplinary approach covered in Chapter 9, "Multidisciplinary Team Approach." This approach is a much more detailed level of problem-solving and calls for observing the student in multiple settings, reviewing his or her school records, interviewing the parents, and so forth.

TIER 3

What this book does not cover is the bottom tip of the pyramid, Tier 3 interventions. These interventions must be conducted by someone with extensive training in dealing with complex behavioral problems, and they require a full-fledged functional behavior assessment. In the medical analogy, this is the point when, if the student still has a headache that has not responded to early intervention or to multiple targeted interventions, it's time to call in the neurosurgeon. In most school districts, this part of the triangle is probably well in place. This book is about designing and implementing universal prevention and layers of early and targeted intervention problem-solving to better meet the needs of all students.

FUNCTION-BASED APPROACH

Another important B-RTI concept that you'll encounter in this book is the function-based approach to problem-solving. The premise is simple: Chronic repetitive behavior usually serves a purpose for the individual exhibiting it. The behavior's function serves to help the individual either get something he or she wants (such as attention) or avoid something (like a difficult assignment). However, a third possibility is that the behavior exists simply because the opposite/positive behavior that you expect to see is not in the student's repertoire.

For example, a student who lacks basic social skills may be disrespectful, but the function of the disrespect is neither to get nor to avoid something—it simply happens because the student has no positive alternatives in his repertoire of skills. So the purpose of a function-based approach is to develop a hypothesis about why the student exhibits the behavior, then tailor the intervention to the hypothesis (O'Neill et al., 1997; Sprick & Garrison, 2008; Sugai et al., 2000).

If the student makes inappropriate remarks in class and the hypothesis about the function is that he does this to get adult attention, then reducing the amount, duration, and intensity of attention given in response to his inappropriate comments while concurrently providing lots of attention to the student when he is behaving appropriately would be a logical function-based intervention plan. For the disrespectful student who you hypothesize exhibits this behavior because she lacks social skills, a logical function-based intervention plan would involve teaching and practicing basic social skills, gently correcting disrespectful behavior by modeling more appropriate responses, and providing descriptive, positive feedback when the student exhibits respectful behavior. The goal is that students will have their needs met without resorting to misbehavior.

FOCUS ON THE GOAL

The B-RTI approach is, at its core, about service delivery. You should not necessarily have a specific set of steps that say, "Take this action at this time." It is very important to remain flexible. It is also vital that B-RTI should never be about the process—getting a particular student through a series of interventions until he reaches the one the teacher wants. Many teachers view interventions as simply a hoop-jumping process they must get through before they can refer a student to a special education program or an alternative placement. This approach is rooted in "not-my-problem" thinking and needs to be part of the cultural change.

True B-RTI is about making a good-faith effort to find a solution that will help a student behave more responsibly and, accordingly, become a better student. It is always about achieving the intended end result—it is never about which steps are taken along the way.

Our B-RTI model is independent of a school district's process for referring students to special education programs. Our model can operate parallel to a district's framework, but we do not advocate for any specific point at which a student is referred.

CONCLUSION

Creating B-RTI processes is a lot of work, especially when your goal is to "meet the needs of *every* student." Yet this is the crux of why a comprehensive B-RTI approach is needed. As recently as 50 years ago, public schools were charged with educating only a percentage of students to the point of high school graduation. Disciplinary procedures consisted mainly of punitive approaches, and if these were unsuccessful, the next steps were suspension and expulsion. This did not necessarily change behavior, but from the schools' perspective it was very effective: "If Johnny is a pain, don't let Johnny come to school—problem solved. Besides, Johnny will probably be fine and can get a job somewhere."

Now schools are charged with, and held accountable for, keeping *all* students in school and successfully educating them (IDEA, 2004; NCLB, 2001). This has required a fundamental shift in the nature of behavioral support practices. Schools must reach and motivate a segment of the population they never had to reach before (Walker & Sprague, 2006). This is a fundamental change in what schools must do to support positive behavior outcomes, and B-RTI may be the best model to effectively implement that change.

CHAPTER 2

Universal Prevention

The Role of the Leadership Team

Positive Behavioral Support (PBS) requires the implementation of universal practices, or interventions, for districtwide, schoolwide, and classroom levels. Without these processes in place, there is great potential that the problem-solving resources in the school will be overwhelmed by the sheer number of students exhibiting behavior problems (Stewart, Benner, Martella, & Marchand-Martella, 2007; Walker, 2004; Walker et al., 1996).

To recap, the basic definition of PBS is changing the system to meet the needs of the student while also helping the student fit successfully into the system. Universal practices are broad-based polices and procedures that change or structure the system so that it meets the behavioral and emotional needs of most students (Commission on Chronic Illness, 1957; Gordon, 1983; Horner, Sugai, Todd, & Lewis-Palmer, 2005; Sprick, Borgmeier, & Nolet, 2002). These policies are preventive in nature and should address school safety, civility, motivation, behavior, discipline, and climate (Nelson, Martella, & Marchand-Martella, 2002; Walker et al., 1996; Walker & Shinn, 2002). From a staff development standpoint, universal behavioral practices address every aspect of school that is not academic, including parent and community involvement.

DUTIES OF THE LEADERSHIP TEAM

Such a monumental task requires a building-based leadership team to take responsibility for shaping and overseeing these practices (George & Kincaid, 2008; Grimes, Kurns, & Tilly, 2006; McDougal, Clonan, Martens, & Nastasi, 2000; Sugai et al., 2008). This chapter, which is a condensed version of information that appears in *Foundations: Establishing Positive Discipline Policies* and *CHAMPs: A Proactive and Positive Approach to Classroom Management*, outlines the many responsibilities of the leadership team. The first task, or set of actions, in this chapter is to ensure that such a team exists and is fully functional in providing direction and creating unity among the staff for implementing evidence-based practices related to safety, discipline, motivation, climate, and so on.

This team is charged with ensuring that the school has an ongoing cycle of continuous improvement in each of these nonacademic areas. We don't use the word *continuous* lightly. Working toward school improvement can never stop. The goal of behavior support is not just the absence of misbehavior. Behavior support also seeks to teach students positive behaviors and to create a climate in which every student can be successful (Colvin & Fernandez, 2000; Horner et al., 2005; Sprick, Garrison, & Howard, 1998). In a school's dynamic environment, there is no such thing as *maintaining*—if you're not moving forward, you're losing ground. Task 2 in this chapter describes this continuous improvement cycle and provides guidance to the team about how to implement the cycle and get staff to actually implement effective practices throughout the school.

The leadership team also has to manage the maintenance of these practices and teach the users (all staff) how to implement and get full benefit from the policies and procedures. For universal practices to be effective, the leadership team must also work with the staff to design policies that teachers are willing to adopt and implement (Duchnowski, Kutash, Sheffield, & Vaughn, 2006; Elliott, Witt, & Kratochwill, 1991; Lane, Beebe-Frankenberger, Lambros, & Pierson, 2001). Without teacher support, the *practice* part of universal practices will never be a reality; you'll have universal theories instead.

In addition, a key element of universal practices is ongoing effort to encourage parental involvement in the school, increasing the partnership between staff and parents—not just when problems occur but also as part of shaping the climate and culture of the school to be inviting and inclusive of families. The team should also guide the staff in how to increase the school's connection with the community. A school should not be separate from the neighborhood and businesses, but rather a central part of that broader community.

> In a school's dynamic environment, there is no such thing as *maintaining*—if you're not moving forward, you're losing ground.

This leadership team is responsible for designing and managing the universal practices and B-RTI structures in the building, and that includes the classrooms. Although the team will never be involved in evaluating teachers, the team does need to create a schoolwide expectation that effective practices carry into each classroom. Task 3 in this chapter describes the type of universal behavior support that needs to be implemented in every classroom. This involves making sure that all teachers implement sound classroom management practices—what the research has taught us in the last 40 years about what really great teachers do differently than adequate or struggling teachers.

This set of tasks is both demanding and challenging. To meet these challenges, the team needs time to meet. We recommend that the team meet weekly or every other week and periodically take a full day to meet away from campus to reduce interruptions and prevent members from being pulled out of the meeting. In the early years of getting these processes established, we meet with teams for two full days every quarter to provide training and time to work on building implementation plans for all the tasks delineated in this chapter. After the first two years of learning these processes, we recommend at least one full day in the fall and one in the spring to maintain the cycle of continuous improvement.

Throughout most of this chapter, we describe building-level practices. However, there are great benefits when these universal behavior support procedures are implemented throughout the entire school district (George & Kincaid, 2008; Nersesian, Todd, Lehman, & Watson, 2000). Those readers with district-level responsibilities can read this chapter with a view toward how to institutionalize universal PBS throughout all schools within their district. This chapter ends with suggestions about ways to accomplish this (Task 4).

Task 1: Create a Behavior Leadership Team

The first step in establishing universal practices is to pull together a leadership team whose main responsibility is the implementation and continuous refinement of behavior support procedures (Dunlap et al., 2000; George, Horrower, & Knoster, 2003; Sprick, Garrison, & Howard, 2002; Sugai & Horner, 2006). In all but very small schools (say, fewer than 300 students), this team should focus exclusively on implementation of behavior support processes, not on case management of individual students. In Chapter 3, we describe the importance of problem-solving personnel and structures that do focus on case management of individual students. One such structure is a problem-solving team that we call an intervention planning team (IPT). For example, if a student is not succeeding in school, a teacher may refer the student to the IPT. The team and the teacher may then determine that the student—Kwesi—needs an individualized behavior support plan to help him manage and complete homework. In this chapter we describe a different team—what we call the behavior leadership team (BLT). This team will not focus on the individual student (in this case, Kwesi), but may determine by looking at data that 30% of students in the school are struggling with managing and completing homework. The BLT may subsequently decide to set a goal with the staff that within one year they will design and implement a variety of school-wide behavior support procedures to raise this rate of completion from 70% to 90%.

> The first step in establishing universal practices is to pull together a leadership team whose main responsibility is the implementation and continuous refinement of behavior support procedures.

ASSEMBLE THE TEAM

To be most effective, this leadership team will consist of six to nine staff members, including a school-based administrator and representatives of the entire staff (George et al.,

2003; Scott & Nelson, 1999; Sprick, Howard, et al., 1998). The suggestion of six to nine is based solely on considerations of group dynamics. If the team gets too large, it becomes difficult to sit around a table and discuss issues. However, if the team is too small—say, only three or four members—perspective may be too narrow and staff members may not feel adequately represented when new policies and procedures are discussed.

The school principal must be actively involved with this team because support from the top is imperative to its success. Without the principal's involvement, the probability of fragmentation among the staff in implementing any particular policy or practice is very high (Kincaid, Childs, Blasé, & Wallace, 2007). In large schools, particularly secondary schools, one of the building's assistant principals may be the administrator who actually serves on the team, but this will be effective only if the principal is willing to regularly and visibly vocalize his or her support for the process.

Representation on the team must mirror the staff as closely as possible. Because general education teachers make up the largest percentage of the staff, there must be an adequate number of general education teachers on the team. In a high school, this representation of general education teachers might be organized by departments, grade levels, teachers with common planning periods, or professional learning communities, depending on how the lines of organization and communication work within the school. There should be at least one special education teacher who represents the special education staff. Once representation of teaching staff has been assured, thought needs to be given to making sure that every member of the school staff is directly connected to a member of the team.

The leadership team should represent a cross section of the staff and not be limited to teachers and administrators. The more diverse the perspectives you have on the team, the more likely it is that the team will generate creative solutions to a broad array of school problems. Consider including staff members who have extensive training—school counselors, school psychologists, and behavior specialists—but also involve passionate teachers, administrators, and a few nonacademic staff such as the school nurse or lead maintenance person. It may also be helpful to have a parent or community liaison on the team. This person can serve as a link from the school to the community by providing input during meetings, soliciting feedback and ideas from the community, and promoting community involvement activities.

Note that every job role in the school cannot actually serve on the team. For example, there may be a custodian on the team. However, if there is not, someone on the team must represent the custodial staff. This could be a general education teacher who represents the ninth grade teachers and the custodial staff. Whenever issues are discussed that affect the custodial staff (e.g., restroom issues), this team member should be thinking about how to involve the custodians in analyzing the problem, brainstorming solutions, and supporting any new policies and procedures that are adopted that affect restrooms.

Because general education teachers make up the largest percentage of the staff, there must be an adequate number of general education teachers on the team.

KEEP THE TEAM ON TRACK

To help the leadership team stay organized and meet regularly, we developed a nine-point Schoolwide Behavior Support Checklist (Reproducible Form 2.1). It covers basic concepts such as meet on a regular basis, keep minutes, and assign tasks. The checklist also outlines the broad areas of the team's responsibilities: reviewing data, developing Guidelines for Success, classroom management, and more. Consider printing a copy of this checklist from the CD included with this book and fill it out as you read the remainder of Task 1 and move on to Task 2.

> ## ☀ *PBS Models*
>
> There are several proven models of schoolwide approaches to PBS. *Safe & Civil Schools* has developed the program titled *Foundations: Establishing Positive Discipline Policies*. Other models include:
>
> - *Positive Behavior Intervention and Support*, developed by George Sugai, Robert Horner, and colleagues at the University of Oregon.
>
> - *Project Achieve*, developed by Howie Knoff and published by Sopris West.
>
> - *BEST Behavior*, developed by Jeff Sprague and Annemiecke Golly and published by Sopris West.

✔ **Checklist Item 1.** As we described earlier in this chapter, a leadership team, including active involvement of the building principal, represents the entire staff.

✔ **Checklist Item 2.** The team meets on a regular basis and uses its time efficiently—starting and ending on time, keeping minutes, assigning tasks, etc. If team members don't meet, or are inefficient when they do meet, the process for improving schoolwide behavior support will stop (Pearce & Herbik, 2004). Every individual in a school is extremely busy each day trying to do his or her best to meet the needs of the students. Without a functional team, there may be little or no energy put into asking the question: What can we do to make the school a safe, inviting, and inspirational place for staff, students, and parents? It is up to the team to meet regularly and operate efficiently to guide the staff in doing just that.

Continued on p. 22

Reproducible Form 2.1 (p. 1 of 2)

SAMPLE

SCHOOLWIDE BEHAVIOR SUPPORT CHECKLIST

Item	Component or Process	In Place?	Actions
1	A leadership team, including active involvement of the building principal, represents the entire staff.	✓	
2	The team meets on a regular basis and uses its time efficiently—starting and ending on time, keeping minutes, assigning tasks, etc.		schedule team for year.
3	The team involves the staff in a continuous cycle of improvement that includes: a) collecting data, b) setting priorities, c) revising existing practices, d) adopting new policies or procedures, and e) ensuring implementation by staff.		Need to orient new staff members.
4	Review meaningful data to identify strengths of current behavior support practices and areas needing improvement.		
	4a. Annually, the team guides the staff in collecting and analyzing staff, student, and parent perceptions of existing policies and practices as well as overall school climate.		Prepare parent survey. Copy last year's staff survey results for team.
	4b. Annually, the team (with help from staff and students) conducts observations of all common areas.	✓	
	4c. The administrator provides quarterly summaries of disciplinary referrals so the team can analyze trends based on location, type of offense, time, date, and so on.	✓	Distribute next summary by 11/10.
5	This data is used to identify new priorities for improvements and assess the efficacy of current and past priorities.		Get input from staff—cafeteria or morning arrival as next priority.

 Reproducible Materials Blank copies of the forms are provided on the CD. Permission is given for individual teachers, administrators, or other school personnel to reproduce any form labeled "Reproducible Form" for in-district use.

Reproducible Form 2.1 (p. 2 of 2)

SAMPLE

SCHOOLWIDE BEHAVIOR SUPPORT CHECKLIST

Item	Component or Process	In Place?	Actions
6	For any given priority, revision proposals are developed for new policies and procedures. Any revision proposals are presented for feedback to the entire staff.		
	6a. Guidelines for Success (or equivalent) have been developed and are used as the basis for rules, procedures, and lessons.	✓	
	6b. Common areas have been assessed with regard to safety, civility, and efficacy and improved as needed. In secondary schools, particular attention is paid to hallway/passing time issues.	✓	*Need to review how well new playground rules are working.*
	6c. Procedures for coordination among administration, counseling, and teaching staff regarding severe misbehavior have been assessed and improved as needed.	✓	
	6d. An analysis has been conducted to determine gaps in the school's efforts to create school connectedness and to meet all students' basic needs.		*Are we doing enough to welcome/and orient students moving in mid-year?*
7	Any revision proposal will be implemented only after being adopted by the staff.		
8	The team will monitor implementation of new policies and practices, refining implementation until a subsequent review of data indicates that specific priority has been largely resolved.		
9	A classroom management model has been adopted, training and coaching provided, and reasonable accountability created.		*Need more suggestions for dealing with non-compliance.*

Adapted from *Foundations: Evidence-Based Behavioral Strategies for Individual Students* (Sprick, Garrison, & Howard, 2002)

Reproducible Materials Blank copies of the forms are provided on the CD. Permission is given for individual teachers, administrators, or other school personnel to reproduce any form labeled "Reproducible Form" for in-district use.

Task 2: Establish Practices of Continuous Improvement

The leadership team's first responsibility is to design universal practices and establish a continuous cycle of improvement based on those practices. To that end, this task will cover the remaining items from Reproducible Form 2.1. The main responsibility of the team is to create and maintain a cycle of continuous improvement. This is an enormous task with hundreds of details, but the underlying principle is simple: First, establish your expectations for students, then organize all settings to make success likely for students, and then continuously teach those expectations and reward students for meeting them. As simple as this may sound, it is at least as complex as what a hospital must do—continually work to ensure that the organization is implementing the most up-to-date, research-based practices while paying attention to thousands of small but important details (such as the accuracy with which medications are dispensed to patients) and accomplishing all of that in the most humane, supportive manner possible.

Many effective policies and practices may already be in place, but the leadership team has the opportunity to review and revise these polices regularly to ensure that they continue to be effective and that better policies and practices replace those that are not effective.

✔ **CHECKLIST ITEM 3**. The team involves the staff in a continuous cycle of improvement in which the team and staff:

1. Collect and *review* data.

2. Use that data to *prioritize* a manageable number of things to improve.

3. For any given priority, develop a proposal to *revise* existing policy or practices.

4. Continue to revise based on staff feedback until the staff is ready to *adopt* the new policies or practices.

5. Once new policies are adopted, ensure that all staff *implement* them.

Figure 2.1 provides a graphic representation of this concept—what we refer to as the improvement cycle. The main responsibility of the behavior leadership team is to institutionalize this cycle into the culture of the school. The remainder of this task provides suggestions on how to implement this cycle.

Figure 2.1
The Improvement Cycle

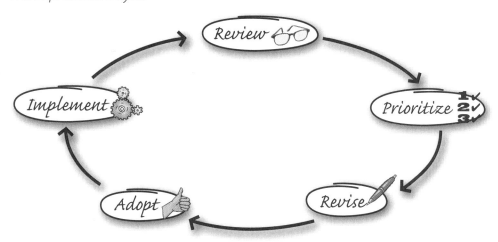

✔ **CHECKLIST ITEM 4**. The cycle begins with the review of meaningful data about safety, discipline, and climate to determine both strengths of current practices and gaps or weaknesses that need to be addressed. Before establishing or revising any universal practices, the leadership team should collect and/or review school-based data to share with the staff. This data will guide decision making (Horner, Sugai, & Todd, 2001; Irvin, Tobin, Sprague, Sugai, & Vincent, 2004). Item 4 from the Behavior Support Checklist says, "Review meaningful data to identify strengths of current behavior support practices and areas needing improvement." Specifically, this involves reviewing data from surveys (Item 4a), observations (Item 4b), and patterns of disciplinary referrals (Item 4c) to identify the major discrepancies between how you want students to behave and how they actually behave. Using these and any other relevant data sources, the team will share data with the staff in preparation for moving on to the next step of the cycle: setting a manageable number of priorities for improvement (but more on that later).

Surveys (Checklist Item 4a). Conducting surveys is an excellent way to gather information because respondents can give truthful opinions and remain anonymous. It's an opportunity to ask students: Do you feel safe in the hallways? Do you feel respected? Do you know what is expected of you? It also creates an opportunity for staff to contribute their perceptions on what types of problems are occurring and where. Giving staff and students the same survey is a great way to analyze the perceptions of each group and see how well they match up—or don't.

For example, one school conducted staff, student, and parent surveys (from templates found in *Foundations*). One item asked: Teachers treat students with respect. Agree or disagree. The results were startling: 100% of staff said they treated students with

> Review meaningful data to identify strengths of current behavior support practices and areas needing improvement.

respect, but only 45% of the students agreed. The leadership team knew that the disparity in perceptions had to reflect a reality in the classroom, so they conducted focus groups with students to find out exactly what the problem was. Whenever data is confusing, as in this case, focus groups are an excellent way to find out what's really going on. One strategy is to randomly choose 10 students from each grade level in the building, then meet with each group. It's important to promise the students confidentiality and no repercussions in exchange for their honesty.

In this case, the focus groups revealed that students perceived the frequent use of sarcasm by staff as disrespectful. Teachers proactively worked to change the way they spoke to students, and in the next year's survey, 89% of students agreed that teachers treated students with respect.

We recommend that the leadership team survey the staff and students every year if possible. If not logistically feasible, survey the staff every year and the students every other year. Getting feedback from parents is also useful, and if possible, we recommend surveying parents at least every three years. Although the surveys in *Foundations* are more extensive, a simple survey for staff and students asks respondents to agree or disagree with five basic statements about each of the major locations in the school (see Reproducible Form 2.2).

Adapt the survey in Reproducible Form 2.2 in any way necessary to make it directly applicable to your school. For example, high schools will probably need to say courtyard or commons instead of playground. If no hallways exist, substitute breezeways. For elementary schools, surveys are probably most useful for third grade and up.

Direct observation (Checklist Item 4b). This point may seem obvious, but the best data you can collect on student behavior comes from directly observing behavior beyond the classroom. The leadership team is tasked with shaping expectations for hallways, bathrooms, playgrounds, cafeterias, outdoor athletic fields—every place on the school property that students access. On an annual basis, the team should enlist teachers and other staff members to directly observe each of these common areas and report the behaviors they encounter. Assign pairs of staff to specific areas during critical time periods and arrange for their classes to be covered while they're collecting observation data. For example, if two teachers are to observe in the cafeteria, they will need someone to supervise their usual responsibilities during this time. Don't forget arrival and departure zones and times. Assign teachers to observe these zones for a 25-minute period at the beginning and end of each day. These areas are critical because they represent students' first and last school experiences each day. Be sure to assign at least one male and one female to observe hallways so that entering restrooms can be part of hallway observations.

The best data you can collect on student behavior comes from directly observing behavior beyond the classroom.

Reproducible Form 2.2

SAMPLE SCHOOL SURVEY

Put a ✔ in each box for which the statement is true.

	on school grounds before school	in the classrooms	on the playground	in the halls	in the bathrooms	in the cafeteria	on school grounds after school	on the bus	walking to and from school
1. Students feel safe.									
2. Students treat other students respectfully.									
3. Students are taught how to behave responsibly.									
4. Students treat staff respectfully.									
5. Staff treat students respectfully.									

Reproducible Materials Blank copies of the forms are provided on the CD. Permission is given for individual teachers, administrators, or other school personnel to reproduce any form labeled "Reproducible Form" for in-district use.

Much of what teachers report will not be news (food throwing at the corner table in the cafeteria), but some of the information will highlight new problems that need to be addressed. For example, in one school a teacher assigned to observe the playground noticed that the assistants supervising the playground were standing together talking. From this observation, the leadership team was able to clarify playground expectations and craft a policy for the playground supervisors: Divide the playground into zones and have each supervisor circulate in his or her zone to observe students. In addition to providing general feedback about behavior across school settings, these observations may also reveal concerns as specific as the length of time students have to wait in line for lunch, unpleasant levels of noise and horseplay in bus loading areas, "bullying" by some students, or isolation of certain students. All of these pieces of observational data gathered by the leadership team can help inform and shape the school's universal policies and practices to better meet the needs of all students.

Disciplinary referral patterns (Checklist Item 4c). Wherever patterns of misbehavior exist, there is an opportunity to employ preventive strategies (Cooper, Heron, & Heward, 2007). The leadership team needs to analyze disciplinary referrals and determine whether patterns exist, form hypotheses about what is shaping those patterns, then craft universal practices that will prevent or at least minimize disciplinary problems. If your school already uses the School-Wide Information System (SWIS, May et al., 2003), this is a great place to start sorting for disciplinary patterns. Even when the patterns are expected (e.g., December and the last month of school are difficult months in most schools, with many referrals during this time), the team can use the information to plan additional supports for those students and compare the effectiveness of one year's supports with the next year's. In addition to confirming hypothesized patterns, teams can use office discipline referral data to better understand new problems (e.g., who's getting the referrals, what time they are occurring, and in what setting/apparatus).

Leadership team members may discover that what they find contradicts what they hear from staff. If you ask teachers on what day of the week they have the most behavioral problems, most will say that Friday is their most challenging day. Yet many buildings will find that according to referral patterns, Thursday has the most discipline referrals, and Mondays and Fridays have the least. From this information, leadership team members can develop a hypothesis. In this case, they may guess that the high referral pattern is a function of teachers being more tolerant on Mondays and Fridays because they just had a great weekend or are looking forward to one. On the other hand, Thursday may have the greatest number of discipline referrals because it corresponds to peak teacher frustration with student behavior.

There is an opportunity here for the leadership team to present this hypothesis to teachers, get their feedback, then design polices and plans that will address the problem. The goal of universal practices is to create a school environment that is safe,

> The leadership team needs to analyze disciplinary referrals and determine whether patterns exist, form hypotheses about what is shaping those patterns, then craft universal practices that will prevent or at least minimize disciplinary problems.

civil, and *consistent* for teachers and students alike (Colvin, Kame'enui, & Sugai, 1993; Lewis & Sugai, 1999; Sprick et al., 1992). Students need to know that behavior expectations for Monday are exactly the same as behavior expectations for Thursday. Teachers need to know that if they're feeling a little frayed as the week wears on, the school has support systems in place to help them. However, what constitutes a referral to the office should be based on student behavior, not adult emotion.

Once the leadership team has discovered the spikes in student misbehavior (which often correlate with holidays and special events), the team can establish a calendar for re-teaching behavior expectations. Reading the rules once at the beginning of the school year isn't sufficient. If your school is doing a good job of establishing universal expectations, the level of information can be overwhelming. Re-teach expectations in manageable chunks throughout the school year. Think about a sports coach who re-teaches basic expectations and plays periodically throughout the season. It is not that the team did not learn these things initially—periodic re-teaching sustains and enhances performance over time.

Other data sources. The previous section described three major sources of data that a behavioral leadership team should examine: surveys, direct observations, and office discipline referrals. However, you should also ask if there are any other useful data sources to include in this review step. Focus groups, for example, were mentioned earlier. Or you may want to consider your school's injury reports. By looking at locations where injuries occur, such as stairwells or hallways, the team may identify a priority that needs to be focused on. Safety is key to a positive school environment. If the data reveals that your school has a rising level of violence, it may be time to re-evaluate the implementation (including teaching and rewarding behavior) of your universal PBS strategies as well as to consider implementing periodic anger management training and conflict resolution for students as part of your universal practices. If the data indicates that four students were injured on stairways during the previous year, the leadership team needs to observe students' behavior in stairways, then design policies that will make the stairs safer.

One school had such a problem. Through observation, team leaders discovered that middle school students (who haven't learned to drive yet) were prone to cut across the stair landings, sometimes colliding with other students. So the team recommended painting traffic flow lines on all the landings—visually teaching students to stay to the outside when making a left turn. The school reduced the number of injuries and potentially created better future drivers at the same time.

Summary. The team collects, reviews, and compiles various sources of data. They then prepare summary reports of this information to present to staff. Next, the team guides the staff in discussing this data to prepare to take action, specifically: What is the staff going to work to improve? That takes the team to the next step of the cycle: Prioritize.

> Reading the rules once at the beginning of the school year isn't sufficient . . . periodic re-teaching sustains and enhances performance over time.

✔ **CHECKLIST ITEM 5**. The next stage of the improvement cycle is to use the collected data to get staff agreement on what problems or concerns need to be addressed and to put those concerns into some sort of hierarchy from most to least urgent. This means that the team's job is to unify the staff in defining the school's priorities for the year regarding behavior support efforts.

What is the staff ready and willing to work to improve? Those priorities should include specific areas where the school (or teaching staff) needs improvement, as determined by the data collection. This again goes back to the discrepancy between how you (and the entire staff) want students to behave and how they actually behave. For example, one school may prioritize bullying prevention, particularly on the playground, while another school may prioritize improving efficiency and orderliness in the cafeteria and arrival/dismissal areas, while another school may establish the priority to reduce insubordination and disrespect in all locations of the school at all times of day, and yet another school may address apathy and lack of motivation. What the school focuses on will be based on multiple data sources and what the staff as a whole is excited about improving.

If you've put together a great leadership team, its members will be enthusiastic and may even rally the staff to want to fix everything at once. Having 17 goals for the year, however, isn't realistic. So the team must analyze the data, present the data to staff, and get the staff to agree on the priorities for the next period of time—say, a semester. Choosing two or three main areas to focus on at any one time is a practical approach that will more likely produce the necessary improvement.

Once a given priority is set, summarize for the staff the data that led to the conclusion that this item needed to be a priority and set a timeline for improvement. For example, if 25% of students disagreed with the statement, "Students feel safe in the restrooms," a goal could be that within a semester, 95% agree with that statement.

✔ **CHECKLIST ITEM 6**. In the next stage of the improvement cycle, revised procedures will be discussed for each agreed-upon priority. Once new policies and procedures have been developed, they will be presented for the staff to consider adopting, but adoption will be discussed later in this chapter. For any given priority, the proposed revision will involve policies and procedures that are different from what staff have been doing in the past, because, as the old adage says: If we keep doing what we have always done, we will keep getting what we have always gotten. Another way of stating this is that the school's current policies and procedures (what the staff is actually doing, not just what is written in a file drawer) are perfectly suited to generate students' current behaviors and attitudes. Because there is both data and agreement from staff that the problem needs to be addressed, the staff must also be willing to explore what they can do differently to facilitate improvement in the behavior of the students.

> Choosing two or three main areas to focus on at any one time is a practical approach that will more likely produce the necessary improvement.

ROADMAP FOR REVISION

One approach to addressing any concern is to target for revision the five areas of improvement, one from each of the STOIC variables (Structure, Teach, Observe, Interact, Correct) discussed in the previous chapter. An example using this STOIC strategy for improving a school's cafeteria might look like this:

*S*tructure. Change from two lunch shifts to three to reduce crowding. Improve the record-keeping process so students do not need to stand in line as long as they do now. Put more condiments on tables so there is less need for students to move to another table or to pass a ketchup bottle among 25 students at long rows of tables. To further reduce time in line, have students enter the cafeteria and go directly to tables, then excuse each table to get food.

*T*each. Provide systematic lessons to teach:

- Entry procedures

- Quiet conversation at tables

- Behavior when standing in line

- Making efficient choices at the salad bar

- Basic manners when interacting with food service personnel, cafeteria supervisors, and other students

- How to accept a compliment or a behavior correction (gentle reprimand) from a cafeteria supervisor

- Exit procedures

*O*bserve. Train cafeteria supervisors to:

- Position one supervisor at the door as students enter the cafeteria.

- Assign one supervisor to excuse students at tables to get their food.

- Circulate throughout assigned zones to ensure that all tables are supervised.

- Continue to supervise as students are dismissed and exit so students do not think that once excused from the table, they are free to do whatever they want.

*I*nteract. Train all adults in the cafeteria (food service workers, custodians, supervisors) to greet students, be inviting, and provide age-appropriate positive feedback to all students.

*C*orrect. Train all adults in the cafeteria to gently and immediately correct any behavior that violates the expectations that have been taught (see the bulleted list under "Teach"). That is, if a student does not say "thank you" when given something by an adult, that adult is expected to calmly and immediately say, "What do you say when someone gives you something?" Or if a student is repeatedly too loud and gentle reminders are not sufficient, the student may be required to sit at an assigned table for the reminder of the lunch period. Supervisors will be trained to avoid power struggles and to use a range of corrective consequences.

CATEGORIES TO TARGET FOR IMPROVEMENT

On the Schoolwide Behavior Support Checklist (Reproducible Form 2.1), Item 6 addresses the revision stage of the improvement cycle. This item is subdivided into Items 6a through 6d. These represent four major categories for revising schoolwide policies and procedures. In working with leadership teams from several thousand schools during the last 20 years, we have found that schools may benefit from working on each of these categories on an ongoing basis as their data indicates a need for improvement. After describing each category of policies and procedures that may benefit from revision, we will get back to the improvement cycle with suggestions for the two remaining steps, Adoption and Implementation.

Craft Guidelines for Success (Checklist Item 6a). One of the most effective universal practices that a school can put into place is development of overarching Guidelines for Success. These guidelines are, in essence, goal statements that summarize the skills or traits that define the school's culture and communicate what teachers, students, and parents value. The leadership team must be the guiding force in developing a process that includes input and ownership from staff students and parents. As a starting place, ask yourselves: What broad traits do we want to emphasize?

An excellent example, shown in Figure 2.2, comes from Interlake High School in Bellevue, Washington, where the leadership team chose "Integrity, Humanity, and Scholarship" as the school's guiding principles (Sprick, 2006). With these three carefully chosen words, the school's staff were able to not only sum up their expectations for students but also give students a cultural identity that they could be proud of and want to live up to.

Figure 2.2

Interlake High School's Guiding Principles

You could say that these Guidelines for Success have a spiritual component that goes beyond a set of rules. Guidelines for Success are the message that you will preach to your students. We use the word *preach* purposefully, because preaching is recursive; it means communicating the same core messages over and over—using passion, knowledge, and charisma to get others to value the same things that you value. Your guidelines need to be value statements that every staff member and student in your building or organization can be passionate about on the first day of school, the last day of school, and every day in between. Imagine how powerful it is for a student to hear again and again from every adult they encounter for four years the importance of integrity, humanity, and scholarship. Guidelines for Success can become part of your students' characters—traits they will remember, and hopefully be influenced by, for the rest of their lives.

Address the common areas (Checklist Item 6b). STOIC variables need to be addressed for all of a school's physical locations that are used by students and supervised by a variety of adults. These locations include:

- arrival areas
- halls/stairs/breezeways
- restrooms
- playground
- courtyards
- cafeteria
- dismissal areas

Although assemblies and how-to-behave-with-substitute-teachers are not physical areas, we consider them common areas in that they can benefit from clear procedures for both staff and students, as outlined by the STOIC variables. How to address these common areas is beyond the scope of this chapter, but the cafeteria example provided earlier offers a sense of breadth and depth that we suggest you duplicate as you develop revision proposals for a common area that has been identified as a priority. Note that secondary schools may need to be especially vigilant about developing and implementing procedures that address the passing times between classes—the combined issues of hallway behavior, restroom behavior, and tardiness to class. See the *START on Time!* box for information about a program that when implemented well can reduce tardiness to class by up to 95% (Sprick, 2003).

✥ START on Time!

Another resource that leadership teams can employ is the *START on Time!* 10-Point Checklist (see Reproducible Form 2.3). This universal practice has proven to reduce tardiness and in-school absenteeism by up to 95% in secondary schools—from inner cities to suburbs to Indian reservations (Sprick, 2003). When used properly, *START on Time!* will give your school the same 95% response rating. Experience shows that when schools follow only five points on the list, they get only a 50% reduction in tardiness. Some schools even skip the lessons, but this is counterproductive. If you have the time and resources to do only one thing, the lessons are most important. Equally important is to teach and re-teach the expectations to your students throughout the school year.

Develop policies for addressing severe misbehavior (Checklist Item 6c). Severe misbehavior is especially frustrating to staff. Policies and procedures need to ensure that staff feel a sense of safety and support and at the same time take student needs into account. Following is a list of questions that must be addressed so that there is seamless support when dealing with severe behavior problems and behavioral safety issues. Again, it is beyond the scope of this chapter to provide answers to all these questions, but for more information you can peruse *Interventions: Evidence-Based Behavioral Strategies for Individual Students* and *Foundations: Establishing Positive Discipline Policies*.

- What categories of behaviors are severe enough that the student should be removed from the classroom? (By implication, all other behaviors will be managed in the classroom by the classroom teacher.)

- What types of consequences can be assigned by a teacher within the classroom to nonreferrable categories of behavior?

Reproducible Form 2.3

START ON TIME! 10-POINT CHECKLIST   SAMPLE

For Items 1–3, ask a building administrator for these documents.

For Items 4–8, observe at least two different passing periods during the day.

For Items 9 and 10, talk to several teachers during the day.

	No Evidence	Some Evidence	Full Evidence
1. A map, list, or table provides documentation for preplanning the distribution of adults in different locations—providing full coverage of all places where students might be during passing times.	0	5	(10)
2. A printed schedule defines which staff members and which administrative/security staff members are assigned to which locations for each passing time.	0	5	(10)
3. Lesson schedules and lesson plans are provided for teaching hallway/restroom/tardiness expectations to all students at the beginning of the year with appropriate review throughout the year.	0	(5)	10
4. During the passing time, adults are visible throughout the corridor supervising classrooms and the hallway.	0	(5)	10
5. Adults in the hallways are interacting in friendly and supportive ways with students.	0	5	(10)
6. Adults in the hallways intervene with any and all perceived misbehavior. If no misbehavior is observed, mark "Full Evidence."	0	(5)	10
7. When the bell rings, teachers immediately close their doors, do not allow students to enter, and begin class as soon as the door is closed.	0	(5)	10
8. Any students not in class are swept by an adult within two minutes of the bell ringing. If no students are in the hall, mark "Full Evidence."	0	(5)	10
9. All swept students are required to fill out the START on Time! form that will be sent to parents.	(0)	5	10
10. Administrative/Security staff check in with staff on the sweep to manage any paperwork and to take over code-of-conduct violations.	0	(5)	10
Add the sum of point values for each column:	0 +	30 +	30
How many students were observed in a major hall 30 seconds after the bell rang? ☐ 2 or fewer ☑ 3 to 7 ☐ 8 or more		=	60 %

If two or fewer students are tardy and implementation is less than 70%, there is probably no need for improved implementation.

If tardiness appears to be a problem and implementation is less than 80%, some additional planning and/or staff development may be warranted.

Reproducible Materials Blank copies of the forms are provided on the CD. Permission is given for individual teachers, administrators, or other school personnel to reproduce any form labeled "Reproducible Form" for in-district use.

- When sending a referral to the office, what sort of paperwork and other actions (e.g., contacting parents) is the teacher required to follow?

- What processes will administrators follow when getting and processing referrals? How will the referring teacher know what has been done, and what is he or she expected to do or not do when the student returns to class?

- What is the role of the school counselor in dealing with severe and chronic misbehavior? School social worker? Nurse? District behavior specialist? Other?

- How should staff to respond to behavioral emergencies such as threats, fights, or a student who gets physically out of control?

- How should staff respond if a student refuses to follow a direction? (e.g., "No, I am not going to come in from recess!")

Ensure that all students' basic needs are met (Checklist Item 6d). Your school should be a great place for every individual student you serve. Every student has these needs:

- Physical and emotional safety

- General acceptance

- Adult attention, encouragement, and positive feedback

- Respectful correction when mistakes are made

- Academic success

- Sense of emotional connectedness to the school because it provides a sense of purpose and belonging

We encourage the leadership team to think every several years about a range of individual students, from the outstanding to the actively troubled to the passively troubled to the average, may-fade-into-the-background student. Then for each of those types of students, ask if the school is a great place. If the answer may be "no" (for the sake of clarity, in this case let's say for the average student in a high school), the team should guide the staff in using the STOIC framework to develop suggested policies and procedures that will address the problem.

For example, relative to Structure, perhaps the school needs to develop a broader array of clubs, intramural sports, service opportunities, work experiences, adult mentors, school-based jobs, and so on. For the T in STOIC, students need to be taught what is available through active marketing to encourage participation in this rich array of structures. For example, does the coach of the track team encourage all students who might be interested to come to an orientation to learn about the benefits of being part of the track team? Staff can also be trained to watch more closely for those uninvolved students (observe), to make more frequent and encouraging contact with those students (interact), and to respond to the student who is not getting involved (correct). For example, staff can be encouraged to do things like this: If you know a student is interested in track, but you find out he did not go to the orientation meeting, talk with the student privately after class about why he didn't go to the orientation and even offer to intercede with the coach to find out if it's not too late for him to get involved.

✔ **CHECKLIST ITEM 7**. Once the leadership team has crafted a proposal for any given priority, it is imperative to present the proposal to the staff for their approval. This is the adoption stage of the improvement cycle. Without teacher support, universal practices, no matter how carefully designed, are not likely to succeed (Elliott, Witt, Kratochwill, & Callan-Stoiber, 2002; George et al., 2003). If teachers are forced to implement a proposal they don't fully support, they are more likely to fail to implement it, and the plan will fail. One school spent six months drafting proposal after proposal that the staff rejected until the team came up with exactly the right plan. Our experience indicates that those leadership members and teachers who give the most consideration to their universal practices have the most success in the long term.

The school principal, as a member of the leadership team, should be a crucial component in the adoption process. The principal's role is to communicate with teachers, and his or her main message needs to be this: "Staff, consider this proposal carefully. You do not have to adopt it. If it isn't adequate, make suggestions and send it back. Do not adopt anything you don't fully support. Because once these practices are adopted, it is my job to ensure that they are implemented by each and every teacher."

✔ **CHECKLIST ITEM 8**. In addition to crafting the proposal and getting it adopted, the leadership team must ensure that the policies are implemented. Experience has taught us that in most schools, some small percentage of the staff may be passively resistant to new policies and procedures. Even if the proposal is adopted, the leadership team must work to pump up support for implementation. Teacher enthusiasm is key to making universal practices effective. If even one teacher fails to implement the policies, that nonsupport can derail the proposal. If the lack of implementation is not addressed, it can lead other teachers to think, "If Mrs. Smith isn't doing it, why should I?" The passive resistance will spread to other teachers. Here again, the principal has a role and must step in, take that teacher aside, and respectfully enforce compliance.

> Without teacher support, universal practices, no matter how carefully designed, are not likely to succeed.

It is better to have no policy at all (e.g., no dress code) than to have one that only seven out of ten teachers enforce. Inconsistency of implementation communicates very unclear information to the students about what is truly acceptable and unacceptable in the school.

Task 3: Provide Classroom Management Support

✔ **CHECKLIST ITEM 9**. In addition to designing universal practices that create an ongoing cycle of schoolwide improvement, the leadership team has another equally important task—to provide the training, administrative support, and coaching that teachers need for classroom management (George & Kincaid, 2008; Sprick, Knight, et al., 2007; Sugai & Horner, 2006). As a member of the leadership team, the most difficult aspect of your job is to take on the task of classroom management and share it with your colleagues, who are your peers. For universal classroom management to be effective, it must be supportive and nonevaluative. Initial training is not enough; effective classroom management also typically requires continuous support and feedback from the leadership team (Adelman & Taylor, 1997; Grimes et al., 2006; Sugai et al., 2008; Taylor-Greene et al., 1997). We have also concluded that the process needs to involve everyone who has a role in the classroom. What we describe next is a condensed version of material in *CHAMPs: A Proactive and Positive Approach to Classroom Management* and *Coaching Classroom Management*.

THREE ROLES FOR CLASSROOM BEHAVIOR SUPPORT

A classroom management model that engages all educational staff comprises three groups of people who each have a role to play: building-based administrators, coaches, and teachers.

Administrators. The main role of principals and assistant principals in classroom management is to choose the approach. This may mean determining whether to use a schoolwide or districtwide model, or it may mean leading the school to adopt a currently existing program. The advantage to having a schoolwide standard is that it creates a common language, giving administrators the opportunity to clarify their expectations for outcomes. Without a unified approach, the staff lacks a common language, and it may be difficult for teachers, especially new teachers, to understand expectations.

The outcome of classroom management should always be defined by student engagement. The evaluation of classroom management should not be about the details or steps taken—it should be about the results. As administrators, your goal for student engagement in the classroom should be 90%. Anything less than that means the classroom management approach needs work. With only 80% engagement in a classroom of 30 students, six students are off task. Neither the leadership team members nor the teachers have the time to design and implement individual interventions for that many students. An unacceptable level of student engagement must be viewed as a classroom management problem.

So the second main task of administrators is to conduct frequent classroom walkthroughs and provide feedback to teachers based on observations. Conducting observations and providing feedback once a year is not enough because it gives only a single snapshot in time. Administrators need to conduct multiple spot checks across time to observe how well teachers are keeping their students engaged throughout the year. During walkthrough visits, administrators should be mainly assessing whether student engagement is at least 90%. In addition, the observation can capture a snapshot of positive-to-negative ratios of interactions. These interaction ratios can be used to determine whether teachers are attending to responsible behavior at least three times more often than attending to misbehavior. This ratio of positive to negative interactions is important because research has shown that the behaviors we pay attention to tend to increase over time (Cooper, 1987). This fits with the STOIC acronym in that structure, teaching, and observation should result in 90% engagement or better, and the ratio of interactions examines the teacher's distribution of positive *interactions* as compared with corrective *consequences*.

If a principal observes that a teacher consistently has an inadequate level of student engagement or is not being sufficiently positive, it is the administrator's role to discuss those observations with the teacher, insist that the teacher make improvements, and offer all the resources the school has available to support the improvements. Those resources should include a cadre of coaches trained in effective classroom management practices. Administrators should encourage teachers who need help to seek out a coach to work with. Then the administrator's role is to step back and let the teacher take the initiative to make the best use of the available resources.

Coaches. The role of coach can be filled by anyone who has an opportunity to be in the classroom with teachers in a supportive, nonevaluative role. Coaches can be literacy coaches, school counselors, school psychologists, or behavior specialists.

The key word here is *nonevaluative*. For teachers and coaches to establish a supportive, *trusting* relationship, there must be an understanding that their interactions will be confidential and not reported back to administrators. To be effective, coaches must not be viewed as the classroom management police. Their role is to respond to the teacher's request for help, then offer observation, guidance, and support. The leadership team and administration must create a supportive culture and communicate this concept clearly to teachers so that they feel comfortable asking for coaching assistance when they need it.

Coaches can support teachers in a variety of ways, including demonstration teaching, co-teaching, and observation with feedback (Codding, Feinberg, Dunn, & Pace, 2005; DiGennaro, Martens, & McIntyre, 2005; Noell et al., 2005; Sterling-Turner, Watson, & Moore, 2002). To assist coaches, we offer a classroom checklist that covers key areas of effective classroom management (Reproducible Form 2.4 on the next page).

This tool provides an efficient, effective, and objective way for coaches to monitor a classroom and identify problem areas for the teacher to address. Checklist in hand, the coach can say something like, "Mrs. Johnson, I see that you have posted classroom rules, Guidelines for Success, and expectations, but I noticed that your students

During walkthrough visits, administrators should be mainly assessing whether student engagement is at least 90%.

Reproducible Form 2.4

SAMPLE

CLASSROOM MANAGEMENT STOIC CHECKLIST

Variables	Questions to guide discussion	Y	N	Comments
Structure/ Organize the classroom for success.	1. Is the room arranged so you can get from any part of the room to any other part of the room relatively efficiently?	Ⓨ	N	*Ending routine needs work—some students aren't waiting until they are dismissed.*
	2. Can you and your students access materials and the pencil sharpener without disturbing others?	Ⓨ	N	
	3. Does the schedule create consistency, variety, and opportunities for movement?	Ⓨ	N	
	4. Do you have effective beginning and ending routines?	Y	Ⓝ	
	5. Have you defined clear expectations for instructional activities?	Ⓨ	N	
	6. Have you defined clear expectations for transitions between activities?	Ⓨ	N	
Teach students how to behave responsibly in the classroom.	1. Have you created lessons on expectations and explicitly taught them for classroom activities and transitions?	Ⓨ	N	*Reteach start and end routines. Increase positive reinforcement of students who follow rules.*
	2. Have you created lessons and explicitly taught expectations for classroom routines and policies?	Ⓨ	N	
	3. Have you provided teaching and reteaching as needed? (Think about a basketball coach reteaching particular plays or patterns.)	Y	Ⓝ	
Observe student behavior (supervise!)	1. Do you circulate and scan as a means of observing/ monitoring student behavior?	Ⓨ	N	*Try to visit each group at least twice during independent work.*
	2. Do you model friendly, respectful behavior while monitoring the classroom?	Ⓨ	N	
	3. Do you periodically collect data to make judgments about what is going well and what needs to be improved in your management plan?	Ⓨ	N	
Interact positively with students.	1. Do you interact with every student in a welcoming manner (e.g., saying hello, using the student's name, talking to the student at every opportunity)?	Ⓨ	N	
	2. Do you provide age-appropriate, non-embarrassing feedback?	Ⓨ	N	
	3. Do you strive to interact more frequently with every student when he is engaged in positive behavior than when he is engaged in negative behavior?	Ⓨ	N	
Correct irresponsible behavior fluently— that is, in a manner that does not interrupt the flow of instruction.	1. Do you correct consistently?	Ⓨ	N	*Add supervised lunch to menu?*
	2. Do you correct calmly?	Ⓨ	N	
	3. Do you correct immediately?	Ⓨ	N	
	4. Do you correct briefly?	Ⓨ	N	
	5. Do you correct respectfully?	Ⓨ	N	
	6. Do you have a menu of in-class consequences that can be applied to a variety of infractions?	Ⓨ	N	
	7. Do you have a plan for how to respond to different types of misbehavior fluently?	Ⓨ	N	

Copyright © 2009 Pacific Northwest Publishing

 Reproducible Materials Blank copies of the forms are provided on the CD. Permission is given for individual teachers, administrators, or other school personnel to reproduce any form labeled "Reproducible Form" for in-district use.

might benefit from increased prompting and feedback. One strategy you might try is to circulate through the room more frequently. This might allow you to prompt more responsible behavior from your students and more readily acknowledge the responsible behavior you see."

Teachers. The teachers' role, the most important of the three, is to implement the core practices of effective classroom management. For teachers, classroom management is a complex and lifelong learning task. Training and coaching are a continuous part of the practice. There are several classroom management models to choose from, but we offer *CHAMPs: A Proactive and Positive Approach to Classroom Management* as an exemplar.

The CHAMPs Model. The principles outlined in *CHAMPs* offer teachers a series of decisions about which variables to adjust to help students be successful. Within the classroom, the STOIC variables—Structure, Teach, Observe, Interact, and Correct—are constantly in play, and effective classroom management is about successfully manipulating these variables. The Classroom Management STOIC Checklist (Reproducible Form 2.4) is a condensed version of the information offered in *CHAMPs*. The checklist follows the STOIC structure and provides a useful framework for effective classroom management.

*S***tructure.** The first five guidelines in the checklist help create a classroom environment that is structured for success.

- Complete a classroom management plan or syllabus (see the Syllabus section that follows for more detail).

- Post classroom rules.

- Post Guidelines for Success.

- Post expectations for major activities.

- Arrange the physical setting to allow easy supervision.

*T***each.** The next three guidelines offer good practices for what and how you teach:

- Schedule activities and lessons designed to create variety and engagement.

- Teach and re-teach age-appropriate lessons on behavioral expectations, as needed.

- Include *CHAMPs* expectations in lessons on behavioral expectations, as needed. *CHAMPs*, which stands for *Conversation*, *Help*, *Activity*, *Movement*, and *Participation*, is a resource from *Safe & Civil Schools* that outlines the details of what we have to teach kids about our classroom expectations.

Another key factor in the Teach variable is that instructors must periodically re-teach their expectations. Too many teachers think that going over the rules once at the beginning of the year is adequate. It's not. Teachers must think more like athletic coaches who practice the fundamentals with their charges again and again.

*O*bserve. To observe students in the classroom, teachers should do the following:

- Circulate throughout the classroom unpredictably to prompt responsible behavior.

- Visually scan to monitor alignment with expectations.

*I*nteract. The fourth variable in STOIC, Interact, involves some of the most important classroom management practices. A later section covers student-teacher interactions in more detail, but here are the three guidelines from the classroom checkup.

- Provide frequent noncontingent attention.

- Provide age-appropriate, nonembarrassing, positive feedback.

- Maintain at least a three-to-one ratio of interactions (attention to positive behavior versus attention to negative behavior).

*C*orrect. Appropriate corrections are fluent and do not interrupt the flow of classroom instruction. These two guidelines cover this management practice.

- Implement preplanned consequences for rule violations and other chronic misbehavior.

- When misbehavior occurs, correct calmly consistently, briefly, and immediately.

Positive and negative interactions. Positive and negative interactions reflect the Interact and Correct variables in STOIC. Although there is no universal agreement for the exact ratio, most research shows that to be effective, positive interactions must significantly outnumber negative ones (Brophy & Good, 1986; Rosenshine, 1971; Sprick, 2006; Sprick, Garrison, et al., 1998). Positive interactions create motivation; students work harder for teachers who are interested in them. Contingent praise has been correlated with increases in task engagement, correct academic responding, compliance, and reduction in problem behaviors (Alber, Heward, & Hippler, 1999; Gunter & Jack, 1993; Sutherland, Wehby, & Copeland, 2000). A simple "Good morning, James" tells the student that you know who he is, you care about him, and you expect him to participate in your classroom experience.

Although some researchers suggest a ratio as high as nine to one, teachers should ideally offer a minimum of three positive interactions for every negative or corrective action. If teachers pay more attention to misbehavior than to appropriate behavior, the corrections may inadvertently serve as a positive reinforcer (ultimately increasing misbehavior) for students who are starved for attention.

Appropriate corrections, although labeled negative interactions, should be minimal. Spending too much time on a correction or becoming emotionally charged are both counterproductive. As coaches, school counselors, and teachers, you can anticipate the misbehaviors you expect to encounter and plan in advance what you will say. Preplanned corrections will be smooth, nondisruptive to other students, and non-embarrassing for the misbehaving student. For example, if a student shouts out a smart-aleck response to a question, all that the staff member needs to say is, "Justin, that made me feel disrespected, so we will talk about it after class, but now I'm going to continue with my lesson. As I was saying . . . "

The same preplanned strategy can be used with students who are off task. If, during independent study, a student is not doing her work, you can quietly ask if she is having problems. If she says, "You can't make me do this work," agree with her. Say something like, "You're right, I can't, but I would like you to do the assignment. Excuse me, but another student needs my help." Then walk away, giving yourself and the student time to reassess your strategies. In this scenario, the correction has been minimal and nonconfrontational.

As leadership team members, you can apply the STOIC model to help teachers improve their classroom management. Ask yourselves: How can we improve the classroom *structure* to help teachers be successful? Which teachers would benefit from more *teaching*/training in Tier 1 interventions? How often should we *observe* teacher-student interactions in each classroom? Is our ratio of positive-to-negative *interactions* with a particular teacher supportive of success? How can we give teachers *corrective* feedback in a preplanned, supportive way?

Effective classroom management is always defined by student engagement *and* respect. Everybody in the classroom deserves to be treated with dignity and respect. It is imperative not only that students show respect for teachers but that teachers show respect for students. If a teacher has a high rate of engagement but belittles students, that teacher needs coaching. Treating a student with disrespect may not only damage the student's motivation in that classroom, but also affect every subsequent class the student attends.

Classroom Management Plan. Elementary teachers may benefit from summarizing their classroom management strategy using the two-page Reproducible Form 2.5: Classroom Management Plan. By filling out this form before the school year begins, the teacher thinks through how he will handle the issues outlined in the form. An additional benefit is that the completed form can be included in the teacher's folder for substitute teachers as a compact summary of how the teacher manages behavior.

Classroom Syllabus. The typical secondary classroom is incredibly complex. There are scores of policies, procedures, rules, and expectations (Sprick, 2006). Some procedures apply to the specific teacher and how she wants assignments turned in. Other policies reflect the schoolwide practices designed by the leadership team. In total, it's a massive amount of information that teachers and students are responsible for. Consequently, we've developed a classroom Syllabus Template (Reproducible Form 2.6 starting on p. 45) to help teachers gather all this information into a single document that details how their classes operate and what they expect from students. This document—which includes grading polices, assignment turn-in procedures, absence policies, Code of Conduct violations, Guidelines for Success, and many other details—will run seven to ten pages long.

Our recommendation is to turn the syllabus into a lesson plan and teach it to your students in manageable chunks. On day one of school, pass out page one to your students and teach the information on that page. On day two, repeat the process with page two. Then repeat the entire process a few months into the school year. In our experience, teachers who follow this recommendation have great success with their students.

Task 4: Infuse Universal Behavior Support throughout the District

Instituting the improvement cycle within any given building (all of the things discussed so far in this chapter) is extremely challenging. When done well, it can create an environment that is life altering for many students. However, all too often the development and implementation of these practices is not well documented. In addition, the implement cycle can be overly specific to a single person. In such a case, if the principal or a key member of the leadership team leaves the employ of the school, the improvement cycle can cease, and within a year or two all of the gains can be lost.

Continued on p. 48

Reproducible Form 2.5 (p. 1 of 2)

CLASSROOM MANAGEMENT PLAN

SAMPLE

Teacher: Mr. Kuske

Guidelines for Success

1. Be responsible.
2. Always try.
3. Do your best.
4. Cooperate.
5. Treat everyone with dignity and respect.

Rules

1. Arrive on time with all materials.
2. Keep hands, feet, & objects to yourself.
3. Follow directions.
4. Stay on task during work times.

Teaching Expectations

1. Teach students how to handle transitions between activities and lessons.
2. Teach students how rules relate to each different type of classroom activity.
3. Conduct lessons on study strategies.
4. Teach and review grading procedures with a course syllabus.

Monitoring

1. Use frequent scanning and proximity management to keep in touch with what students are doing.
2. Provide weekly printout to each student with current grades and missing assignments. Conference with students as necessary.
3. Keep track of misbehavior with the Weekly Record form.

Encouragement Procedures

Class:
- Verbal feedback
- Group activities, e.g., game time or time outside
- Cooperative groupings—train to encourage each other

Individual:
- Verbal feedback
- Frequent noncontingent acknowledgement
- Written feedback: notes on papers, certificates, thank-you notes
- Lottery tickets toward drawing (only some weeks, to maintain variety)
- Parental contacts
- Free homework pass
- Call the Top Guns at home, highest male and female on each test
- Individualized contracts as necessary

Possible Corrective Consequences

- Verbal reprimand
- Time owed after class
- Restitution
- Proximity management
- In-class timeout
- Principal notification form
- Keep a record of the behavior
- Parental contacts
- Disciplinary referral

Reproducible Materials Blank copies of the forms are provided on the CD. Permission is given for individual teachers, administrators, or other school personnel to reproduce any form labeled "Reproducible Form" for in-district use.

Reproducible Form 2.5 (p. 2 of 2)

CLASSROOM MANAGEMENT PLAN

1. Procedures for Assigning Classwork and Homework

All assignments will be written on the board each day. In addition, assignments will be written on an 8.5" x 11" sheet of paper and placed in the Absent: What You Missed basket. When a student returns after an absence, the student can pick up each day's assignments and any handouts or papers from this basket. In addition, all long-term assignments will be written on the daily assignment list on the board (e.g., science projects due in two days.)

2. Procedures for Managing Independent Work Periods

A. Any time a student is developing a pattern of not completing work, I will meet with the student privately to determine if the work is beyond the student's ability. If so, I will modify assignments or adapt instruction to help the student be successful.

B. I will not schedule seatwork periods that last longer than 30 minutes without creating some change in activity that allows students to move about somewhat.

C. During the first two weeks of school, I will directly teach students how to behave during independent work periods.

D. I will provide guided practice (doing 10% to 25% of the assignment together as a classwide teacher-directed activity) before expecting students to complete any new type of task independently.

E. When students have questions, they can flip up a question mark flag that I will place on each desk.

3. Procedures for Collecting Completed Work

During the first month of school, I will collect all homework and classwork. Students will put their completed assignments on their desks, and I will go around and collect them. After the first month, I will have students put classwork into a basket and check off on a wall chart that they have handed it in. I will continue to physically collect homework from students at least until after winter break.

4. Procedures for Keeping Records and Providing Feedback to Students

I will enter all grades into my computer grade program. I will send a weekly printout of current grades, missing assignments, and record of absenteeism/tardiness home with students. A parent (guardian) will be asked to sign and return.

I will also keep a class chart of Percentage of Homework Handed in On Time as a way to provide feedback and to motivate students to get their homework in on time.

5. Procedures and Policies for Late or Missing Assignments

Any assignment that is turned in late will receive an immediate 10% penalty (a 100-point lab will have 10 points deducted from the score earned).

No assignment will be accepted beyond one week late.

Parents will be informed on my Weekly Grade Report of any missing assignments.

 Reproducible Materials Blank copies of the forms are provided on the CD. Permission is given for individual teachers, administrators, or other school personnel to reproduce any form labeled "Reproducible Form" for in-district use.

Reproducible Form 2.6 (p. 1 of 3)

SYLLABUS TEMPLATE

Teacher: Ms. Alvarez, 9th grade Remedial Reading

Classroom Goals (Write your classroom goals in the form of what students will be able to successfully do at the end of the year or semester.)

By the end of the year, you will be able to:

• Read long multisyllabic words and learn to use new vocabulary words

• Understand what you read

• Write complete sentences and well-organized paragraphs

• Read aloud smoothly, with expression

Guidelines for Success (Write your list of the attitudes and traits that you feel will ensure your students' success.)

Success in this class takes:

Preparation
Responsibility
Integrity
Dedication
Effort

Classroom Rules (Outline the important student behaviors that will ensure your class runs efficiently.)

1. Arrive on time, with paper, pencil, and books.

2. Follow directions the first time.

3. Stay on task during all work times.

4. Class ends when I dismiss you.

Activities (Outline the activities that students will be engaging in during a typical week.)

Teacher-directed instruction (large group)

Station activities:

Partner practice (fluency, vocabulary, projects)

Mastery checks with teacher

Computer practice

Independent practice (writing activities, worksheets, etc.)

Grades

(**Grading scale:** Outline the percentage cutoffs for A's, B's, and so on.)

900 total points possible for the semester. A = 800–900 points, B = 700–800 points, C = 600–700 points, D = 500–600 points, F = below 500 points.

(**Relative value:** Outline the relative weight of homework, quizzes, tests, papers, behavior/effort on the final grade.)

50% class participation (you can earn 10 points per day for a total of 450 points), 30% written work (27 assignments worth 10 points each), 20% performance on mastery checks (18 short checks worth 10 points each)

Reproducible Form 2.6 (p. 2 of 3)

SYLLABUS TEMPLATE

Classroom Procedures

1. **Entering the classroom**
   (Outline exactly what students should do from the time they enter the room until the bell rings for class to begin.)
   Be in your seat when the bell rings. Have all your materials ready. Start work on the activity on the board or at your desk until I signal for your attention.

2. **Tardy to class**
   (Identify your definitions of on time and tardy and identify the consequences for being tardy.)
   If you enter the classroom after the bell rings, you are tardy and will lose one participation point for the day. All tardies are reported to the attendance office.

3. **Paper/pencil**
   (Identify what students should have to write with. In addition, specify what a student should do if he or she does not have this tool and what, if anything, you implement as a consequence.)
   If you forget your pencil or paper, you may borrow some from the basket at my desk. Return pencils at the end of class, and replace paper you use when you bring your own.

4. **How to find out what the daily assignments are**
   (Identify how you will assign work and how students will know what they are to do each day. Also define how they should keep track of what they need to do for homework and long-range assignments.)
   All students will have a folder on the counter by the window. I will put a weekly assignment sheet in your folder every Monday. The sheet will list all tasks you will work on during the week.

5. **Turning in assignments**
   (Identify where and how students turn in classwork and homework. Specify if students are to check off completed work they have turned in.)
   For the first two weeks of class, I will collect class and homework assignments. After that, you will place completed work in the tray by the door.

6. **Returning assignments to students**
   (Detail your policies on how you will return completed work to your students.)
   I will return graded assignments to your folder.

7. **Finding out grade status**
   (Review your grading system and explain whether you will give students a weekly grade report or if you expect them to track their grades themselves. Also identify when and how a student can approach you to discuss their current status in the class.)
   A grade report will be placed in your folder each week. It will show your current grade in the class, any missing assignments, and a progress report showing your current reading level.

Reproducible Form 2.6 (p. 3 of 3)

SYLLABUS TEMPLATE

8. **Student responsibilities after an absence**

   (Outline what students will need to do when returning after an absence: (1) How to find out what you missed; (2) How long you have to make up your assignments; (3) What to do if you miss a test.)

   > Your weekly assignment sheet will list independent practice and vocabulary assignments for the days you missed. You will have as many days as you were absent to make up your assignments. I will reschedule any mastery checks you miss.

9. **Late, missing, or incomplete assignments**

   (Outline the maximum number of late assignments you will accept, along with penalties and time limits for late work.)

   > Late assignments will lose one point for each day they are late, but must be turned in within five days of the due date. I will accept no more than six late assignments. I will place any incomplete assignments in your folder, and you will have three days to complete them with no penalty.

10. **Communication procedures with parents/families**

    (Identify if you will have any regular communication with families that you initiate. Provide information on when, where, and how family members can get in touch with you.)

    > You can earn three bonus points each week you return your weekly grade printout signed by a parent or guardian.

11. **Ending class**

    (Specify how you will end class, any responsibilities your students may have, and how you will dismiss students.)

    > One minute before class ends, I will ask you all to return to your seats for final announcements. After the bell rings, I will dismiss the class by rows.

12. **Consequences for classroom rule violations**

    (List the range of corrective consequences that you may assign if rules are violated.)

    > Depending on the frequency and severity of the misbehavior, you may receive one or more of the following consequences:
    >   Loss of a participation point, change in seating assignment, time owed after class, detention, parental contact, office referral
    > If you feel a consequence is unfair, you may make an appointment to discuss the situation with me.

13. **Consequences for Code of Conduct violations**

    (Inform students that you must follow through with disciplinary referrals for violations of schoolwide rules, including dress code, unexcused absences, threats, and so forth. Make sure to get this information from your principal or assistant principal.)

    > If you break a rule that is covered by the Code of Conduct in your student handbook (possession of illegal substances, fighting, etc.), I will refer the situation to the office for the administrator to handle.

This template is derived from *Discipline in the Secondary Classroom: Proactive Classroom Management in Grades 9–12*, (Sprick, 2006).

Reproducible Materials Blank copies of the forms are provided on the CD. Permission is given for individual teachers, administrators, or other school personnel to reproduce any form labeled "Reproducible Form" for in-district use.

It does not take long for a great and very positive school, through inattention and lack of resolve, to turn into a mediocre and very negative school.

The district should take responsibility for ensuring that PBS practices are infused throughout the entire district. One way to accomplish that is through ongoing training of the leadership teams (Sprick, Garrison, et al., 2002; Sugai & Horner, 2006; Sugai et al., 2008). Numerous districts that have been implementing *Foundations* for many years conduct an annual training in the fall. All leadership teams, including all new members, attend a session at which they are reminded of their team's role and are given time to review their data from the past year and set up a tentative plan for implementing the improvement cycle for the coming year. At this training, teams are also charged with developing a plan for orienting any staff new to their school to the full range of behavior support procedures that are in place in the building.

District staff can also encourage implementation of behavior support by making it part of the district conversation with building administrators. When the person the principals report to (the superintendent of a small district or the area superintendents of a large district) asks about the progress of behavior support, the chance that the building administrator will view this as important is increased. If the principal's boss never asks, the principal may think it is unimportant and lose focus. If the principal loses focus on the improvement cycle for behavior support, staff will eventually lose focus as well. Talking Points/Questions (see the box and Reproducible Form 2.7 on pp. 50–51) is a guide that we developed to encourage this conversation between central office staff and building-level administrators. Essentially, it is a list of questions to the principal about details of the improvement cycle.

CONCLUSION

The most challenging aspect of universal prevention for school staff is to keep every single student (and, ideally, parent) engaged—not just the students who are easy to interact with and those who are starved for attention, but all of the average students as well. Universal prevention—and the cycle of continuous improvement—must strive to make school a great place for all the students who too easily slide under the radar of teacher attention. To see how truly challenging this goal can be, try this visualization task:

> *Picture student A. This student is a high achiever. He gets good grades, excels in music, is a star on the basketball team, and has lots of friends. He's probably good looking and a social extrovert who interacts easily with everyone. Now visualize student B. She is the starved-for-attention student who constantly acts out. This student demands, and gets, attention from adults every day.*
>
> *Now picture student C. This student works hard to get straight C's. He doesn't play a musical instrument, he's not an athlete, he doesn't speak up in class, and he is probably not considered physically attractive. This student does not stand*

out in any way. Yet this student represents most of the students in your school.
This student needs as much attention and support as students A and B.

One of the leadership team's most important tasks is to communicate this truth to staff members: All students deserve the same standard of education, and we have the responsibility to support the outcomes of all students. Every student has a need for recognition, acknowledgment, purpose, belonging, and competence. We are likely to be more successful at creating this school culture if we continually seek feedback and embed it within the community context. Creating this school culture in which all students feel they belong is especially important. An increasing body of research indicates that students' emotional connectedness to school is directly related to their choices about activities involving drugs and violence (Bonny, Britto, Klostermann, Hornung, & Slap, 2000; Glover, Burns, Butler, & Patton, 1998; McNeely & Falci, 2004; Resnick et al., 1997; Yan, Beck, Howard, Shattuck, & Kerr, 2008).

 A leadership team must not only communicate the *every-student* concept to teachers but also observe and evaluate whether all students are getting their needs met, and then design and implement universal practices to ensure that they are. This process is a cycle of continuous improvement and must be ongoing. The process should include *reviewing* the data and policies currently in place, *prioritizing* the areas that need the most improvement now, *revising* anything that's not acceptable or not working, and *adopting* new policies, new attitudes, and new ways of approaching problems. Then *implement* those practices across the board—every staff member, every day, is committed to making the plan work and the school a better place. And never stop this process. There are always things that can be done to make the school a little bit better for each individual student.

Reproducible Materials

Copies of these reproducible forms appear on the CD.

Reproducible Form 2.1: Schoolwide Behavior Support Checklist

Reproducible Form 2.2: Sample School Survey

Reproducible Form 2.3: START on Time! 10-Point Checklist

Reproducible Form 2.4: Classroom Management STOIC Checklist

Reproducible Form 2.5: Classroom Management Plan

Reproducible Form 2.6: Syllabus Template

Reproducible Form 2.7: Talking Points/Questions

👁 TALKING POINTS/QUESTIONS

Principals should be introduced to this concept, the talking points, and the purpose in a general meeting so all principals know that no one is being singled out and that this process is simply part of the partnership between central administration and each campus.

The purpose of this process is to ensure that each campus maintains a continuous improvement process related to safety and civility.

Begin each visit by reasserting that this is not a "gotcha" process. It is intended to identify strengths to celebrate and target areas for improvement in the safety, civility, culture, and climate of the school. Use Reproducible Form 2.7 as a discussion guide and record of your notes.

1. **Let's discuss (examine) your most current safety/civility data.** This can include annual surveys, quarterly observations of common areas, patterns of disciplinary referral, Foundation Implementation Tool (FIT), *Foundations* and/or *CHAMPs* rubrics, and so on.

2. **Based on that information, what are your strengths to celebrate?** How do you know? Have you involved staff, students, parents, central office, and community in the good news? Have you and your staff formally adopted the new policies/procedures? Have you archived the new policies/procedures in a staff handbook and your *Foundations* notebook?

3. Based on your data, **what are your current priorities for improvement?** Why did you select these priorities? For each priority, describe the outcomes you are hoping to achieve.

4. Have you developed a STOIC intervention plan for addressing each priority (structure, teach expectations, observe/monitor, interact positively, correct calmly)? **Describe the intervention plan.** Are there any things the central office can assist with—barriers to reduce, needs to address, information to provide?

Thank the principal for his or her commitment. Summarize what you (central office) have said you would do to provide support. Ask if there are any questions you have neglected to ask. Invite the principal to e-mail or call you if he or she thinks of any related issues or things you can do.

Follow up with the principal several weeks later:

5. **How are things going with** . . . (each major priority)? How do you know?

To keep dialogue about the cycle going, return to question one and ask about any more recent data and whether it indicates a change in priority.

Reproducible Form 2.7

TALKING POINTS/QUESTIONS

Date: ___10/13___   **Area Superintendent:** ___Dr. Dixon___

School: ___Chavez Elem.___   **Discussion Participants:** ___Akiko Morimoto (Principal),___

___Dr. Dixon___

1. **Let's discuss (examine) your most current safety/civility data.**

   Referrals for in-school and out-of-school suspensions are down 15% from this time last year. Student survey last spring indicated many students don't feel safe on playground and before/after school. New cafeteria rules have almost eliminated behavior problems during lunch.

2. Based on that information, **what are your strengths to celebrate?** How do you know? Have you involved staff, students, parents, central office, and community in the good news? Have you and your staff formally adopted the new policy/procedures?

   New cafeteria rules for students and increased adult supervision have dramatically reduced lunchtime behavior problems. Rules are outlined in staff handbook and taught to all students at the beginning of the school year.

3. Based on your data, **what are your current priorities for improvement?** Why did you select these priorities? What outcomes do you want to achieve?

   Before/after school and playground behavior were selected based on student survey showing many don't feel safe at those times. Goal is for next survey to show 80% of students feel safe at those times and places. Secondary priority is developing schoolwide Guidelines for Success.

4. Have you developed a STOIC intervention plan for addressing each priority? **Describe the intervention plan.** How can the central office help?

   Currently developing the intervention plan for before/after school and playground behavior. School would like to investigate district resources for before and/or after programs to provide more structure for students who arrive early and/or stay late.

Follow-up (Date: _____)
5. **How are things going with each major priority in question 4 above?** How do you know?

 Reproducible Materials Blank copies of the forms are provided on the CD. Permission is given for individual teachers, administrators, or other school personnel to reproduce any form labeled "Reproducible Form" for in-district use.

CHAPTER 3

The Framework

Building a Behavioral Response to Intervention

Most students are well served by a broad framework of universal polices, procedures, and programs that outline a school's expectations for students. But for some students, these universal polices and classroom management structures are not enough, and they have difficulty meeting academic or behavioral expectations (Carr et al., 2002; Gresham, 2004; Walker et al., 1996). When these students slip through the broad safety net of universal prevention, it is crucial to have in place a second level of netting—a response-to-intervention framework that ensures that student needs will be met in the most time- and cost-efficient manner possible (Sprick & Garrison, 2008; Sprick et al., 1992; Sugai et al., 2008). This chapter outlines how to create a B-RTI framework that consists of problem-solving processes and a protocol of evidence-based interventions that will give your school or district the preparedness and flexibility to respond to a variety of student needs with a variety of effective interventions. Establishing and institutionalizing problem-solving processes and a protocol of interventions require the leadership team from any individual school to coordinate with district personnel and community resources to build a continuum.

Note: Throughout this book we refer to the "intervention plan" or "intervention," although these terms encompass the requirements of a BIP (behavior improvement plan). Thus, if a BIP is required by law, an intervention that stems from the processes described in this book would be the student's BIP.

The first category, problem-solving processes, essentially looks at who is involved in analyzing the nature of the problem and what type of processes they should follow to develop recommendations for the type of intervention needed. As shown in Figure 3.1: Components of B-RTI, we suggest a range of options that moves from the type of problem-solving done by a general education teacher in a few minutes after school through several more collaborative and time-consuming problem-solving processes to a full and complete FBA guided by the most highly trained behavior analyst available to the district.

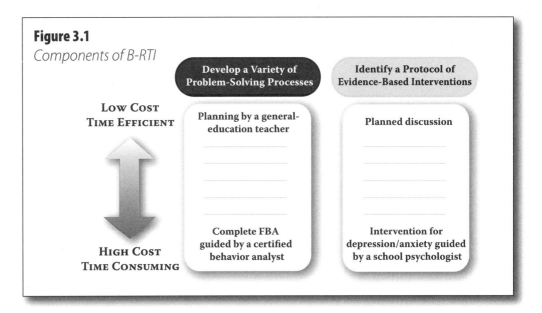

Figure 3.1
Components of B-RTI

Develop a Variety of Problem-Solving Processes

Identify a Protocol of Evidence-Based Interventions

LOW COST TIME EFFICIENT

HIGH COST TIME CONSUMING

Planning by a general-education teacher

Complete FBA guided by a certified behavior analyst

Planned discussion

Intervention for depression/anxiety guided by a school psychologist

The second category considers the type of intervention plan that will result from the problem-solving processes, regardless of the setting the student is in. That is, who will work with the student and what interventions will be implemented. A category that we do not address in this book considers the type of placement—general education or special education. As stated earlier, we leave it to the reader to determine whether and how these B-RTI processes relate to referral, assessment, and placement for special education. Keep in mind that the goal is to meet the student's needs in the most time- and cost-efficient manner possible.

The vertical arrow in Figure 3.1 points both up and down. The down portion of the arrow is intuitively obvious. If a process and set of interventions are unsuccessful (i.e., the student's problems are not responsive to intervention at that level), the problem-solving process will take on a greater degree of structure, as will the intervention(s) that is a result of that process.

However, the arrow also points up, meaning that when a student's difficulties respond positively to the current intervention, a move to less-structured interventions should occur if there is a reasonable chance of continued success when the previously implemented supports are modified or faded. It is our hope that this chapter will encourage building-based behavior leadership teams and district-level personnel to examine their current problem-solving processes and the types of interventions staff have been trained to implement. The goal is to determine strengths and areas for improvement in your current service delivery relative to the social, emotional, and behavioral needs of students. This chapter also serves as an introduction to the subjects in the subsequent chapters in this book. For example, one of the problem-solving processes we suggest is training a variety of people and positions within the school and district as interventionists—personnel who can guide the process of problem identification, intervention design, and implementation. Chapters 6 and 7 provide detailed information that these interventionists may find useful.

Task 1: Develop a Variety of Problem-Solving Processes

The problem-solving process involves problem identification, analysis, intervention design, and progress monitoring (Deno, 2002; Grimes & Tilly, 1996; Kratochwill, Elliott, & Callan-Stoiber, 2002; Reschly & Ysseldyke, 2002). In this section, we address the question of who is involved in the problem-solving process. In a B-RTI structure, there should be a range of processes—from low cost and time efficient to very high cost and time consuming—so that the intensity of the process matches the intensity of the need (Howell & Nolet, 2000; Ysseldyke & Christenson, 1988). Using the medical metaphor from a previous chapter, the first time you have a headache, you usually do some problem-solving and decide on a simple intervention such as taking a couple of aspirin. This process involves only one person who decides on a simple treatment plan, which, if effective, solves the problem. Contrast this with the person who consults a neurologist, who may use data from CAT scans, MRIs, complex lab tests, and collaboration with a neurosurgeon. One process takes minutes and costs almost nothing. The other process may take weeks or months of problem identification and analysis before an intervention plan is determined and has costs that probably run into six figures. One process is not better than the other—the different processes, we hope, match the intensity of the need. Now think about a continuum. Before the situation got to the neurologist, in all probability the person with the headache spent time with an internist or general practitioner who tried a variety of interventions to see if the person's headache would respond—changes in diet, different medications, allergy tests, etc. We advocate that within a school there be a similar continuum (Gresham, 2004; Horner et al., 2005; Walker & Shinn, 2002).

Figure 3.2 shows a sample of such a continuum, and the text that follows describes each item on the continuum. As you read these suggestions, analyze the current organization and use of resources within your building and set up a plan for filling in any gaps in the layers of problem-solving.

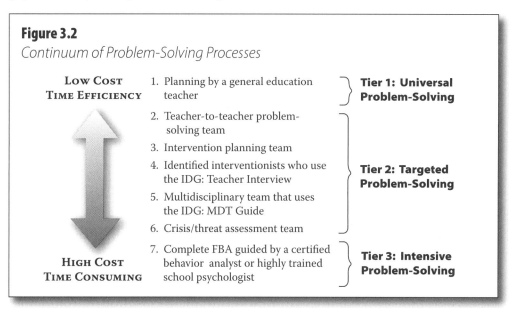

Figure 3.2
Continuum of Problem-Solving Processes

LOW COST
TIME EFFICIENCY

1. Planning by a general education teacher

Tier 1: Universal Problem-Solving

2. Teacher-to-teacher problem-solving team
3. Intervention planning team
4. Identified interventionists who use the IDG: Teacher Interview
5. Multidisciplinary team that uses the IDG: MDT Guide
6. Crisis/threat assessment team

Tier 2: Targeted Problem-Solving

7. Complete FBA guided by a certified behavior analyst or highly trained school psychologist

Tier 3: Intensive Problem-Solving

HIGH COST
TIME CONSUMING

TIER 1: UNIVERSAL PROBLEM-SOLVING

We suggest that all teachers be trained in basic problem-solving for behavior problems and be familiar with a set of basic interventions. We also suggest that schools put this level of problem-solving into operation by stating in policy and staff handbooks that the first level of problem-solving for when a student is not meeting behavioral expectations is planning and intervention by the general education teacher.

Planning by a general education teacher. In our medical metaphor, the teacher who tries a series of interventions is similar to the person with a headache who takes a couple of aspirin. If that does not work, the person may try lying down to rest in a quiet place. If the headache continues, the person may try a couple of different over-the-counter pain relievers. If those do not work, he may try allergy medication. All of these are self-help problem-solving processes and interventions. Eventually, if the headache does not respond to these interventions, this person may go to a doctor, but that is usually not the first layer of problem-solving

One goal of staff development is to ensure that when a student is exhibiting academic or social behavioral difficulties, all teachers understand that they must play an active role, in fact a pivotal role, in preventing the development of problems and in problem-solving to support the student's needs (Kellam & Anthony, 1998; Patterson, Reid, & Dishion, 1992; Scheuermann & Hall, 2008; Walker, Ramsey, & Gresham, 2004). This staff development function is ongoing because there is always more to learn about how to help students improve behavior (Guskey, 1999; Quinn et al., 2001; Stager, 1995). Here, we offer two prerequisite concepts that staff must operate from to be effective problem-solvers. The first is that behavior is highly malleable—it can be changed (Baer, Wolf, & Risley, 1968; Heward, 2005; Quinn et al., 2001; Scheuermann & Hall, 2008). When teachers fully understand this concept, they are well on their way to becoming active problem-solvers, not passive problem-admirers. If a teacher does not understand and operate from the belief that behavior can be changed, she is more likely to view any intervention as doomed to failure. ("That is just the way this student is!") The best problem-solvers in the building are those who know that although this may be the behavior we see now, this student's behavior can improve dramatically with the right intervention plan. Starting with the concept that behavior can be changed gives educators great confidence. No matter how difficult or problematic a student's behavior may be, there is some combination of variables that can be changed in such a way that the student makes dramatic progress toward more responsible behavior.

Another prerequisite concept for teachers to be problem-solvers is a recognition that they need to manipulate the variables that are within their control and not worry about those outside their control (Martella, Nelson, & Marchand-Martella, 2003; Scheuermann & Hall, 2008). As obvious as this sounds, some teachers get so mired in concerns about a student's home life or getting a student labeled ADHD that they may blame the student and fail to see other ways the problem can be solved (Walker, 1995). Although school social workers or school psychologists may eventually be

> If a teacher does not understand and operate from the belief that behavior can be changed, she is more likely to view any intervention as doomed to failure. ("That is just the way this student is!")

involved in the home situation or in coordinating with physicians for a diagnosis, teachers cannot wait for someone else to take care of the problem. They should first try a variety of promising practices to see if the problem responds to simple intervention. In Task 3 within this chapter, we suggest a set of early-stage interventions that all teachers should be trained to implement before they ask for collaborative assistance. Each of the subsequent layers of problem-solving processes is collaborative in nature, involving more than just the classroom teacher functioning as an independent problem-solver.

TIER 2: COLLABORATIVE PROBLEM-SOLVING

Tier 2 interventions are collaborative and planned in conjunction with a building-based interventionist or problem-solving team but are implemented by typical school personnel, most commonly the classroom teacher. The collaboration may involve several individuals or may include only the teacher and an interventionist who work within an outcome-focused model of service delivery (Feldman & Kratochwill, 2003; Kratochwill et al., 2002). As stated earlier, we use the term interventionist to mean anyone who is involved in planning an intervention. An interventionist can be a teacher, school counselor, behavioral specialist, special education teacher or consultant, or administrator. Note that we listed a special education consultant as possibly being part of this team. In many districts, special educators are becoming more involved in the preventive aspects of Tier 2 processes, which, if successful, reduce the likelihood that a student will need special education services to be successful. All interventionists should be trained in the full range of interventions that your school or district has in place as a B-RTI framework. The goal of Tier 2 is to create a range of collaborative problem-solving structures and a range of personnel who can assist with problem-solving (Sprick et al., 1992; Walker & Sprague, 2006). We suggest the following four levels.

1. **Teacher-to-teacher problem-solving (uses the 25-minute planning process)**

   In this structure, teachers are grouped together by grade level or by a small learning community. On a regular basis they discuss the needs of a particular student. For example, in a high school organized by house, all the teachers who work with a particular group of students—for example, 125 freshmen—meet weekly for common planning. One week, they meet about instructional issues, and the next week they discuss individual students who are not making adequate progress. In this type of scenario, all teachers are on one of these teams, and so every other week everyone is practicing the problem-solving process. These teams can be trained to use the 25-minute planning process presented in detail in Chapter 8.

2. **Intervention planning team (uses the 25-minute planning process)**

   Although this team may be called different things in different districts (TAT, CARE, SST, etc.), it is a group that meets regularly to conduct problem-solving for behavioral or academic issues for individual students. Any teacher who has a student that she is concerned about can refer the case to the team. We call this team the intervention planning team (IPT). This team may include teachers but may also have a few expert participants such as a school counselor, administrator, and/or school social worker. For this team to be maximally effective, all team members must have some training in basic problem-solving, behavior functions, and a range of research-based interventions, while some team members have more specialized skills or in-depth knowledge (Benazzi, Horner, & Good, 2006; Nelson, Roberts, Mathur, & Rutherford, 1998). In Task 3, we suggest a menu of evidence-based interventions these team members should be trained to design and help implement. This team can be trained to use the 25-minute planning process presented in detail in Chapter 8.

3. **Identified interventionists (use the IDG: Teacher Interview)**
   In most schools, several job roles can be designated to play a role in problem-solving for behavioral issues: department chairs, school counselors, school social workers, school psychologists, instructional coaches, and administrators. Each of these people can be trained in basic behavioral consultation—that is, how to help teachers with problem-solving and intervention design. Chapters 6 and 7 provide detailed guidance on how to function as a behavioral interventionist and how to use a protocol we call the Intervention Decision Guide: Teacher Interview as a process for efficient collaborative planning. If all of the people who function as interventionists are trained in the same processes and in the same set of evidence-based interventions (similar to the list we provide in the second half of this chapter), the building develops a common language around problem-solving and intervention, which may increase the effectiveness and efficiency of planning and providing supports (Rones & Hoagwood, 2000; Sugai & Horner, 2006).

   Having a range of people who can function as interventionists gives teams or administrators (whoever is assigning interventionists to specific cases) flexibility in delegating tasks and may also provide teachers with a choice of who they want to work with to support individual students. With a range of interventionists, there is less likelihood that cases will be on waiting lists or that things will come to a stop when the only person serving as an interventionist is out with an illness. In addition, with a range of interventionists, there can be greater matching of the style and expertise of the interventionist to the particular case at hand. In the next chapter, we talk about how interventionists interface with different teams, but the basic concept here is that these people are similar to the general practitioner in medicine. They may guide a series of different interventions in hopes of finding something successful without going to more-expert levels of problem-solving.

> With a range of interventions, there is less likelihood that cases will be on waiting lists or that things will come to a stop when the only person serving as an interventionist is out with an illness.

As a reminder, we are not taking a position on when, where, or how these problem-solving processes relate to special education issues of setting and type of intervention. Although what we describe as Tier 3 may overlap into special education issues, it is our hope that the process will become fluid enough that if a special education student might benefit from a 25-minute planning meeting, there would be some hesitation to move that student to a different structure. By the same token, a student who is not identified as special education but who exhibits high-intensity crisis behaviors would immediately rise to the attention of a crisis or threat assessment team. As a final example, a student who is receiving special education services for speech/language issues and who begins to exhibit behavioral problems may go through one or more of the Tier 2 problem-solving structures as opposed to having that problem tackled by an entire multidisciplinary team.

4. **Multidisciplinary team (uses the IDG: MDT Guide)**

   This team is made up predominantly of experts such as special education teachers, school psychologists, school counselors, administrators, school social workers, and, when appropriate, players from other agencies such as mental health, juvenile justice, district-level truancy, and so on. This more-expert team may decide that a more comprehensive, community-based view of the problem is needed to adequately support the student. Chapter 9, "Multidisciplinary Team Approach: Using the Intervention Decision Guide," provides suggestions about what information this team may need to collect. Note that we are not suggesting time or resource constraints at this level. Because the problem has been resistant to easier solutions, part of problem-solving may involve observations of the student in multiple settings; systematic records review; interviews with the student, all staff who work with the student, and family members; and coordination with other agencies that the family may benefit from being involved with (Barnhill, 2005; Dishion & Stormshak, 2007).

TIER 3: INTENSIVE PROBLEM-SOLVING

A problem may considered intensive because of its severity and immediacy or because it has been resistant to other interventions. It is beyond the scope of this book to provide information about these intensive levels, but in most districts a few key personnel have been designated to perform these functions and have been given training through the state department of education or a regional service center.

Crisis/threat assessment team. The school should have adopted a set of policies, procedures, and record-keeping standards related to threats or incidences of violence (Greene, 2005; Sandoval, 2002). One part of those policies should include a building-based team that can convene immediately whenever there is a threat. This team's job is to determine whether the threat is a transient or a substantive threat. For any substantive threat, this team will involve either a district-level crisis team and/or relevant authorities. For information about such policies and practices, see *Interventions: Evidence-Based Behavioral Strategies for Individual Students*, specifically "Intervention G: Managing Physically Dangerous Behavior/Threats of Target Violence."

Note that because of the intensity of behaviors such as a threat by a student to harm herself or someone else, the situation demands an immediate jump to a Tier 3 level of intensive problem-solving. B-RTI is not a rigid set of hoops wherein every situation goes through Tier 1 and Tier 2 problem-solving. Crisis situations must be addressed immediately without any delay related to referral processes or tiers or paperwork considerations.

Complete FBA. This protocol is guided by a certified behavior analyst or highly trained school psychologist. A complete FBA may have been done by the multidisciplinary team in Tier 2, but if no intervention has yet been successful, it may be time to turn the process over to the most highly trained personnel that the district has available (Crone & Horner, 2000). These experts with the most training should be protected from being deluged with cases that might be handled with a less intensive Tier 2 level of problem-solving and professional expertise. In the medical example, the FBA is analogous to referring the situation to a neurosurgeon who will guide all subsequent problem solving-processes and intervention implementation.

Problem-solving processes for behavior can result in all personnel seeing that they play a role in helping individual students improve behavior whenever the universal prevention procedures have not been sufficient. The remaining chapters in this book focus on these Tier 2 problem-solving structures.

Task 2: Identify a Protocol of Evidence-Based Interventions

This task addresses what will actually be implemented to help the student be successful in whatever setting she is placed. In other words, what are the specific interventions that staff will be trained to implement effectively and with fidelity? We divide this task into three sections. The first is a brief description of our suggestions for early-stage interventions—those things that all teachers should be trained to implement as part of universal, Tier 1 problem-solving. The second section describes group-based support programs that are discussed in more detail in Chapters 10 and 11. In the third section, we describe a set of highly structured interventions—those things we suggest that all Tier 2 interventionists and problem-solving team members should become skilled in implementing. How to design and implement these early-stage and highly structured interventions is the focus of the book *Interventions: Evidence-Based*

Behavioral Strategies for Individual Students. In addition, *The Teacher's Encyclopedia of Behavior Management: 100 Problem/500 Plans* may be of use to teachers and administrators as they design early-stage interventions. Districts may wish to develop their own protocol of evidence-based interventions. It is simply our contention that districts need an agreed-upon menu of interventions that become the outcome of problem-solving processes.

TIER 1 INTERVENTIONS

As noted in earlier chapters, we advocate a three-tiered intervention framework. Behavioral specialists structure this model in slightly different ways, with some considering only universal prevention as part of Tier 1. In our three-tiered model, Tier 1 includes not only universal policies (see Chapter 2) but also a layer of problem-solving interventions that all staff members should be familiar with.

Tier 1 interventions come into play when the schoolwide and classroom behavior support polices are simply not working for an individual student. These interventions are the base of the framework and can be planned and implemented by a general education teacher. As part of your framework, we advocate developing a set of simple interventions that school staff should try first. If you adopt these six interventions as the base of your B-RTI framework, you must also implement systematic inservices to train all teachers in how to conduct these interventions. Following are the interventions that we believe should be included in your protocol.

Planned Discussion. As a first step, planned discussions are meant to ensure student compliance with the teacher's basic classroom management plan. The operative word for this intervention is *planned*. These discussions should not take place immediately after misbehavior. They should be thought out in advance to give the teacher an opportunity to determine:

- What is the real nature of this problem?

- Why is it happening?

- What exactly do I want this student to do differently?

Planned discussions give the teacher and student a chance to talk about the problem. We list this intervention first because of our belief that no behavior problem should ever be a function of ignorance. It's important to ensure that the student knows exactly what is expected and what the problem is.

Academic Assistance. This intervention assesses and ensures that a student's behavior problem is not a function of academic skill deficits. Behavior problems often result from a student's inability to efficiently or effectively complete the work that is expected (Ervin et al., 2006; Nelson, Benner, & Mooney, 2008; Scheuermann & Hall,

2008; Walker, 2004). And equally as often, teachers assume that a student can do the work "if he'd just try." Some students are masterful at making something they can't do look like something they don't want to do. For these children, it is easier to act willful and angry than admit to themselves or to their teachers that they lack competence. So it's important to take the time to determine whether a student needs academic help and, if the student does, to provide an academic intervention alongside the behavioral intervention.

Goal Setting. This intervention takes a broad, general idea of the problem and puts it in it writing along with specific observable behaviors that the student can exhibit. Goal setting is well substantiated in the research literature for both academic and behavior problems (Conte & Hintz, 2000; Copeland & Hughes, 2002; Miller & Kelley, 1994; Ruth, 1996; Walker & Fabre, 1987), and we advocate using it as an effective early-stage intervention.

Systematic Data Collection. If the teacher has tried the first three interventions without success, the problem may be considered chronic. To effectively understand and address chronic problems, data collection is necessary (Alberto & Troutman, 2006; Baer et al., 1968; Fox & Gable, 2004). When a patient sees a doctor for a medical problem, the first thing the doctor does is collect data. When do the headaches occur? How long have they been happening? Without systematic information, treatment objectives can't work. In addition, often the act of collecting data on a particular behavior, charting that data, and regularly discussing that data with the student and parent has great potential, in and of itself, to improve the behavior of concern. This phenomenon is known to researchers as the Hawthorne effect—when the behavior or disease that you're studying improves just because it is being studied (Landsberger, 1958). Researchers hate the phenomenon because it muddies the data, but for teachers, it's a boon to be taken advantage of. Often, simply collecting data and debriefing with the student will function as a successful intervention.

The most important reason for collecting data is to create a basis from which to measure success. Without data, it may be difficult to recognize success because often it doesn't look like the miracle you were hoping for. If an intervention reduces a student's disruptive behavior by 40%, that is a significant improvement. But the student is still acting out, so without the data to measure the reduction, the intervention may not seem successful and may be tossed out.

Increase Positive Interactions. This simple intervention can be used in conjunction with any of the other interventions to boost their effectiveness. Often when a student exhibits a pattern of misbehavior, the ratio of interactions with that student can get heavily weighted to the negative side. Simply increasing the number of positive interactions in tandem with data collection, for example, can result in overall improvements in levels of appropriate and inappropriate behavior (Scheuermann & Hall, 2008).

STOIC Analysis. Although it can be implemented by a single teacher, this is a comprehensive, multifaceted intervention. The first step is to analyze the function of the behavior, then address that function with each component of STOIC (Sprick & Garrison, 2008). If the function of the behavior is to get more attention, for example, look first at Structure. Can you move the student to another place in the classroom where he'll get more attention? Then address Teach and Observe. Can you teach him how to get more positive attention? Can you observe the student more frequently so that you notice when he's asking for attention in a positive way? That leads to Interact. Is there an opportunity to increase positive interactions with the student? And last, examine your Corrections. Are they consistent, immediate, and brief?

STOIC
S = Structure
T = Teach
O = Observe
I = Interact
C = Correct
See pp. 39–40 for more details.

TIER 2 TARGETED INTERVENTIONS

Your buffet of interventions should offer—as main courses—various group-based programs that are relatively easy to set up and plug at-risk or struggling students into. By having these programs in place as part of your framework, teachers can easily refer at-risk students into an existing program rather than designing an individual response for every student whose needs aren't being met (Colvin et al., 1993; Hawken & Horner, 2003; Lewis, Sugai, & Colvin, 1998; Walker et al., 1996). Some of these structures may already be in place in your school or district.

Check and Connect. One program, often referred to as Check and Connect, is a simple but powerful card-carry system in which students are given the opportunity to receive structured (positive) feedback throughout the day as well as check in and out with an adult in the building (Hawken & Horner, 2003; March & Horner, 2002; Neyhart & Garrison, 1992; Warberg, George, Brown, Churan, & Taylor-Greene, 1995). This program allows the teachers in a grade level or learning community to decide which three behaviors they believe are most important to evaluate for struggling students, thus giving the teachers design control of the intervention. All students placed in the program carry a card that lists those three behaviors. That keeps the evaluation process simple for teachers, who each may have several students in the program. This program gives students responsibility for picking up the card, getting it signed, and taking it home to their parents. This is an effective program for many students (Filter et al., 2007; Hawken, MacLeod, & Rawlings, 2007) and one we recommend that all schools have in place. For more detailed information about this program, see Chapter 10: "Connections: A Schoolwide Check-and-Connect Plan."

Mentoring. Another simple program that should be part of your framework is mentoring. Mentoring programs recognize that misbehavior is often a function of a need for attention and that many students need more attention than they typically receive from adults in the school. Establishing a cadre of mentors who are willing and able to provide individual attention for students whose problem behavior appears to be maintained by adult attention may be a simple but powerful way to address student needs from a functional perspective. For more detailed information on mentoring and other schoolwide programs, see Chapter 11, "Other Targeted Interventions: Mentoring and Other Ready-to-Implement Programs."

Meaningful Work. Providing a student with a specific and meaningful job within the school can be a great way to meet a student's basic needs, whether it is a need for attention, for purpose and belonging, or simply to get to school on time. Often, giving a student a responsibility will motivate the student to rise to the occasion. It is important to have a range of jobs available to meet various student needs and personalities, and it is important to have a cross section of the student population participating in the program. First, you want to avoid stigmatizing the jobs program as something for only problem children. Second, the high-achieving, adaptive student workers model appropriate and desired student behaviors.

PASS Program—Structured Support in the General Education Classroom. In this option, there is a classroom within the school run by a skilled teacher with knowledge of behavioral issues. This class is the home base for students when needed, but for the most part, those students are in a general education classroom with support from the PASS teacher as needed. Following is a description of this model, which was developed by Jim Poole and Dr. Hope Caperton Brown (in press):

> *PASS is based on the belief that many behaviorally at-risk students and those identified with serious emotional/behavioral disabilities benefit behaviorally and academically when their educational placement is in mainstream settings rather than self-contained or segregated programs. Theoretical support for placing behaviorally disordered students in inclusive environments derives from the social learning theory of Albert Bandura (1977) and the social-ecological theory of Urie Bronfenbrenner (1979). Specifically, these theories emphasize the effect of environments (including peer groups) on behavior. Additionally, the program's practice of placing students in inclusive settings is influenced by research (Dishion, Spracklen, Andrews, & Patterson, 1996) that indicates the presence of an iatrogenic effect/contagion of placing students with antisocial behaviors together in segregated settings.*

Homework Room. This piece of your framework is not meant to be homework detention, but instead a place where students can get help with homework during lunch and before and after school. The key to making homework rooms effective is to have enough academically competent people available to provide immediate help when a student needs it. If a student has to wait 10 minutes to get his question answered, he won't likely come back.

Structured Recess/Structured Lunch. Think of this program as Recess 101, similar to driving school for adults. When a student has too many problems on the playground for too long, the student can be placed in a structured/staff-supervised recess to learn or relearn the "rules of the road."

Social Skills Training Classes. For students who have skill deficits, teaching students the social skills they lack can be an effective means of changing behavior (Gresham, 2002; Strain, Guralnick, & Walker, 1986; Terpstra & Temura, 2008). The biggest drawbacks to these programs are that they often take time away from academic instruction and that they are not likely to be effective if not carefully designed and implemented based on student skill needs (Gresham, 2002). Chapter 11 provides suggestions for ways to organize the delivery of teaching social skills to targeted students.

First Step to Success. First Step to Success (Walker, Severson, Feil, Stiller, & Golly, 1998) is a standardized, packaged intervention that allows interventionists to organize and implement the intervention with little or no outside support. First Step for Success is designed for children who begin school exhibiting signs of antisocial behavior and is considered a packaged intervention because it consists of multiple components implemented in a standard format for all participating students. Research has documented that First Step to Success is well liked by teachers and parents and that it is effective in improving academic engagement and decreasing antisocial behavior in young students

Students Targeted for Special Attention. This program allows interventionists to single out students who need lots of additional attention. It can be as simple as showing a student's photo at a staff meeting and asking teachers to make a special point of interacting positively with the student at every opportunity, even something as simple as a brief "hello" in the hallway. The cumulative effect can be tremendous for the targeted students.

TIER 2 INDIVIDUALIZED INTERVENTIONS

At the next level, interventions are more complex, collaborative in nature, and planned in conjunction with a building-based interventionist or problem-solving team.

Managing Physically Dangerous Behavior and Threats of Targeted Violence. This is an intervention to help staff design a proactive plan for responding to intense misbehavior that creates a risk of physical injury. In this intervention, guidance is provided for making decisions about when and how to clear a room or use physical restraint. Data regarding dangerous incidents will be collected, charted, and analyzed to determine whether progress is being made. Above all, the primary intent of this intervention is to keep students and staff safe; consequently, other interventions will be needed to help the student learn alternative, productive behaviors.

Managing Severely Disruptive Behavior. This is another intervention that is designed to prevent one student's behavior from infringing on her classmates' ability to learn. This intervention involves developing agreements between the teacher and the school administrator about what behaviors are severe enough to warrant removal of the student from the room and what procedures will be instituted if the student refuses to leave. Because this code-red intervention is strictly implemented in response to problem behavior, other interventions should be implemented concurrently to help the student learn more responsible behaviors.

Managing the Cycle of Emotional Escalation. This intervention describes a predictable cycle of escalation that occurs with emotional behavior such as tantrums, refusal to comply with instructions, aggression, and confrontation. Understanding the stages of this cycle allows school personnel to analyze patterns in a student's acting-out behavior, identify when the student is beginning to escalate, and intervene quickly and appropriately before the student reaches the boiling point. Learning to interrupt the cycle in a fluent manner can bring a student back to a calm state before the student reaches the peak, out-of-control behavior that might otherwise portend a potentially explosive code-red situation.

Cueing and Precorrecting. A simple but powerful intervention, cueing involves increasing the student's own awareness of the negative behaviors in which he tends to engage (Colvin, Sugai, & Patching, 1993; Lewis, Colvin, & Sugai, 2000; Yu, Darch, & Rabren, 2002). For example, a teacher and student may work out a system in which the teacher can covertly signal the student that she is bragging in a way that may be alienating other students. Precorrection is similar to cueing, but instead of reacting to a student's problem behavior, a teacher will remind the student not to exhibit the problem behavior or to exhibit a desired behavior before the problem happens. Precorrection is most effective when the teacher has a good idea of which situations are likely to trigger the unacceptable behavior, as in the case of a student who habitually argues with the teacher when directions are presented.

Self-Monitoring and Self-Evaluation. This intervention can help students gain control over their own behaviors. A commonplace example of self-monitoring is the things-to-do list that many adults write daily and then check off as each item is completed. Self-monitoring can be used to reduce misbehavior, such as disruptions, or it may be used to increase positive behavior, such as work completion. Self-evaluation procedures are designed to improve the quality or consistency of a particular behavior such as cooperation, participation, or neatness of written work by having the student rate the behavior on a scale with descriptors for each item on the scale (Alberto & Troutman, 2006; Daly & Ranalli, 2003; McConnell, 1999; Reid, 1996; Van Leuvan & Wang, 1997). Self-evaluation can also stimulate discussion and help a student and teacher reconcile differing views of the student's behavior and performance.

Positive Self-Talk and Attribution Training. This intervention can reduce chronic negativity. If the negativity is directed toward other people, things, and events (as opposed to merciless self-criticism), simply teaching the student positive statements to replace the negative statements can change the student's behavior. Eventually, this intervention may also lead to changes in the student's attitude and self-talk (the words people silently say to themselves). If the individual's negativity is primarily directed inward (self-criticism), the problem may be one of attribution—that is, do you attribute successes and failures to things within your control or things that are out of your control? Attribution training (or retraining, as it is sometimes known) helps the student learn to attribute successes to herself ("I got a good grade because I studied hard") rather than external forces or happenstance ("I got a good grade because the test was too easy").

By the same token, this intervention can help the student learn to ascribe mistakes, difficulties, and failures to things outside herself or outside her control. ("I forgot about band rehearsal, so I didn't give myself the time I needed to do a great job on my homework," as opposed to "I always do badly at homework because I am stupid.") Refocusing self-talk and reframing attribution may improve a student's confidence level, sense of self-efficacy, motivation, and, in some cases, tendencies toward depression or anxiety (Burnett, 1994; Burnett & McCrindle, 1999; Meichenbaum & Goodman, 1971; Philpot & Bamburg, 1996).

Teaching Replacement Behavior. A useful component of almost any behavior intervention plan, this intervention is based on the idea that behaviors can be learned. Just as a coach knows with certainty that ongoing teaching, practice, and feedback will help a team improve, a teacher can also help a student improve his behavior by teaching more positive and responsible behaviors to replace the problem behavior (Alberto & Troutman, 2006; Bandura 1977; Cashwell, Skinner, & Smith, 2001; Sugai & Lewis, 1996; Weissberg & Gesten, 1982). More than simply telling a student to exhibit a particular behavior, teaching replacement behavior shows students how to master a particular behavior and incorporate it into daily life.

Functional Communication. This intervention is useful for any student who does not know how to get his needs met by communicating those needs appropriately. Instead, the student engages in misbehavior to get them met. In conjunction with a multidisciplinary team and with the guidance of a school psychologist, speech/language clinician, and/or occupational therapist, the teacher must first ascertain that the problem is communication based and then design an alternative communication system for the student to get his needs met in positive and responsible ways instead of by misbehaving (Carr & Durand, 1985; Miltenberger, 2004; Richmond, Mancil, Conroy, & Alter, 2006).

Structured Reinforcement Systems. When a student does not seem interested in improving a particular behavior, this is a useful intervention. By creating a structure of points, tokens, or other age-appropriate means of tracking positive performance, the teacher can introduce incentives and rewards for positive behavior. By earning points or tokens, the student can accumulate enough to spend on desired interactions, activities, or other tangible items. Although it is important for students to learn to behave appropriately without external rewards, this is a temporary intervention designed to move students in a more positive direction (Broughton & Lahey, 1978; Cruz & Cullinan, 2001; McGoey & DuPaul, 2000).

Defining Limits and Establishing Consequences. This intervention acknowledges that reasonable consequences for misbehavior are both appropriate and necessary for the well-being of all students and staff, although most interventions should focus on providing positive support (Alberto & Troutman, 2006; Horner, 2002; Lerman & Vorndran, 2002; Scheuermann & Hall, 2008). It is important to establish a range of consequences with pros and cons, so you can decide which consequence to apply to various situations. Teachers must also learn how to define problem behavior by delineating limits—that is, by clarifying the lines between behavior that is always appropriate (and always encouraged), behavior that is acceptable only to a point or at certain times, and inappropriate behavior that will always receive a clearly defined consequence. Setting clear limits is the only way to ensure that consequences will be applied fairly, consistently, and equitably, which greatly increases the likelihood that consequences will be effective (Cook, Landrum, Tankersley, & Kauffman, 2003; Sprick, 2006).

Relaxation and Stress Management. This intervention is geared toward the teacher rather than the student. If a student's misbehavior is making a teacher tense, angry, or frustrated, it can be difficult, if not impossible, for the teacher to calmly and consistently implement any other interventions. By learning to physically relax, mentally decompress, and keep the student's behavior in perspective, the teacher can more positively and effectively instruct her students—not just the challenging students, but all students.

Internalizing Problems and Mental Health. This intervention addresses those quiet problems that often go undetected, such as students who may be anxious or depressed. It provides proven intervention strategies that fall into three broad categories (Merrell & Buchanan, 2006):

- Emotional education

- Behavior change

- Cognitive change

Even without previous training in counseling, teachers and other school personnel can try several effective strategies for helping troubled students. These techniques may be useful in working with a student who is sad, withdrawn, worried, or nervous. At the same time, school staff must learn to identify when a problem is severe enough to warrant referral to a mental health professional.

CONCLUSION

A B-RTI framework requires an organized continuum of problem-solving processes and a protocol of interventions. This framework allows a match between the intensity of the student's needs and the processes and interventions that will be used to ensure that those needs are met. If your district has gaps in either of these areas, consider using this chapter to work with building- and district-based leadership to fill those gaps in your B-RTI framework. Regardless of whether a student is identified with disabilities or whether the student is in general or special education, a student's intensity of need should be matched by the nature or the problem-solving processes and by the type of interventions that are the result of those processes.

CHAPTER 4

Develop a Process

Linking Needs to Available Resources

Designing a behavioral response-to-intervention (B-RTI) framework is only one step in the process of meeting every student's needs and ensuring that all students "fit successfully in the system." A framework is only a structure on which applications and actions can be based. For B-RTI to be effective, the school or district must also establish the connections that link students' needs to the resources that have been made available through the work of the leadership team in establishing universal practices and a B-RTI framework (Curtis & Stollar, 2002; Gresham, 2004; Knoff, 2002, 2008; Sprick, Garrison, et al., 2002). In other words, it isn't enough to create an ideal structure for student success—you also must build bridges that link students to the structure you've created, and you must send out invitations to teachers and put up "Open for Business" signs. This chapter outlines the steps the leadership team can take to create those links and invitations.

THE EIGHT-POINT TASK LIST

We mentioned earlier that the work of a leadership team is never done. The role of linking needs to resources also falls under the leadership team's purview. This eight-point task list will help guide the team through the linking process:

1. Develop a set of indicators (red flags) that signal a need for collaborative problem-solving.

2. Develop a process for requesting assistance.

3. Identify available resources (personnel and processes) for providing collaboration in meeting students' behavioral needs.

4. Identify a case manager.

5. Identify the tools and processes for Tier 2 interventions.

6. Establish a staff development plan.

7. Remove roadblocks to collaboration.

8. Actively involve parents.

We'll discuss each step in detail, providing specific examples and sample forms, when appropriate.

Task 1: Develop a Set of Indicators (Red Flags)

The most important task in this process is to identify those situations that should alert the system that a student has a significant need and there is work that needs to be done immediately. In other words, identify the student-based conditions that indicate a need for the system to launch one or more of the processes of collaborative problem-solving. These red flags can cover a wide range of potential problems, but their primary function should be to act as a systemwide alert to academic failings and disciplinary problems of any individual student (Deno, 1985; Irvin et al., 2004).

Any time the number of students flagged as needing collaborative services begins to overwhelm the system, more work needs to be done on improving universal prevention, the topic covered in Chapter 2 of this book. For example, if so many students in a high school fail two or more classes in the first quarter that there are not a sufficient number of interventionists (school counselor, school psychologist, problem-solving team, etc.) to provide collaborative assistance, the system has a clear indication that schoolwide improvements need to be made to increase academic success. Whenever too many students hit a red flag alert for individual intervention, you should assume that your entire system needs work in that particular area (Colvin et al., 1993; Sprick, Garrison, et al., 2002; Sugai, Horner, & Gresham, 2002, Taylor-Greene et al., 1997).

Academic failure. For example, any time a student fails two classes within a given period of time (say, a quarter or semester), that situation should serve as a warning that the student needs an immediate intervention. A team should be created and a plan of action implemented. Failing several classes soon becomes failing a whole grade level. The longer this goes without remedy, the greater the gap becomes between the student and grade level peers, to the point where there is a high probability that the student will not graduate from high school (Alexander, Entwisle, & Kabbani, 2001; Christle, Jolivette, & Nelson, 2007; Griffin, 2002; Perez-Johnson & Maynard, 2007; U.S. General Accounting Office, 2002). When schools or districts have academic red flags in place, they can prevent the long-term academic failures that lead students to drop out of school.

In addition to failing grades, any other academic indicators in place in your district can and should be used as red flags that initiate collaborative support efforts. For example, if your district does regular progress monitoring of oral reading fluency, DIBELS (Good & Kaminski, 2002), or curriculum-based assessment measures, those data sources can have threshold levels established that indicate a need for problem-solving to begin (Good, Simmons, & Kame'enui, 2001; Kaminksi & Good, 1996).

Disciplinary referrals. Identify the number of disciplinary referrals that signals a need for proactive planning. In other words, a specific number of referrals should launch the system into problem-solving mode because the referrals have not been sufficient to solve the problem. For example, whenever a student has three disciplinary referrals in a single semester, it should signal that the student needs a targeted or comprehensive intervention. Sugai, Sprague, Horner, and Walker (2000) recommend three levels of analysis of office discipline referral data that parallels the three-tier intervention model. Students with zero or one referral are likely benefiting from universal supports, students with two to five referrals are likely to need a targeted intervention, and students with six or more need a comprehensive, individualized evaluation and support plan. Every school or district can choose its own threshold number (and time period, such as during one month or one semester), but we recommend three. Two referrals may not represent a significant or long-term problem, especially if they occur months apart. But three disciplinary referrals within a specific time frame such as a nine-week quarter signal that, for that student, disciplinary action is not enough to correct whatever is going on. For most students, the real consequence of a referral is the reaction they get at home from their parents, not whatever the principal uses as a consequence. That's what makes referrals effective—they notify parents and get them involved, then the parents or guardians reinforce the value that such behavior is not tolerated.

Identify the number of disciplinary referrals that signals a need for proactive planning.

When a student receives a third referral within a nine-week period, it should be a red flag that the student does not perceive referrals in a negative way and may even enjoy the attention surrounding a trip to the front office. So it becomes the staff's responsibility to design an intervention that will help the student learn to function at a higher level of accountability. The intervention must include alternative strategies that don't fall under the Correction variable (such as those aligned under the other STOIC variables: Structure, Teach, Observe, Interact) because it should already be clear that corrective action alone is not effective. By launching into collaborative problem-solving, the system can seek to design interventions that will reduce the problem behavior, which will in turn reduce future office referrals for this student.

Detention referrals. Another example of a red flag that can be generated somewhat automatically by a database is when a student hits a certain number (six, for example) of after-school or lunchtime detentions. If your school does not have a lunchtime detention, problem-solving room, or other such consequence, we are not suggesting you need one. Rather, if there is such a setting in your school, we suggest that its records be kept in a database so the system will be alerted that this corrective intervention is not working for any student who is repeatedly on its receiving end. Again, the school or district can choose the number that sets off the alert, but the number needs to be built in to the database system—along with the date, time, location, and reason for correction—and needs to reflect the point at which the student's behavior is a call for proactive planning, even if a teacher has not asked for help with the student.

Chronic absenteeism. Another red flag that can be embedded within the system is an alert for absenteeism. Once a student has been absent for a specific, predetermined number of days during a semester, the response should be automatic, and a team should move into action. Students who drop out of school don't reach that point overnight; they often practice not coming to schools for months or years first (Alexander et al., 2001; Christle et al., 2007). A preset alert within the attendance database can be the first step toward preventing that student from becoming a statistical casualty.

Our experience in schools has taught us that there is a fair degree of variability in average daily attendance. In one urban district, high-poverty high schools are averaging 91–92% attendance, only slightly below the average of lower-poverty schools. In another urban district, all of the high schools are averaging 75% to 80% average daily attendance. We suggest you investigate your school or district's average daily attendance to determine if absenteeism should be viewed as a universal system-level problem or if daily attendance can be a signal for helping individual students.

Task 2: Develop a Process for Requesting Assistance

The leadership team's second task is to design a process for teachers to use when they have a request for assistance. The concept of red flags (Task 1) is designed to ensure that student needs are met. This second step is designed to ensure that the system is fully ready to help and support teachers, whether or not a student's problems have risen to red flag status. The team's priority should be to make it easy for busy teachers to request and receive the assistance they need—without creating a cumbersome bureaucracy that makes the process difficult. We have two forms available as models: an informal request for assistance (Reproducible Form 4.1) and a more formal request (Reproducible Form 4.2).

The details of how your problem-solving systems work—including who collects the forms and how they come to the attention of the leadership team—may already be established by your district. However, if systems are not in place, plan to construct clear and consistent processes to ensure that the needs of staff, students, and parents are met within your systems for problem-solving and intervention design and implementation. Again, this is an opportunity to communicate with teachers and make them aware of the resources available. One way to accomplish this is to send out an invitation at the beginning of the school year that notifies teachers about the school or district's resources and outlines the brief process for requesting assistance: what forms to use, where to locate them, and who to give the completed forms to.

Task 3: Identify Resources

In addition to developing efficient request-for-assistance processes and identifying a set of automatic red flags that signal students' academic, disciplinary, or emotional needs, the leadership team must also identify and document the resources (individuals, teams, and organizations) available in the school or district to respond to those needs. In other words, who are the interventionists who will provide the collaborative problem-solving processes that are discussed throughout this book? Those resources may include grade-level colleagues, small learning communities, intervention planning team members, school counselors, behavior specialists, literacy coaches, school psychologists, county mental health experts, child protective services, and others. The names of these positions may vary from district to district and state to state, but the idea here is that you will build a menu of people and/or teams who are available to provide support for problem analysis, intervention design, implementation, and follow-up (Feldman & Kratochwill, 2003; Kratochwill & Pitman, 2002; McEvoy & Welker, 2000).

Plan to construct clear and consistent processes to ensure that the needs of staff, students, and parents are met within your systems for problem-solving and intervention design and implementation.

Continued on p. 78

Reproducible Form 4.1

SAMPLE INFORMAL REQUEST FOR ASSISTANCE

Date: __11/3__

To: __Ms. Vargas__

From: __Mr. Kavanaugh__

Position: __3rd Grade Teacher__

Re: __Sam Jefferson__

. . . .

Brief description of the problem:

Playground misbehavior – pushing, shoving, arguing with other kids.

__X__ This is an informal request for assistance. (I'd just like some ideas at this point.)

_____ This is a request for formal assistance. (The problem may be serious enough for a structured intervention plan.)

Reproducible Form 4.2

FORMAL REQUEST FOR ASSISTANCE

Referring Person: _Mrs. Iwanaga_   Position: _6th grade teacher_   Date: _3/12_

Student: _Melinda Krych_

Grade: _9_   DOB: _____   Sex: M (F)

. . . .

Check the Type of Problem Behavior:

Academic	Social	Communication	Self-Help	Health
❏ Reading	❏ Aggression	❏ Language	❏ Dressing	❏ Vision
❏ Spelling	☒ Noncompliance	❏ Fluency	❏ Hygiene	❏ Hearing
❏ Writing	❏ Truancy	❏ Articulation	❏ Other:	❏ Physical
☒ Study Skills	❏ Tardiness	❏ Voice	_____	❏ Other:
❏ Other:	❏ Withdrawal	❏ Other:	_____	_____
_____	❏ Disruptions	_____		_____
_____	❏ Social Skills	_____		
	❏ Self-Managemt			
	❏ Other:			
	_____			
	_____			

Provide a Specific and Observable Description of the Problem:

Has turned in only two of 15 homework assignments. She now disrupts class by calling assignments "stupid".

Provide a Specific Description of the Problem Context:

Where:

When:

With Whom:

Other:

Provide a List of Previous Remediation Attempts (if any):

1.

2.

3.

Reproducible Materials Blank copies of the forms are provided on the CD. Permission is given for individual teachers, administrators, or other school personnel to reproduce any form labeled "Reproducible Form" for in-district use.

These resources should be listed in your school handbook along with a statement that highlights the collaborative nature of your staff. The statement could say something like, "We are a collaborative staff who work together as professionals." Teachers need to know that if the first person they turn to is not the correct person to assist them, that professional will recommend another professional. This collaborative nature, and the documentation of it, reinforces for the staff that asking for help and using resources is not considered a sign of weakness but instead is a sign of teaching strength. The idea is that when a culture of teamwork and collaboration among school personnel is created, the combined knowledge results in increased problem-solving efficiency (Feldman & Kratochwill, 2003; Hilty, 1998; Kratochwill & Stoiber, 2002). Schools must also do more to advertise to students that direct assistance is available to them as well. This is what we mean by putting up "Open for Business" signs. Students need to be made aware that they can ask for help when they're being bullied, when they have trouble passing classes, or simply when they need assistance getting to school on time. Staff members also need to know that they have support anytime they need it.

Task 4: Identify a Case Manager

The fourth task in the process of linking needs to resources is to identify one of the interventionists (from the list created earlier) to serve as a case manager. A case manager is assigned to a specific student and has responsibility for ensuring an orchestrated, coordinated, and sustained response. The case manager works to ensure that problem-solving processes are initiated quickly, that all relevant parties are actively included (at the very least, the teacher(s), student, and parents), and that an intervention is designed, implemented, and evaluated for efficacy (Gravois, Knotek, & Babinski, 2001; Gravois & Rosenfield, 2002; Rosenfield & Gravois, 1996). If the intervention is successful, the case manager continues to monitor to ensure that the school's universal practices are sufficient for the student to be successful. However, until that point is reached, the case manager remains linked to the student as an advocate to make sure that if one level of problem-solving does not lead to success (response to intervention), other resources will be brought to bear. This advocacy for the student by someone who is knowledgeable about all the people and processes available may even occur across years so that the student's needs are not lost in the shuffle of moving from one sort of problem-solving process to another. Without this case manager concept in place, it is possible that the student and the parent will be moved from the school counselor to the school psychologist to the behavior specialist, with no one within the system coordinating the situation.

> A case manager is assigned to a specific student and has responsibility for ensuring an orchestrated, coordinated, and sustained response.

In addition to being an advocate for the student in any given year, the case manager needs to be an advocate for the teacher. The teacher is likely to be the main implementer of the intervention, so he must feel that he is an active part of all processes and decision-making. Given this need for the case manager to support the teacher, active thought should be given to pairing case managers and teachers who are likely to work well together. Consider gender, age, race, and style issues, then try to create a match that would appear to result in a positive and mutually respectful relationship.

Deciding how to identify the case manager is a part of the process that needs to be predetermined. The case manager should not be a classroom teacher who is directly connected to the student and/or problem, but the role could be filled by one of the intervention planning team members who may, in fact, be a general education teacher.

Whoever is assigned the role should stay in touch will all aspects of intervention planning, even if the intervention moves to subsequent tiers. The case manager not only ensures that team members involved in the intervention follow through on the action chosen, but in effect also becomes an advocate for the student throughout the process. Ultimately, the case manager's job is to ensure that this particular student does not fall though any cracks in the system (Rosenfield, 1987; Rosenfield & Gravois, 1996). (See Chapter 8, "The 25-Minute Planning Process," for more information.)

Task 5: Identify the Tools and Processes for Tier 2 Interventions

Although not every red flag or teacher request for assistance will require Tier 2 interventions, it is important to establish in advance the tools and process that you want in place when B-RTI moves to that level (Colvin, Kame'enui, et al., 1993; Lewis et al., 1998; Walker et al., 1996). In addition, the leadership team is also charged with training the staff members who will be involved in interventions in how to use the tools and processes established. Years of experience have led us to the development of three intervention planning tools that we recommend as a starting point: (1) the teacher interview process (see Chapter 7); (2) the 25-minute planning process (see Chapter 8); and (3) the multidisciplinary team approach (see Chapter 9).

Your school or district can use these tools as they exist, modify them to meet your specific needs or structure, or start from scratch and develop your own. Whichever approach you chose, the leadership team should have these or similar processes in place before the first red flag or teacher request occurs. Tier 2 interventions are too critical for the student and too resource-dependent for the district to leave to last-minute plans. (This step is discussed in detail in Chapter 3.)

👁 BEHAVIOR IMPROVEMENT PLAN (BIP)

There is a legal requirement for children with emotional/behavioral disabilities that after an FBA (functional behavior assessment) is completed, a BIP will be developed and implemented. A BIP is a set of strategies that support children in learning new acceptable behaviors and abstaining from inappropriate behaviors. Throughout this book we refer to the "intervention plan" or "intervention," although these terms encompass the requirements of the BIP. We chose these more generic terms because BIP may refer to a legal requirement for students with disabilities, whereas the term "intervention plan" includes any plan developed to help a child improve behavior, whether that child is receiving special education services or not. Thus, if a BIP is required by law, an intervention that stems from the processes described in this book would be the student's BIP.

Task 6: Establish a Staff Development Plan

As a leadership team, you not only identify the five or six Tier 1 interventions (school-wide universal practices) that your building or district will focus on for the year, but also establish a staff development plan to facilitate the implementation of those Tier 1 interventions (Kratochwill, Volpiansky, Clements, & Ball, 2007). In other words, you can't just say, "Here's what we're going to work on this year." You will be more likely to experience success when you provide staff members with the protocols, the training, and the common language they'll need to accomplish the goals they've agreed to meet (Colton & Sheridan, 1998; Sheridan & Kratochwill, 1992).

The acronym STOIC and its variables (Structure, Teach, Observe, Interact, and Correct) are a good starting point as a common language for improving school culture. The concept of function-based intervention (determining why a student misbehaves and tailoring the intervention to the reason) must also be widely understood by general education teachers, special education teachers, and school support specialists such as school psychologists and case managers (Scheuermann & Hall, 2008; Sprick, Knight, et al., 2007). The terms Tier 1 and Tier 2 interventions must also be part of the district's language and the staff's common knowledge.

Which staff members will get which training? Who will provide training? When will training sessions be scheduled? These questions and more must be asked and answered by the leadership team as it establishes a staff development plan. Staff development must also include ongoing support for teachers beyond the initial training (Gingiss, 1992; Kratochwill et al., 2007; Scott, McIntyre, Liaupsin, Conroy, & Payne, 2005). Again, active communication comes into play here. The staff development plan can include refresher training sessions, periodic memos to teachers about resources and support available, and scheduled meetings with individual teachers or with grade-level groups to give them an opportunity to communicate their needs.

The leadership team is also charged with establishing a menu of Tier 2 interventions that planning team members can use at that level of B-RTI. See *Interventions: Evidence-Based Behavioral Strategies for Individual Students* for a comprehensive list of Tier 2 interventions to choose from. Or your team can consult other sources if your needs go beyond the scope of what that book offers.

In addition, as part of the staff development plan, the team must determine which staff members will receive training on which interventions. This process connects back to the first task of identifying the resources, or players, who will be available to participate in collaborative problem-solving. The team must examine the backgrounds of school counselors, behavior specialists, and assistant principals to assess the level of training they already have in Tier 2 interventions and determine how much more they need and who will provide it.

Task 7: Remove Roadblocks to Collaboration

Another important task in the process of linking student needs to available resources is to lay the groundwork for a collaborative, problem-solving culture (Denton, 2003; Joyce & Showers, 2002; Kratochwill et al., 2007; Rones & Hoagwood, 2000). The leadership team must actively remove any roadblocks to collaboration that exist in the school, building, or district. Building bridges between students and the structures you've created for them is effective only if the roads are clear and traffic flows freely.

The greatest roadblock to collaboration in any school or district is fear. If teachers fear that requesting help or admitting they don't know how to handle a student's problems will stigmatize them as substandard teachers, they will not reach out for the collaboration available to them. As members of the leadership team, administrators must actively, repetitively, and convincingly communicate to teachers that asking for help will always be viewed in a positive light. Administrators, as educational leaders promoting collaborative school systems, must also walk the talk and actively support and praise teachers who fill out those request-for-assistance forms and who follow through on actively participating in collaborative problem-solving (Boscardin, 2005). If the forms are a roadblock, make them optional in the earliest stages of requesting help. Asking for help needs to be easy and uncomplicated. Teachers today are tasked with educating every student who walks through the door, regardless of the student's motivational level or support at home (IDEA, 2004; NCLB, 2001). If a teacher mentions to a school counselor while passing in the hallway that she could use a little assistance with Jason, treat that request as seriously as if the teacher had initiated a formal process. If the relationship is informal—just a casual talk in the hall—the interventionist should always end the conversation with a willingness to move to a more formal level by offering to get the teacher a copy of the referral form. Interventionists need to remember that anything more than one casual talk in the hall should have paperwork documenting the problem-solving process. Otherwise there is potential for misunderstanding at a later date. The teacher could say, "I asked for help and never got any assistance," while the interventionist is thinking, "I never got a request for help from this teacher." When in doubt, document, but make this process as easy and inviting for the teacher as possible (Knoff, 2002).

> As members of the leadership team, administrators must actively, repetitively, and convincingly communicate to teachers that asking for help will always be viewed in a positive light.

Communication is the key component of this task (Bergan & Kratochwill, 1990; Rosenfield, 2004, 2008). Advertise your resources and services in your teacher handbook. Figure 4.1 shows a sample of a page from a staff handbook that emphasizes collaborative problem-solving. This approach allows the principal (at the beginning of each year) to emphasize that collaboration and professionalism are inseparable and to introduce any new personnel to each other and to the various people who function as interventionists.

Figure 4.1

Page from Staff Handbook on Collaborative Problem-Solving

Collaborative Problem-Solving: The Highest Form of Professionalism

We, the staff of Hamilton Middle School, are committed to meeting the academic and social/emotional needs of all students. However, we recognize that some students come to us with severe challenges. To meet these needs, we must work together, sharing expertise and support.

Following is a list of positions and, more importantly, the wonderful people who are available to assist teachers in their ongoing efforts to help every student achieve his/her fullest potential. Use these resources!

> Dr. Arizmendi, Principal
>
> Mrs. Uesugi, Assistant Principal
>
> Mr. Spenser, Literacy Coach
>
> Ms. Jenson, Speech/Language Clinician
>
> Dr. Jones, District Standards Coach
>
> Mr. Griffith, Chairperson of the Intervention Planning Team (IPT)
>
> Mrs. Wong, New-Teacher Mentor
>
> Ms. Stevenson, Behavior Specialist
>
> Mr. Torres, New-Teacher Mentor
>
> Mr. Torgeson, School Psychologist
>
> Ms. Younger, School Counselor Mentor

You can also make 30-second announcements in staff meetings. A quick "Don't forget the resources we have available if you're having any difficulty" will suffice. The only way to establish a culture of collaboration and overcome teachers' fear of asking for help is to communicate at every opportunity that your building or district encourages, perhaps even rewards, such requests (see Figure 4.2).

Peer-to-peer communication can be your most effective advertising strategy. If a teacher has used the intervention planning team's services and experienced successful results, you can ask that teacher to provide a testimonial about his experience to other teachers in a faculty meeting. Having a teacher openly discuss his experience of asking for help, getting other staff members involved, and benefiting from the process is likely to be a powerful motivator for other teachers to do the same (Knoff, 2002).

Figure 4.2
Sample Promotion

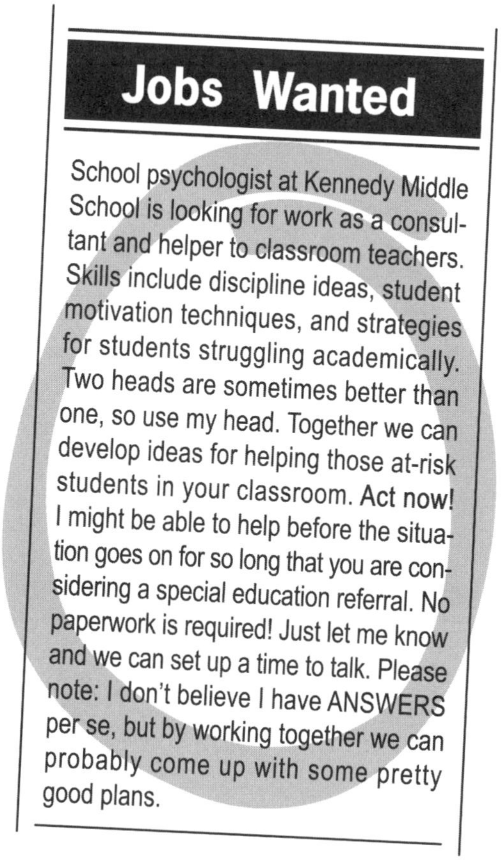

Jobs Wanted

School psychologist at Kennedy Middle School is looking for work as a consultant and helper to classroom teachers. Skills include discipline ideas, student motivation techniques, and strategies for students struggling academically. Two heads are sometimes better than one, so use my head. Together we can develop ideas for helping those at-risk students in your classroom. **Act now!** I might be able to help before the situation goes on for so long that you are considering a special education referral. No paperwork is required! Just let me know and we can set up a time to talk. Please note: I don't believe I have ANSWERS per se, but by working together we can probably come up with some pretty good plans.

Task 8: Actively Involve Parents

Finally, the leadership team must decide at what point the planning team will link to the student's parents or guardians and get them involved in the intervention process. This process may involve a series of decisions, and the policies may be school, building, or district based. The team should check with district guidelines to determine whether a parental notification policy is already in place.

If such guidelines are not in place, we recommend that if an intervention goes beyond a planned discussion, it's prudent to involve parents and get their written permission to proceed with an intervention (see Reproducible Form 4.3: Parental Permission). This request for permission is separate from the formal consent processes involved in special education processes and 504 evaluations—those in which you are bound by law to follow due process and specific timelines. This is for earlier-stage problem-solving efforts, and the goal is to provide documentation that parents were informed and invited to actively participate in both problem-solving processes and intervention design.

Reproducible Form 4.3

PARENTAL PERMISSION

SAMPLE

Dear _Mr. and Mrs. Torres_____ :

Parent or Guardian Name

We would like to develop a plan to support _____Felipe_____

Student Name

To assist us in developing the most useful plan possible, we would like your permission to informally assess your child's behavior and work habits. This process may include any or all of the following:

_– classroom observations_____

_– self-monitoring activities_____

_____

_____

_____

_____

After we gather preliminary information, we will ask to meet with you to discuss the information and how to proceed to ensure that your child is successful in school. We hope to work with you as partners in creating a positive school experience for your child.

Please sign the slip below and return it to school by _____12/1_____. As soon as the assessment has been completed, we will be in touch.

Thank you for your assistance.

Sincerely,

- -

_____ has my permission to informally assess _____ 's academic skills and work habits, and to develop a plan of assistance.

_____   _____

Signed (Parent or Guardian)   Date

Early and proactive involvement of parents has many potential benefits. Conjoint consultation (involving parents, teachers, and consultant/team) has been perceived by both parents and teachers as more acceptable than either parent or teacher problem-solving in isolation (Freer & Watson, 1999). Involving parents and teachers with the consultant to solve problems can foster improved communication between home and school, may increase treatment effects, and can promote maintenance of treatment effects over time (Gortmaker et al., 2004; Sheridan et al., 1996). For example, parents may have access to powerful reinforcers that the school cannot provide, and they may be able to play an important role in problem-solving and supporting intervention implementation at home and at school because they know the student well and may have insights to the student's behavior that staff have not considered (Rones & Hoagwood, 2000).

The person who initiates the parent contact is a district-by-district decision. Ideally, the student's teacher will have been in contact with the parents about the problem long before it reaches the point of needing a problem-solving team. It's important to keep parents informed and involved at every step so they're not blindsided by an out-of-nowhere call from a school counselor or interventionist asking them to come in for an intervention meeting. It's also important to work actively with your special education department in the event that your intervention leads to a special education referral.

TEST YOUR SYSTEM

The last step in this linking process is to use hypothetical student scenarios to test the system. With a scenario in mind, work through the steps to see where the system may break down. Determine what can be done to improve your team's plans and policies. Look critically at your system's links between the red flags for students and the resources available. Consider whether a student could fall through the cracks or get lost in the shuffle. If so, modify aspects of your current service delivery to repair those cracks and eliminate the possibility that a child and family may get shuffled from one person or team to another with no one serving as an in-system advocate. Some student scenarios to consider when you test your system are:

- A quiet student who is academically adequate but completes only 70% of assignments

- A very able, socially skilled student who has a drastic change in behavior

- A student who makes a threat

- A student who has a history of fighting

- A student who never completes homework

- A student who is absent one or two days a week

> Consider whether a student could fall through the cracks or get lost in the shuffle. If so, modify aspects of your current service delivery to repair those cracks.

CONCLUSION

This task list for linking student needs to available resources is comprehensive and will take time to work through—and it is only one set of many responsibilities that the leadership must follow through on. Yet it may be the most important. By building links and bridges between students and the assistance they need, your leadership team is creating a safety net that will keep students from falling through the cracks.

 Reproducible Materials

Copies of the following reproducible materials appear on the CD. Permission is given for individual teachers, administrators, or other school personnel to reproduce these forms for in-district use.

Reproducible Form 4.1: Informal Request for Assistance

Reproducible Form 4.2: Formal Request for Assistance

Reproducible Form 4.3: Parental Permission

CHAPTER 5

Data-Driven Decisions

Create a Culture and Process of Data Collection

Within the B-RTI process, collecting and interpreting behavior data is an essential component if a school expects to have successful interventions. And yet data collection and analysis is often the weak link in the process (Lewis, Hudson, Richter, & Johnson, 2004; Quinn et al., 2001; Whelan, 2005). Somehow, the reported side effects of data collection have caused many teachers and problem-solving teams to cringe. For some educators, data collection is an unpleasant, aversive task, or at the very least overwhelming. The good news is that teachers and teams are becoming more efficient and skillful in collecting academic data through benchmark testing, universal screening, curriculum-based assessment, and state accountability testing. Analyzing academic data is fast becoming a prerequisite skill for all teachers. However, social behavior data is a whole different creature. Many educators see social behavior data as the "evil twin" to academic data.

As noted earlier in this book, there aren't any behavioral interventions that are guaranteed to work every time. In many respects, attempting behavioral interventions is like gambling in that you don't know for sure whether you will be successful. The key to being successful is to be relentless and savvy. Being savvy is where data plays such a critical role. Data will help the classroom teacher and/or problem-solving team throughout the B-RTI process—from the initial problem identification to the eventual evaluation of the intervention plan (Batsche et al., 2005; Fuchs & Fuchs, 2007; Shinn, 1989; Sulzer-Azaroff & Mayer, 1991; Upah, 2008). Thus, data collection and analysis needs to be demystified so that the classroom teacher and problem-solving team can effectively and efficiently use data.

This chapter is designed to provide practical information and strategies to help the classroom teacher and the problem-solving team see data as their ally, not their nemesis. This chapter will also look at systematic data collection from all angles of the B-RTI process, starting with the role of data for the classroom teacher during the early-stage interventions at Tier 1 and moving on to how data is collected and analyzed for an intervention developed by an intervention planning team or multi-disciplinary team working at Tier 2 or Tier 3. The initial focus of this chapter is the rationale for data collection. Next, it covers certain prerequisites to how and when to effectively collect data. A number of data collection tools (from simple to complex) are described. Finally, we provide information about what to do with data after it is collected—how to interpret, when to share, and how to document.

RATIONALE FOR DATA COLLECTION AND ANALYSIS

There are compelling reasons for data collection and analysis in Tier 1 and Tier 2 of the B-RTI continuum. First, the entire thrust of federal and state-level RTI initiatives is to implement interventions that have been proven to be effective. In other words, evidence-based interventions are those in which data has shown that intervention has successfully addressed misbehavior (Kratochwill & Shernoff, 2003; NCLB 2001; Sprick & Garrison, 2008; Walker, 2004). Furthermore, a teacher or problem-solving team implementing an evidence-based intervention must collect data to evaluate both the consistency of implementation and the intervention's effectiveness for that particular student (Algozzine, Ysseldyke, & Elliot, 1997; Fuchs & Fuchs, 2007; Howell & Nolet, 2000; Kratochwill & Stoiber, 2000; Ysseldyke et al., 2006). When looking at the fundamental findings about effective behavior management as illustrated by the acronym STOIC, the O conveys the vital importance of observing and monitoring student behavior (a.k.a. collecting data).

In addition to helping you evaluate the effectiveness of an intervention, systematic data collection plays essential roles throughout the entire intervention process. The initial data collection provides a baseline of information—frequency, duration, latency, and intensity—about the misbehavior (Alberto & Troutman, 2006; Casey, Skiba, & Algozzine, 1988; Upah, 2008). Remarkably, the mere act of collecting data can be an effective intervention that results in a decrease of the target behavior. There are several possible reasons, including:

- The well-documented Hawthorne effect (Landsberger, 1958) causes short-term improvement.

- The student wasn't aware the behavior was a problem for the teacher.

- It is human nature to shape up when you know someone is watching.

- Collecting data conveys that the teacher is serious about addressing the problem.

- Data collection increases the amount of attention the student receives from the teacher.

- Data collection communicates the teacher's concern and care for the student.

Regardless of the reason, collecting data can sometimes end up being an effective intervention. The major benefit of data collection is that it provides insights and uncovers trends about the student's misbehavior, which in turn can lead to understanding the function (reason) for the misbehavior and to identifying a potentially effective intervention (Alberto & Troutman, 2006; Merrell, 2003; Scheuermann & Hall, 2008; Sprick & Garrison, 2008; Sugai & Tindal, 1993).

Another reason for collecting data is the role of data in shaping perceptions. When dealing with student misbehavior, the perceptions of the teacher(s), administrators, parents, and even the student are critical. How they feel about a student's problem will decide what is done and how it is done. Is the problem minor or serious? What are the reasons or functions for the behavior? Which interventions might work? Is the intervention working? Has the intervention successfully met the stated goal? To answer these and similar questions, the teacher and other staff members will likely form an opinion or impression. The key is whether the opinion or impression is based on valid data. Without data, there is no way to confirm that perceptions or impressions are correct. For example, a teacher who has struggled with a student's out-of-seat wandering for five months may respond to a question about whether the intervention is working by saying, "Things have not improved." If all you have are the teacher's perceptions, the intervention is evaluated on those perceptions only. With data, there is objective evidence to demonstrate the effect of the intervention (Alberto & Troutman, 2006; Baer et al., 1968; Scheuermann & Hall, 2008). For example, the same teacher now has data that shows a decrease in out-of-seat wandering by 40% after two weeks. For this teacher, the perception that the misbehavior still exists is accurate, but the data clearly shows that the intervention is having a positive effect.

Better yet, data can help shape the teacher's perceptions by showing her that the intervention is affecting the student's behavior. Gaining such insight can be an empowering experience for the teacher, who now realizes that she has the power and tools to influence how the student decides to behave. Gaining that insight is highly reinforcing. An objective evaluation that reveals the effect of the intervention on the student's behavior can cause a teacher to stick with an intervention, try other interventions, have more positive expectations about the student (which is correlated with improved student outcomes), and feel better about herself (Scheuermann & Hall, 2008; Shinn & Bamonto, 1998; Sulzer-Azaroff & Mayer, 1991). All of those outcomes enhance the likelihood that the intervention will continue to be implemented with fidelity and that it will subsequently succeed.

> Without data, there is no way to confirm that perceptions or impressions are correct.

PREREQUISITES FOR DATA COLLECTION AND ANALYSIS

Initial data collection at Tier 1 needs to be simple and easy for the classroom teacher to accomplish. At this stage, classroom teachers often say, "I don't have time to collect data! His misbehavior and teaching the other 24 students take up every second of my day!" Having the time and energy can be a real challenge for the teacher, especially when he is frustrated and feels overwhelmed. The best way to respond to this frustration is to identify simple data collection methods and tools. In addition to selecting simple methods, following are several considerations to address before starting to collect data.

Task 1: Identify the Target Behavior

First, the teacher needs to objectively identify which misbehavior will be the focus of the intervention (Alberto & Troutman, 2006; Bergan & Kratochwill, 1990; Kratochwill, 2008; Sprick & Garrison, 2008; Thompson, Symons, & Felce, 2000). As easy as that may sound, it can be hard to objectively describe a student's behavior without injecting subjective impressions. For example, "He is so immature" and "She acts like a five-year-old" are both subjective statements. Making subjective statements is normal, but it is virtually impossible to collect valid data based on such impressions. Table 5.1 compares subjective descriptions that can't be measured (from a data collection perspective) with objective statements that can be measured.

The teacher needs to take the subjective impression of the student's behavior and break it down into objective descriptions of what the behavior looks and sounds like. The goal is to describe behavior in such detail that it can be easily seen or heard by the teacher or any other third-party observer (Alberto & Troutman, 2006; Scheuermann & Hall, 2008; Thompson et al., 2000). One way to achieve this objectivity is to use a T-chart (Sprick, Garrison, et al., 1998). Table 5.2 illustrates how T-charts yield objective, observable descriptions of behavior.

Once you have a clear description of what the problem behavior looks and sounds like, it is helpful to also describe what appropriate behaviors (i.e., replacement behaviors) should look and sound like. For example, appropriate behaviors for the student described in the sample T-chart could include the following:

- Stay two to three feet away from other students when angry or frustrated.

- Talk with students and teachers in a quiet voice without using profanity.

- Tell the teacher that he is starting to feel angry or frustrated.

- Go to a designated spot in the classroom for cool-down time.

- Take 10 deep breaths when feeling angry.

Table 5.1

Comparison of Subjective and Objective Behavior Statements

Subjective (Unmeasurable)	Objective (Measurable)
Bad attitude	• Makes disrespectful comments to the teacher and other students. • Says she always messes up when writing and spelling.
Unmotivated	• Doesn't complete classwork or homework. • Doesn't answer questions in class. • Reads a book when assigned to do math problems.
Off in his own world	• Stares out the window. • Doodles on his paper. • Plays quietly with items in his desk.
Poor self-image	• Makes negative statements about self, such as "I'm stupid!" and "I can't read!"
Attention-deficit problems	• Fidgets while sitting in chair (rocks her chair, sits on her feet). • Gets out of her chair and wanders around the room. • Makes tapping noises with a pencil on the desk or her foot on the leg of the desk.
Emotional problems	• Responds with angry verbal outbursts when asked to read. • Cries when frustrated. • Doesn't interact with students when approached.

Table 5.2

Sample T-Chart

Identify Problem Behavior: Adam's aggressive behavior when angry	
How Does It Look?	**How Does It Sound?**
• He hits other male students with his fist. • He pinches female students until they cry. • He kicks male and female students in the shins or steps on their feet. • He sometimes throws objects (pencils, book, rulers, etc.) at students from four to six feet away.	• He often yells and screams when he hits, pinches, kicks, or throws objects. • His yelling sometimes includes profanity.

Developing a description of replacement behaviors makes it easier for the teacher and any other staff member to determine whether a behavior needs a positive or negative consequence. If struggling to identify the problem in a measurable way, the teacher can consider keeping an anecdotal record for a few days. To do this, use a voice recorder, computer, or notepad to record what the student does. Specify what happened, when it happened, and what might have caused it to happen.

Task 2: Identify Behaviors to Document

Identify which specific misbehaviors will be observed and recorded for the purpose of data collection. If the goal of the intervention has already been established, the targeted misbehaviors or positive replacement behaviors should be clearly related to the goal (Alberto & Troutman, 2006). Select the data collection methods that are best suited to generate the data needed to evaluate the goal of the intervention. For example, if the goal of the intervention is to reduce a student's blurt-outs by 30% at the end of two weeks, the teacher will need to keep a simple frequency count each day. It is imperative that the teacher and/or problem-solving team establish realistic short-term goals for improvement. Eliminating all blurt-outs within two weeks is not realistic. Furthermore, the teacher needs to anticipate that the frequency of the blurt-outs may actually increase during the first two to four days of the intervention because students often test the teacher at first to see if she will consistently implement the plan.

Task 3: Identify Interpretation Rules

In addition to selecting collection methods that will provide the data needed to evaluate the effectiveness of the intervention, consider setting some general interpretation rules for the data. By establishing data decision rules before starting the implementation, the teacher or problem-solving team is better prepared to understand what the collected data means. For example, if the goal is to reduce blurt-outs by 30% by the end of two weeks, data collection rules could include increasing the goal if the improvement is greater than 50% after two weeks. Likewise, if the behavior improves by less than 10%, the rules could entail modifying the positive and negative consequences and using precorrections. The classroom teacher will likely need the case manager or interventionist to assist in establishing realistic data decision rules.

Task 4: Identify Documentation Protocols

To help interpret the data and identify meaningful trends when using any data collection method, it is important to always document the following information:

- Actual date of the observation

- Day of the week (In case the wrong date is recorded, having the day of the week will help identify the actual date. It also makes it easy to see if there is any trend for when the misbehavior occurs—for example, it almost always occurs on Thursdays and Fridays.)

- Time of day

- Length of the observation

- Location in the room or school

- Activity that the student should be doing

Task 5: Identify Third-Party Observation Rules

We recommend the following considerations when planning observations by a third party. These observations are typically conducted in the classroom by a case manager, interventionist, or member of the problem-solving team as part of a Tier 2 or Tier 3 intervention. The purpose of the observations may be to collect initial baseline data, monitor progress, and/or evaluate the implementation of the intervention plan.

Coordinate with the teacher. Notify the classroom teacher ahead of time before conducting any observations in the classroom. Have the teacher identify times and/or activities that should provide opportunities to observe the target behavior(s). Ask the teacher to describe the planned activity during the selected observation period, including how long it should last. Also, decide ahead of time if more than one observation is needed to obtain sufficient data.

Identify a comparison. Consider selecting another student with whom to compare the target student's data. This can provide a normative benchmark for interpreting the frequency, duration, latency, and intensity of the target student's behavior in that teacher's classroom. Ask the classroom teacher ahead of time to select a comparison student of the same age, gender, and developmental level. Another criterion might be to select a student of the same ethnicity if that appeared to be an important variable in the student's behavior. Whenever observing the target student, systematically record data on the comparison student. Given the complexity of recording data for two students, it is likely that a classroom teacher won't be able to collect comparative data while teaching; however, the teacher could provide descriptions of a comparison student when compiling anecdotal records, keeping a journal, or rating the student's behavior on an intensity scale. If the selected comparison student leaves the room during the observation, the observer should quickly select another student who is similar to the comparison student with regard to age and gender.

Inconspicuous location. When entering the room, the third-party observer shouldn't talk with the teacher. By sitting in an inconspicuous location, the observer will have a front or side view of the student. This allows the observer to see if the student is looking at the teacher, talking, working on an assignment, etc.

Preparation. The observer should come prepared with a clipboard, a watch with a second hand, pen or pencil, and several copies of any observation forms being used. The observer needs to be familiar with how to use the selected observational forms and needs to know which target behavior(s) to record.

Length of observation. Determine ahead of time how long the observation should last. Typically, 15 minutes is a minimal time to observe, while observing for more than 30 minutes in one setting is atypical. Besides recording data on the identified target behavior(s), the observer should also record brief anecdotal notes about how the teacher responds to the student's misbehavior, the teacher's ratio of interactions with the student, and the overall climate of the classroom.

Watch all students. During the observation, the observer should scan the room and look at all the students in addition to focusing on the target student and any comparison student. Staring only at the target student invariably results in the target student noticing the observer and deviating from her normal behavioral routine.

Ignore all students. The observer should ignore all of the students by not talking with them or smiling; otherwise, the students may be inclined to walk up to the observer and start talking. If necessary, use gestures (head shaking, pointing a finger) to redirect students. If the observer is well known to the students, have the classroom teacher tell the students ahead of time that the observer will be in the room to watch the teacher and that the teacher expects the students to ignore the observer.

Verify behavior. Following the observation, the third-party observer should verify with the teacher whether the behavior of the target student and the other students in the classroom was typical. It is important that this is verified to increase the validity of your observation. Otherwise, you may find out (too late) that the observation was not typical and the data is not useful. If for some reason the observation is not typical, it is critical to schedule a followup observation.

Task 6: Select a Data Collection Method

There is a wide range of data collection methods to consider using during the B-RTI process (Alberto & Troutman, 2006; Sprick & Garrison, 2008). Some are relatively simple and easy to use; others are more complicated and time intensive. For a Tier 1 intervention by the classroom teacher (who will also collect most of her own data), adopting a simple, easy method is highly recommended, unless the teacher is already experienced in using more complicated methods. As the student moves into Tier 2 or Tier 3, it becomes more important to collect increasingly comprehensive data, and there are staff resources available to deploy more complicated methods (Gresham, 2004; Harn, Kame'enui, & Simmons, 2007; Walker et al., 1996). The data collection methods described in this chapter are arranged to reflect the complexity of usage, with the simpler methods presented first. Note that our list of data collection methods is not meant to be all-inclusive. The methods and data forms described in this chapter were originally presented in *Interventions: Evidence-Based Behavioral Strategies for Individual Students*. (We have renumbered the forms sequentially for this book.)

In a Tier 1 intervention, the classroom teacher will typically have sole responsibility for collecting and reporting data. It is important that the teacher select a simple method, preferably one that yields objective data. In a Tier 2 or Tier 3 intervention, the interventionist and/or problem-solving team will work collaboratively with the teacher to select the appropriate data collection methods. We recommend that at least one method during a Tier 2 intervention involve the classroom teacher. There are several potential advantages to having the teacher initiate and report one data method during a Tier 2 intervention: The teacher will be more comfortable with collecting and reporting data she initiates, and the teacher may be more objective in assessing the effect of the intervention plan (Skiba, Deno, Marston, & Casey, 1989; Sulzer-Azaroff & Mayer, 1991).

The selected method may yield subjective data (e.g., it uses a rating scale) or provide objective data (e.g., a simple frequency count). It is essential that the data collection method used during progress monitoring and evaluation yield useful data tied directly to the behavioral goals established for the intervention plan. In some cases, the data collection methods used in establishing a baseline for a specific behavior may not be appropriate to use for monitoring progress and evaluating the intervention. For example, a teacher who collected baseline data by analyzing a month of office referrals and anecdotal notes would likely find using a simple frequency count and daily rating scales more helpful in assessing the effectiveness of her intervention plan to decrease verbal outbursts and use of profanity in the classroom.

Collecting and recording existing data. The easiest sources of data are permanent products that already exist with the teacher or the school (Alberto & Troutman, 2006; Scheuermann & Hall, 2008). This data method is ideal for a classroom teacher attempting a Tier 1 intervention because it is simple. Another advantage is that it could also be used in conjunction with another data method when implementing a Tier 2 intervention. Following are examples of possible existing data sources that could be used for collecting relevant behavior data:

- Grade book

- Attendance record

- Tardy record

> It is important that the teacher select a simple method, preferably one that yields objective data.

- Class homework or assignment sign-in sheet

- Classroom incentive point system

- Behavior grading records

- Daily report card system

- Office referral forms

- Referrals to detention or in-school suspension (ISS)

- Anecdotal notes

Each of these sources yields valuable information that could provide a data picture of a specific behavior (Sprick, Garrison, et al., 1998). For example, the teacher's grade book may be an excellent source for data about a student's work completion rate—the number of assignments completed versus the number assigned. A classwork or homework sign-in list provides useful data about the number of assignments completed and submitted. From this type of data, a percentage of work completed week-by-week could be compiled. Poor attendance and tardiness can be problem behaviors, and the data could be easily collected and recorded from an existing database maintained by the teacher or the school. For specific behavior data, reviewing an elementary teacher's records for a classroom incentive point system or a secondary teacher's behavior grading system could provide daily frequency information about specific misbehaviors. A daily report card system is another excellent source of behavior data. (See Chapter 10 for detailed information about how to set up and implement a daily card-carry system.) Summarizing the frequency and intensity of misbehavior leading to referrals to the office, detention, ISS (in-school suspension), or OSS (out-of-school suspension) can provide a data picture of more serious misbehavior in the classroom.

An advantage to accessing these existing data sources is the possibility of comparing the target student's behavior with either a comparison student or even a class/grade average. For example, the behavior grading system revealed that a target student exhibited a weekly average of sixteen misbehaviors for four weeks compared with the class average of two misbehaviors. Furthermore, computing a class average for a specific behavior (e.g., tardies, incomplete classwork or homework) can help establish a realistic goal for the intervention plan.

Anecdotal or journal records. Having the teacher keep anecdotal notes or a behavior journal on the target student is another effective data collection method (Alberto & Troutman, 2006). Although not as simple as analyzing existing data records, this method can be easy for a teacher because she chooses the time to write her observations. The teacher can jot down the observations throughout the day when the misbehavior occurs or record the observations at the end of the period or the day. These confidential writings provide the teacher with a vehicle to describe the misbehaviors and issues that confront the student each day or each period (see Figure 5.1). We recommend that teachers maintain the records or journal for at least three days, if not longer.

A daily report card system is another excellent source of behavior data.

Figure 5.1

Anecdotal Record of Jin-Luen's Behavior

	10/2 Notes on Jin-Luen
8:25	Jin-Luen told the class that her father is a pilot in the Navy and that he is away on a secret mission. (untrue-her father is unemployed and lives out of state)
9:30	Jin-Luen told me that she didn't have her homework because some boys stole it from her this morning. (true?)
10:45	Jin-Luen was quietly crying at her desk.
12:30	Jin-Luen claimed that she could not participate in PE because she sprained her ankle at lunch. It wasn't swollen, but I sent her to the nurse to get it checked out. The nurse didn't know for sure, so we let her sit out PE. (true?)
1:10	She said she didn't want to do her work.
2:15	When I was collecting the reading assignments, Jin-Luen said she already turned in the completed assignment. I asked her to find it in the stack and she couldn't. She claimed I lost it. (untrue - I happened to see the incomplete assignment hanging out of her book. She then denied lying and said she was just confused.)

Information from anecdotal records or a behavior journal will often contain both objective data (how many times a student was out of his seat) and subjective impressions ("Sara was so demanding today."). One advantage of this data method is that its wide range of information can yield insights into patterns of both misbehavior and appropriate behavior. A disadvantage is that this method may require extensive time each day to make notes. By the same token, some teachers find that the act of writing anecdotal records or a behavior journal gives a positive and appropriate outlet for their frustration while also helping to identify important insights about how their behavior influences the student's behavior. The greatest challenge of working with anecdotal records or a behavior journal is that it can be very time consuming to process all of the written information and generate a summary of the behavior data.

Weekly Misbehavior Recording Sheets. Another simple and easy data collection method for the classroom teacher during Tier 1 is using a daily/weekly recording sheet to track the frequency of rule violations and other misbehaviors by the entire class or by an identified group of students (Sprick, Garrison et al., 1998). The derived data is most useful in establishing a baseline for a particular student. It can also be used by the teacher to monitor progress of a specific behavior as well as for a summative evaluation of a Tier 1 intervention.

The Misbehavior Recording Sheet (Daily) (Reproducible Form 5.1) is designed for hourly recording by a teacher who has the same students for the entire day, such as an elementary or special education teacher. The Misbehavior Recording Sheet (Weekly) (Reproducible Form 5.2) provides a full week of data collection and is useful for secondary teachers who have students for only one class period. Both forms require the teacher to create and use a behavior coding system when using the form. Following is an example:

Codes: D—Disruptive behavior such as using profanity, disturbing others

O—Off task (not working, staring out of the window, etc.)

T—Talking when not appropriate

When the forms are used for monitoring progress or evaluating the intervention, the code should be modified to reflect the target behaviors being addressed by the intervention.

For the daily recording sheet, the teacher can record the data one of three ways:

1) Keep a running tally when the misbehavior occurs.

2) Periodically record the data every two or three hours.

3) Record at the end of the day.

Keeping a running tally provides the most accurate data. On the weekly recording sheet, the secondary teacher could record the data one of two ways:

1) Keep a running tally when the misbehavior occurs.

2) Record at the end of the period.

Again, keeping a running tally provides the most accurate data. At the end of the week, the teacher should total the number of recorded misbehaviors. The teacher could also differentiate the number of different misbehaviors by using a special behavior coding system for the target student and a comparison student. Summarizing the differentiated data based on codes can be quite useful when looking at the target student and could generate an average or median for the class as a whole.

The weekly form is intended for a full week of data collection and is useful for secondary teachers who have students for only one class period. In the samples provided, Scott Henry is the focus of a data collection and debriefing intervention. His teacher tracks misbehavior by week using the weekly Misbehavior Recording Sheet. A frequency count of his misbehaviors from this form is placed on a weekly chart to track his misbehavior. For the week of November 3, eight misbehaviors were tallied. On

Reproducible Form 5.1

MISBEHAVIOR RECORDING SHEET
(Daily by Student Name)

SAMPLE

11/12   Art museum field trip

Date   Reminders

Name	1st Hour	2nd Hour	3rd Hour	4th Hour	5th Hour	Total
Anderson, Chantel				T		1
Baker, Ruben						0
Bell, Justin						0
Cabrezza, Melinda		T		T	T	3
Cummings, Teresa						0
Demalski, Lee			T			1
Diaz, Margo						0
Etienne, Jerry						0
Fujiyama, Kim						0
Grover, Matthew						0
Henry, Scott	DDT	DO		DT	T	8
Isaacson, Chris						0
Kaufman, Jamie						0
King, Mark						0
LaRouche, Janel				T		1
Morales, Marie Louisa				T		1
Narlin, Jenny						0
Neely, Jacob	D					1
Nguyen, Trang						0
Ogren, Todd	TT			T		3
Pallant, Jared						0
Piercy, Dawn				O		1
Reaes, Myra						0
Thomason, Rahsaan		T			T	2
Vandever, Aaron						0
Wong, Charlene						0
Yamamoto, Junko				O		1

Codes: D – Disrupton   O – Off task   T – Talking

Reproducible Materials Blank copies of the forms are provided on the CD. Permission is given for individual teachers, administrators, or other school personnel to reproduce any form labeled "Reproducible Form" for in-district use.

Reproducible Form 5.2

MISBEHAVIOR RECORDING SHEET
(Weekly by Student Name)

SAMPLE

Week of 11/3 _____ On Wed. remind about Fri. test
Date   Reminders

Name	Mon.	Tue.	Wed.	Thur.	Fri.	Total
Anderson, Chantel				T		1
Baker, Ruben						0
Bell, Justin						0
Cabrezza, Melinda		T		T	T	3
Cummings, Teresa						0
Demalski, Lee			T			1
Diaz, Margo						0
Etienne, Jerry						0
Fujiyama, Kim						0
Grover, Matthew						0
Henry, Scott	DDT	DO		DT	T	8
Isaacson, Chris						0
Kaufman, Jamie				D		1
King, Mark						0
LaRouche, Janel				T		1
Morales, Marie Louisa				T		1
Narlin, Jenny						0
Neely, Jacob			O	O		2
Nguyen, Trang						0
Ogren, Todd	TTD	D	OO	T		7
Pallant, Jared						0
Piercy, Dawn			T	O	T	3
Reaes, Myra						0
Thomason, Rahsaan	TT		T	T	TT	6
Vandever, Aaron						0
Wong, Charlene						0
Yamamoto, Junko		T		OT		3

Reproducible Materials Blank copies of the forms are provided on the CD. Permission is given for individual teachers, administrators, or other school personnel to reproduce any form labeled "Reproducible Form" for in-district use.

days such as a field trip day when an escalation in problem behavior is anticipated, the teacher chooses to record behavior in more detail using the daily Misbehavior Recording Sheet.

Rating scale. In this data collection method, the teacher rates the quality or intensity of a behavior on a simple scale. It is another easy data collection method that can be used by the classroom teacher during a Tier 1 intervention to collect baseline data, monitor progress of a targeted behavior goal, and evaluate the outcome of an intervention. Rating scales can also be used as one of several data collection methods for a Tier 2 or Tier 3 intervention (Gresham, 1985; Merrell, 2003; Walker et al., 2004). Though more subjective than some of the other methods, a rating scale can be made more objective by a consistent application of judgments over time and across activities. When establishing a baseline, the teacher can use three behaviors a student exhibits during different activities as a measure to build an overall picture of the student's behavioral pattern and identify possible points of intervention.

When using a rating scale for progress monitoring or evaluating an intervention, it is beneficial for the interventionist or case manager to help the teacher discuss and establish a broad rubric of what each rating point should look and sound like for the target student. For example, what would taking notes and verbally participating in a designated classroom activity look and sound like for the target student? Once a rubric is established, the teacher's ratings should be more objective.

The following rating scale sample (Reproducible Form 5.3) shows whether a student received a point for each of three behaviors and whether she exhibited those behaviors appropriately during an activity. One week's worth of data can be recorded on one page.

Reproducible Form 5.3

RATING SCALE

SAMPLE

Alita	3	Mr. Johns	6
Student	Grade/Class	Teacher	Period/Time

SUBJECT

MONDAY		reading	history	lunch	math	music	language
Behavior	uses appropriate language	① 0	① 0	① 0	① 0	① 0	① 0
	cooperates with others	① 0	1 ⓪	① 0	① 0	① 0	① 0
	problem-solves positively	① 0	1 ⓪	① 0	① 0	① 0	① 0

TUESDAY

Another example is ranking a particular behavior on a scale—for example, from 1 to 5. If each rating has a specific descriptor, this type of form is called an anchored rating scale. A partially anchored scale may have descriptors for only the first and last rating numbers. A fully anchored scale may be more objective. Another use for an anchored rating scale is to have the teacher self-assess the fidelity of implementing the intervention plan. The questions could address how consistently the teacher feels she followed the plan that day and its effectiveness in addressing the student's target behavior. As described in "Intervention K: Self-Monitoring and Self-Evaluation" in *Interventions: Evidence-Based Behavioral Strategies for Individual Students*, rating scales may be completed by a teacher, the student, or both. Although any rating scale is admittedly more subjective than some of the other methods, the body of information can provide another useful window into a student's behavior over time. The sample (Reproducible Form 5.4) shows an anchored scale to assess a student's class participation.

Reproducible Form 5.4

SAMPLE

PARTICIPATION EVALUATION RECORD

Justin	_11_	_Mr. Mathison_	_12/6_
Student	Grade/Class	Teacher	Date

Rating Scale:
0 = Did not participate verbally and did not take notes
1 = Participated verbally at least once but did not take notes
2 = Took notes but did not participate verbally
3 = Participated verbally at least once and took notes

Directions: For each subject, circle the number that best describes your level of participation.

Subject	Monday	Tuesday	Wednesday	Thursday	Friday
Science	0 ①2 3	0 ①2 3	0 1 ②3	0 1 2 3	0 1 2 3
Health	⓪1 2 3	⓪1 2 3	0 1 2 3	0 1 2 3	0 1 2 3
English	0 1 ②3	0 1 2 ③	0 1 2 3	0 1 2 3	0 1 2 3
Math	⓪1 2 3	0 ①2 3	0 1 2 3	0 1 2 3	0 1 2 3
Art	⓪1 2 3	0 ①2 3	0 1 2 3	0 1 2 3	0 1 2 3
History	0 ①2 3	0 1 ②3	0 1 2 3	0 1 2 3	0 1 2 3

 Reproducible Materials Full-page blank copies of forms are provided on the CD. Permission is given for individual teachers, administrators, or other school personnel to reproduce any form labeled "Reproducible Form" for in-district use.

Basic frequency count. The most common type of behavioral data collected is a frequency count (also known as event recording). It simply entails counting the number of occurrences of a positive or negative behavior. The types of behavior best suited for a frequency count include interrupting, blurting out in class, hitting, out-of-seat activity, talking back, initiating contact with classmates, throwing objects, responding to directions the first time they are given, and a whole range of academic concerns (e.g., number of teacher questions answered). For this method, the behavior must have a clear beginning and a clear end that are both easy to judge (Alberto & Troutman, 2006). A frequency count is simple enough that the classroom teacher can easily use it to collect baseline data, monitor progress of a targeted behavior goal, or evaluate the intervention plan during a Tier 1 intervention. The classroom teacher may also use the frequency count during a Tier 2 intervention. Furthermore, the basic frequency count can be used by a third-party observer any time during a Tier 2 intervention.

The simplest way to keep a frequency count for an individual student is by totaling a tally of hash marks, which can be kept on a card in the teacher's pocket or on a sheet of paper attached to a clipboard. The nice thing about structuring a frequency count this way is that the teacher or third-party observer can add columns as different behaviors are noticed and need to be recorded. There might be a column for disruptions, another column for the number of times the student remembers to raise his hand, and a third column for the number of times the student leaves his seat inappropriately.

A frequency count requires that the teacher or third-party observer carry materials on which to record hash marks. If that is awkward or impractical for the classroom teacher, consider alternatives such as a golf counter or hand tally counter. Another alternative is for the teacher to put a handful of paper clips in one pocket. Each time the student exhibits the targeted behavior, the teacher moves a paper clip to a different pocket. The disadvantage of these methods is that the teacher may be limited to counting only one behavior for a single student.

Some interventionists recommend always counting desired positive behaviors instead of negative behaviors that need to decrease. This is a nice idea, but it's not always easy to do. The teacher or third-party observer could, for example, count the frequency that a student raises his hand instead of counting the frequency that he blurts out answers, but opportunities for hand-raising vary from day to day. This means the count may show a positive increase in hand-raising that masks the negative reality that the student is also blurting out more often. In this example, the teacher or third-party observer may want to count both behaviors, which allows the computation and display of a percentage of raised-hands versus blurt-outs for the total number of opportunities the student had to respond. In some cases, it is not feasible to count a positive behavior. If classroom disruptions are the concern, for example, it would be very difficult to count the absence of those disruptions or the times when a student is not being disruptive. The simplest solution is to count the number of disruptions the student causes, as shown in the following sample (Reproducible Form 5.5).

> A frequency count is simple enough that the classroom teacher can easily use it to collect baseline data, monitor progress of a targeted behavior goal, or evaluate the intervention plan during a Tier 1 intervention.

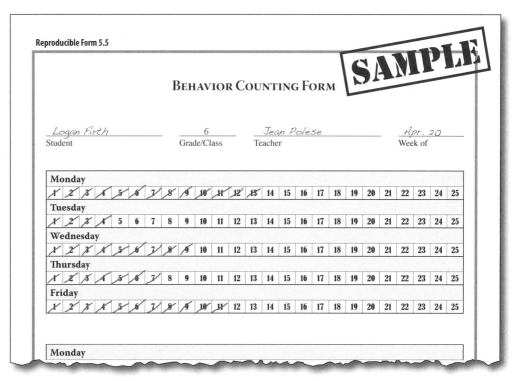

Reproducible Form 5.5

BEHAVIOR COUNTING FORM SAMPLE

Logan Firth	_6_	_Jean Polese_	_Apr. 20_
Student	Grade/Class	Teacher	Week of

Monday

| 1 | 2 | 3 | 4 | 5 | 6 | 7 | 8 | 9 | 10 | 11 | 12 | 13 | 14 | 15 | 16 | 17 | 18 | 19 | 20 | 21 | 22 | 23 | 24 | 25 |

Tuesday

| 1 | 2 | 3 | 4 | 5 | 6 | 7 | 8 | 9 | 10 | 11 | 12 | 13 | 14 | 15 | 16 | 17 | 18 | 19 | 20 | 21 | 22 | 23 | 24 | 25 |

Wednesday

| 1 | 2 | 3 | 4 | 5 | 6 | 7 | 8 | 9 | 10 | 11 | 12 | 13 | 14 | 15 | 16 | 17 | 18 | 19 | 20 | 21 | 22 | 23 | 24 | 25 |

Thursday

| 1 | 2 | 3 | 4 | 5 | 6 | 7 | 8 | 9 | 10 | 11 | 12 | 13 | 14 | 15 | 16 | 17 | 18 | 19 | 20 | 21 | 22 | 23 | 24 | 25 |

Friday

| 1 | 2 | 3 | 4 | 5 | 6 | 7 | 8 | 9 | 10 | 11 | 12 | 13 | 14 | 15 | 16 | 17 | 18 | 19 | 20 | 21 | 22 | 23 | 24 | 25 |

Monday

 Reproducible Materials Full-page blank copies of forms are provided on the CD. Permission is given for individual teachers, administrators, or other school personnel to reproduce any form labeled "Reproducible Form" for in-district use.

The Happy Cat/Sad Dog form is a basic frequency count for monitoring the behavior of younger students (Sprick & Garrison, 2008) (Reproducible Form 5.6). The advantage of using this format is that it might be easier for the teacher to record and share the data with the student. Note that the top half of the form shows happy cats while the bottom half shows happy dogs, giving both cat fanciers and dog lovers among your primary-age students equal opportunity to indicate positive behavior with the animal pal of their choice.

Countoons/Public posting. A countoon can be used to count positive behavior, negative behavior, or both. It is a data collection method for teachers to use primarily for monitoring the progress of specific target behavior goals and evaluating the effectiveness of the intervention plan, although the form can also be used initially to establish the baseline of a target behavior. This method of recording frequency data is most appropriate for younger students in grades K–3. Because the countoon is designed to be publicly posted in the student's classroom or other setting, it is important to make sure that it is OK with the student or students involved. In the case of public posting, consider counting only positive behaviors. Data reporting should never be embarrassing to a child. A natural use would be in resource rooms or special education classrooms in which most, if not all, students have a behavioral or academic goal that is being recorded and charted. In this way, the countoon doesn't stand out as odd or appear to single out one particular student.

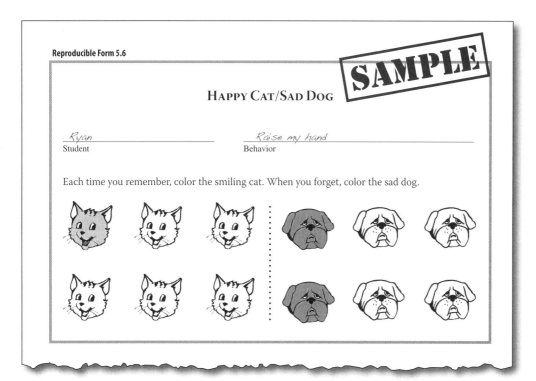

The countoon shown in the sample Reproducible Form 5.7 is for a student who makes frequent negative comments. Obviously, a teacher can be creative by designing clever and appealing countoons for a student. The reproducible version of the form (found on the CD) includes a template for the teacher to create her own.

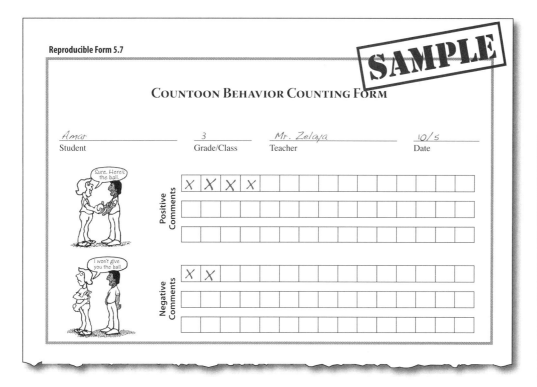

Advanced frequency count. Advanced frequency count is a more complicated data collection method, which means it will be used primarily by a third-party observer during a Tier 2 or Tier 3 intervention. Most interventionists and case managers have already had extensive training in how to conduct advanced frequency counts and will likely have specialized forms that they prefer to use. Given that advanced frequency counts are time intensive, it is unlikely that a classroom teacher will have the time or experience to attempt this method. Advanced frequency counts are effective for collecting baseline data, monitoring the progress of a specific behavior goal, and eventually evaluating the intervention plan at Tier 2 or Tier 3.

As shown in Figures 5.2 and 5.3, the data is differentiated between two or more variables. Figure 5.2 focuses on Alexa's argumentative behavior with both the teacher and the classroom assistant. Figure 5.3 reports bothersome behavior for Colin during independent work, cooperative groups, and transitions. To refine the data further, one-letter codes can be used to indicate more specific information about the target behavior, such as A for a.m., P for p.m., T for inappropriate talking, and O for being out of the seat inappropriately. Using such a coding system requires the observer to carefully watch the student to collect accurate data, but it doesn't take any more time to record than a simple frequency count. The coding system can yield discrete and useful information that would not be possible to glean from most observation methods.

Figure 5.2

Anecdotal Record of Alexa's Argumentative Behavior

	Notes on Alexa's Arguing — 11/4 (frequency)
	With Teacher: AA PPPP With Assistant: AAAA PPPPPP PPPP
9:05	Mr. Yarborough (asst.) told Alexa to clean up the Science Ctr. when she finished. Alexa argued it was a mess before she got there. They went back and forth several times until Alexa was almost shouting. I went over to see what was going on. Alexa told me to stay out of it and started arguing with me.
9:50	When I was collecting the science papers, Alexa told me that I didn't give her enough time to finish. I reminded her that she should take the work home as homework just like everyone else, but she kept demanding that I explain why I never give enough time to finish assignments.
1:00	I told the students they needed to hand in their long-term project proposals. Alexa asked why I didn't remind them yesterday. I told her I had reminded them yesterday, but she kept insisting I hadn't. After a few back and forth exchanges, several other students told her I was right. That silenced her.
3:15	This afternoon was typical. Alexa didn't think that she should have to do the art project, she didn't want Mr. Y to correct her work, she didn't know that we had given out book order forms, and on and on.

Figure 5.3

Anecdotal Record of Colin's Bothersome Behavior

	Colin's Bothersome Behavior — 4/3 (frequency count)
	Ind. Work AAAAAA AAAPP PPPPP PP **Coop. Group** PPPPP PPPPP **Transitions** AAAAA PPP PPPPP PPPP
	NOTES: Transition – As Colin is moving to join his cooperative group, he pokes Blaine in the arm, knocks Belinda's books off her desk, and pulls Maria's hair.

These are examples of frequency counts that use anecdotal notes and do not require the use of a dedicated form. To create a dedicated form for an advanced frequency count, the observer could adapt Reproducible Form 5.5: Behavior Counting Form by expanding the size of the recording boxes to permit the recording of several codes and by including a blank code box in which to list the different codes being used during the observation.

Duration recording. When a behavior does not occur regularly but tends to last a long time, duration recording is an effective data collection method. Instead of counting the frequency of the behavior, the observer determines the duration of the behavior to see how long the student engages in that behavior (Alberto & Troutman, 2006; Scheuermann & Hall, 2008). For example, Brenda was out of her seat only two times during a 30-minute reading period, but she was out for an average of five minutes each time (Reproducible Form 5.8). This method can provide valuable data about a whole range of behaviors, including being out of the seat, wandering around the room, crying, whining, tantrums, thumb sucking, staring/daydreaming, independent work, verbal outbursts, getting ready to work, and responding to a teacher's direction. Similar to the frequency count, duration recording requires that the behavior have a clear beginning and a clear end that are both easy to determine. Duration recording requires using a stopwatch or a watch with a second hand to jot down the time each occurrence begins and ends. When using a stopwatch, don't reset it after each instance. Simply stop the time and restart it if the behavior begins again. At the end of the period or day, the stopwatch will have recorded the cumulative amount of time the student engaged in the behavior. Divide this total time in minutes or seconds by the number of behavioral episodes that occurred to compute the average duration of the behavior.

Duration recording can be more complicated than frequency recording because the observer needs immediate access to a timing device when the behavior starts and

Reproducible Form 5.8

SAMPLE

DURATION RECORDING

Brenda Vasquez	_7_	_Mr. Timmens_	_1/10_
Student	Grade	Teacher	Date

Reading	_getting out of seat_
Period/class	Target behavior

Time Started: _1:46_   Time Ended: _1:50_   Total Time: _4 minutes_

Comments:

Time Started: _2:02_   Time Ended: _2:08_   Total Time: _6 minutes_

Comments:

Reproducible Materials Full-page blank copies of forms are provided on the CD. Permission is given for individual teachers, administrators, or other school personnel to reproduce any form labeled "Reproducible Form" for his or her in-district use.

ends and must also record these times. After being trained, a classroom teacher or a third-party observer could use duration recording for the purposes of collecting baseline data, monitoring the progress of a specific behavior goal, and eventually evaluating the intervention plan at Tier 1 or Tier 2. If the teacher or third-party observer is also observing a comparison student, clearly record at the bottom of the form that student's duration times for similar behaviors.

Latency recording. Latency recording is designed to track the amount of time a student takes before responding to a teacher directive (Alberto & Troutman, 2006). For example, the teacher says, "Derrick, return to your seat and sit down," and Derrick sits down three minutes and 30 seconds later (Reproducible Form 5.9). Thus, the data shows that three minutes and 30 seconds is the latency of his response. Latency recording is an excellent data collection tool for any behavior in which the student habitually fails to follow a teacher's direction or doesn't begin to work right away. For students who are described as scattered, disorganized, defiant, or passive aggressive, latency recording can yield valuable insight into the behavior. Similar to duration recording, latency recording requires the observer to use a stopwatch or a watch with a second hand. The observer jots down the time of day when the direction is issued and the time of day when the student engages in the appropriate behavior related to the teacher directive. To determine the average amount of time the student takes before complying, add the amount of time the student took in responding to each directive

Reproducible Form 5.9

SAMPLE

LATENCY RECORDING

Derrick Dunn   5   Mrs. Brandon   3/26
Student   Grade   Teacher   Date

Math   25 minutes
Period/class   Time observed target behavior

Direction Given: 10:31:20   Student Complied: 10:34:50   Total Time: 3 min, 30 sec.

Teacher Direction:
Sit down

Direction Given: 10:35   Student Complied: 10:38   Total Time: 3 minutes

Teacher Direction:
Get out your math book

and divide that total of minutes or seconds by the number of times latency recording was done. Latency recording is also more complicated than simple frequency recording because, again, the observer needs to have immediate access to a timing device and record-keeping form. When also observing a comparison student, clearly record her latency times for the same teacher directions at the bottom of the form. A classroom teacher or a third-party observer could use latency recording for collecting baseline data, monitoring the progress of a specific behavior goal, and eventually evaluating the intervention plan at Tier 1 or Tier 2.

Interval recording or scatterplot. Sometimes, the student's misbehavior is situational, happening more in some situations or at particular times. Interval recording involves marking whether the behavior occurs during a particular time interval. This method is often used when the target behavior occurs at such a high rate over an extended period of time that it is difficult to obtain an accurate picture. Interval recording has been used with behaviors ranging from task engagement to disruption/aggression to thumb sucking (Carter & Horner, 2007; Friman, 2000; Reinecke, Newman, & Meinberg, 1999). Instead of recording the actual frequency of a behavior, interval recording yields an estimated percentage of how often it occurs. This can be an effective data collection method for such behaviors as talking at inappropriate times, talking back to the teacher, and repetitive motor behaviors such as vocal tics or thumb sucking. To conduct interval recording, first select the time interval to observe the student. Typically, the observational interval is 10–30 seconds and is almost never more than one minute. Next, the observer records observations for five seconds by noting whether the behavior occurred at any time during the observational interval.

Having a watch with a second hand is mandatory. If more than one behavior is being targeted during the observation, identifying and using a behavior code is essential. Following is a sample code for collecting data about a student's off-task behavior.

P for passive off-task: This behavior includes not looking at the teacher or instructional materials during group or individual instruction and not looking at or working on the assigned task. It may also include looking around the room, working on nonassigned work, or playing quietly with small objects.

V for verbal off-task: This behavior includes talking with other students without permission, making disruptive noises, or talking to oneself loud enough to disturb other students.

M for motor off-task: This behavior includes being out of the seat or assigned area without the teacher's permission, walking around the room, crawling on the floor, and sitting in another student's chair without permission.

O for on-task: This behavior includes looking at the teacher or instructional material during group or individual instruction and working on or attending to the assigned work.

When doing interval recording, scatterplots are often used to report the data. Scatterplot is a fancy name for a data collection form that shows the relationship between two variables, such as the occurrence or lack of a behavior during a particular activity in a particular time interval (Alberto & Troutman, 2006). Typically, interval recordings and scatterplots are used by a third-party observer only during Tier 2 and Tier 3 interventions because of the complexity of collecting and recording the data as well as graphing the subsequent scatterplot. Interventionists and case managers often have had training and experience in how to conduct interval recording and create a scatterplot. The sample scatterplot in Reproducible Form 5.10 combines interval recording and frequency counts by recording a tally of the number of target behaviors that occur each day during each activity and transition. In this case, two weeks of observation show Mondays to be problematic and demonstrate that reading, lining up, and hallway behaviors are problematic across all days. Collecting such detailed information has tremendous potential for aiding in design of an intervention plan as well as for monitoring progress of a specific behavior goal and evaluating the intervention.

Reproducible Form 5.11 on the CD is an interval/scatterplot for one week that records the time of day the behaviors occur.

Not all reproducible forms on the CD are displayed as samples in this chapter. Skim through the Reproducible Materials section at the end of the chapter to determine which data collection and debriefing format is best suited to the student's needs.

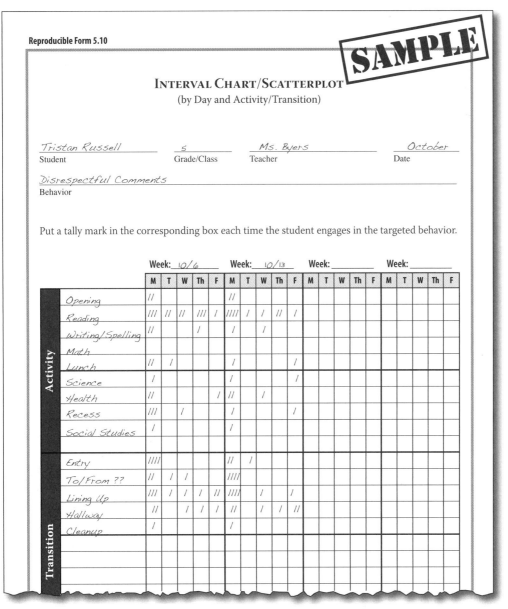

Reproducible Materials Full-page blank copies of forms are provided on the CD. Permission is given for individual teachers, administrators, or other school personnel to reproduce any form labeled "Reproducible Form" for his or her in-district use.

Task 7: Summarize and Report Collected Data

Once the data is collected, the focus shifts to interpreting it. Collected data should never be used to blame either the student or teacher; instead, the data must be used to help answer questions and solve problems (Alberto & Troutman, 2006; Scheuermann & Hall, 2008). This data-driven focus requires the teacher at Tier 1 and the interventionist and/or problem-solving teams working with the teacher at Tiers 2 and 3 to implement the following steps.

STEP 1 — Summarize the Collected Data

Raw data can easily be overwhelming. It is crucial that the data be summarized in an easy-to-read and understandable format. A simple graphic format is preferred because most people find a visual illustration easier to understand and better for highlighting trends and patterns. Possible formats to consider include table, bar graph, line graph, pie chart, or scatterplot. Select the format that will be best understood by participating staff members, parents/guardians, and students.

It is helpful to display behavioral changes across time to illustrate the student's progress. Such illustrations can be powerful tools when meeting with a teacher, student, or parent regarding the outcomes (for both student target behaviors and teacher fidelity behaviors) from the intervention (Alvero, Bucklin, and Austin, 2001; Casey et al., 1988; Noell et al., 2005; Scheuermann & Hall, 2008). The person summarizing the data may employ statistical techniques such as drawing the line of best fit, either by hand or automatically using a spreadsheet application such as Excel. Using this type of software allows the observer to automatically chart the data and to keep a record of the data so that meaningful statistics can be generated later.

A key question to ask is whether the collected data shows any trends across time. This generally depends on the format in which the data was entered in the first place. Data collected on separate sheets of paper is of little use for conducting a cogent analysis. Separate data sheets or forms should be brought together in one place as a chart. Frequency counts, duration records, and rating scales should be summarized on a chart to help the teacher, problem-solving team, parents, and even the student make sense of their significance across time. On the other hand, interval recording and scatterplot forms steadily reveal more information as you enter your observations. The relationships between the variables on the x and y axes will become clearer as more data points are filled in. These forms may be useful without transferring the data to a separate chart, but by the time the data has been collected for more than a week or two, the data and the trend will probably need to be displayed on some type of graph or chart.

> Frequency counts, duration records, and rating scales should be summarized on a chart to help the teacher, problem-solving team, parents, and even the student make sense of their significance across time.

For example, graphing the number of intervals each day that the student was successful shows progress over two or three months and perhaps correlates anomalies in the graph with events that occurred in class (e.g., there was a substitute teacher for three consecutive days), at school (e.g., school started late for two consecutive days because of inclement weather), or in the student's life (e.g., the student's grandmother was in the hospital). If significant events occurred during the intervention or if the intervention was modified by the teacher or team, insert simple phase change lines on the summary chart/graph/scatterplot to indicate the event or the change in how the intervention was being implemented.

STEP 2   **Make Sense of the Data**

As powerful as data is, it is meaningless if you do not put it into its proper context (Baer et al., 1968; Deno, 1985; Howell & Nolet, 2000). This is where the classroom teacher plays an important role. The case manager or interventionist needs to ask the teacher if the data is representative of the student's typical behavior. Does the data make sense? If not, the interventionist or case manager needs to ask questions that will identify what variables interfered with data collection and decide whether additional data collection is needed. Comparing the data to some normative standard is also important when attempting to understand what the data means. How did this student compare to the class average for completing homework? Or, how did the target student's duration or latency behavior compare with a student of the same age and gender?

Another variable in interpreting data during progress monitoring and intervention evaluation is whether the intervention was implemented with fidelity (Gresham, 1989, 2000; McIntyre, Gresham, DiGennaro, & Reed, 2007; Quinn et al., 2001; Wood, Umbreit, Liaupsin, & Gresham, 2007). This is especially important when the intervention was not successful. For a Tier 1 intervention, it will be more difficult to objectively assess the fidelity because the teacher is implementing the plan by herself. It is possible to prompt the teacher to assess or rate the consistency of how she implemented the different components of the intervention on a daily basis. For example:

- Did the teacher work to increase the daily quantity of non-contingent attention provided to the target student?

- Were verbal reprimands delivered fluently?

- Did the teacher ignore the behaviors selected for planned ignoring?

By responding to a self-assessment, the teacher can gain some valuable insights into the fidelity of her intervention. Another option for assessing fidelity of a Tier 1 intervention is to have the case manager or interventionist ask the teacher some questions during the initial stages of Tier 2. Sample questions include:

- Was there consistency of daily implementation?

- Was there a substitute teacher during the intervention?

- Was the student absent during the intervention?

- Were there any major schedule disruptions (e.g., field trips, assemblies, or early closings)?

For a Tier 2 or Tier 3 intervention, the active involvement of the case manager or interventionist provides several opportunities to assess the fidelity of the intervention. Those opportunities include data collection methods (e.g., classroom observations), interviews with the target student, and collaborative planning and debriefing with the classroom teacher.

Once the data has been discussed, the teacher and/or problem-solving team need to address whether the intervention met the established improvement goal. The collected data should provide a clear indication whether a short-term goal or the eventual goal was met. Depending on the outcome, decisions should be made about what to do next to intervene with the student. Options include the following:

- If the intervention is working, continue its implementation for another two to four weeks.

- Continue the intervention as designed, but adjust the implementation to ensure that it is implemented with fidelity.

- Revise the intervention to make modifications needed to address weaknesses. Implement the revised intervention for another two weeks and continue to collect data.

- Change the focus of the intervention to address other target behaviors. Implement the new intervention for another two weeks and continue to collect data.

- Refer the student to the appropriate level of Tier 2 or Tier 3, including a referral to determine eligibility for special education.

- Begin to phase out the intervention because of its successful impact on the target behavior. Set a gradual phase-out schedule.

See Chapter 9, page 244, for a more detailed list of next-step options.

STEP 3   Share the Data

The collected data needs to be shared with various people throughout the B-RTI process. At Tier 1, the teacher should first inform the student that data is going to be collected to establish a baseline. Carefully explain to the student that the data is being collected not as a punishment but as a way to help the student and teacher understand the significance of the problem (its magnitude or severity) and what everyone involved might do to try to make things better. Tell the student how the data will be collected so that the teacher's actions and the data will not be a secret. For example, when counting the frequency of disruptions, tell the student, "Paul, that's disruptive," when he is causing a disturbance and then mark the record form. Both of these actions provide feedback that can help the student self-regulate future behavior. The teacher needs to be overt and open without causing embarrassment.

After the baseline data is collected, the teacher should use a summary graph or chart to show the student how he is doing. At this point, the teacher should share her intervention plans to address the identified target behavior. Once the intervention is started, the teacher should meet regularly with the student (at least weekly) to share the data collected during progress monitoring. Again, use a summary graph or chart that visually illustrates whether the student is making progress in improving the target behavior. Finally, the teacher should meet with the student to discuss the data used to evaluate the intervention and to share the recommendations for what will happen next.

The teacher will want to consider sharing the data from the Tier 1 intervention with the parents. Depending on the severity of the student's misbehavior and the level of parent involvement, it is feasible for the teacher to share summaries of the data from initial baseline to progress monitoring and final evaluation. In other Tier 1 situations, it may be more appropriate for the teacher to share only data from progress monitoring and final evaluation.

Above all, data-sharing meetings with the student and parents should be encouraging. Even if the collected data show that things might be getting worse, the focus should be on exploring ideas from the student, parents, and teacher about what might improve the situation. Remember, it is not unusual for a behavior to get worse before it gets better (Lerman, Iwata, & Wallace, 1999; Watson, 1967). Make suggestions, or better yet ask the student, "Is there anything I can do to help you make this better, to help turn this around?" By putting herself on the student's side, the teacher is taking on the essential role of a coach: "Yes, we may have lost a couple of close games, but I know you have what it takes. This next week can be our best yet, and I'm committed to helping you make that happen."

At Tier 2, whenever a third-party person has collected data, the interventionist or case manager needs to share and discuss that data with the classroom teacher. Not only will the teacher receive the data collected by the third-party observer, it is likely that the teacher will also share the data that she has collected thus far. This collaborative sharing of data provides the opportunity for the teacher and case manager or interventionist to discuss the implications derived from analyzing the data (Haager & Mahdavi, 2007; Kratochwill, 2008; Miller & Kraft, 2008; Upah, 2008). As for sharing the data with the student and parents, it is important to establish a schedule for who will share what data. Similar to Tier 1, the shared data must be in a simple visual format with the focus on having positive expectations and looking for ideas and suggestions for how to help the student improve.

Above all, data-sharing meetings with the student and parents should be encouraging.

STEP 4 **Maintain the Data**

It is important to decide where to keep collected data so it won't be lost. This is especially true for data that is recorded on slips of paper rather than on forms. In this case, the teacher or case manager should enter the data on a master chart, preferably on a daily basis. Slips of paper are easily misplaced, and a teacher or case manager doesn't want to negate several days of data collection by being careless. Furthermore, collected raw data and summary charts or graphs should be stored in a confidential folder that the teacher starts in Tier 1 and the case manager or interventionist continues to use during Tier 2.

If the Tier 1 intervention is successful, the teacher should ask the principal or multidisciplinary team leader if any state or district guidelines cover how long raw data and summary data charts or graphs should be maintained before being destroyed. The teacher should also ask the principal or multidisciplinary team leader if any state or district guidelines address whether summary data charts should become part of the student's permanent school records.

When a student is referred to Tier 2 or Tier 3, the school or district should establish the expectation that copies of data summaries will be attached to the referral paperwork. These data summaries will help the interventionist, intervention planning team, or multidisciplinary team gain an immediate perspective on the student's presenting behavioral issues and the outcomes from attempted interventions.

CONCLUSION

For B-RTI to be effective, data collection is a critical component throughout the entire process (Brown-Chidsey & Steege, 2006; Fuchs & Fuchs, 2007; Gresham, 2005; Kratochwill, 2008). In fact, data is required if evidence-based interventions will be implemented during B-RTI. From the initial data collection by the classroom teacher at Tier 1 to establish a baseline of the target behavior to the collection of data to evaluate a Tier 2 intervention, data needs to drive decisions about how to help the student (Alberto & Troutman, 2006; Casey et al., 1991; Howell & Nolet, 2000; Scheuermann & Hall, 2008). Perhaps the greatest challenge in establishing this data-driven process is helping classroom teachers become comfortable and skillful in collecting and understanding social behavior data (Heward, 2005). As classroom teachers become more data savvy when dealing with behavior, B-RTI will have a stronger platform for helping teachers and schools successfully meet the needs of all students, especially those students who are struggling to adjust.

Reproducible Materials

Copies of the following reproducible materials appear on the CD. Permission is given for individual teachers, administrators, or other school personnel to reproduce these forms for in-district use.

Reproducible Form 5.1: Misbehavior Recording Sheet (Daily)

Reproducible Form 5.2: Misbehavior Recording Sheet (Weekly)

Reproducible Form 5.3: Rating Scale

Reproducible Form 5.4: Participation Evaluation Record

Reproducible Form 5.5: Behavior Counting Form

Reproducible Form 5.6: Happy Cat/Sad Dog and Happy Dog/Sad Cat

Reproducible Form 5.7: Countoon Behavior Counting Form

Reproducible Form 5.8: Duration Recording

Reproducible Form 5.9: Latency Recording

Reproducible Form 5.10: Interval Chart/Scatterplot (by Day and Activity/Transition)

Reproducible Form 5.11: Interval Chart/Scatterplot (by Day and Time)

Reproducible Form 5.12 Interval Chart/Scatterplot (by Day and Behavior)

Reproducible Form 5.13 Scatterplot Data Collection

CHAPTER 6

The Interventionist

A Summary of Skills and Responsibilities

The term *interventionist* sounds technical and specific, but in fact it simply means one who intervenes. We use the term broadly as well—any third-party staff member who is involved in designing an intervention is an interventionist. By third party, we mean someone besides the student and teacher who will assist with problem analysis, intervention design, implementation, and follow-up. An interventionist can be another teacher, a school counselor, an assistant principal, or a behavior specialist. Also, any member of a problem-solving team is considered an interventionist. As discussed in Chapter 4, we suggest that as soon as collaborative processes begin (either through red flags or a teacher's request for assistance), one interventionist be assigned as the case manager who will serve as an advocate for the student's needs and who will remain case manager until there has been a positive response to intervention, meaning there is no longer a problem.

The job of an interventionist can be complex and challenging. Ensuring high-quality services for students, staff, and families requires an interventionist to be knowledgeable about the range of possible interventions. He or she needs to know which interventions will have the highest probability of success, how to apply procedures to specific situations, and how to combine interventions into multidimensional solutions (Allen & Graden, 2002; Kratochwill & Stoiber, 2000; Merrell & Buchanan, 2006; Task Force on Promotion and Dissemination of Psychological Procedures, 1995; Zins & Erchul, 2002). Although necessary, this technical knowledge is not enough to develop the working relationships required to produce and implement interventions. It is the interventionist's interpersonal skills that determine his effectiveness (Allen & Graden, 2002; Bergan & Kratochwill, 1990; Feldman & Kratochwill, 2003; Kratochwill et al., 2002; Rosenfield, 2002, 2008; Rosenfield & Gravois, 1996).

> An interventionist can be another teacher, a school counselor, an assistant principal, or a behavior specialist.

This chapter describes those skills—communication, case management, self-evaluation, and reflection—and outlines the basic responsibilities of an interventionist. Although much of this content is embedded throughout other chapters, the information in this chapter may be useful for an interventionist who wishes to review and/or analyze his own skills and practices.

OVERVIEW

An interventionist functions first and foremost as an advocate to safeguard the needs of the student and to ensure that intervention processes work smoothly and in a timely fashion. However, she also serves as an advocate for teachers and families (Auster, Feeney-Kettler, & Kratochwill, 2006; Kratochwill, 2008; Zins & Erchul, 2002). Therefore, the interventionist must possess the communication, interpersonal, and management skills needed to:

- Actively listen to others

- Communicate effectively with staff, students, and families

- Recognize and respond to different individual's strengths, limitations, needs, and biases

- Balance competing interests and bring people together to work through the unique conditions of each problem

The interventionist is anyone who is working collaboratively with the teacher, student, and family to design an intervention. The case manager is usually the first interventionist who works on a given case and stays on as advocate for the student and for the teacher even if the case moves along to involve other interventionists or problem-solving teams. For example, a school social worker is assigned as case manager, but the interventions tried are not effective. The teacher, parent, and case manager jointly decide to ask the district's special education consulting teacher to help with designing the next intervention. In this case, the special education teacher is the interventionist, but the school social worker stays involved as case manager to make sure that the teacher, student, and parents get their needs met in this new problem-solving and intervention design process.

COMMUNICATION AND INTERPERSONAL SKILLS

Becoming an effective interventionist is a lifelong learning task. Each situation and every relationship requires specific communication skills and provides a unique opportunity to learn. The effective interventionist continuously fine-tunes her ability to collaborate with students, staff, and parents. The effective interventionist must be diplomatic at all times and with all participants. She must be able to get those involved in the process to look at the situation from others' perspectives. The effective interventionist must be a skilled listener, and, in a typical meeting, will do more listening than talking.

Skill 1: Actively Listen to Others

The skilled interventionist processes and retains what others say to her. She pays attention to the content of what is being said as well as to the tone of voice and body language of the speaker. She asks questions to help her fully understand the problem, and she clarifies and paraphrases what she hears.

- What else did he do?

- You felt angry, but the student seemed to get quiet.

- Why do you think that happened?

- What have you tried?

- I'm sure that's frustrating.

Active listening can help an interventionist determine whether a staff member is ready to look at problem resolution or simply wants to vent frustration. It's important to let the teacher vent, even though some of the teacher's frustrations with the student may be beyond the scope of anything the interventionist can assist with. The teacher needs to feel that he has been heard. Making suggestions too soon tends to elicit a "Yeah, but . . . " response. If teachers aren't given an opportunity to describe all the problems and solutions they've tried, they are bound to feel resentful and may not put much faith in the collaborative process. Active listening helps the interventionist create a climate of trust and collaboration (Duhamel & Tabot, 2004; Lasky, 2000; O'Shea, Algozzine, Hammittee, & O'Shea, 2000). However, active listening also entails knowing when to move things along. If the teacher begins to reiterate the same content—the venting has given way to perseverating on the problem—the interventionist needs to summarize the teacher's major concerns, then start directing the conversation to other parts of the problem-solving process. This is somewhat like the Goldilocks story: You want to avoid listening too little, but you don't want to listen so much to the problem that there is no time to seek solutions. Find that balance that is just right.

Teacher:	Jim and Terry are probably the toughest of the bunch.
Interventionist:	What do they do?
Teacher:	They are real leaders, but unfortunately they lead the class in the wrong direction. When I give a direction, they just ignore me. You'd think I was speaking a foreign language.

Interventionist:	That would be frustrating. It must make teaching really hard.
Teacher:	I'd like to get them split up, but the principal said that they were careful with placements last year and that neither of the boys would mix any better in any of the other classrooms.
Interventionist:	Does it look like you have to live with the situation?
Teacher:	Yeah.
Interventionist:	Have you found anything that makes a difference?
Teacher:	I tried separating the boys. That helps a bit.
Interventionist:	Good. Tell me a little more about what they do. Maybe we can put our heads together and come up with some ideas for making this year more livable and helping these students learn to behave more responsibly.

Through active listening, the interventionist may be able to assist with the planning and implementation of interventions that directly help troubled students. Active listening may also result in the interventionist serving as a general resource to teachers who are having difficulties managing a difficult student or group of students. By encouraging teachers to discuss what they would like their classes to be like, an interventionist can often suggest strategies that will assist in creating that vision.

Interventionist:	It sounds like you've tried a lot of things—keeping the kids in at recess, calling their parents, working on rules. I'm sure that it's disappointing when things don't work out.
Teacher:	It is really frustrating! I got into this profession because I wanted to teach. With this group of kids I feel like I'm a combination babysitter–prison guard. They aren't mature enough, or their values aren't strong enough, to trust them with any kind of responsibility.
Interventionist:	You do have a challenging group this year. I've worked with several of these kids in the past. The two of us might be able to work out some strategies that would help improve the situation. As you know, there aren't any magic tricks with these kids, but we might find some things that would help them gradually move in the right direction.

At a later meeting:

Interventionist:	How have things been going?
Teacher:	Actually, not as bad. I talked to Jim about the tutoring he did last year. His eyes lit up and he was almost friendly the rest of the day.
Interventionist:	That's great. Perhaps things are beginning to turn a bit.
Teacher:	I'm not sure it will last, though. One of the other kids began picking on Jim, and then we were into problems again. Sometimes it feels like a losing battle with this group.
Interventionist:	There are dozens of stumbling blocks. A lot of your kids may not have good models at home. If you had the ideal class, what would it be like?
Teacher:	The ideal class? That's interesting. It would be a group of kids who respect each other—and me. They would be engaged in their work, take pride in their accomplishments, and have fun.
Interventionist:	Would you be interested in working together to create that vision? I don't think it's impossible. Hard maybe, but together we might be able to turn this whole group around. I have two or three intervention ideas in mind that we might study together. We could sift through the strategies and pick some that might have merit.

Skill 2: Use Everyday Language to Discuss Problems and Share Perceptions

The skilled interventionist is careful to use language that staff, parents, and students are comfortable with. Technical jargon or confusing language may create barriers to collaboration (Allen & Graden, 2002; Bergan & Kratochwill, 1990). For example, an interventionist with a school psychology background may be tempted to use phrases such as *intermittent reinforcement* and *antecedent event*. This vocabulary reflects useful concepts from the science of behaviorism, but these same ideas can be described in everyday language. Contrast the following two statements:

Interventionist 1:	If you watch Norm carefully, the antecedent event to his agitation seems to be Mrs. Harper approaching him. I wonder if we can figure out why.

> **Interventionist 2:** If you watch Norm carefully, he seems to get agitated whenever Mrs. Harper approaches him. I wonder if we can figure out why.

A teacher listening to Interventionist 1 might think, "Figure out what? I have no idea what he's talking about!" On the other hand, a teacher working with Interventionist 2 is more likely to respond, "That's interesting. Do you suppose that Norm just doesn't trust adults?"

Skill 3: Discuss Problems and Share Perceptions in a Value-Free Manner

Language that conveys particular biases or philosophies may hinder effective communication. Value-laden terminology can inadvertently create barriers that are difficult to tear down. It's important to use neutral, objective language and to talk about directly observable behaviors (Allen & Graden, 2002; Rosenfield, 1987, 2008). A discussion that is focused specifically on the needs of the student is more likely to engage the teacher. Contrast the following two comments:

> **Interventionist 1:** Karla needs a developmentally appropriate environment. She needs to be able to stretch and move physically.
>
> **Interventionist 2:** I wonder if Karla is just one of those kids who have a difficult time staying still. Do you think we could structure her workspace so she could move but not bother the other children?

The first interventionist has risked putting the teacher on the defensive. If the teacher hasn't adopted a developmentally appropriate philosophy, she might wonder, "Is the interventionist saying that my classroom is not developmentally appropriate? I think it's developmentally appropriate to teach children to stay on task and not prevent others from working." In future discussions, the teacher may feel the interventionist is judging her against the unknown standards of a developmentally appropriate practice.

On the other hand, by keeping the conversation focused on the needs of the student and the situation, the second interventionist has involved the teacher in problem-solving: "Maybe we could create a space for Karla to move about while she is working and also teach her not to bother other students."

Skill 4: Work with Staff and Parents as a Collaborator Rather than an Expert

The effective interventionist acts as a resource. She is there to provide support, assistance, and guidance to teachers, students, and/or families as they design intervention plans. She may ask questions and offer suggestions, but as much as possible, she should avoid telling people what they ought to do. When an interventionist grandstands, working relationships may be jeopardized and the interests of students may be sacrificed. The effective interventionist collaborates with others to jointly resolve problems and avoids setting herself up as an expert (Allen & Graden, 2002; Brown, Pryzwanksy, & Schulte, 2000; Gutkin & Curtis, 1999; Kratochwill, 2008). This well-known citation summarizes the problem with experts: Human experts and rabbits have much in common. First, they multiply at a prolific rate. Second, they are both highly susceptible to infection—rabbits catch myxomatosis and experts catch "expertosis." The symptoms are common to both: The head swells and the patient goes blind.

Interventionist:	Our goal is to help Cindy be more responsible for her work.
Teacher:	Yes, I really think the problem is that Cindy just doesn't care.
Interventionist:	I like the idea of teaching Cindy to care about her work. As we look at strategies, we'll need to be careful to determine what she can do. Academics are still very hard for her. Mrs. Walker, if you can give examples of assignments she's had problems with, we can go through and try to identify whether her problems were related to can't do or won't do.
Teacher:	I guess a good example would be this paper. She was supposed to look up words in the glossary and copy definitions. She lost her place and copied parts of the wrong definition several times.
Interventionist:	Let's take a look at the words and their definitions. You know, Mrs. Walker, this is just a guess, but I wonder if Cindy understands the words she was copying.
Teacher:	I hadn't really thought about that. I don't know. I know she can read them.
Interventionist:	The glossary has some pretty hard definitions.
Teacher:	If that is a problem, what are we going to do?
Interventionist:	We're going to have to try to find a balance between teaching Cindy to compensate for her academic problems and providing her with adaptations to the assignments. Perhaps by combining some motivational techniques and adjusting assignments, we can help Cindy care more about her work.

Skill 5: Be Aware of and Sensitive to the Various Participants

Throughout intervention planning and implementation, an interventionist must be sensitive to the needs and abilities of individual students, parents, and teachers. Each person brings unique characteristics to the situation.

Through observation, interviews, and assessment, the effective interventionist can develop and provide an objective view of the needs and abilities of each student who is brought to her attention. During intervention planning and implementation, the interventionist serves an important role—helping to clarify realistic expectations for students. What works with some students may not work with others.

The effective interventionist is also sensitive to the needs of the teacher—providing services before the intervention, during intervention planning and implementation, and following the intervention (Kratochwill & Stoiber, 2002; Watson & Sterling-Turner, 2008). One of the primary roles of the interventionist is to help reduce teacher isolation and encourage collaboration. Students with behavior problems often create stress for teachers. When dealing with challenging situations, teachers need an opportunity to talk to someone who is nonjudgmental. The interventionist needs to ask, "How else can I help you?"

The interventionist can also protect the teacher if planning becomes unrealistic. Interventionists with regular classroom teaching experience can sometimes anticipate when a teacher may have difficulties implementing an intervention. If an interventionist hasn't had classroom experience, she can actively work at understanding the demands of the classroom and anticipating where problems might occur. The interventionist might say something like, "I love this part of the plan, but when I try to imagine doing this with 25 other children in the room, I think I would forget. Mr. Sherman, do you see that as a potential problem?"

Through good communication, an interventionist can also help teachers identify what is going well. Working with high-risk students requires patience and endurance. During the setbacks that are bound to occur, a teacher may need an interventionist to objectively look at data, recognize that progress is being made, and communicate that success to the teacher (Allen & Graden, 2002; Howell & Nolet, 2000; Schuermann & Hall, 2008; Skiba, Deno, Martson, & Casey, 1989).

> If an interventionist hasn't had classroom experience, she can actively work at understanding the demands of the classroom and anticipating where problems might occur.

All interventionists should know whether they are expected to report to the principal or district administrators about cases they are working on. If the principal expects an interventionist to report his involvement with a teacher, the interventionist needs to let that teacher know in advance. It is very damaging to a collaborative relationship for the teacher to assume she is telling the interventionist things in confidence only to learn later that he is reporting about the collaboration to the principal. Some interventionists may have a job role in which the collaborative relationship allows for confidentiality, such as a school counselor, whereas another job role, such as a school psychologist, may have requirements to report to the administrator. Clear, honest, before-the-relationship-begins communication is essential.

....

Teacher:	Clay really blew it today. I had to send him to the office.
Interventionist:	What did he do?
Teacher:	He started to pull on Megan's ponytail, and they got into a major argument.
Interventionist:	That must be really frustrating.
Teacher:	I don't think what we're doing is really helping.
Interventionist:	How long has it been since you had to refer Clay to the office?
Teacher:	I don't know. Maybe three or four weeks. It has been a while, hasn't it?
Interventionist:	Do you remember what he did that time?
Teacher:	That was the time he chased the kids and was threatening to kick them. I guess he has made progress, hasn't he?
Interventionist:	Given that this involves office referral, Mrs. Ruiz may be involved at various points. I just want to remind you that Mrs. Ruiz does not ask me about the cases I work on with teachers. She may choose to ask you, but my relationship with you is between you and me. She likes to support the notion that you can tell me things without having to worry about what I might say to her about you or this concern you have with Clay.

An interventionist must also be sensitive to the needs of different families. What is realistic for one family may be entirely unrealistic for another. It is important for the interventionist to make sure that requests made of a family do not ask more than the family can deliver. She can help the family by providing direct assistance and offering suggestions.

Teacher: Jason is failing because he never gets his homework done. He can do the work; he just chooses not to. I think we need to get his parents involved in this. It's their responsibility.

Interventionist: I agree that it's their responsibility. Let's brainstorm some other possibilities, though. Then we can talk pros and cons.

Teacher: What is there to discuss? You call the parents. If they don't get the kid to do his homework, it isn't our problem.

Interventionist: I know that this kind of problem is very hard because we want students to assume responsibility for their work. The fact is that Jason hasn't learned to do that, and it appears that his parents won't or can't help. I spoke with Jason's dad last week. He works at night, and it sounds like the mother spends her evenings in the bars. If we all work together, I think we can help Jason. His parents love him, but neither seems to be able to help right now. The first suggestion I have would be to get Jason involved in Alateen.

Finally, when there are conflicts of interests, the effective interventionist keeps focused on the intervention plan. For example, if a teacher wants a disruptive child to be removed from his classroom, but the interventionist does not feel this is in the best interests of the student, she might handle it as follows:

Teacher: I really can't tolerate Jeffrey any more. He has disrupted my class more times than I care to remember. He's disrespectful and obnoxious, and I don't want him returned.

Interventionist: I know that Jeffrey has really caused problems. I am sorry we were not there to help sooner.

Teacher: I don't think it would have done any good. I've tried everything with that kid. Nothing works.

Interventionist: I'm sure you have. What I'd like to do with you today is work through a plan for what types of misbehaviors should result in the student being sent to the office and what types should be handled in the classroom. I know the vice-principal wants to have as much handled in the classroom as possible so the student does not miss out on instruction. Let's talk through a plan, then run it by Mr. Corderra to see if you and he are on the same page about when and when not to send the student to the office. Does that sound OK to you? Then part of the plan will be to consider a special education referral, but we also need to figure out a plan to keep your classroom livable while we are doing that.

RESPONSIBILITIES OF THE INTERVENTIONIST

An interventionist often serves as the case manager or facilitator for collaborative problem-solving teams (e.g., a teacher and interventionist; a teacher, parent, and interventionist; a teacher assistance team (TAT) or intervention planning team (IPT); a pre-referral team; a care team; a grade-level team). Regardless of the composition, whenever a group jointly designs and implements an intervention plan, someone must assume responsibility for coordinating the process. The role typically falls to the interventionist and includes a subset of responsibilities, which we will discuss as tasks that the interventionist typically handles during any intervention:

Task 1: Respond Promptly to Requests for Assistance

Once a request has been made, the effective interventionist moves quickly to determine the urgency of a problem. If the problem involves physically dangerous behavior, it is important to move to emergency procedures without delay. When the problem is severe—the teacher can no longer cope or teach the student—an interventionist should schedule a meeting within a day of the request to determine next steps. For less severe problems, the interventionist should try to schedule a meeting within a week.

Task 2: Organize Meetings

After determining with the teacher the format for the intervention planning and who should participate, the interventionist should take responsibility for contacting those involved. Depending on the urgency of the problem, she should provide as much notice as possible. It can also be useful to send notices about the meeting a day or so in advance to remind all participants about time, location, purpose, and who else will be in attendance.

Task 3: Set and Maintain a Positive Tone for the Meeting

An effective interventionist is not only familiar with the three planning formats discussed in Chapters 7, 8, and 9, but also takes an active role in conducting the meetings. The interventionist can set the tone for collaborative meetings by welcoming and introducing each participant: "Mrs. Miller, I know you've met Rob and Nancy Johnson. I appreciate everyone taking the time to meet. I know there have been a lot of phone conversations, and I think it will be good to sit down together." Pay particular attention to making the parent(s) feel comfortable. Remember that they are probably nervous, may be defensive, may have had bad experiences in schools, and are quite likely outnumbered at the meeting. Anything and everything you can do to make them feel like partners in the process will go a long way toward securing their active input and participation.

The interventionist should also make a statement regarding the purpose of the meeting. Conflicts can be prevented when a clear focus on the needs of the student has been established. Briefly acknowledging any past differences and summarizing common goals allows the interventionist to move the discussion directly to productive ground.

Interventionist:	Despite past differences, we're meeting today to focus on what we can do to help Andrew have a better year. The Johnsons have shared their concerns with me, and I've also spoken with Ms. Miller. You all have the same goals for Andrew and his class. You'd like to see a respectful atmosphere in the classroom. You'd like to have the kids learn as much as possible, which means that they need to become engaged and work hard on their assignments and activities in class. Let me explain some of the strategies Ms. Miller and I are working on to improve the classroom atmosphere. First, Ms. Miller has designed some classroom rules that we'll share with you. To teach students how to follow the rules, we have been working on role-playing and some other things. Ms. Miller can explain what we are doing with the whole class.

Task 4: Keep Meetings Moving Along

Intervention planning meetings can easily become too lengthy, with inordinate amounts of time spent complaining or hashing and rehashing ideas. Although participants may be enthusiastic during the meeting, later they may resent the amount of time invested. The effective interventionist develops the skill of encouraging involvement but keeps the discussion focused and moving along. Both the IDG: Teacher Interview (Chapter 7) and the 25-minute planning meeting (Chapter 8) offer the interventionist a structure in which to do this.

Task 5: Don't Spend Too Much Time on Consequences for Misbehavior

Although consequences for misbehavior are often a necessary part of an intervention plan, they are unlikely, in isolation, to have an effect on problems that involve moderate to severe misbehavior (Skiba & Peterson, 2000). Consequences for misbehavior should be designed to limit the reinforcement that follows problem behavior. Usually by the time a teacher makes a referral, the most common consequences for misbehavior have been tried. An effective interventionist will direct the group to put the majority of its time into planning proactive interventions—those that teach and reinforce the student's appropriate behaviors—rather than interventions that focus on consequences for the misbehavior (Alberto & Troutman, 2003; Horner, 2002; Lerman & Vondran, 2002; Nelson, 1996; Scheuermann & Hall, 2008).

Task 6: Clarify Responsibilities and Summarize the Plan

The interventionist can facilitate implementation by providing all participants with a written summary of the planning meeting and a list of their responsibilities. When summarizing plans, the interventionist should watch for inconsistencies, omissions, and potential glitches or places where the participants might need additional assistance. If materials are needed, the summary should specify them. Interventionists can help overburdened teachers by providing or developing any materials needed to implement the plan.

Task 7: Ensure the Plan is Fully Understood by Participants

When an intervention is fairly complex or involves new skills, the interventionist can rehearse the plan with participants. Exploring questions about what might happen is also useful. (What might happen if . . .? What might you do when . . .?) A dry run may help participants clarify parts of the plan and work out any glitches. The interventionist can also offer to model the new procedures, giving the teacher a chance to learn by watching.

Task 8: Offer Support as Needed

It is the interventionist's role to seek feedback and offer support to all participants. Offering support also means making changes and adjusting the intervention until all participants feel that they are supported in the process and that progress is being made.

It is also typically the interventionist who presents the plan to a student. The interventionist can answer questions and help the teacher and student work out the details of the plan. She can give examples and have the student and teacher practice or role-play relevant parts of the plan. When explaining a plan to a student, the interventionist should have the student paraphrase the information. If the student doesn't have the language skills to paraphrase, the interventionist should ask questions to make sure the student understands the plan.

Finally, when an intervention plan involves teaching the student a new skill, the interventionist can either provide the instruction or offer to take the teacher's class while the teacher instructs the student. Sometimes, a student is asked to demonstrate the new skill in context. When time permits, the interventionist can provide on-site coaching—prompting the student to use the new skill and giving feedback.

Task 9: Monitor the Fidelity of Implementation

The interventionist must make judgments about the fidelity of implementation. Is the intervention being implemented the way it was designed? If yes, and the intervention has not worked over a period of weeks, the intervention needs to be modified. If, however, the intervention is not being implemented correctly or consistently, it is not reasonable to assume that it is not working (Duchnowski et al., 2006; Gable, Hendrickson, & Van Acker, 2001; Moncher & Prinz, 1991; Peterson & McConnell, 1996; Witt, VanDerHeyden, & Gilbertson, 2004). The intervention may stay the same, but it make take more work with the teacher to get the intervention actually implemented. To go back to a medical metaphor, you cannot know whether the antibiotics will work if you do not take the medication. This creates a tricky political balance. You do not want the teacher to feel like you are checking up on him, but you owe it to the student to ensure that if an intervention is unsuccessful, some thought is given to whether it was the intervention or the implementation.

Task 10: Provide Follow-Up During and After the Intervention

The interventionist assumes primary responsibility for monitoring implementation—scheduling brief check-ins, arranging follow-up meetings, evaluating student progress, and supervising decisions about maintaining, modifying, or fading interventions. The interventionist also typically assumes primary responsibility for post-intervention follow-ups. Even when a student has been successful and the intervention is faded, it is important for someone to follow through with both the student and the teacher. Without continued monitoring, students and teachers may find themselves falling into old habits. By conducting periodic post-intervention follow-ups, the interventionist can provide the support needed to keep the student (and teacher) on track (Fuchs & Fuchs, 1986; Noell et al., 2005; Rodriguez, Loman, & Horner, in preparation; Witt et al., 2004).

SELF-EVALUATION AND REFLECTION

To enhance his effectiveness, the skilled interventionist continually evaluates his knowledge, the quality of his interpersonal skills, and his ability to help others design and implement successful interventions. As part of this self-evaluation, the effective interventionist engages in reflection—analyzing goals, activities, and relationships as well as the outcomes of his collaborative efforts. Following are some practices used by an effective interventionist:

Keep a confidential journal. A confidential journal allows an interventionist to record thoughts, impressions, and events that might not be appropriate to keep in a student's file. As the interventionist works on cases, the act of writing provides an opportunity to explore ideas, pose questions, think about possible solutions, and make predictions. While writing, an interventionist can consider why certain procedures were effective or ineffective.

Keeping a journal also provides a vehicle for reviewing cases. Journal entries give the interventionist a way to examine the accuracy of past predictions and impressions, identify patterns, and track progress. When a journal has been kept over a long time, the interventionist can track his own professional growth.

Work with a study group. An interventionist does not always have others he can talk to about being an interventionist because of the issues of trust and confidentiality. Like other professionals, though, she needs opportunities to talk freely with others who share similar responsibilities. A study group can provide interventionists with the same support they give to staff, students, and parents. It can provide a structure for interventionists to meet and share cases, discuss ideas and procedures, explore problems, and celebrate successes.

When school counselors, school psychologists, and special education resource teachers act as interventionists in a district, these professionals might meet in small study groups once a month. The agenda may involve presentations of case studies. Following is a possible agenda for conducting a case study analysis:

1. Briefly present the situation, demographic information, and the reason for referral. Include the age of the student, grade, classroom structure, statement of the problem, and the teacher's goal.

2. Identify how the request for assistance was made. Was it made by a teacher or parent? Or was it the result of an automatic referral process such as follow-up on an existing problem or excessive office referrals?

3. Provide any relevant background information.

4. Identify what has been tried and the results.

5. Identify concerns, successes, and difficulties encountered.

6. Brainstorm additional strategies, resources, and ideas.

It's important to get all staff members involved in intervention training, so the interventionist should also facilitate study groups among grade-level teachers. By having a group of grade-level teachers construct lessons and teach an intervention to a larger group, those teachers learn the intervention in a deeper way than they would have if they had simply been part of an audience (Guskey, 1994; Massarella, 1980; Scott et al., 2005).

Make sure that all study group members know that confidentiality and adhering to professional standards is essential. When presenting cases, do not use the real names of teachers, students, or parents. Nothing undermines the effectiveness of a collaborative relationship more than a teacher hearing from someone else that her situation was discussed as a case study.

Facilitate training for collaborative problem-solving groups. Teacher assistance teams, multidisciplinary teams, pre-referral teams, or care teams might meet monthly to work on improving the quality of the service they provide to staff and students. The group might work on the efficiency of their meetings as well as the effectiveness of their intervention plans. Each month the group might study one of the interventions outlined in the book *Interventions: Evidence-Based Behavioral Strategies for Individual Students*.

Ask for direct feedback. The reflective interventionist may ask teachers, parents, and administrators with whom he has worked to provide feedback about the collaborative problem-solving process. What was helpful? How could the process be improved? By asking both general and specific questions, the interventionist gains insights into improving the process and his role in it.

Conduct staff surveys. Surveys can yield valuable information for developing procedures to meet the needs of staff and students. To ensure a high rate of response, staff members can be asked to fill out a confidential survey during a staff meeting and drop it into a box as they leave the meeting. See Reproducible Form 6.1 for a sample survey.

Market your services. Another form of communication that an interventionist must excel at is publicizing her services. An interventionist needs to continuously make other staff members aware of her expertise and willingness to help. Simply saying to a teacher—"I may be able to assist you with this"—is the first step in marketing intervention services.

Reproducible Form 6.1

INTERVENTIONIST SAMPLE SURVEY

Dear Staff:

Please take a minute or two to respond to the survey below. Your responses will be anonymous. Your honest opinions will assist us as we continue to develop collaborative problem-solving relationships.

1. Have you received assistance with a student this year? Y Ⓝ

   (If your answer to question 1 is Yes, please continue with questions 3–10. If your answer to question 1 is No, please complete question 2 only.)

2. If No, why not?

   __X__ Did not have any severe problem students

   _____ Did not know consultation services were available

   _____ Prefer to handle things on my own

   _____ Do not feel comfortable with _____, but did seek assistance
   from someone else in the school

	Not at all 1	Somewhat 2	Generally 3	Very much so 4
3. The interventionist was quick to respond to my concerns.	○	○	○	○
4. The interventionist was sensitive to my concerns.	○	○	○	○
5. The interventionist was easy to work with and listened to my ideas about how to solve the problem.	○	○	○	○
6. Working with the interventionist was time efficient.	○	○	○	○
7. The plan that was developed was organized and had clearly defined roles and timelines.	○	○	○	○
8. The plan that was developed was practical (e.g., the amount of teacher time required was realistic).	○	○	○	○
9. Adequate follow-up/support (e.g., modeling and coaching) was provided after the plan was developed.	○	○	○	○
10. The plan developed was effective (e.g., student behavior improved).	○	○	○	○

Reproducible Materials Blank copies of the forms are provided on the CD. Permission is given for individual teachers, administrators, or other school personnel to reproduce any form labeled "Reproducible Form" for in-district use.

The interventionist can also seek out testimonials (Figure 6.1) from teachers she has helped. Having a teacher speak out in a staff meeting about his or her positive experience with an intervention process is a great way to encourage others to request, and benefit from, assistance. Those testimonials can also be included in printed material that the interventionist distributes periodically to remind the staff that intervention and support services are available in their building or district.

Figure 6.1
Sample Testimonial

Why I Love the Problem-Solving Team

One of my students used to interrupt me constantly while I was teaching. No amount of verbal reminders or consequences seemed to make a difference. So I submitted a request for help. (It was easier than I thought it would be!)

A member of the problem-solving team met with me right away. In 15 minutes, we had plans for a self-monitoring intervention. It was great. My student learned to correct herself, and all I had to do was pay more attention to her before and after class. This was a rewarding experience, and I'll never again hesitate to ask for help. Rating: ☆☆☆☆☆—**Sandra Daly, Teacher, November 2007**

CONCLUSION

No matter how skilled an interventionist is, there is always more to learn. By striving to learn more each year—to improve communication and observation skills and be more sensitive to the needs of staff—the interventionist can become more proficient in both her technical knowledge and her ability to share that knowledge with staff.

 **Reproducible Materials**

A copy of the following reproducible material appears on the CD. Permission is given for individual teachers, administrators, or other school personnel to reproduce this form for in-district use.

Reproducible Form 6.1: Interventionist Sample Survey

CHAPTER 7

Teacher Interview

Using an Intervention Decision Guide

The Intervention Decision Guide (IDG) was developed as a tool for interventionists to use when meeting with teachers to discuss a student in need. In its early form, the IDG was simply a set of standardized questions that had proved effective in eliciting useful information about the student. When this protocol is followed, the teacher interview serves as a rudimentary functional behavior assessment that gives the interventionist and teacher a foundation for developing a potentially effective first-step intervention. Simply by bringing two heads together to discuss the situation, the IDG assures that the outcome will be better than if the teacher or the interventionist acted alone.

The objectives of the IDG, however, go beyond decision-making. One of this tool's primary purposes is to include and support the teacher in the intervention process. By taking the time to gather as much information as possible from the teacher (who may not have even asked for help), the interventionist or case manager greatly increases the likelihood that the teacher will feel vested in the process and be willing to faithfully implement the intervention that is chosen (Bergan & Kratochwill, 1990; Rosenfield, 2008).

The importance of getting and giving teacher support lies in the fact that the success of any intervention is highly influenced by the teacher's ability and willingness to consistently implement it (Duchnowski et al., 2006; Gresham, MacMillan, Beebe-Frankenberger, & Bocian, 2000; Luborsky, McLellan, Woody, O'Brien, & Auerbach, 1985; Walker & Sprague, 2006). All too often, the time spent planning the "perfect" intervention can be lost because the plan is never consistently implemented. It is not uncommon for only portions of a well-designed intervention to be implemented or for implementation to last only a couple of days. Without treatment fidelity or consistent implementation of an intervention as planned

(Gresham, 1989; Noell, Gresham, & Gansle, 2002), it is difficult to distinguish whether a lack of improvement in the student's behavior is a result of an ineffective intervention or poor implementation of a potentially effective intervention (Gresham, 2000; Wood, Umbreit, Liaupsin, & Gresham, 2007).

Working with the teacher to assess her preferences and determine any additional skills or support she may need may improve fidelity of implementation. This partnership *framework* emphasizes collaboration between teacher and interventionist to create or adapt an intervention to fit both the teacher's and the student's needs (Power et al., 2005; Sprick, Knight, et al., 2007). It is important that consultants work in alliance with the teacher to carefully define the problem and develop an intervention that fits her preferences and skills. These steps, which are incorporated in the IDG, will increase the likelihood of avoiding obstacles related to inconsistent intervention implementation (Bergan & Kratochwill, 1990; Kratochwill et al., 2002; Perepletchikova & Kazdin, 2005).

The teacher, who works with the student every day, is also the best source of information about the student and can offer insights into the student's behavior and motivation. Empowering the teacher by hearing, valuing, and including her perspective is the first step toward a successful implementation (Beutler, Moleiro, & Talebi, 2002; Cormier & Nurius, 2003; Kerkorian, McKay, & Bannon, 2006; Tryon & Winograd, 2002).

The IDG is time and resource efficient. If the teacher and interventionist can plan an effective and easy-to-implement intervention, then more extensive processes—such as direct observation, records review, or interviews with others—can be skipped or saved for later, if needed. The IDG can be also used to help develop comprehensive and specialized intervention plans for high-risk students.

The IDG tool guides interventionists through a four-stage process of planning an intervention that will best address the target student's problem and needs. The stages are:

- Background—reason for the referral and description of the problem

- Preparation—possible interventions to consider

- Intervention design—summary of intervention, responsibilities, and final plan

- Implementation—notes from follow-up sessions

This chapter describes how to implement the process outlined on Reproducible Form 7.1, the Intervention Decision Guide: Teacher Interview. This form appears on pp. 140–143, and a blank reproducible version is available on the CD. Permission is given for individual teachers, administrators, or other school personnel to reproduce any forms labeled "Reproducible Forms" for in-district use. Consider printing a copy of this four-page reproducible to refer to as you read this chapter. When the form is printed front and back on 11" x 17" (tabloid size) paper, it can serve both as a guide to your interview with the teacher and as a place to make notes. Our goal is that this form will be a useful tool as you work with teachers to develop interventions to help students improve their behavior.

In Chapter 4, we suggest that as soon as a student's situation moves into Tier 2, collaborative problem-solving, someone should be assigned as a case manager to provide support and monitor the intervention process to make sure that the student's needs are met. In most cases, this will be the same person we describe in this chapter as the interventionist, because this will be the person who first works with the teacher on the relatively simple and time-efficient process of the IDG: Teacher Interview. However, if the intervention developed at this stage does not help, the case manager will continue to stay with the situation, serving as an advocate for the student and the teacher and bringing in other, more structured problem-solving resources.

The top of the form includes basic information about the student and the names of the interventionist and teacher(s). Be sure to include whatever information may be needed later to demonstrate how this intervention interview fits as part of a comprehensive file—especially the date and the participants involved in the interview planning process.

Stage 1: Background

In the early stages of intervention planning, it is essential to gather all relevant background information that will inform crucial decisions about which procedures to use. This information will largely come from a meeting between an interventionist and the teacher. This may be a self-contained two-person process, or the IDG interview may be used in advance of multidisciplinary or planning team meetings. In this initial meeting, the goal is to use the information the student's teacher has at his fingertips to design an intervention that best addresses the student's problems and needs. Because the IDG provides structure but no time limits, the interventionist must skillfully guide the process—not spending so much time that the meeting drags on, but enough time to gather needed information and develop a sound intervention plan that the teacher is willing to implement. The more information the interventionist or team has and the more clearly the problem is defined (using the objective language of behaviors rather than child-deficit language), the greater the likelihood that the interventionist and the teacher can develop an intervention plan that is responsive to the needs of the student (Rosenfield, 1987, 2008; Tombari & Bergan, 1978; Tryon & Winograd, 2002).

In this initial meeting, the goal is to use the information the student's teacher has at his fingertips to design an intervention that best addresses the student's problems and needs.

Continued on p. 144

Reproducible Form 7.1 (p. 1 of 4)

SAMPLE

INTERVENTION DECISION GUIDE: TEACHER INTERVIEW

Student: _Jake Stillwell_   Age: _10_   Grade: _5_   Beginning Date: _4/21_

Interventionist: _Mr. Bickman_   Teacher(s): _Ms. Thompson, Mr. Gill_

Stage 1: Background

1. Reason for referral and description of the problem: _Jake plays pencil hockey at his desk & flicks rubber bands. He also has severe anger problems & resorts to loud arguing with peers and teachers at a moment's notice. Jake doesn't have many friends & when he isn't exhibiting anger, he isn't interactive at all._

Code Red: Is it an emergency situation? _No_

The behavior is a threat to physical safety.	**Intervention G:** *Managing Physically Dangerous Behavior*
The behavior is so disruptive the teacher cannot teach.	**Intervention H:** *Managing Severely Disruptive Behavior*

2. Are there situations that seem to set off the problem behavior? _When Jake's mother is sick, he becomes easily agitated. During independent work time, Jake gets restless and starts to bother other students._

3. Where do the problems tend to occur? _Jake has problems in all school settings, but most are in the classroom because that's where he spends the most time._

4. When do the problems tend to occur?
   Times of day: _More frequent in (but not limited to) the morning._
   Days of week: _There doesn't seem to be a pattern._

5. How often do the problems occur? How long does the behavior last? How intense is the problem?
   The problems occur almost daily. The behavior lasts until a teacher intervenes.

6. Is the student psychologically and neurologically capable of controlling his or her behavior? Is there evidence to support this opinion? _There is no medical paperwork to suggest that Jake's problem is neurological, but his teachers think he may not be able to control himself at times. There is only observation of his abrupt outbursts of anger to support this opinion._

7. Is the student aware of the problem? _Yes. Both teachers have discussed the problem with Jake, and he has expressed an understanding of learning to control the problem._

8. Does the student seem motivated to improve the behavior? _Jake says he wants to make changes, but his teachers say they don't see any effort._

9. What is the function of the problem behavior? What seems to be maintaining or reinforcing the student's misbehavior?

   ☒ Ability   ❏ Awareness   ❏ Adult attention   ❏ Peer attention
   ❏ Power or control ❏ Escape or avoidance   ❏ Competing reinforcers   ☒ Other _venting_
                       (task difficulty/discomfort)   _frustration_

Notes:
   Jake's behavior problems are escalating and becoming unmanageable.

Reproducible Form 7.1 (p. 2 of 4)   *Teacher Interview (continued)*

SAMPLE

10. Strengths of the student (list at least three):

academically adequate, a hard worker, gets most of his work done, good baseball player

11. The teacher's goal or desired outcome:

What would the teacher like to have happen?
Jake shows respect for other students.

What can't the teacher live with any longer?
verbal hostility toward and harassment of other students

12. Methods for evaluating intervention effectiveness:

frequency count of disruptions (in place)
add rating scale (1-3)

13. Notes on parental involvement:

Contact date(s): *4/23*

Notes on the contact(s): *Called mother. She can't participate because of poor health.*

What would the parents or guardians like to have happen?
She supports whatever interventions are necessary to address Jake's behavior problems

14. Other interventions tried and their results (in particular, Interventions A–F):

For each: *D – Data Collection*

Are copies of this information available? *yes*
How successful were the interventions?

15. Other information the teacher is aware of:

Input from other adults who know the student (teachers, assistants, specialists, school counselors)

Third-grade teacher suggests providing the custodian as a mentor for Jake. Time spent with custodian could be positive reinforcer.

16. Review of the student's records:

Reproducible Materials Blank copies of the forms are provided on the CD. Permission is given for individual teachers, administrators, or other school personnel to reproduce any form labeled "Reproducible Form" for in-district use.

Reproducible Form 7.1 (p. 3 of 4)

SAMPLE

Stage 2: Preparation

Possible Interventions to Consider:

Presenting Behavior	✓ if true	Intervention	Date of implementation	Effectiveness (+/−)
Several or many students in class misbehave.		**Preintervention:** *Classroom Management*		
The student may not know what is expected.		**Intervention A:** *Planned Discussion*		
The student may have an underlying academic problem.		**Intervention B:** *Academic Assistance*		
The student has difficulty with motivation and may not understand how to reach a goal.	✓	**Intervention C:** *Goal Setting*		
The student's behavior appears to be chronic and resistant to simple intervention.	✓	**Intervention D:** *Data Collection & Debriefing*		
The student gets a lot of attention from adults or peers for misbehavior or failure.	✓	**Intervention E:** *Increasing Positive Interactions*		
The reason the behavior is occurring chronically needs to be analyzed and incorporated into the intervention plan.		**Intervention F:** *STOIC Analysis & Intervention*		
The student's escalating behavior is physically dangerous, or poses a threat to physical safety.		**Intervention G:** *Managing Physically Dangerous Behavior*		
The behavior is so severe that the teacher cannot continue to teach.		**Intervention H:** *Managing Severely Disruptive Behavior*		
The student is impulsive and has difficulty maintaining emotional control.		**Intervention I:** *Managing the Cycle of Emotional Escalation*		
The student seems to be unaware of when he/she engages in inappropriate behavior.		**Intervention J:** *Cueing & Precorrecting*		
The student has some motivation to change or learn new behaviors.	✓	**Intervention K:** *Self-Monitoring & Self-Evaluation*		
The student makes negative comments about him- or herself and others.	✓	**Intervention L:** *Positive Self-Talk & Attribution Training*		
The student does not know how to meet expectations.		**Intervention M:** *Teaching Replacement Behavior*		
The student cannot or will not communicate verbally.		**Intervention N:** *Functional Communication*		
The misbehavior is a firmly established part of the student's behavior.		**Intervention O:** *Structured Reinforcement Systems*		
It is difficult to be consistent with the student because it is not always clear when the student has crossed the line between appropriate and inappropriate behavior.		**Intervention P:** *Defining Limits & Establishing Consequences*		
Consequences for misbehavior seem necessary but do not seem to work.				
Teacher feels anxious, worried, discouraged, or angry about one or more students.		**Intervention Q:** *Relaxation & Stress Management*		
The student seems anxious, lethargic, or depressed.		**Intervention R:** *Internalizing Problems & Mental Health*		

TIER 1 / TIER 2

Reproducible Materials Blank copies of the forms are provided on the CD. Permission is given for individual teachers, administrators, or other school personnel to reproduce any form labeled "Reproducible Form" for in-district use.

Reproducible Form 7.1 (p. 4 of 4)   *Teacher Interview (continued)*

Stage 3: Intervention Design

1. Selected intervention(s):

2. Summary of responsibilities for implementing the plan:

3. Summary of the final plan:

Stage 4: Implementation

1. Initial follow-up notes:

2. First follow-up meeting:
    Date:
    Purpose:

    Summary:

3. Second follow-up meeting:
    Date:
    Purpose:

    Summary:

 Reproducible Materials Blank copies of the forms are provided on the CD. Permission is given for individual teachers, administrators, or other school personnel to reproduce any form labeled "Reproducible Form" for in-district use.

STEP 1   **Start the IDG Meeting**

Convene the meeting by welcoming the classroom teacher or teachers and establishing an atmosphere of support and advocacy for the student. It is essential to remember that teachers of at-risk students are frequently dealing with high levels of stress and anxiety. During this meeting, you will need to actively work to put the teacher at ease, helping her realize that you are there in an effort to collaboratively find a solution, not to judge the teacher's past methods (Beutler et al., 2002; Cormier & Nurius, 2003; Wickstrom & Witt, 1993). Sit next to the teacher rather than across from her. This will take away certain intimidation factors and avoid the sense that the meeting is an interrogation. You are simply taking notes, not writing anything that is a secret. Allow the teacher to see the form so that she can go back and ask questions or clarify the process. This will also allow the teacher to see how the IDG form guides your discussion toward key information. The teacher will see that you are trying to be respectful of her valuable time and that you view the meeting as a collaborative effort— a sense of "we are going to work together on this."

If the student has had ongoing problems and the intervention process will be conducted and implemented by a planning team, designate a case manager who will conduct this initial meeting with the teacher. Familiarize the teacher with the 25-minute planning process (Chapter 8) and explain that the background information gathered on the IDG will inform decisions made in the planning team meeting. This will help the teacher see that any intervention chosen by the planning team will attempt to fit the nature of the problem, the teacher's abilities and style, and any other factors that may be relevant.

Because the teacher is doing most of the talking, you will mostly likely take notes and record general information at the top of the form: student name, age, grade, beginning date of intervention planning, and so on. But if a teacher seems uncomfortable with the process, offering to let the teacher record the information may give him a sense of participation and control.

STEP 2   **Determine the Reason for the Referral and Get a Description of the Problem**

This step should be viewed as an opportunity to allow the teacher to explain any and every problem that is occurring with the student. Although the intervention plan will later be narrowed to address only the one or two behaviors that are of most concern, it is essential to determine the breadth of the student's problems. Ask the teacher to tell you anything and everything about the situation that resulted in the request for help. To prompt the discussion, ask questions such as: What does the student do? What frustrates you? Tell me more about what goes on every day.

> It is essential to remember that teachers of at-risk students are frequently dealing with high levels of stress and anxiety.

At this stage, the interventionist needs to achieve a balance between giving the teacher room to vent and discouraging any unproductive cycling on the problem. The goals are to ensure that the teacher has an opportunity to describe the full range of the problem and concerns about the student without getting mired in uncontrollable aspects of the problem. (Chapter 6 provides suggestions on active listening for the interventionist.) It is a challenging balance—the interventionist needs to move things along while recognizing that if the teacher feels too rushed or in any way "bullied" in the process, she is less likely to view the interventionist as an ally.

Teachers often feel they aren't listened to by interventionists, who may attempt to immediately identify and address the most critical problem. Those with extensive behavioral training need to proceed with caution, putting aside training that says, "We must be dealing with an observable behavior." It will be far more productive in the early parts of the interview to be a good listener and to acknowledge the range of problems that arise with the student. This can further set the stage for collaboration and goal setting (Creed & Kendall, 2005; White & Mullis, 1998). This may also help the teacher and interventionist identify categories of problem behavior for a later stage of planning. Once the teacher has presented the full scope of the student's problems, let him know that eventually it will be necessary to determine the one or two major behaviors or categories that will be addressed first with an intervention. Ask the teacher to reflect on which behaviors are of greatest concern as you continue working through the Intervention Decision Guide. If the teacher begins to vent or repeat the same content about the problem, gently prompt the teacher to move on to the next step in gathering background information.

Case Study: Severe Anger Problems

Jake is a fifth-grade student whose severe anger problems have come to the attention of the school counselor, Mr. Bickman. Acting as an interventionist, Mr. Bickman sets up a meeting with Ms. Thompson and Mr. Gill, who co-teach Jake's fifth grade class.

At the start of the meeting, Mr. Bickman thanks the two teachers for bringing Jake's problem to his attention and commends them for their willingness to find a solution to Jake's behavior issues. Mr. Bickman explains the purpose of the Intervention Decision Guide and places it in front of him so both teachers can follow along as he takes notes.

Ms. Thompson and Mr. Gill identify several problems as they give an overview of their experiences with Jake in the classroom.

> Teachers often feel they aren't listened to by interventionists, who may attempt to immediately identify and address the most critical problem.

STEP 3 Determine Whether the Situation Involves Code-Red Emergency Behavior

Explicitly ask the teacher whether the student's behavior is currently, or may eventually be, physically dangerous or severely disruptive. If this question is not directly asked, the interventionist runs the risk of missing warning statements about such behavior, in which case the teacher may be unprepared to handle a volatile situation. Under *code-red* circumstances, you will skip simple intervention strategies and move directly to the protocol that your district has in place for handling severely disruptive or dangerous behavior. If your district lacks such a policy, see "Intervention G: Managing Physically Dangerous Behavior" and "Intervention H: Managing Severely Disruptive Behavior" in our *Interventions* book. All of these protocols can help you develop emergency plans for dealing with out-of-control students. Physically dangerous or highly disruptive behaviors should be treated like a potential fire in the school—emergency procedures must be prepared and in place before the problem occurs (Jimerson & Furlong, 2006; Richtig & Hornak, 2003; Sprick & Garrison, 2008). Teachers should have the same confidence in their ability to deal with dangerous or severely disruptive students that they have in the fire drill preparation, with procedures that are thoroughly preplanned and rehearsed.

Once temporary procedures have been put in place for defusing or responding to code-red situations, continue with the Intervention Decision Guide to develop a long-term intervention plan that will help the student learn appropriate behavior.

 Case Study Continued »

> *When the interventionist, Mr. Bickman, asks if Jake's behavior is physically dangerous or severely disruptive, Ms. Thompson says no. Mr. Gill hesitates, then replies that although Jake's behavior has never been violent, he fears his volatility could eventually lead to violent behavior. Mr. Bickman and the two teachers agree to review the school-based emergency plan but decide that an individualized emergency plan for Jakes' potentially physically dangerous behavior is not necessary at this time.*
>
> *Mr. Gill also mentions that Jake's level of emotion makes teaching difficult. Jake sometimes spontaneously yells things out when his behavior is escalating. Mr. Bickman makes a note that they will need to come back and address Jake's disruptive behavior later in the meeting.*

❧ *Removals & Referrals*

Whether a student's behavior is severely disruptive or just a major annoyance is a judgment call that depends largely on the classroom teacher's skills and tolerance level. Because your district protocol (or Intervention H) may involve the removal of the severely disruptive student from the classroom, independent confirmation of the student's disruptive behavior is recommended. The nature of confirmation may include direct observation by the interventionist or administrator, complaints from parents or other students, or reports of severely disruptive behavior in other settings.

It's important for the interventionist to get an administrator involved in any decision about whether to remove a student from the classroom. Inexperienced teachers may not be aware of the building administrators' perspective on removing students from the classroom and sending them to the office as disciplinary referrals. In some cases, the teacher may think he is doing the right thing—removing the student to prevent disruption of other students' education—when in fact the administrator may be thinking, "Why is he sending me all these referrals? He should be handling this level of misbehavior himself." If this misunderstanding continues, the new teacher may be at risk for bad performance evaluations. The interventionist may need to act as a mediator and facilitate a discussion between the teacher and the administrator to help them come to an understanding about what types of behavior should be handled in the classroom and what behaviors, from the administrator's perspective, should be sent to the office.

STEP 4   Identify Trends in the Student's Problem Behavior

The next questions in the Background section of the IDG guide you and the classroom teacher to look for trends in the student's behavior by determining the when, where, and how of the behaviors. When you look at situations that may set off the student's problem behavior, the function of or reason for the misbehavior may emerge (O'Neill et al., 1997; Repp, 1999; Sprick & Garrison, 2008). These behavior trends may also help in later planning stages with tasks such as determining when intervention procedures will be used, how often behavior will be monitored, and so on. It's important to work through each of the questions in this section, making it clear to the teacher that she doesn't have to come up with something for each trend or pattern. There may not be enough information to answer one or more of these questions, but it is useful to think through each one.

> When you look at situations that may set off the student's problem behavior, the funtion of or reason for the misbehavior may emerge.

It will be helpful at this stage in the IDG to gently ask the teacher if she has any data that might show trends in the student's behavior. Monitoring forms, scatter-plot data, and any other collected information will be extremely useful in this stage of intervention planning. This information may help identify trends in the student's behavior, which will allow the intervention plan to address the function of the student's misbehavior. You can use the collected data as you work through the following questions to analyze trends in the student's behavior. If the teacher does not have any data, proceed to the next steps to gather the teacher's subjective perceptions of patterns in the student's behavior.

Are there situations that seem to set off the problem behavior? Identify any situations that seem to trigger problem behavior. Begin to focus the discussion on the student's main problems and ask the teacher to consider whether these behaviors are set off by certain precipitating or escalating events. If the student fights with peers, what sort of interactions precipitate a fight? If the student is overly defiant of authority, what events occur before the insubordinate acts? When specific triggers are identified, the intervention can be focused on teaching the student to manage his behavior under those conditions or to avoid situations that result in problems (Bambara & Kern, 2005; Conroy, Asmus, Sellers, & Ladwig, 2005; Kern & Clemens, 2007; O'Neill et al., 1997). If a teacher can identify triggers such as giving the student too much time to work on his own or after the student has been at his dad's house for the weekend, the teacher can also begin to anticipate and help prevent problem behaviors.

 Case Study Continued »

Interventionist: (Mr. Bickman)	We need to start narrowing down our view of Jake's behavior. I'm going to ask some questions that might help us get at whether there are trends for some of Jake's problems. Have you noticed any situations that seem to precipitate or set off Jake's problem behavior?
Teacher 1: (Ms. Thompson)	I've noticed that Jake does worse during individual work times. I think when he has too much time on his hands, he begins to fidget or get in other kids' space.
Teacher 2: (Mr. Gill)	Jake's mom is also in and out of the hospital a lot. We can anticipate that whenever she is having trouble, we'll see much more acting out from Jake.

Where do the problems tend to occur? Try to determine whether the student exhibits the problem behavior in multiple settings or whether the behavior is isolated to one location. Do problems occur only in the classroom? Does the student have difficulty in the halls or in special settings like the library and music room, the playground, or the cafeteria? Do the parents report similar problems at home? When problems are pervasive across all settings, the misbehavior may be firmly ingrained in the student's repertoire or the student may not have the expected behavior in his repertoire. On the other hand, if the problem occurs only in one or two settings, there may be something specific about the setting that results in problems.

When do the problems tend to occur? Look to see if there is a pattern in the timing of the misbehavior. Do problems occur during certain times of the day? Are mornings better than afternoons? Do problems tend to occur more frequently on certain days? If a pattern is detected, it may help with intervention planning. For example, if a student has tantrums and angry outbursts more frequently on Mondays, weekends may be hard for the student. She may be tired. Her home situation may be particularly disruptive on weekends. The student may feel torn after custody visits. Given this situation, the interventionist can try to collaborate with parents to help reduce stress on weekends as well as identify school-based intervention strategies for Mondays—for example, giving the student a chance to check in with the school counselor for a welcoming visit upon arrival at school on Monday morning.

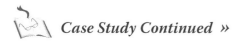 *Case Study Continued* »

> *Mr. Bickman, the interventionist, asks about trends in the when and where of Jake's behavior. He asks if there is any data from previous interventions or simple daily tracking that might help with this analysis. The teachers have collected data on the frequency of Jake's disruptions, but they agree that there doesn't seem to be a pattern to the time or place. Jake acts out mostly in the classroom, but both teachers have heard about negative interactions with teachers and peers in the hall and on the playground.*

How often do the problems occur? How long does the behavior last? How intense is the problem? Knowing the frequency and duration of problems can also be critical information for planning interventions (Alberto & Troutman, 2006; Scheuermann & Hall, 2008; Sulzer-Azaroff & Mayer, 1991). If a young student throws tantrums once or twice a week, the problem may not be severe. However, if tantrums last for 60–90 minutes each, the student may need an intensive intervention plan. Other information that may be worth considering is the intensity of the behavior: Is it sometimes more intense than other times, and have any trends or patterns been noticed? If the problem involves not following directions, discuss the latency between when a direction is given and when the student complies with it. Sometimes it is useful for the teacher or interventionist to record data about the problem before planning an intervention or implementing a plan. (See Chapter 5 for information and forms for data collection.)

> Knowing the frequency and duration of problems can also be critical information for planning interventions.

Is the student psychologically and neurologically capable of controlling his behavior? Is there evidence to support this opinion? If a student has psychological or neurological impairments that make controlling behavior difficult or impossible, it will be necessary to coordinate with the student's family physician, specialists within the district, or other professionals about how to accommodate the student in a way that allows her to experience success. For example, a student with Tourette syndrome has a neurological disorder that will not respond to intervention. On the other hand, a student with Attention Deficit Hyperactivity Disorder (ADHD) is likely to be capable of making moderate behavioral changes. It is a disservice to the student to fail to offer interventions that will help her succeed. Again, the interventionist has an opportunity to act as a mediator who gathers information from the student's doctor as well as the teacher and to facilitate a conversation that will result in a plan to help the student make the changes that she can.

Is the student aware of the problem behavior? Determine whether the teacher believes that the student is aware that his behavior is a problem. Unless there is a prior record of a planned discussion, goal-setting contract, or other such indicator that the student has been directly addressed about the problem, this will be a subjective perception given by the teacher. Sometimes a teacher may feel that constant nagging should be sufficient to convey behavioral expectations to the student, but in reality, the student has no idea he is doing anything wrong. In other cases, the problem may have been addressed, but the student simply disagrees that the behavior needs to change.

For example, the teacher may be concerned because a student is being argumentative and insubordinate. However, in some cases, this could be a cultural style difference between the teacher and the student. The student may not even know that the teacher finds the student's behavior argumentative and perhaps even frightening. As the interventionist, listen to the teacher's perception about whether the student is aware of the teacher's concern. But if the teacher declares, "She knows that behavior is unacceptable," keep open to the possibility that some part of the eventual intervention plan may involve directly teaching the student to become more aware of the behavior that concerns the teacher, which in this example might mean learning to talk to the teacher in a quieter voice with less confrontational body language.

Does the student seem motivated to improve the problem behavior? The student's motivation to change his behavior is another essential factor to take into account in intervention planning (Bandura, 1986; Brophy, 1986). If a student has no motivation to change, it will affect the intervention selection process because you must tailor the choice of intervention to the needs of the student. For example, "Intervention K: Self-Monitoring and Self-Evaluation" from *Interventions* is a powerful tool, but it is likely to be effective only when the student has some motivation to want to do better.

Consider the student who has no desire to complete work and no motivation to improve, yet is placed on a self-monitoring form for his completed assignments. Picture

---

Sometimes a teacher may feel that constant nagging should be sufficient to convey behavioral expectations to the student, but in reality, the student has no idea he is doing anything wrong.

this student's great joy each day when he checks off "nothing accomplished today" on the form. In this case, self-monitoring may actually reinforce the student's poor level of participation. Interventions should instead be tailored to increase the student's motivation, possibly through extrinsic positive reinforcement within a structured reinforcement system.

What seems to be maintaining or reinforcing the student's misbehavior? This question will help you and the teacher take into account the function of the student's misbehavior. Every behavior that occurs repeatedly serves some function—escape, gaining attention or some other reinforcer, competing/multiple reinforcers, venting frustration or anger—for the individual who exhibits the behavior (Cooper et al., 2007; O'Neill et al. 1997; Scheuermann & Hall, 2008). It is important to identify what the student seems to achieve through the behavior. Ask questions such as: What's in it for the student? Does the student control situations? Does the student handle frustration or anger by misbehaving? Does the student get out of doing work?

For example, if the student consistently gets teacher attention for misbehavior, she may enjoy the adult contact, even though it is negative. If misbehavior consistently leads to removal from the room, this removal is probably satisfying to the student at some level. Perhaps the student struggles academically and hides deficiencies by getting kicked out of class, or maybe the student gains peer attention for his rebellious behavior. It is not always possible to determine the specific events or situations that reinforce and perpetuate the problem, and any ideas about the misbehavior's function will always be a guess or hypothesis. However, this discussion process may lead to useful insights that will assist in intervention planning.

Following is a list of possible functions that may be factors in the student's problem behaviors, along with a brief description of what to look for in considering whether that function may be a factor in any given situation. Use this list to help the teacher develop a hypothesis about why the behavior may be occurring.

Ability. As discussed earlier, sometimes a behavior occurs because the student does not have the neurological or physiological ability to behave the way the teacher would like. When this is the case, behavioral intervention will not attempt to change the student's behavior, but must instead make accommodations for the behavior. In other cases, the problematic behavior may occur because the student lacks the information or skill to exhibit the more appropriate behavior. This is also an ability issue, but one in which behavioral intervention holds great promise for helping the student learn new behaviors. For example, if the student has never learned how to accept a reprimand or an academic correction, he may argue with the teacher because he has no other behavior in his repertoire for responding to this type of situation. If the student never exhibits the positive behavior the teacher wants, there is a fair chance that ability issues may play a role. When this is the case, at least part of the intervention plan will need to include teaching replacement behavior so the student learns to exhibit the new skill—much like learning a skill in a sport.

> Every behavior that occurs repeatedly serves some function for the individual who exhibits the behavior.

Awareness. Information about this was presented in the previous section to help the teacher explore the possibility that the student is able to exhibit the positive behavior but may not know that she is exhibiting the problem behavior. For example, the student may talk incessantly (the proverbial "running off at the mouth" problem), but have no awareness when she is doing this. She is fully able to not talk, but she is not aware how frequently she gets into this verbal state or how long it lasts. If the student is able to control the behavior when corrected, but seems surprised when corrected, it may be an awareness problem. With these types of problems, cueing and signaling, along with some form of self-monitoring or self-evaluation, may be especially useful interventions.

Adult attention. Some students are starved for adult attention. For these students, the form of the attention may not matter—reprimands and compliments both involve an adult providing attention. If this is the function, the teacher may describe the student as needy, demanding, helpless, or aggravating and may even say, "He drives me crazy." If the student is currently getting a lot of adult attention when he misbehaves, there is an excellent chance that the attention itself is perpetuating the problematic behavior. When this is the case, the crux of the intervention plan will be reducing the frequency, duration, and intensity of attention the student receives in response to misbehavior while concurrently drastically increasing the frequency, duration, and intensity of adult attention the student receives when exhibiting positive behavior.

Peer attention. A student may exhibit misbehavior to get attention and/or approval from peers. This may be in the form of showing off for peers by being the class clown or disruptive influence. In other cases, it may be exhibiting behavior that elicits disapproval from peers. ("She just seems to love annoying the other students in class.") If the chronic misbehavior gets lots of attention from peers, either positive or negative, it is a reasonable hypothesis that the peer attention may be reinforcing the problematic behavior.

Power or control. Sometimes a student's behavior serves to give the student a sense of control over some aspect of life. This could include negative behaviors such as arguing, insubordination, and overtly refusing to follow directions. It could also include passively negative behaviors such as just doing nothing. For example, when given a direction, the student does not argue but also does nothing to comply and even just passively stares off into space.

> Simple attention-seeking behavior often responds to an intervention in which the adults give less attention to misbehavior (ignoring) and more attention to positive behavior.

This is a somewhat controversial issue in the behavioral field because many experts suggest that a hypothesis that differentiates power from other forms of attention does not imply differences in intervention. We have found that simple attention-seeking behavior often responds to an intervention in which the adults give less attention to misbehavior (ignoring) and more attention to positive behavior. If the student likes exhibiting behaviors that make adults frustrated and angry, however, we have found that when the behavior is ignored, the student is likely to accelerate the intensity of the behavior into something that cannot be ignored, such as hitting other students.

In this case, a more useful intervention may be to implement a consequence for the misbehavior, but also to implement a proactive plan that gives the student a sense of importance and power, such as a highly visible school job (see Meaningful Work in Chapter 11). When the student gains a sense of power in positive ways, he has less need to exert power in negative ways.

Escape or avoidance (task difficulty or discomfort). This may involve trying to get out of difficult, stressful, or uncomfortable situations. The most obvious example is the student who misbehaves to avoid work that is too difficult. If the student is unable to do assigned work, she is in a position to misbehave and cover up that she cannot do the work, or she can behave appropriately, in which case she and everyone else will know that she is not able. Exhibiting misbehavior may make it appear that she does not *want* to do the work, when in fact she is not *able* to do the work. Another example of escape would be when a student who is afraid to go out to recess exhibits behavior that results in an office referral because the safety of the office is far more attractive than facing the recess situation. When escape may be the possible function, the intervention will need to reduce the fear or stress of the situation the student is avoiding while concurrently teaching the student the skills needed to handle the situation. That is, the intervention must have a strong skill-building component to ensure that the student is learning behaviors that will allow her to handle the type of situation that has been problematic.

Competing reinforcers. This function simply means that the student is not exhibiting the desired behaviors because doing something else is more fun. For example, a kindergarten student may not do an assigned task, such as participating in centers, simply because he would rather be playing with puzzles. This is probably a less frequent function than the others already mentioned, but should be considered as a possibility. When this may be the case, the intervention will need to restrict access to the competing reinforcer (make it less accessible) while concurrently increasing the reinforcing aspects of the desired behavior through increased attention and possibly with the addition of a structured reinforcement system.

Other. Although the functions listed are the most common, keep open to any and all possibilities. For example, the student may exhibit emotional outbursts on Monday not because of what occurs in school on Mondays, but rather to vent frustration and anger over things that occurred at home on the weekend. Or a student may misbehave at the end of the week and especially before vacations because of anxiety about the upcoming separation from the security of school and a caring staff. Remember that whatever you and the teacher come up with here is simply a hypothesis, not a diagnosis. As you move toward intervention selection, keep your hypothesis in mind and design an intervention that will address the function, making it possible for the student to succeed and get her needs met in positive ways. If the intervention that you develop and implement is not successful, you may wish to revisit your function hypothesis as one part of the analysis about where to go next with the intervention plan (Crone & Horner, 2003; Ingram, Lewis-Palmer, & Sugai, 2005; Newcomer & Lewis,

2004; O'Neill et al., 1997; Sprick & Garrison, 2008). That is, maybe the intervention did not work because the student is not seeking attention but rather lacks the skill to exhibit the appropriate behavior. So the next intervention might put more emphasis on teaching replacement behavior.

 Case Study Continued »

Teachers Mr. Gill and Ms. Thompson suggest that Jake probably uses mis-behavior to get attention. The noise-making and fidgety behavior, especially during independent work, point to Jake's attention-seeking habits. They also believe that he is not entirely in control of his emotions, so volatile situations occur when Jake tries to vent frustration and anger about personal situations such as when his mom is sick.

STEP 5   List at Least Three Student Strengths

It is essential at this stage of intervention planning to identify the student's positive attributes. It is easy for the teacher of an at-risk student to become so frustrated by the everyday battle of interacting with and teaching the student that the teacher forgets that the student has positive qualities. The power of any intervention will be greatly increased by focusing on student strengths and the possibility of change rather than highlighting the frustration of working with such a student (Seligman, 2002; White & Epston, 1990).

Listing student strengths may also change the nature of how the problem will be addressed. Consider the teacher who describes her eighth-grade student by saying, "He's a smart aleck. He always makes these rude comments." Without hearing the student's strengths, the interventionist might move directly to a plan to reduce the frequency of this student's disruptions. However, when asked about the student's strengths, the teacher identifies that the student is very academically capable, is quite funny, and thinks on his feet. The problem is that the student sometimes uses his verbal wit and abilities to make cruel comments. He wields a level of power with his sharp, fast, and on-target humor that can make people either laugh or cry. To be effective, the intervention should increase the strength and power the student feels by using his strengths in positive ways. As a result of building on strengths, the problematic mis-behavior may just go away, and the strength-based behaviors are more likely to take over more of the student's behavioral repertoire (Karwoski, Garratt, & Ilardi, 2006; Seligman & Csikszentmihalyi, 2000; Tedeschi & Kilmer, 2005).

> The power of any intervention will be greatly increased by focusing on student strengths and the possibility of change.

Case Study Continued »

> *Jake's teachers identify him as academically adequate. They list one of his strengths as being a hard worker. Although he doesn't earn A's, his work is always at least average. Mr. Gill mentions that Jake gets most of his work done, and when he isn't angry, his interactions with adults seem to be fine. Ms. Thompson notes that Jake is on the baseball team and is a good player.*

STEP 6 Determine the Teacher's Goal for the Student

The purpose of this section is to clarify what the teacher hopes to accomplish through the intervention. This is a pivotal point in the intervention planning process. The focus shifts from what is known about the past up to this point to what the teacher wants things to be like in the future. The skilled interventionist recognizes this juncture and carefully guides the teacher toward developing a clear, reasonable, and achievable goal for the student's behavior.

Narrow the goal. If the intervention won't solve all of the student's problems and the teacher can pick only one or two major categories, what would he or she most like to see change? If you are dealing with a student who has many problems, where are you going to start? It is important to identify objectives that will allow the student to focus on one or two areas of improvement and to remember that objectives should be ambitious but obtainable (Alberto & Troutman, 2006; Howell & Nolet, 2000). Overly ambitious goals might be revised to reflect more intermediary goals. With multidimensional problems, limit the scope of what everyone hopes to accomplish. For example, if the student needs to get to school on time, use better hygiene, stay on task, learn to complete academic work, learn new social skills with peers, and learn to work cooperatively in the classroom, having intervention goals to change each of these would be overwhelming. By narrowing objectives and beginning with obtainable goals, troubled students have a greater chance of success. Once the student experiences success, many secondary problems resolve themselves and/or the positive momentum makes the other problems more amenable to future intervention efforts.

Because the purpose is to clarify the teacher's goals, the interventionist should determine not only what the teacher hopes to accomplish but also what the teacher "can't live with any longer." Listen carefully to find out what the teacher wants. When a teacher feels cut off, the collaborative nature of planning may be damaged.

> With multidimensional problems, limit the scope of what everyone hopes to accomplish.

By listening to and writing down all the things the teacher says, you imply that you value the teacher's perceptions. Although the objectives may need to be adjusted later to ensure they are obtainable goals, it is important to get the teacher's perspective on what are the most disruptive and "impossible to live with" behaviors (Tharp & Wetzel, 1969). Ask the teacher to think about what behaviors most get in the way of teaching effectively. Student success is determined to a large extent by the teacher's perceptions. Therefore, an intervention must focus not only on improving student behavior but also on addressing any misbehaviors that the teacher cannot tolerate. Conduct the process as an advocate for the student but also make it clear that you are an equal advocate for the teacher—that you want the intervention process to be win–win for both parties (Kratochwill et al., 2002; Feldman & Kratochwill, 2003).

Establishing the goal of the intervention will be a cooperative process that at this stage is largely determined by the teacher. Encourage the teacher to be a bit selfish in this stage of planning—"What do you need to get out of the intervention?"—because any intervention that has teacher support will have a greater likelihood of success. However, if the teacher wants to change too many of the student's behaviors, you may need to help the teacher narrow the scope of the initial intervention. Often, focusing on and improving one pivotal behavior will have a positive effect on several other problem areas (Stokes & Baer, 1977). On the other hand, if the intervention plan tries to focus on too many goals, it may be overwhelming to the student, but it is even more likely to be overwhelming to the teacher (Forman & Burke, 2008). Other recommendations for selecting target behaviors include (Hawkins, 1986):

- Choose the most pivotal behaviors.

- Choose behaviors with more general utility over highly specific behaviors.

- Focus on building appropriate behaviors.

- Consider behaviors that will give the student increased access to naturally occurring reinforcers and/or behaviors that the student would like to improve.

Work for clarity. When the behaviors to be changed can be narrowed and specified as much as possible in this stage of planning, it makes the next steps significantly easier. The goal of the intervention must be a specific observable behavior, such as "Help Mark learn stay in his seat during class," and not a general label or conclusion, such as "Stop Mark from being so fidgety." Encourage the teacher to use objective descriptions of the student's situation and to avoid jargon and generalizations. By moving from subjective labels or conclusions to objective descriptions of the problem, logical objective goals are more likely to emerge (Crone & Horner, 2000; Deno, 2002). Following are some specific examples of each:

An intervention must focus not only on improving student behavior but also on addressing any misbehaviors that the teacher cannot tolerate.

Conclusions	Objective Descriptions	Goal of Intervention
Sara is really lazy.	Sara has completed only one of eight assignments and has not turned in any homework.	Sara will complete in-class assignments and homework.
James is totally out of control at recess.	James run through the games other students are playing. He pushes others, and he will not follow directions of the playground assistants.	James will follow directions of the playground assistants, and for two weeks during recess he will be assigned to a specific game that will be monitored closely by one of the assistants.
Mariah doesn't seem to have any confidence.	Mariah does not ever talk with other students and talks with adults only when they initiate the contact.	Mariah will learn social skills that will result in her initiating interactions with both students and adults.

Prompt the teacher to use numbers to describe the severity of a problem. The use of numbers is objective and can help define the goal of the intervention. Stating timelines and degrees of goal accomplishment is also useful. For example, if a student has fits of anger and tantrums 10–15 times a day, it would be unrealistic to try to eliminate all outbursts within a week. Success would be impossible. Instead, the goal might be to reduce the average number of tantrums each week for the remainder of the year. The following are a few examples of possible goal statements with timelines:

- Within four weeks, the student will be able to complete at least 80% of her classwork every day.

- Within two weeks, the number of disruptive acts will be reduced by 50%, and within two months, the number of disruptive acts will decrease by 80%.

- The student will learn to stay calm and manage his anger without screaming, hitting, or engaging in aggressive acts. Each month, the number of disruptive incidents will be lower than in the previous month.

Stating the goal of the intervention in observable and measurable terms establishes criteria that the interventionist and teacher can use to determine the success or failure of the intervention. If the goal can't be counted or measured somehow, it may be too broad or subjective. The interventionist should guide the teacher in redefining her goal for the student's behavior.

If the goal can't be counted or measured somehow, it may be too broad or subjective.

Case Study Continued »

Interventionist: (Mr. Bickman)	At this point, I'd like to find out what you hope to accomplish with an intervention plan. I'd like to get your input on what you see as the most immediate things you would like us to work on with Jake. Which behaviors would you like to see Jake focus on changing?
Teacher 1: (Ms. Thompson)	I know what I don't want him to do, but there are too many things to try and change all at once.
Interventionist: (Mr. Gill)	Let's begin with what you would like Jake to accomplish.
Teacher 1:	I guess I'd like to see him less desperate for attention. I want him to feel valued and happy with his talents. I think he wouldn't alienate the other students as much. He wouldn't feel as much anger and need to turn to hostility. It might reduce some of his annoying little behaviors like the pencil hockey. I don't think Jake recognizes his strengths. He is a good student and a good athlete. I hate to see all of that go to waste. Learning to value himself isn't very specific, but I really want to lobby for that goal.
Interventionist:	Let's think about how that broad goal could be translated into something more specific. Would you consider it progress if Jake were to make fewer disparaging comments (self-putdowns) while increasing the frequency with which he makes positive comments about himself and his abilities?
Teacher 2:	Sure, I think that would be great progress.
Interventionist:	I have that down for a start. Now let's think about what you would rather not live with anymore.
Teacher 2:	I can ignore the rude comments to me, but I don't want Jake to bother the other kids. Some of them have learned to ignore his comments, but others are really bothered by his hostility.
Interventionist:	That helps narrow this down. Would you say the least tolerable behaviors involve verbal hostility toward and harassment of other students?

Teacher 2:   Yes.

Interventionist: We might also say that a goal for what we want to happen is for Jake to respect other students. He can show respect by reducing the annoying and rude behaviors. We can define examples of these in a few minutes. We can monitor to see if he reduces the sarcastic comments and teasing and if he works on not grabbing things from others. I think we should consider creating a timeline for how much progress we would like to see from Jake once the intervention begins. This will help us figure out if the intervention is successful. I see from his previous frequency count that he is rude or disruptive an average of 15 times a day. We need to figure out a reasonable reduction number we think Jake could achieve over the next couple of months.

STEP 7   Identify Methods for Collecting Data and Evaluating Progress

Look at the goal that was developed in the previous step and determine how data will be collected and recorded to track the intervention's progress. This is where behavioral training comes into play, because you will need to come up with a clear, definable, measurable goal and recommend a process for measuring intervention effectiveness. If the goal is not defined in terms of measurable and observable behaviors, it is important to go back to Step 6 and redefine the goal.

Identify at least one source of objective data collected on the goal behavior or on each separate goal, if there is more than one (Alberto & Troutman, 2006; Crone & Horner, 2000). You may simply be able to continue or modify monitoring procedures that are already in place, or you may need to develop a new system. To effectively monitor intervention plans and avoid misperceptions in the data, two independent means of evaluating progress are recommended. When selecting evaluation procedures, try not to overburden teachers. Objective data collection might include any of the following methods.

Quality ratings. Ratings on the quality of student behavior can provide valuable information. Although this procedure has a subjective aspect, rating scales are usually accompanied by criteria for judging student behavior, which makes the evaluation more specific and clear. Following is a sample rating scale (Figure 7.1) for a student who is learning to follow directions.

> Identify at least one source of objective data collected on the goal behavior or on each separate goal.

Figure 7.1
Sample Rating Scale

Please rate the student's behavior between 8:30 and 11:30 a.m.

5 = Followed all directions pleasantly and cooperatively

3 = Followed some directions pleasantly and cooperatively

1 = Failed to follow directions and was uncooperative

Monday____ Tuesday____ Wednesday____ Thursday____ Friday____

Work products. When the goal of an intervention is to increase the quality or quantity of a student's work, the evaluation procedures should consider the student's work. The data used may include the percentage of assignments completed, test scores, grades, and number of written words in a journal. In most cases, this does not require additional work for teachers, only periodic analysis of data already collected. In other words, a teacher's grade book may provide a major source of data on any problem that involves work products.

Self-monitoring data. Some intervention plans involve student self-monitoring. For example, a student may record the number of times he raises his hand and the number of times he blurts out in class without raising his hand. The teacher or interventionist may also need to conduct periodic assessments to ensure that the student is accurately recording his own behavior. The data that the student collects should also be monitored by the teacher or interventionist to assess improvement. For example, initial data may show that the student blurted out answers 10 times during a half-hour discussion and never raised his hand. After implementation of the district's intervention for self-monitoring and self-evaluation, the student's data may show that he raised his hand 50% of the time and blurted out responses 50% of the time. Although this is not perfect, the student is clearly making progress. (For more information about a self-monitoring intervention, see Intervention K in *Interventions* or consult other evidence-based sources.)

Data from a reinforcement system. If the intervention plan includes a reinforcement system, this system will provide information about the effectiveness of the intervention. Any reinforcement plan should include a method for determining whether the student earns a reinforcer. For example, the teacher may give the student a plus mark for every 15-minute period in which the student behaves positively and a minus symbol for every 15-minute period in which the student engages in misbehavior. The total number of pluses and minuses can be charted each day to determine the student's degree of success. It is likely that your district has a protocol in place for structured reinforcement, but if not, see "Intervention O: Structured Reinforcement Systems" in *Interventions* for more information about how to set up such a system.

Frequency data. During observation, a count can be taken whenever the student engages in a particular behavior (e.g., the number of times the student gets out of her seat in a day or the number of times the student interacts disrespectfully with the teacher). The teacher might make a simple tally of the number of times the student engages in the behavior. To take frequency data, for example, the teacher might carry a small index card in her pocket. Whenever the student engages in the targeted behavior, the teacher makes a tally mark on the card. If the student engages in tantrums, the teacher might keep a record on her calendar of the number of tantrums per day.

Duration data. Evaluation information might also include the amount of time a student engages in a particular behavior—a duration count. For example, if a student engages in tantrums, the teacher might record the number of tantrums—a frequency count—and use a stopwatch to track the duration of each tantrum. At the end of the day, the teacher has a record of the amount of time the student spent in temper tantrums. "Joey had three tantrums today for a total of 58 minutes."

Latency data. Sometimes it is appropriate to note latency—how much time it takes for a particular behavior to begin after a stimulus occurs. For example, if a student has trouble following the teacher's directions, it may be appropriate to record the length of time between when the instruction was given and when the student begins to comply.

Audio or video records. Audio or videotapes can provide effective documentation of changes in student behavior. Recordings are made both before the intervention is implemented and then at periodic intervals after implementation. Pre- and post-intervention tapes can be examined to determine whether there are qualitative and/or quantitative changes in student behavior. Frequency, duration, and latency data can be obtained from recordings.

If you are considering recording as a part of the plan, be sure to check with your building or district administration to determine any policy or legal restrictions on doing so. Some jurisdictions have strict confidentiality restrictions on the use of audio and video recording—whether you can do it, and if you can, what you can use the recording for and what you cannot. Make sure your actions comply with district policy and state law.

The interventionist can also ask the teacher if he would like an objective, systematic observation for additional data. Observations can yield information regarding the frequency of a negative behavior, the amount of time the student engages in the behavior, and the length of time that elapses between the stimulus and when the student engages in the behavior. Each of these procedures—frequency, duration, and latency—yields important objective data that will help evaluate the effectiveness of an intervention. To determine progress, observations should be scheduled to take place before the intervention begins and then periodically after its implementation. To increase the usability of data collected by outside observers, it may be helpful to schedule observations for times when the student has the greatest difficulty, with follow-up observations scheduled for the same time periods and for the same lengths of time (Hintze, Volpe, & Shapiro, 2008; Salvia & Ysseldyke, 2004). See "Intervention D: Data Collection and Debriefing" in *Interventions* as one source of information about effective methods and tools to collect and evaluate data.

👁 SUBJECTIVE PERCEPTIONS

One method of evaluating the effectiveness of an intervention is to gather subjective impressions from the teachers, parents, and students involved. Is the situation better, the same, or worse? This is the easiest and least time-consuming evaluation procedure. Although subjective perceptions alone are not sufficiently reliable, a clear picture of the intervention's effectiveness generally emerges when they are used in conjunction with another evaluation procedure.

If subjective impressions are used as a measure of effectiveness, the plan should specify how, when, and from whom opinions about student progress will be solicited. Anecdotal records and/or interviews provide subjective evaluations. For example, the interventionist might conference with the teacher and student after two, four, and six weeks of implementation to determine how the intervention is working.

 Case Study Continued »

Although Jake's behavior is already being monitored by a simple frequency count, the interventionist and teachers decide that they want to change the monitoring procedure to take into account the intensity of each disruption. They decide to continue counting disruptions and add a rating scale in which each disruption is ranked as 1) minor, 2) moderate, or 3) angry/hostile. This system allows the intervention team to see if progress is being made in terms of a reduction in either the frequency or the intensity of disruptions. If the total frequency remains the same but the number of angry/hostile interactions decreases, progress is being made. With a simple frequency count, it might be easy for the team to overlook this progress. Similarly, if the record shows a decrease in the frequency of disruptions but an increase in the number of times Jake reaches level-three intensity, it probably indicates that the intervention is not working as planned.

After realizing that monitoring and recording the frequency and intensity of the disruptions will be challenging, Jake's teacher Mr. Gill agrees to have "reducing the disruptions" be the goal of intervention. He agrees that the other concerns about self-putdowns and increasing positive self-statements can be less important for now but might be a second intervention plan when the disruptions are under control.

This frequency/level information will be supplemented by periodic meetings that include the interventionist, teachers, and Jake to gather subjective data about each of their perceptions about the intervention.

Interventions rarely run a smooth and gradual course toward success; therefore, it is important to identify trends that will help determine whether the intervention is having a positive effect on student behavior. To recognize such trends, it may be useful to graph the evaluation data. Types of behavior that can be counted and graphed include:

- Number of times each day the student uses profanity

- Number of minutes spent in timeout each day

- Total number of minutes owed for delays in following an instruction

- Number of pluses, which represent specified periods of time on task, earned during the day

- Average ratings of "how hard I worked" for 15-minute periods throughout the school day

- Percentage of assignments completed

Graphs visually depict trends and help teachers determine whether their subjective impressions match what is happening (Alberto & Troutman, 2006; Alvero et al., 2001; Scheuermann & Hall, 2008). When a student's behavior is especially stressful for a teacher, data may be needed to help the teacher recognize progress. If a teacher is feeling despair, burnout, and a sense that her efforts are not making a difference, visual information that depicts progress can encourage the teacher to continue her efforts. Evaluation and graphing information will be used in Stage 4: Implementation to determine whether the student is making progress. For more information about data collection, see Chapter 5, "Data-Driven Decisions."

It is important to identify trends that will help determine whether the intervention is having a positive effect on student behavior.

STEP 8 Make Notes on Previous and Future Parental Involvement

Parental contact and involvement are necessary components of intervention planning. All too often, an interventionist brought into planning realizes that the teacher has never interacted with a student's parents. It is essential to try to bring parents in as partners in the earliest stages of the process. Parents have a right, both legally and ethically, to know when their child is having a problem. Such contact will also let parents know that the staff is concerned enough to initiate intervention planning and may result in interventions that are more effective than those developed without input from parents. By this point, parents should have been contacted and permission obtained for intervention planning. If this has not been done, contact the parents immediately before any further planning or action takes place.

Make note of what interactions with parents have been like in the past. How have parents reacted to indications that their student needs to change his or her behavior? What levels of support have been shown? Include any information that may have been provided by parents in previous contacts. Regardless of their level of current involvement, families should be brought into the process as much as possible. It is well known that children whose parents are involved consistently do better in school (e.g., Henderson & Mapp, 2002). You may be working with families who can't or won't function as partners, but they need to be invited nonetheless. Their wishes should be explored and their input valued.

Sometimes, parents will argue about whether a problem even exists. In these situations, you need to gently try to get the parents on board. At other times, you may encounter parents who actively contradict the school's position that the behavior is a problem. ("You bet he slugs other kids! We tell him if anybody gets in his way to go after that sucker!") In this case, you will need to bring the family, student, principal, and possibly the police together (in the rare situation that a parent threatens the staff's physical safety) to explain that there are consequences in school and in life for problematic actions, despite the encouragement the student gets at home. "I know your dad has said . . ., but at school, we call it *assault*, and there are serious consequences." Even in these circumstances, school personnel should try to the best of their ability to involve the parents as partners, explaining the school's position and trying to get the parents on board (IDEA, 2004; Miller & Kraft, 2008; NCLB, 2001; Ysseldyke et al., 2006).

Families should be
brought into the process
as much as possible.

If involving the family seems difficult for whatever reason, consider involving the school's social worker. Although the teacher probably does not have time available to work on family-related issues that go beyond the student's classroom issues, the school social worker may know of district and community resources that may assist the family. Providing this highly skilled assistance may eventually make it easier for the family and the school to work as partners, moving together toward the student's success in school.

Case Study Continued »

> *Jake's mother has been contacted about the intervention planning meeting. She agrees that Jake needs help and wants the best for her son, but she says she cannot participate in the intervention planning and implementation because of her ill health. Jake's mother gives the planning team signed permission to try whatever interventions are necessary to address Jake's behavior problems. Mr. Bickman, the interventionist, makes note to talk about the home situation with a district-based social worker to determine if now is the time to involve a school social worker or if that would be premature at this stage.*

STEP 9   **List Other Interventions Tried and Their Effectiveness**

List any interventions that have been tried to date, how long they were implemented, and if they were successful. As you move through this section, actively work to prevent teachers from feeling defensive or alienated. If no action has been previously taken, make it clear to teachers that this is OK and that the information will help determine whether to start with one of your district's established early-stage interventions (or our Interventions A–F). If any interventions have been attempted with the student, ask to look at any records, contracts, or other data or forms that were collected during the intervention. It may be useful to contact the student's previous teachers to find out whether they had success with any interventions. When designing an intervention, it important to capitalize on anything that worked in the past and to avoid interventions that have proven ineffective.

❈ SCHOOLWIDE RTI

If your school is implementing a schoolwide response-to-intervention system, encourage teachers to keep a complete file on any student with whom an individualized intervention was attempted—both what worked and what did not. This will allow any subsequent intervention planning to be efficient because relevant information will already be collected and ready for review.

> When designing an intervention, it is important to capitalize on anything that worked in the past and to avoid interventions that have proven ineffective.

 *Case Study Continued* »

Mr. Bickman, the interventionist, notes that Jake drove his fourth-grade teacher crazy, but in third grade, he seemed to be OK. Mr. Bickman offers to talk to the third-grade teacher and ask if there was anything specific she did in working with Jake. This teacher mentions that Jake loves hanging out with the school custodian. She suggests making the custodian a mentor and using time with him as a positive reinforcer.

STEP 10   Make Note Of or Attach Any Other Relevant Information

This is the time to throw any other information on the table for consideration. Do you or the teacher know anything else that might be useful to consider? Ask the teacher if she has heard anything from other adults or students that should be looked into more thoroughly. Find out if the teacher has information about the student's medical history or involvement with outside agencies. It is important at this stage for all information to be considered and kept in play. As interventions are designed, implemented, redesigned, and re-implemented, any and all information about the student may prove to have value.

If you are conducting this meeting as a background session before a 25-minute planning period with an intervention team, conclude the meeting with the teacher at this time. Inform the teacher that the team will consider many intervention options at the planning meeting but that the first seven minutes will be used to review the problem, trends/patterns, and any data that was uncovered in the current meeting. If the intervention planning is conducted one-on-one, continue to the next stage of the intervention process.

Stage 2: Preparation

The third page of the Intervention Decision Guide includes a list of 19 possible interventions to consider, but your school or district may have its own list of protocols from which to choose. The first seven pre-interventions are easy for classroom teachers to implement and should probably be tried first before more intensive interventions are considered. Every teacher should be trained in these interventions, and, hopefully, some of them will have been attempted with the targeted student before the intervention planning meeting was called. For example, if nine students in a classroom are all having the same problem, the teacher must first look at his classroom management and try a universal pre-intervention. If eight out of nine of the students respond well to the change, designing an individual intervention for the remaining student becomes a manageable task. If the teacher has already implemented other early-stage interventions without seeing progress from the student, some of those interventions may be now included in the process of intervention consideration. But they will probably be supplemental to more intensive, highly structured interventions that have not yet been implemented. If early-stage interventions have not been implemented, they should be actively considered during current planning because they represent some of the most powerful and easy-to-implement interventions.

The next 12 interventions on the IDG target more severe and ingrained problems. They are designed to work with students whose behavioral problems require more intensive intervention. Intervention specialists such as school psychologists, special education teachers, administrators, and anyone involved in an intervention planning team should be well versed in Interventions G–R, but classroom teachers are not likely to be trained in these methods. These interventions will probably be implemented by or with the assistance of an interventionist, not solely by the classroom teacher. If your district uses any other approved interventions, you may wish to bring these to the table for consideration. You will also want to modify the IDG to reflect your district's list of evidence-based interventions.

STEP 1   Determine Which Interventions Might Be Applicable

Read through each statement in the first column. Each is a descriptor of the type of behavior that might be best addressed by the intervention listed in the next column. For each problem descriptor that matches behaviors the student exhibits on a regular basis, put a check mark in the "applicable" column. Leave the column blank if the statement is false. Another option would be to mark each statement as either true (T) or false (F).

Marking interventions as applicable does not mean you will implement every one of them. In some cases, only four interventions may appear to be applicable to the problem, and in other cases you may end up with 15 check marks on the first pass. As a general rule, it is somewhat better to have more checked interventions because it is likely that the initial intervention plan will include up to three interventions for a combined, multifaceted approach. If these fail and there are nine other interventions worth trying, you have fallback options. If only three interventions are marked, this puts great pressure on the success of the initial intervention.

STEP 2   Mark Any Interventions that Have Been Tried Previously

If any of the interventions have already been tried, indicate the date and effectiveness. Determine the following:

- Does the teacher believe the intervention was run long enough?

- Were there glimmers of success?

- Should the effort be part of a comprehensive intervention, or abandoned?

- Is any other relevant information available?

If the intervention was successful, or the teacher thinks it might be successful in combination with other interventions, mark the "applicable" column to include the intervention for consideration. Before abandoning any intervention as ineffective, determine whether it was implemented with fidelity for at least two weeks. Any intervention needs to be given that much time to assess its effectiveness.

Stage 3: Intervention Design

This stage of the planning process may take less time than information gathering, but it is a critical process. At this stage, the interventionist's skills come more into play in describing how some of the interventions might actually be implemented and suggesting combinations of interventions that may be particularly powerful in addressing the function of the misbehavior. Though the interventionist may provide suggestions, the teacher still has a deciding role in what the final intervention plan includes.

STEP 1   **Select the Interventions to Try First**

From the list of checked interventions on page three of the IDG, choose one to three interventions to implement. Selecting appropriate and effective interventions requires a thorough knowledge of the interventions. Interventionists should have training in all 19 of the interventions as well as in any other district-approved interventions. If you are not familiar with some of the interventions, it will be useful to take a day or two to become more familiar with them by reading through the corresponding chapter in *Interventions* or other comparable resources.

If the teacher is involved in this planning stage, explain more about each of the possible interventions: "If this is what you want to accomplish, let me tell you a little about each of the interventions that might help achieve the goal. We will work together to select interventions that have the highest likelihood of success and are acceptable given your needs and time constraints." The teacher may also wish to look at the intervention more closely, either in the *Interventions* summary or by exploring the corresponding chapter. At this stage, you will give huge credibility and decision-making power to the teacher. While you, as an interventionist, will guide the decisions, you are essentially saying to the teacher, "This is your intervention. I will help and guide you, but you will be living with it on a daily basis, so your input is essential."

When selecting interventions to implement, determine whether the intervention is related to the identified goal or desired outcomes. Next, determine whether the intervention seems manageable for both the student and the teacher and whether it is appropriate to the situation and the student. Finally, try to balance the following, sometimes competing, variables:

The amount of time and effort required from the teacher. Even the most cooperative teachers are likely to be overwhelmed by interventions that are too difficult to manage (Elliott, 1988; Galloway & Sheridan, 1994; Perepletchikova & Kazdin, 2005; Rones & Hoagwood, 2000). Classroom teachers cannot implement an intervention that makes it impossible to meet the needs of other students or the normal responsibilities of teaching. Furthermore, the ability of teachers to implement intervention strategies will vary greatly. When considering an intervention, think about how intrusive the intervention will be (i.e., how much teacher time and effort will be required). If an intervention seems unwieldy or if it would put undue stress on the teacher, it would not be wise to use that intervention.

For example, in some cases an intervention such as "Intervention J: Cueing and Precorrecting" is easy for a classroom teacher to implement. "It will be easy for me to cue Casey. When she begins to whistle, I can just put my finger to my lips." For some problems, however, the intervention may require too much vigilant attention from the teacher. "To prevent Eric from a full-blown tantrum, I need to catch his fidgeting symptoms early on. I honestly don't think I could monitor and cue him in time without disrupting my ability to teach."

A related issue is a teacher's willingness and readiness to work on an intervention. The interventionist should try to assess how frustrated the teacher is with the student and the problem situation. The greater degree of teacher frustration, the more the interventionist should look for solutions that do not require too much work from the teacher. Similarly, if the teacher seems resistant to an intervention for any reason, it is probably prudent to look for other options, because without high levels of classroom support, interventions are not likely to be implemented consistently (Finn & Sladeczek, 2001; Gable et al., 2001; Gunter & Denny, 1996; Rones & Hoagwood, 2000).

The amount of support available to the teacher. Given the right resources, interventions that seem unmanageable for the teacher to implement may, in fact, be possible. One way to avoid overburdening a classroom teacher is to have an administrator, special education teacher, school counselor, school psychologist, well-trained teacher assistant, or interventionist implement highly structured interventions. For example, if the teacher cannot manage cueing Eric's fidgety symptoms but a classroom aide is

> Determine whether the intervention seems manageable for both the student and the teacher.

scheduled in the room for 90 minutes a day, the aide might be assigned to monitor the student and cue when he shows his first escalating tendencies. Of course, this covers only the 90 minutes, but if the intervention shows dramatic progress, the teacher may see that the cuing process is not as difficult to do while teaching as she first assumed. Similarly, if "Intervention M: Teaching Replacement Behaviors" seems like it could have a high probability of success but is too time consuming for the teacher, the school counselor might be designated to conduct daily lessons.

The degree of student responsibility and motivation. Select interventions that encourage the student to assume the greatest amount of responsibility for change, but make sure that these interventions provide enough support and structure for success. Interventions with less support—requiring students to be more independent and responsible for change—take less time to set up, implement, monitor, and fade. Because students are required to take more responsibility, they are more likely to attribute success to their own abilities rather than feeling that adults made them change. These more independent interventions tend to be appropriate for relatively mild behaviors (ones that do not require a large change from the student), for more mature students, and for behaviors the student is motivated to change. For example, if a student interacts inappropriately with peers but wants to be accepted, "Intervention K: Self-Monitoring and Self-Evaluation," along with some instruction on how to interact positively with peers, might be appropriate. On the other hand, if the student does not seem to care whether other students like him, a more teacher-guided intervention such as "Intervention O: Structured Reinforcement Systems," along with instruction on how to interact, might be more appropriate.

Other interventions provide high degrees of structure and support for ensuring student success. They tend to require more effort and support from teachers and other involved adults. More time is required to set up, implement, monitor, and fade the intervention. However, because of the structure and support provided, there is a higher probability of success, especially with less mature or more troubled students. These interventions are appropriate when students have a long history of problem behavior and/or have fairly severe problems that are likely to be resistant to change. For example, a severely disruptive and impulsive student may not change her behavior based on the low structure provided in "Intervention A: Planned Discussion," because this intervention essentially requires that students hold themselves accountable for their own behavior. This student might respond better to the support provided in "Intervention O: Structured Reinforcement Systems" or "Intervention I: Managing the Cycle of Emotional Escalation."

> Select interventions that encourage the student to assume the greatest amount of responsibility for change.

STEP 2   **Summarize the Roles and Responsibilities of Everyone Involved**

To complete the planning process, the interventionist should summarize the plan in writing, listing each person's responsibilities. Good intentions and the best-laid plans are easily lost in the everyday bustle of school responsibilities, so you must clearly communicate that it is essential for each person to follow through on his or her part of the intervention plan (Crone & Horner, 2000; Rosenfield, 2008). The danger is that if one person says he will take care of an aspect of the plan and then forgets, the intervention may fall through the cracks and not get started for a month or more. In the life of a troubled student, this month is a critical time, and the delay may lead to a loss of essential learning and progress.

STEP 3 **Finalize the Intervention Plan**

Set times for follow-up meetings and observations, then tie up any other loose ends. Ask the teacher if you can check in after the first day or two of implementation to discuss progress and anything that was not anticipated. Schedule follow-up meetings at one-week intervals to look at data and assess the intervention plan. Does it need to be modified, increased, or faded? Once the plan is finalized, ask if there are any questions and indicate that a written summary of the plan with each person's responsibilities will be sent to all relevant team members. Although the IDG provides only two spaces for follow-up meetings, inform the teacher that you plan to continue the intervention process until the student is no longer having problems and that the people involved will do everything possible to reduce the possibility that the student will fall through the cracks. Conclude the meeting with words of encouragement and thank all participants for their assistance.

Stage 4: Implementation

The IDG has set the stage for a carefully designed, targeted intervention plan. During implementation, it is important for staff to follow through with their responsibilities. If any member of the intervention team is unable to continue with his or her responsibilities for any reason, it is essential that a replacement be found immediately so that support for the student continues throughout the process. The support provided by collaborative planning groups and individuals can ultimately make the difference in whether an intervention plan works or not.

STEP 1 **Check in With the Teacher at the Start of Implementation**

After the first day of implementation, the interventionist should conduct a quick check-up with the teacher. If there are any glitches in the plan or procedures that need clarification, they can be taken care of quickly. If necessary, schedule observations or assistance before the initial follow-up meeting that takes place a week after implementation begins.

> It is essential for each person to follow through on his or her part of the intervention plan.

STEP 2 Evaluate and Modify the Plan as Needed

In all subsequent follow-up meetings, the interventionist and the teacher will evaluate progress and make modifications to the plan, as needed. As a general rule, interventions should be scheduled to run at least two weeks. If the student is absent during part of that time, the intervention should continue for a longer period. In addition, follow-up must involve regular meetings with the teacher, the student, and the family to review data being collected to determine if the situation is getting better, staying the same, or getting worse (Crone & Horner, 2000; Kratochwill, 2008; Rosenfield, 2008).

Guidelines for maintaining, modifying, and fading plans are as follows:

Develop a new intervention plan if the student makes no progress or gets worse. When a student shows no progress over the course of a week or two, the plan may need to be redesigned. However, before abandoning a plan, look carefully at the data. If a student has been making good progress but blows it one day, a teacher may feel the student hasn't made any progress at all, when in fact the objective data shows the student has been making progress on most days. Evaluation information and the support of the interventionist can help the teacher and student stay on course.

Modify the plan to provide more support if progress is slow or comes to a halt. Because intervention planning involves trial and error, it may become apparent that the student needs more assistance. When you make changes to the plan, it is important that you make note of the planned changes and the date they will begin. This will allow you to make an objective decision about the effectiveness of the modified intervention.

Maintain the intervention plan if the student is making good progress. If the student is steadily progressing toward a goal, the plan should be maintained until the student demonstrates continuous and consistent success in achieving the goal. You want to ensure that the student has experienced a period of success long enough to make sure that the more naturalistic reinforcers in the setting (e.g., grade, praise, increased attention) are likely to maintain the behavior without additional intervention supports. This period may be a few weeks, but it is more likely to be a couple of months or the rest of the school year. With a student whose language skills are fairly sophisticated, the student can be part of the process of deciding if the intervention can be faded successfully.

Fade the intervention when there is a high probability that the student can maintain success. Fading is accomplished by gradually providing less structure and support. Some intervention plans are automatically faded as the student becomes successful. For example, cueing might be used less and less as a student demonstrates success on her own. Eventually, the cueing could be stopped completely.

CONCLUSION

Although the IDG can serve as a rudimentary functional behavior assessment, it is primarily a means of gathering as much information as possible from the most direct source and using it to form an initial plan. The teacher interacts with the student day after day. She is the one who is experiencing the problem, and she is the one who will carry out the initial intervention. The teacher's information, input, buy-in, and full participation are crucial to the success of any intervention in her classroom (e.g., Gable et al., 2001; Kratochwill et al., 2002; Roach & Elliott, 2008). The IDG also serves as guide to brainstorming everything that is known about the student. At this early point, all information is valuable and needs to be documented in a single place so that it stays in play throughout the intervention process.

Reproducible Materials

A copy of the following reproducible material appears on the CD. Permission is given for individual teachers, administrators, or other school personnel to reproduce this form for in-district use.

> Reproducible Form 7.1: Intervention Decision Guide: Teacher Interview

CHAPTER 8

The 25-Minute Planning Process

The Role of an Intervention Planning Team

This chapter outlines the 25-minute planning process, a timed step-by-step format that aids in the collaborative planning of behavioral interventions. This process has a specific structure that allows a problem-solving team (essentially a group of interventionists) to develop a worthwhile plan of action in less than half an hour, and it is appropriate to use when a systematic intervention plan would be helpful. The interventionist and referring teacher may use the 25-minute process for mild to moderate problems. If a problem has been referred to an intervention team, this process can be used as the first step in dealing with moderate to severe problems. Intervention teams are known by many names—CORE, CARE, SST, TAT, SAT, SWAT, RTI. If your school or district has such a team, those staff members may find this planning process useful.

The basic concept behind the 25-minute planning meeting is that team planning of interventions yields better solutions than individual planning (Chalfant, Psyh, & Moultrie, 1979). Without an adequate structure, however, team meetings may fall prey to the drawbacks of collaborative problem-solving. Team intervention planning is inherently more effective than individual problem-solving because two heads are usually better than one. Just as a physician who is puzzled by a medical problem is expected to collaborate with others to diagnose and treat the patient, a teacher who has tried a few interventions on his own should work with others to tackle difficult behavioral issues. Collaborative problem-solving in behavioral interventions is also particularly useful because every individual has specific blinders in the way he or she approaches behavioral interventions. Working with others who are not constrained by the same blinders and limitations is extremely useful.

☞ RESOURCE

If your staff needs training in conducting timed meetings, one tool to consider is our DVD *25 Minutes to Better Behavior, 2nd Edition*. This parallel program can be used as a staff development tool for any problem-solving team to train members in the process described in this chapter.

Case Study: Explore a Broad Range of Options

An interventionist is asked to work with a positive, highly skilled middle school teacher who is trained in adaptive P.E. The target student is a seventh grader with fairly significant developmental delays and cognitive deficits. The student also deals with weight issues, and the other students in the P.E. class tease him unmercifully. Whenever the teacher is nearby, the teasing stops, but as soon as she moves to another part of the room, the goading resumes. The teacher is aware of the problem because the target student does not have strong impulse control. As soon as the teasing starts, he goes ballistic and starts chasing his tormentors around the gym.

After discussing the problem, the interventionist suggests training the student in positive self-talk and how to ignore the teasing. The interventionist recently had success using these same techniques to reduce the teasing of an eighth-grade girl by 80%. During the following weeks, the intervention plan does not seem to be yielding positive results. The teasing still occurs, and the student continues to lose it each day in class. When the interventionist and teacher meet to revise the plan, they fall into the common "Let's do it more" syndrome, trying to improve the intervention by increasing its intensity and applying it systematically, despite indications that the intervention is not helping the student cope with teasing.

Eventually, the problem is referred to the school's problem-solving team. During the 25-minute process step that focuses on brainstorming intervention strategies, another teacher asks, "Have you thought about switching him to the other seventh-grade P.E. class? This might give the student a fresh start. You could prep the class in advance and let them know that because they are a kind and responsible group, you know they will welcome and be respectful of the new student in their class."

The interventionist and teacher agree that this is a great idea and implement it the next day. As soon as the student is moved, he begins experiencing more success. With less teasing to deal with, he is able to ignore it when it does occur.

This example demonstrates that despite the combined behavioral support skills of an interventionist and a teacher, certain intervention possibilities may go unconsidered.

When a team of individuals meets to weigh intervention options, their combined knowledge and perspective is greater than any one person's, so the subsequent interventions will be stronger and more interventions may be tried before possibilities are exhausted.

POTENTIAL DRAWBACKS TO COLLABORATIVE PROBLEM-SOLVING

The rationale behind the 25-minute process is that although collaborative problem-solving is often more effective than individual planning, it does have certain drawbacks if it is not conducted in a structured fashion. The more people involved in the meeting, the more ideas and perspectives will be gained. The concern, however, is that the meeting will become longer and longer as individuals get stuck at certain points in planning. The 25-minute planning process attempts to correct some of these potential problems:

Gripe sessions. Team meetings can easily turn into collective gripe sessions in which the majority of planning time is spent venting complaints about a student or a student's family. These comments can push the meeting to an unnecessary length. There is a point in any planning meeting when it is necessary to say, "Now we know the problems, so what are we going to do about them?" This is significantly easier to do with a predetermined structure and time limits.

Focus on corrections. The meeting's focus may become a discussion of consequences that cycles through menus of corrections that are probably not powerful enough to create lasting change. Members of planning teams often fall into the pattern of "We can try this, but he doesn't care about that . . . We might try this, but it probably won't work because he gets a lot worse punishment at home . . . ." The problem with these conversations is that correction is weak in the spectrum of intervention effectiveness. At best, correction will produce a momentary interruption in negative behavior that provides a chance to create reinforceable opportunities, but it will probably not bring relief from ingrained misbehaviors or yield long-term success (Bambara & Kern, 2005; Scheuermann & Hall, 2008). The 25-minute planning process focuses intervention meeting time on creating proactive plans and allots only a small amount of time for corrective consequences.

Meeting goes on and on. Another risk of collaborative problem-solving is that the meeting will stretch on for hours because of members' excitement and enthusiasm about creating a successful intervention. It is true that an intervention plan will be stronger after 90 minutes of discussion than it will be after 25. However, in the early stages of a problem, long planning meetings that detract from busy teachers' prep, grading, or personal time can leave teachers feeling resentment toward the student who took away important minutes of the day.

Long meetings will probably also leave members feeling like they have *the* plan rather than *a* plan. It's important to keep in mind that whatever the team members come up

When a team of individuals meets to weigh intervention options, their combined knowledge and perspective is greater than any one person's.

with, it is only one plan in an infinite number of plans. If members become overly invested in a single intervention, they may mentally give up on the student if the initial effort is unsuccessful. The sense of finality that may follow a long, open-ended meeting leaves little hope for other solutions to follow. Although a 25-minute plan may be flawed, the probability that members will be willing to try other options is much greater. Therefore, in the early stages of intervention planning, team members should set finite time limits for each stage of the process.

One concept behind B-RTI is that it entails multiple layers of problem-solving that match the intensity of the processes to the needs of the situation (Brown-Chidsey & Steege, 2005; Gresham, 2004; Howell & Nolet, 2000; Sugai et al., 2002). By setting time limits, the 25-minute process creates a problem-solving structure that, if the 25-minute meeting proves ineffective, allows for longer and more intensive processes such as those conducted by a full multidisciplinary team (which may spend two hours discussing one case). However, if every problem were to be worked on with this level of intensity, there would likely be long waiting lists of problems to be addressed.

THE PLANNING TEAM

Intervention planning teams are made up of school personnel who meet to plan and conduct interventions for students whose problems are moderate to severe enough to warrant targeted, structured intervention. Although planning teams should provide support to teachers who have questions about early-stage interventions (interventions that are easy to implement and should always be tried first), more in-depth services and assistance should be reserved for those students who have moved through early-stage interventions without achieving an adequate level of success (Brown-Chidsey & Steege, 2005; Gresham, 2004, 2005; Kame'enui, Good, & Harn, 2005; Sugai et al., 2002). That is, the student's needs were not met with early-stage interventions. Planning team members should be trained in interventions that range from general classroom management strategies to intensive, highly structured interventions. In contrast, because of the limitations on time for professional development, classroom teachers should be expected to learn methods for only the early-stage interventions. Considerations such as the organization of the intervention planning team, who will be involved, and how referrals will be brought to the team should be decided by each school or district according to the school's needs and resources. The following information may assist in these considerations.

Who should be involved in the planning team? Planning teams may be organized in a variety of ways. Your school or district should determine the organization in advance of implementing intensive interventions. If the school does not already have collaborative teams in place, you can talk with other staff in the building about how to get these structures set up. Chapter 3, "The Framework," has information about how to organize the range of problem-solving structures and resources within a building.

Core team. One possible structure is a core team that meets any time a student's behavior has become severe and persistent enough to warrant referral to the team. This core team may comprise several individuals, including school counselors, administrators, school psychologists, special education teachers, and any other teachers or support personnel whose training may help meet students' needs. However, even on an expert team like this, including one or two highly experienced and respected general education teachers is an excellent way to increase the team's credibility with the rest of the teaching staff. Each member of the core team should be familiar with a wide range of behavior management or academic strategies and any school- or district-sanctioned interventions (Allen & Graden, 2002; Kratochwill & Stoiber, 2000; Zins & Erchul, 2002).

Teacher-to-teacher team. Teacher-to-teacher problem-solving teams may also be used to address academic and behavioral concerns about students (Chalfant et al., 1979). These teams may be made up of general education teachers who teach the same subject or grade. If the school has a block structure, each planning team might include teachers who share students. During faculty meetings or predetermined intervention meetings, the team conducts a 25-minute planning process whenever a teacher on the team feels a need for collaborative assistance.

When schools use teacher-based planning teams, it is important that the team be familiar with the same range of interventions that would be used by a core team of administrators, school psychologists, and other personnel who have a wide behavioral intervention repertoire. However, it is unreasonable to expect classroom teachers to get training in or familiarize themselves with a large number of new strategies. If the school uses a specific intervention program or set of strategies, the team can divide up the interventions so that each person is responsible for knowing only a portion of the body of knowledge. In the example shown in Figure 8.1 on the next page, a standard protocol of interventions has been divided among team members. In this case, this list is from *Interventions: Evidence-Based Behavioral Strategies for Individual Students*, but your district may have a different list.

How will the team get referrals? Once a school has determined who will be involved with the planning team or teams, it is important to consider how these teams will get referrals. How and at what point will teachers ask for assistance? Will they make formal requests? Or, if a student has chronic office referrals, will she automatically be brought to the planning team's attention?

Document the red flags that will indicate when a student needs the planning team's expertise. Your district may have a policy in place, or it may fall to the leadership team to establish these protocols. Either way, the most important considerations are that the referral process is easy for teachers to access and that school leadership communicates the availability of this resource to teachers. (See Chapter 4, "Develop a Process," for more information about this subject.)

> Document the red flags that will indicate when a student needs the planning team's expertise.

Figure 8.1

Sample Intervention Assignments for Intervention Planning Team

EARLY-STAGE INTERVENTIONS	A. Planned Discussion B. Academic Assistance C. Goal Setting D. Data Collection and Debriefing E. Increasing Positive Interactions F. STOIC Analysis Intervention	All Team Members
HIGHLY STRUCTURED INTERVENTIONS	G. Managing Physically Dangerous Behavior and Threats of Targeted Violence H. Managing Severely Disruptive Behavior I. Managing the Cycle of Emotional Escalation	Group 1
	J. Cueing and Precorrecting K. Self-Monitoring and Self-Evaluation L. Positive Self-Talk and Attribution Training	Group 2
	M. Teaching Replacement Behavior N. Functional Communication O. Structured Reinforcement Systems	Group 3
	P. Defining Limits and Establishing Consequences	Group 4
	Q. Relaxation and Stress Management R. Internalizing Problems (Depression and Anxiety) and Mental Health	Group 5

BEFORE THE PLANNING TEAM MEETING

The following activities should all take place in advance of sitting down with all participants and attempting to conduct a meeting in 25 minutes.

If the 25-minute process is being used by groups of teachers helping teachers, such as in regular grade-level meetings, these "Before the Planning Team Meeting" steps are probably not necessary. For example, there is no need to assign a case manager because the 25-minute process is being used to generate ideas from teacher to teacher. However, when the process is used by a problem-solving team with more expert members such as a school counselor, administrator, and/or social worker, these steps are very important to ensure that the teacher is comfortable with and fully ready for the meeting.

STEP 1   **Assign a Case Manager**

Before team intervention planning begins, designate an interventionist as the case manager who will meet with the teacher to go over background information about the student and the problem. This case manager will serve as the main liaison between the teacher and the planning team and will usually handle other intervention issues such as observation, evaluation, and contact with parents. The case manager assignment should rotate to a different team member with each new student—this role may be time intensive. Because the teacher and case manager will need to work together closely, it is important to pay attention to staff relations when assigning the role of case manager. Negative associations may hinder the collaborative feel of the intervention and the information gathered. For example, if a teacher has a negative history with the school psychologist, the psychologist should not be assigned as case manager because the teacher needs to trust the interventionist and feel comfortable as she relates sensitive information about her dealings with the student. At the meeting, the teacher and case manager should sit together so the teacher has a sense that they are presenting the case together to the rest of the team and that they have a joint sense of ownership of the problem and the development of an intervention.

STEP 2   **Gather Background Information**

Prior to the planning team meeting, the teacher and case manager should meet to compile as much detailed information about the student, the problem, and the goal for the intervention as time permits. Work through the first section of the Intervention Decision Guide form (Stage 1: Background) to gather all necessary information—the when, where, and why of the student's misbehavior and what the teacher wants to see improve. (See Chapter 7, "Teacher Interview," for detailed information about how to use the form and conduct the background-gathering process.) This step may take 30 minutes or more, but it will help the interventionist and teacher efficiently summarize and relate all relevant background information to other participants during the planning team meeting.

If the teacher thinks it would be useful, the case manager may wish to set up a time to observe the student before the planning meeting. This may allow the interventionist to gather additional information not provided by the teacher. Or in the case of a teacher whose relationship with the student has become hostile, it may allow the interventionist to see trends or positive attributes that the teacher has not seen or shared. This may be a politically sensitive issue, but the interventionist must keep the student's needs balanced against the necessity of collaborating with the teacher. To implement an intervention that will help the student, the problem-solving team must keep the process teacher friendly and supportive.

Once all relevant background information has been gathered, the interventionist should fill out the top of the 25-Minute Planning Process Worksheet (Reproducible Form 8.1.) Either write down the relevant background information or make copies of the filled-out portion of the IDG for each member of the planning team. Then make copies of the 25-Minute Planning Process Worksheet for each participant, including the teacher, parents, and student, if they are going to be involved in the meeting. A blank reproducible version of the worksheet is available on the CD.

 Case Study: Off-Task Behavior

Charlie is a fourth-grade student who is struggling in school because of her constant off-task behavior. Charlie's teacher, Mr. Winfrey, sends a note to one of the designated school interventionists to see if he can get some assistance with Charlie's behavior. Because of her past positive working relationship with Mr. Winfrey, Ms. Trent is designated as Charlie's case manager. They meet for an initial discussion of how to proceed.

Case Manager:
(Ms. Trent)
Mr. Winfrey, I got your note, and I thought we might be able to set up a time to talk about Charlie's behavior.

Teacher:
(Mr. Winfrey)
I need to bounce around some ideas. I'm not getting anywhere and I'm almost at the end of my rope.

Continued on p. 185

Reproducible Form 8.1 (p. 1 of 2)

SAMPLE

25-MINUTE PLANNING PROCESS WORKSHEET

Charlie Metzger   _10_   _4_   _____
Student   Age   Grade   Date

Ms. Trent   _Mr. Winfrey_____
Interventionist   Teacher(s)

....

Starting Time _____

Step 1: Background (5 minutes)   Stop _____

• Describe the presenting problem. Identify when, where, how often, how long, etc. the problem occurs. _Charlie has diffi-_
  culty working independently. She wanders aimlessly and bothers other students.

• Identify student strengths.   _Social skills–she has lots of friends_

• Identify strategies already tried.   _keeping her from recess to finish independent work._

Step 2: Problem/Goal/Data (4 minutes)   Stop _____

• Narrow the scope of the problem and identify a goal. _Wandering around, off-task._
  Goal: Learn to manage work time and space.
• Identify what form of data will be used to track progress toward the goal.   _Self-monitoring system_

Step 3: Corrective Consequences (2 minutes)   Stop _____

Determine whether irresponsible or inappropriate behavior will be corrected or ignored, or whether a consequence will be implemented.
Refer to the menu of possible correct consequences as needed.

  Ignored

Step 4: Responsible and Irresponsible Behavior (4 minutes)   Stop _____

Provide examples of responsible behavior and/or student strengths to encourage. Provide examples of irresponsible behavior to discourage.

Responsible Behavior	Irresponsible Behavior
Any quiet movement within her office space _Raising her hand and asking permission to leave office space (sharpen pencil, turn in work, and so on)_	_Leaving "office" work space without permission_ _Any loud noises, such as pounding her desk._

Reproducible Materials Blank copies of the forms are provided on the CD. Permission is given for individual teachers,
administrators, or other school personnel to reproduce any form labeled "Reproducible Form" for in-district use.

Reproducible Form 8.1 (p. 2 of 2)

SAMPLE

Step 5: Proactive Strategies (4 minutes)   Stop _____

Brainstorm strategies to encourage responsible behavior. (Brainstorm, don't evaluate.) Refer to possible proactive strategies menu as needed.

- Use a point system that allows Charlie to earn points for special privileges.
- Use a check-and-correct card that her parents have to sign every day.
- Have Charlie set goals for her own behavior every day.
- Try self-monitoring system in which Charlie observes and evaluates her own behavior hourly.
- Have the school counselor work with her and teach her responsible behavior.
- Use a question-card strategy.

Step 6: Proactive Plan (3 minutes)   Stop _____

Select a manageable set of proactive strategies to implement.

Self-monitoring office work
Question-card strategy
Positive interactions—mother will read to Charlie before bedtime

Step 7: Final Details (4 minutes)   Stop _____

a. Evaluation: Identify at least two ways to determine if the plan is working.

1. Mr. Winfrey will track positive interactions with Charlie.
2. Charlie will complete self-monitoring form.

b. Support: Identify things other adults can do to assist the student and teacher. (Be specific—who, what, where, and when.)

Office staff and teachers can acknowledge Charlie in noncontingent ways.
Mrs. Metzger will read to Charlie at home before bedtime.

c. Plan Summary: Identify each person's responsibilities and when actions will be taken. Identify who will discuss the plan with the student and when. Schedule follow-up.

Who	Responsibilities	Date(s)
Mr. Ingram	Give Mr. Winfrey self-monitoring booklet	
Ms. Trent	Teach Mr. Winfrey's class to ignore off-task behavior	Tuesday, 9 am
Mr. Winfrey	Set up office space and self-monitoring sheet for Charlie	Monday, lunchtime
	Bulletin board project	Next Monday, after school
	Set up positive interaction monitoring system	

Discussion With the Student

Who _Mr. Trent and Mr. Winfrey_   Date _11/21_   Time _lunch time_

Follow-Up Meeting

Who _Mrs. Metzger, Mr. Winfrey, Ms. Trent_   Date _12/9_   Time _3 p.m._

Case Manager: (Ms. Trent)	Can you fill me in briefly on what the problem is so that we can decide how to proceed?
Teacher: (Mr. Winfrey)	It's hard to sum up, but I guess Charlie's overall problem is not being able to work independently.
Case Manager:	Have you talked to Charlie and her parents?
Teacher:	Yes. Charlie always says she'll try, but nothing changes. Her mom just makes excuses and doesn't have any suggestions.
Case Manager:	Would her mother agree to our setting up a plan for her?
Teacher:	I think so. She's protective, but she wants the best for Charlie.
Case Manager:	Do you want this to go to the child study team?
Teacher:	I don't think this warrants a referral yet, but I do need some help.
Case Manager:	If you can wait a day or two, I'd be happy to schedule a 25-minute planning meeting with the team. You and I should find a time to meet and go through some detailed background information about the problem and what you would like to accomplish with an intervention. Do you think it might be helpful to have me watch to see what she does during independent work times? I know that you are interacting with your other students, so it must be hard to keep an eye on Charlie.
Teacher:	That would be great.
Case Manager:	We should also let Mrs. Metzger (Charlie's parent) know that we would like to develop a plan to help Charlie and that I will be involved in the process. Would you like her to join us in the planning meeting?
Teacher:	I hadn't thought about it. I'll call her and sound her out.
Case Manager:	If she doesn't come to the meeting with us, you can tell her that I'll call and let her know what we've come up with. That way, I can make contact, and she'll know that Charlie has both of us as advocates, not adversaries.

STEP 3   Get Parents' Permission and Invite Them to Participate

It is essential, both legally and ethically, to keep parents informed throughout the intervention process (Comer & Haynes, 1991; Deplantry, Coulter-Kern, & Duchane, 2007; Desimone, 1999; IDEA, 2004; Jacob & Hartshorne, 2007; Miller & Kraft, 2008; NCLB, 2001; Ysseldyke et al., 2006). Parents should be invited to be as involved as they want to be and should be viewed as partners from the earliest stages of intervention planning. In the initial meeting with the teacher, check to make sure he has discussed the problem with the student and parents. If this has not been done, do so immediately before any other steps take place.

Once the parents have been made aware of the teacher's concerns, explain the purpose of the team intervention process and invite parents to participate. When the case manager contacts the parents, it is essential that she explain the time constraints of the meeting and allow the parents to express their concerns in full in advance of the meeting. Otherwise, the parents may take up a large portion of the 25 minutes, leaving very little time to plan the intervention. If the case manager tries to keep the meeting on schedule by cutting the parents off, they may be alienated from the process. A pre-meeting discussion with the parents will avoid both scenarios.

If the student is older, say in high school, you may also wish to invite the student to attend the meeting. The effectiveness of any intervention is likely to be greatly enhanced if the student's input is taken into account (Arra & Bahr, 2005; Carr, Nicholson, & Higbee, 2002).

Be sure to obtain written permission from parents to conduct interventions, regardless of whether the parents choose to be involved in the planning. Some interventions may be unacceptable to certain families because of moral, religious, or other reasons.

> The effectiveness of any intervention is likely to be greatly enhanced if the student's input is taken into account.

STEP 4   Determine Time Limits

It is important to determine in advance whether the planning team will use time limits in the meeting. Although they are not essential, time limits will help keep the meeting productive and a reasonable length. Time limits may feel oppressive at first, so you may wish to set a longer time limit, such as 50 minutes total, for the first one or two times your team implements this process. Then for the next couple of cases, you could make it a 35-minute process. Only after becoming fully familiar with how the process works would you adhere to the 25-minute limit. This will take a lot of pressure off participants while they learn the process. Also, any time team members adequately complete a step in less than the allotted time, they can move immediately to the next step. For example, if they are scheduled for a 35-minute process but two of the steps go very smoothly, they may be done in 30 minutes. This would indicate that the team is getting close to achieving the fluency needed to operate within the 25-minute limit. See Figure 8.2: Time Breakdown for Planning Meeting for how to structure each step for different meeting lengths.

Figure 8.2
Time Breakdown for Structured Intervention Planning Meeting

	Minutes		
Step 1: Background	6	7	10
Step 2: Problem and Goal	2	3	4
Step 3: Responsible & Irresponsible Behavior	4	6	8
Step 4: Consequences	2	3	4
Step 5: Proactive Strategies	4	6	8
Step 6: Proactive Plan	3	4	8
Step 7: Final Details	4	6	8
Total Meeting Time:	**25**	**35**	**50**

STEP 5   Determine Job Roles

The assigned job role for each participant should be included in the written record of the referral/planning process. The problem-solving team should also make a point to rotate jobs so each member has an opportunity to become skilled at various roles and does not get burned out on any one role.

Team leader. Assign one person the role of team leader. The team leader will work to keep the agenda moving and keep participants on track in each step of the process. If conversation begins to stray from the topic at hand or participants begin to cycle on a subject, the team leader should gently prompt the group to return to the designated step.

Timekeeper. If time limits are kept, designate one person as timekeeper. Determine what method will be used to monitor time. One method is to use a timer. When the timer goes off, the timekeeper gently moves the group to the next step in the planning process. You may wish to set the timer for a minute before the time limit so that a one-minute warning can be given. Then reset the timer for one minute and promptly move on when the timer rings. A second method is to note when participants are ready to begin, estimate the start time for each step in advance, and quickly write down stop times for each step. If this method is used, the timekeeper needs to use a stopwatch, digital clock, or digital watch to monitor the time and guide the group though the steps according to the schedule. If the group completes a step faster than the designated time, the additional time can be used in the next step or to reduce the total meeting time.

Recorder. The recorder takes notes on all parts of the discussion. This person should not be the case manager or the referring teacher. These individuals need to be free to think, listen, talk, and participate without having to concentrate on taking notes. When designating a recorder, also consider the person's ability to multitask. The recorder needs to be able to take notes and participate at the same time, because the team will want to benefit from every member's expertise.

Mediator. The role of the mediator requires the most interpersonal skills. This person will function as both an observer and advocate for all participants. Emotions may sometimes run high at these meetings, and the mediator's role is to watch for the body language and facial expressions that indicate a participant feels alienated from or unhappy with the process. The mediator then addresses that person and tries to bring him or her back into the process. For example, if a parent suddenly sits back with arms crossed, the mediator might say something like, "I think Mr. Jones has some concerns about the way we're describing Sam's problem. Let's see if we can clarify and restate it."

STEP 6   Consider Setting Ground Rules

It may be useful to set ground rules with the planning team, either in advance of the meeting or immediately before the discussion begins. Ground rules might include:

1. Meeting will start and end on time.

2. Team members will arrive on time. If someone is late, the meeting will start without that person.

3. Commit to making the student's teacher feel welcomed.

4. All team discussions and disagreements will be respectful.

5. Team members should listen carefully and avoid side conversations.

6. Information discussed during a team meeting is considered confidential and should not be shared outside the team without the team's consent.

7. Team members should treat each other and anyone else attending the meeting with respect.

8. Stick to the agenda and follow time limits.

9. Minutes from the meeting will identify specific tasks to be done, including timelines and who is responsible for which actions.

THE 25-MINUTE PLANNING PROCESS

This section describes how to implement each step of the process shown on Reproducible Form 8.1: 25-Minute Planning Process Worksheet. This worksheet can be found on pp. 183–184 and on the CD that accompanies this book. You might want to print a copy for reference as you read through the remainder of this chapter.

START THE PLANNING MEETING

Convene the planning meeting by setting a positive and collaborative tone. Welcome each participant and establish an atmosphere of support and advocacy for the student. Hand out copies of the 25-Minute Planning Process Worksheet to each group member with the general student information completed. Although the recorder will be the only person to actively take notes on the form, it will be useful for all members to have a copy so they can follow along as you work through each step. If the interventionist has already collected background information from the teacher, you may wish to fill out this information on each participant's planning form before beginning the meeting. This will allow each member to reference the student's history as the team comes up with a plan of action.

If time limits and ground rules will be used, review the procedures. If any participants—such as parents, the student, or new members of the planning team—are unfamiliar with the 25-minute process, explain the format and procedure for structured time limits. Say something like, "When the timer goes off for each step, someone will call time, and we will immediately move on. This may seem rude or rushed at times, but we are using finite time limits that will help us come up with an initial plan of action that we can implement now, then develop further as time goes on. We can discuss any points that don't seem finalized at a later time if we feel it is necessary."

When possible, provide participants the option of following the agenda within the 25-minute period or proceeding without time limits. Without time limits, the meeting will be more casual and responsive to the needs of participants, but it is likely to last much longer. If participants decide to stay within the time limits, the meeting will move very efficiently. However, if the planning format hasn't been jointly agreed on in advance, staff or family members may feel rushed or railroaded into accepting an intervention plan. If family members are involved, special precautions should be taken to ensure that they feel they've been given the opportunity to fully participate (Henderson, Marburger, & Ooms, 1986; Miller & Kraft, 2008; Nord, Brimhall, & West, 1997; Ysseldyke et al., 2006).

> Without time limits, the meeting will be more casual and responsive to the needs of participants, but it is likely to last much longer.

Case Study Continued (Before the Meeting) »

Case Manager: (Ms. Trent)	We've decided to follow a 25-minute agenda.
Parent: (Mrs. Metzger)	What is that?
Case Manager:	The 25-minute format allows us to put together a plan for Charlie quickly, without waiting until we all have more time. Mr. Winfrey has another meeting in about 45 minutes. So if it's OK with you, we'd like to do some fairly focused planning. Then if you'd like, I can talk with you some more later.
Parent:	That would be fine. I know Charlie doesn't like school this year, and I don't see her making good progress.
Teacher: (Mr. Winfrey)	I'm excited about helping Charlie. I don't want her to feel like we are always complaining about her behavior. I'd really like to help.
Case Manager:	I appreciate everyone's cooperation. Mrs. Metzger has agreed to record stop times for each step. Estimated start time is 3:15. Then we'll have six minutes for Step 1, two minutes for Step 2, four minutes for Step 3, and so on. As we're talking, I'll try to gently guide us to the next step when our time is up. You can help me by also watching the time. My apologies in advance for the interruptions.

STEP 1 Background

In this step, the teacher and case manager describe the presenting problem and other relevant background information for the rest of the planning team. This is when the teacher and interventionist summarize the information that was gathered on the IDG. Get the process started by reiterating the nature of proactive planning and describing Step 1.

 Case Study Continued (Student Summary) »

Case Manager:	Mr. Winfrey and I worked through background information on Charlie's problem at our meeting on Thursday. We'll try to give you a summary of some important things we identified in that meeting, but I would like to invite you

to ask questions and help us get a deeper understanding as we move through the information. When we first talked, Mr. Winfrey said that he was worried about Charlie because she has difficulty working independently. As we talk here today, we'll try to get a handle on the problem so we can develop a plan to help Charlie become more independent. In Step 1, we want to discuss the problems, Charlie's strengths, and things that have been tried so far. Mr. Winfrey, why don't you begin by filling us in on what you see in the classroom?

As the teacher and case manager summarize the collected background information, other members of the team should be asking probing questions to gain a deeper understanding of the student's problems and abilities and what the teacher is facing on a daily basis. Discuss in as much detail as possible the student's strengths and what has already been tried, with or without success.

Teacher: Charlie has the greatest difficulty during independent work times. I worry about her because she doesn't seem to be able to get anything done unless I'm standing over her. She wanders aimlessly about, sharpens her pencil, gets a drink of water, and often bothers the other children.

Interventionist: How do the other students respond to her?
(Mr. Ingram)

Teacher: They don't seem to mind her interruptions. Charlie is very likable. She has a good sense of humor.

Interventionist: So one problem is that she wanders and bothers other kids, but one strength is her social skills.

Parent: Yes, Charlie has a lot of friends.

Teacher: Everyone likes Charlie, so she can easily pull other students off task. She doesn't harass anyone.

Interventionist: How does she do during instructional periods?

Teacher: She does better when I'm working directly with her in a small group or even when I'm teaching the entire class, if I remember to call on her often enough.

Interventionist: So being off-task is a problem during independent work, but not when you are around. How is the quality of Charlie's work?

Teacher: (Mr. Winfrey)	She gets it done if I keep her in from recess to do it. She does good work and seems capable, but she wastes so much time in class that she needs the extra time during recess. I don't mind giving up my break once in a while, but it's getting to be an everyday occurrence.
Parent: (Mrs. Metzger)	I think that's one of the reasons Charlie doesn't like school. She really enjoys her time with the other kids at recess.
Case Manager: (Ms. Trent)	We clearly need to come up with a different solution. Mr. Winfrey, is Charlie disruptive when she's at her desk?
Teacher:	When the whole class is working with me, she does fairly well. But during work times, she hums, sings, and talks to the other kids. I have her desk moved away from the other students, but it hasn't done much good because she gets up and bothers the other kids.
Interventionist: (Mr. Ingram)	How does she do in other settings—the hall, playground, music class?
Case Manager:	In P.E. and art she does just fine. Once in a while, she's been a little loud in the hallways and cafeteria, but nothing out of line. The problem is really in the classroom. Let's explore how she does with different activities in the classroom.

STEP 2   Problem/Goal/Data

Narrow the scope of the problem. Determine which behaviors are the most problematic or should be the focus of initial intervention efforts and prioritize them (Crone & Horner, 2000; Hawkins, 1986; Nelson & Hayes, 1979). If the student has hygiene problems, peer relation problems, anger management and self-control issues, academic deficits, and difficulty completing assigned tasks, you will not be able to correct all of the problems at once. A broad-based intervention plan that involves too many changes at once is likely to frustrate the student and teacher and yield fewer positive results. If you narrow the scope of the intervention to a focused plan that is truly manageable, you have the greatest probability of success. There is also a high likelihood that if the student begins to experience success and increased confidence with a targeted intervention, other behaviors may naturally get better without the assistance of an intervention (Angle, Hay, Hay, & Ellinwood, 1977; Hawkins, 1986; Stokes & Baer, 1977). Success breeds success. To identify priorities for the initial intervention, ask the following questions:

> If you narrow the scope of the intervention to a focused plan that is truly manageable, you have the greatest probability of success.

Which behavioral changes will help the student feel successful in the shortest period of time? An intervention plan should initially target changes that have the highest probability of success in the least amount of time. Once the student begins to experience success and to understand the value of positive behavior, the team can focus on more long-term problems that will require greater commitment, motivation, and effort (Ardoin, Martens, & Wolfe, 1999; Belfiore, Basile, & Lee, 2008; Mace et al., 1988; Piazza, Roane, Keeney, Boney, & Abt, 2002). For example, if a student has problems with peer interactions, academic difficulties, and a significant weight problem that is tied to low self-esteem, reducing the student's weight would not be the first target for intervention. Although it might be a worthy long-range goal, success might be difficult to achieve, and results would not be seen for a long period of time. The student is likely to experience success sooner if he works first on improving his peer interactions and academic skills. Once the student begins to experience the sense of satisfaction that accompanies success, helping the student with other problems becomes progressively easier.

Which behavioral changes will help the teacher see improvements in the shortest period of time? The second major consideration in identifying intervention priorities is to address problems that interfere with the teacher's ability to instruct and/or interfere with other students' ability to learn (Hawkins, 1986; Tharp & Wetzel, 1969). The more a problem interferes with the smooth operation of a class, the sooner the problem needs to be addressed. If a problem disrupts the natural flow of a classroom, there is a greater likelihood that the problem will escalate to more serious proportions or breed other problems. For example, a teacher who is frustrated with a particular student's behavior may become less interested in or optimistic about helping the student. As time goes on, the teacher may be less effective in teaching the rest of the class as a result of her stress and frustration with the problem student. In addition, other students may be distracted from learning, so it's important to prioritize interventions that address these types of problems.

 Case Study Continued (Narrow the Focus) »

Case Manager: In this step, we need to narrow the scope of the problems and decide what we think can be realistically accomplished. We don't want to create an intervention that overwhelms Charlie or that swamps Mr. Winfrey with extra work. We've already identified that this is primarily an independent work problem, don't you think?

Teacher: Yes. The more we talk, the more I think this is the biggest problem area.

> The more a problem interferes with the smooth operation of a class, the sooner the problem needs to be addressed.

Identify a positively stated goal. Once a focus has been determined, the team should help the teacher decide whether the goal will be to reduce a particular misbehavior or increase a positive behavior. For example, a student who constantly takes other students' things without asking needs to learn to reduce this behavior. On the other hand, the goal for a student who is painfully reserved in interactions with adults may be to increase positive interactions with adults.

Whether the goal is to reduce a negative behavior or increase a positive one, it's important to state the goal in positive terms. Although many intervention plans are designed to help a student overcome problems, a positively stated goal allows the student to take pride in her accomplishments. For the student who takes other students' things, "learning to be trustworthy by touching only your own things" can help a student develop a sense of self-worth, while "learning not to steal" may simply reinforce the student's sense of untrustworthiness. Similarly, "learning to respect the property of others" is a worthwhile goal, but "learning not to be destructive" is demeaning.

Also work as a team to define the goal in clear, observable terms. The goal should be stated in such a way that it can be measured—it should not be just a broad statement about behavior. For example, "to increase respect in the classroom" is too broad because it does not clarify the specific behaviors that need to change. An alternative statement such as "respond to teacher instructions in a respectful tone of voice or with no verbal reply" would be more appropriate. This level of specificity will help all involved parties clarify and follow the specific expectations of the goal as well as help with monitoring and evaluating the intervention (Alberto & Troutman, 2006; Crone & Horner, 2000; Fuchs, 1995; Howell & Nolet, 2000; Upah, 2008).

 Case Study Continued (Specific, Positive Goal) »

Case Manager: (Ms. Trent)	Let's review what we have identified as Charlie's work-related problem behaviors.
Interventionist: (Mr. Ingram)	Charlie wanders around the room playing with things like the pencil sharpener and talking to others when she should be working. She hums and makes noises at her desk. The net result is that she doesn't get her work done.
Case Manager:	Thank you. Mr. Winfrey, can you identify which behaviors interfere the most with Charlie's success and make it hard for you and the other students to get your work done?

> Whether the goal is to reduce a negative behavior or increase a positive one, it's important to state the goal in positive terms.

Teacher: (Mr. Winfrey)	I guess there are two major problems. She causes problems when she wanders around, and she is very off-task at times. Actually, I guess her biggest problem is wandering around. If she weren't roaming, maybe she'd be more on task, and if she were on task, she'd get her work done.
Interventionist:	What about the humming and other noises she makes at her desk?
Teacher:	They don't seem to bother the other students, and I don't think they would bother me if I knew she was getting her work done.
Interventionist:	If we made the initial focus of the intervention learning to stay in her assigned place, would that seem like a good starting place?
Teacher:	Yes, but what if she does not get her work done?
Case Manager:	Maybe Charlie's goal could be to learn to manage her work time and space. The outcome would be getting her work done.
Teacher:	Sounds good. Mrs. Metzger, what do you think?
Parent: (Mrs. Metzger)	I like that. We have the same problem at home when she does homework. She is all over the place and doesn't get it done.
Case Manager:	Good. Time to move on. We were a few seconds long in this step, so let's try to make it up in the next step.

Determine how to measure intervention effectiveness. Discuss how the success or failure of the intervention will be evaluated. Although subjective perceptions will play some role in this determination and it is important not to overburden teachers with time-consuming data collection methods, it is also necessary to gather objective data (Batsche et al., 2005; Salvia & Ysseldyke, 2004; Scheuermann & Hall, 2008; Upah, 2008). Two independent means of monitoring are recommended. Progress is not always obvious without specific measures, and detailed records will help with future intervention planning. In addition, one of the best tests for whether the goal for intervention is reasonable and behaviorally specific enough is whether intervention effectiveness can easily be measured and evaluated. Evaluation procedures may include counting a behavior, self-monitoring forms, the student's perceptions, observations from the interventionist, discipline referrals, truancy records, the teacher's grade book, records, and rating forms. See Chapter 7, pp. 159–162, for a menu of possible evaluation procedures.

Case Study Continued (Collect Data) »

Case Manager: (Ms. Trent)	We need to identify a couple of ways to determine if the plan is working. Let me suggest some ideas. One possibility would be to monitor the time Charlie spends out of her seat. You start a stopwatch when she leaves her seat, and then stop it when she returns to her space. The next time she leaves, you start the watch again. At the end of the day, you have the total number of minutes Charlie spent out of her seat. We could create a simple chart to record each day's total time, and then we could easily see if she is getting better or worse, or staying the same. Another evaluation procedure would be to see how you are feeling about things. Is this plan working? Is it feasible to maintain, or is it wearing down your patience? We could just have an informal talk about this once a week. A third possibility would be to have Charlie use a self-monitoring system and periodically check it.
Teacher: (Mr. Winfrey)	I doubt I'd remember to start and stop a watch, so I'd prefer not to do that one. It also would be problematic if she gets up for some legitimate reason and then gets distracted along the way. But I think a self-monitoring system would be good, and I will be monitoring work completion anyway, so that can be a measure. I think I'd also like to debrief with you once a week.
Case Manager:	Good. That's all we need for now.

STEP 3 Corrective Consequences

This step does not involve discovering any magic consequences that will solve the student's problem behavior. Corrective consequences tend to be weak interventions for reducing chronic to severe misbehaviors, although they can be effective when used in combination with proactive strategies (Hagopian, Fisher, Sullivan, Acquisto, & LeBlanc, 1998; Hanley, Piazza, Fisher, & Maglieri, 2005). Consequences may *make* a student behave, but they do not encourage the student to become responsible for her own behavior. The most effective intervention plans focus on proactive strategies (Carr et al., 2002; Hieneman, Dunlap, & Kincaid, 2005; Lewis & Sugai, 1999; Munk & Karsh, 1999). Because intervention plans are designed to teach students to be more responsible, only two minutes are given to this step in the 25-minute plan. The team should quickly brainstorm possible consequences and then have the referring teacher select ones that can be implemented consistently. Simply have the teacher choose a reasonable consequence from your menu of possible consequences—verbal reprimand, time out, time owed, ignoring—and move on. The hope is that other aspects of

> Consequences may *make* a student behave, but they do not encourage the student to become responsible for her own behavior.

the intervention plan will be powerful enough to reduce the frequency of behavior so that consequences will rarely be used.

Team members should have some familiarity with the concept of *function*—specifically, that any chronic misbehavior serves some function for the student. As the team explores possible consequences for the student's misbehavior, the hypothesized function should be taken into account and consequences that are likely to reinforce problem behavior should be avoided. For a more detailed explanation of function, see Chapter 7.

Reproducible Form 8.2: Implementing Corrective Consequences provides a menu of possible classroom-based consequences and suggestions for implementing them effectively. Consider having copies of this list available at your team meetings to facilitate this step. If teachers find the list useful, they can take copies with them.

In some cases, there may need to be differential consequences established for different categories of behavior. For example, the plan could involve ignoring a student's disruptive behavior but sending the student to timeout for noncompliance. The teacher should have the final say on what the corrective techniques will be for any given category of misbehavior (except for those behaviors that the administrator has determined should be sent to the office). The team is never telling the teacher what to do—its members are merely helping the teacher explore multiple possibilities.

 Case Study Continued (Establish Consequences) »

Case Manager:	We have two minutes to decide the consequences that will be implemented whenever Charlie engages in the irresponsible behaviors we listed. We aren't going to spend a lot of time on this step because we want to focus more on helping Charlie learn to work independently. Let's brainstorm some possibilities. I'll suggest a couple of ideas. You could ignore Charlie's inappropriate behavior or use gentle reminders. You could also have Charlie go to timeout.
Teacher:	I could have her owe one minute of her recess.
Interventionist: (Mr. Ingram)	How about a point system? If she exhibits an irresponsible behavior, she wouldn't earn a point for that time period.
Teacher:	I could keep her after school.

Continued on p. 200

Reproducible Form 8.2 (p. 1 of 2)

IMPLEMENTING CORRECTIVE CONSEQUENCES

SAMPLE MENU OF CLASSROOM CORRECTIONS

- Give a gentle verbal reprimand.
- Use a proximity correction.
- Keep a record of the behavior.
- Use planned ignoring.
- Reduce points (if using a point system).
- Implement a response–cost lottery.
- Assign time owed from recess or after class.
- Assign time owed after school.

- Assign a timeout at the student's desk.
- Assign a timeout at another location in the classroom.
- Assign an interclass timeout.
- Issue a demerit (3 demerits = afterschool detention).
- Have student fill out a behavior improvement form.
- Require restitution by the student.

TIPS FOR IMPLEMENTING CONSEQUENCES

Implement the corrective consequence consistently. When you implement a corrective consequence only some of the time, the consequence, no matter how severe, is not likely to change the behavior. In fact, it may make things worse than no consequence at all. Any time a student is able to violate a rule and not receive the designated consequence, he is likely to feel a sense of satisfaction. Getting away with misbehavior can be great fun, and the student may like to see how frequently he can engage in the behavior and not get caught. Teachers tend to implement corrective consequences based on an accumulation of misbehavior.

Ensure that the corrective consequence fits the severity and frequency of the misbehavior. Choose a consequence that is mild enough that you will be comfortable implementing it every time the student exhibits an irresponsible behavior. All too often, teachers pick a consequence that is so harsh they are unwilling to implement it when the occasion arises. For example, "LaVona, stop that because I do not want to have to give you a detention" is an indication of inconsistency. In this case, you are letting the student get away with it, but in some cases you may not.

Implementing Corrective Consequences (continued)

Whatever you choose, implement the consequence in the same way for all the behavior within that category and with any student who violates that rule. If you decide to deduct a point, all disruptive acts should result in the loss of one point. Do not create a situation in which some disruptive acts cost one point and some cost three. You will find yourself having to explain why you feel the acts deserve different penalties. If you decide to use time owed as a consequence for a student who tends to be disrespectful, have each infraction equal the same amount of time owed (for example, 15 seconds owed after class). Do not issue 15 seconds in some instances and several minutes in others. Also, keep in mind that a student may exhibit the behavior several times, and you probably cannot assign three detentions to the same student in one class period. But you can impose 15 seconds owed for each incident.

Implement the consequence using a neutral tone. Some students have learned that there is a high probability that they can make adults frustrated, hurt, or angry. For some students, this is virtually an invitation to do so as often as they can. When a student is seeking a sense of power, seeing an adult frustrated or exasperated can be highly satisfying. You must strive to implement corrective consequences unemotionally so your reactions do not give any students the idea that they can have power over you by misbehaving.

Interact with the student briefly at the time of the misbehavior without arguing. When a student breaks a rule, your interaction with that student should be brief. Simply state the rule and state the consequence. The student may ask you to explain and justify. Resist! Explaining transfers the power to the student and lets her know that she can disrupt class by misbehaving and by making you explain yourself. Any explanations should be self-evident from your instruction or can be analyzed in a follow-up with the student later. Sometime during the first few days of school, let students know that if anyone ever wants to speak to you about something they think is unfair, they can make an appointment to see you before or after school. Once you have made this clear, if any student tries to argue, simply remind him that he can make an appointment to see you and then resume teaching.

Although keeping interactions brief may be a difficult at first, you will find that it allows you to keep your focus where it belongs—on teaching and providing positive feedback to all students who are meeting your expectations. Remember that the frequency of your positive feedback must far outweigh that of your negative feedback. Think about the consequence you plan to use for a targeted misbehavior. If you cannot imagine implementing that consequence without lengthy explanations or negotiations at the time of the misbehavior, you should consider a different consequence.

 Reproducible Materials Blank copies of the forms are provided on the CD. Permission is given for individual teachers, administrators, or other school personnel to reproduce any form labeled "Reproducible Form" for in-district use.

Case Manager: (Ms. Trent)	You could send her to take a timeout in my room. From this list, what do you think would be the best option?
Teacher: (Mr. Winfrey)	I don't think keeping her in from recess or after school would work, and if I ignore her, that might be unfair to the rest of the kids. They need to get their work done.
Interventionist: (Mr. Ingram)	Actually, we could teach the other students to ignore Charlie's inappropriate behavior. What do you think?
Teacher:	You know, Charlie really does like attention—withholding it might be the best thing. I will need some help teaching the other kids how to ignore the behavior.
Case Manager:	I can do that. Mrs. Metzger, we won't teach the kids to ignore Charlie, but we will teach them to ignore her off-task behavior during independent work times.
Parent: (Mrs. Metzger)	I understand. Will Charlie?
Case Manager:	We'll make sure to explain this to her very carefully. Great. I think we have a plan for consequences. Mr. Winfrey, Mrs. Metzger, and I can talk after the meeting about how the ignoring plan can be implemented in a way that will be respectful to Charlie. Let's move on to Step 4 now.

STEP 4   Responsible and Irresponsible Behavior

In this step, participants look at the broad goal and clearly define the positive behaviors that will lead to achievement of the goal and the negative behaviors that will detract from it. Identify the line between the responsible behaviors that should be encouraged and the irresponsible behaviors that need to be reduced or eliminated by the application of whatever consequence was identified in the previous step. For some problems, this line is very clear and little time needs to be spent. For example, if a student does not turn in his homework, it is clear that responsible behavior involves handing in the work. With other problems, the line between desired and undesired behavior is very hard to distinguish, making it difficult to teach students expectations and difficult for teachers to implement the plan. For such problems, this step of intervention planning is perhaps the most difficult.

Consider a student for whom the focus of the behavior plan is to decrease disrespectful interactions with adults. If you don't define which behaviors constitute disrespect versus respect, the student will move into a hazy, unclear area in which sometimes a behavior is OK and sometimes it isn't. Teachers will implement the intervention plan inconsistently if this line is not clearly defined. Inconsistency can sabotage any other progress that is made in the intervention. Relative to the goal behavior, you will want only two categories of behavior—acceptable and unacceptable—with no gray areas in between. The interventionist must work with the teacher to be very clear about which is which.

Responsible behaviors include behaviors that are currently in the student's repertoire as well as behaviors that need to be learned, whereas the irresponsible category involves identifying the specific behaviors that will lead to corrective consequences. If the student is working on improving interactions with adults, responsible behaviors might include saying hello in the morning, using a respectful tone of voice, nodding when the teacher addresses the student, and answering patiently when the teacher asks a question. The irresponsible behaviors might include giving the teacher a dirty look, answering the teacher in a sarcastic tone, or mimicking the teacher.

If the student is working on managing his own in-class work, responsible behaviors might include listening to directions, writing down the assignment, getting started right away, and sharpening pencils before class. Irresponsible behaviors might include daydreaming while the teaching is giving directions, not writing down the assignment, and fooling around in the desk rather than getting started on work.

Proactive intervention plans focus on teaching the student responsible behaviors. This step will help adults teach students the behaviors they hope to see for goal achievement while providing clarity for the teacher about precisely when to apply corrective consequences for misbehavior (Alberto & Troutman, 2006; Baer et al., 1968; Fuchs, 1995; Sprick, Garrison, et al., 1998; Telzrow, 1995; Upah, 2008).

Team members should ask probing questions to help the teacher create a clear picture of the boundaries between what is acceptable and what is not. What if you ask the student to do something and he says OK, but his tone of voice is negative or sarcastic? Is that respectful or disrespectful? What if he simply shrugs his shoulders? How about if he responds in an acceptable manner but kicks the chair as he walks away? What if he doesn't respond at all but follows the instruction? It is important to explore as many scenarios and situations as possible to ensure that everyone fully understands what is acceptable and what is unacceptable. The teacher should feel prepared to address many of the student's behaviors, quickly identifying them as positive or negative.

Proactive intervention plans focus on teaching the student responsible behaviors.

Case Study Continued *(Responsible & Irresponsible Behavior)* »

Case Manager: (Ms. Trent)	Our main goal for Charlie is for her to learn to manage her workspace and time during independent work. Now we need to clarify what exactly we expect to see as positive and negative behavior as Charlie works toward that goal. We know that we don't want Charlie to disturb the other kids while they are working. What if she has a question about her work?
Teacher: (Mr. Winfrey)	I let the other kids help each other. I don't mind if Charlie asks a neighbor a question, but I don't want her asking the kids questions unnecessarily. That's going to be hard to distinguish, isn't it?
Interventionist: (Mr. Ingram)	Maybe. We may need to think of a different way for Charlie to get help. I'm going to make a note under proactive strategies to suggest a question card. For now, Charlie may not be able to make the fine distinction between when it's OK to go talk to another student and when it isn't OK.
Case Manager:	Let's talk about out-of-seat behavior. What if her pencil lead breaks? Can she get out of her seat to sharpen it?
Teacher:	That would be fine, unless she abuses the privilege.
Interventionist:	Maybe we should clarify what that means.
Teacher:	It would be irresponsible if she does it all the time or bothers other people on her way to the sharpener. It would also be irresponsible if she used sharpening her pencil as an excuse to get out of her seat and wander around for a long time. Unfortunately, this is another privilege with a lot of qualifiers.
Interventionist:	You may be right. Especially by the time you add in other valid reasons for getting out of her seat, such as getting a drink, turning in her work, or getting materials.
Teacher:	Maybe for Charlie, just being out of her seat is inappropriate, but I hate to be unfair.
Case Manager:	Perhaps when we look at ways to encourage appropriate behavior, we can think of ways Charlie might earn back the privilege. What things she should be doing during independent work times? We'll need to create a clear list of what she should be doing during independent work times and what she should not be doing.

Parent: (Mrs. Metzger)	Charlie's always had a hard time sitting still. I'm not sure she can.
Teacher:	I know Charlie can stay with a task. She does it when I'm with her. But I really don't care whether she is sitting down or not. I just want her to be on task and not bothering others.
Interventionist:	When another student had a similar problem, we defined lines by marking his space with masking tape. We told him he could work in that area, at his desk, on the floor, sitting, or standing. It didn't matter as long as he stayed in that space. We called it his office, and he loved it.
Parent:	I could see Charlie loving that too. Is it possible to do that for her?
Case Manager:	I like that idea. I think it could work.
Interventionist:	Good. I'll write that down under responsible behaviors. Irresponsible behavior would include leaving the office area—and that would be when you would launch into ignoring mode.

STEP 5 Proactive Strategies

Brainstorm proactive strategies to teach and encourage responsible behavior. Come up with as many as possible in the time given—seven strategies at minimum. Be sure to move through each suggestion quickly, not getting stuck on one possibility. Pros and cons of each strategy can be discussed at a later time. The case manager must be assertive at this step to keep the process moving. Consider a broad range of options and be as creative as possible. Consider changing the student's schedule or placement in a room, ratios of interactions, self-monitoring systems, any interventions that team members are familiar with, classroom management strategies, positive reinforcement, and more. The more possibilities for proactive intervention, the greater the likelihood the intervention plan will successfully address the student and teacher's needs. The recorder should write down every suggestion so that all possibilities will be available for future use whether they are used in the initial plan or not. Following are some helpful guidelines for brainstorming.

- Anything goes—don't hold back.

- Write down a summary statement or phrase for every strategy or idea.

- Record the ideas on chart paper, dry markerboard, or a computer and LCD so everyone can see them.

- Any idea or strategy is acceptable.

- Piggybacking (i.e., going in a different direction with someone's idea) is encouraged.

- Members shouldn't look at the referring teacher when offering an idea (looking at the teacher can encourage the teacher to comment on the suggested strategy).

- Each team member should provide at least one strategy.

- Team members should not comment or ask questions about strategies until after the brainstorming.

- After 30 seconds of silence, read the list aloud to stimulate more ideas.

 Case Study Continued (Brainstorm Ideas) »

During brainstorming, the intervention team comes up with several possibilities for the intervention plan. (See Step 5 of Reproducible Form 8.1: 25-Minute Planning Process Worksheet on p. 184.)

STEP 6 **Proactive Plan**

From the list that was developed in the last step, help the teacher choose one to three strategies to implement. The teacher knows the student's tendencies and has to live with and carry out the plan, so the final decision about which interventions will be manageable and effective should be the teacher's. The case manager and planning team should help guide the teacher to a reasonable plan and offer clarification of procedures, as needed. They should be prepared to answer questions such as, "What exactly is attribution retraining, and how will it help my student achieve his goal?"

Case Study Continued (Decide on an Intervention Plan) »

Case Manager: (Ms. Trent)	Let's look at what we have and then decide on one to three strategies to implement.
Teacher: (Mr. Winfrey)	These are all such great ideas. I'd like to do them all.
Interventionist: (Mr. Ingram)	It would be easy to take on too much. We should start with just a few so we don't overwhelm you or Charlie. Then we can re-examine the plan after a few weeks to see if we want to switch to different strategies or add some.
Teacher:	OK. A lot of these suggestions seem pretty easy to implement. Mrs. Metzger, I'd like your input too. I like the masking-tape office. What do you think?
Parent: (Mrs. Metzger)	I think Charlie would like that. Ms. Trent, when we are through, could you help me work out something for Charlie's homework?
Case Manager:	I'd like to do that. Let's finish looking at the list and finalize the school plan. Then you and I can work on a homework plan.
Teacher:	Mrs. Metzger, I'm really glad you came in. I think we can help make this a better year for Charlie. Let's see. We've got the masking tape office. I'd rather not get into a point system.
Interventionist:	Why don't I check the things you want to do?
Teacher:	Check goal setting and self-monitoring. It would be good to get Charlie focused on her own behavior. I'd like to do everything else.
Case Manager:	Let's eliminate a few more—maybe one or two of the more time-consuming ones—and then I think the rest are manageable. Most of this will require time up front, but then the strategies will become fairly routine.
Teacher:	Okay. Let's skip goal setting for now, but let's do a self-monitoring system. I think Charlie would like it. We could set up an assignment sheet for her to monitor her office work. That would keep the focus on work completion.

Interventionist: (Mr. Ingram)	I have several self-monitoring forms that I could leave in your box. They might help you come up with something for Charlie.
Teacher: (Mr. Winfrey)	That would be great. Actually, could I take a look at the intervention chapter that covers self-monitoring? I think it would be helpful. I'd also like to have her help me with something like making a bulletin board. It would give her some extra attention, and we can work on positive interactions. Mrs. Metzger, would you have five or ten minutes to read with Charlie before bedtime?
Parent: (Mrs. Metzger)	Yes. We got out of that habit when she learned to read. She still asks me to read sometimes, though, so I know she would like that.
Teacher:	Oh, and I'd like to do the question-card strategy. That won't be hard to do.

STEP 7   Final Details

Finalize everyone's role and responsibilities. In this step, lay out the final details so that the plan can be implemented successfully. This includes identifying ways in which other members of the planning team can assist with implementation, determining whether other people in or outside of school should be involved, and summarizing each person's responsibilities. Participants in planning meetings often get carried away as they develop proactive plans for students. Enthusiasm runs high in the meeting, but a few days later nothing has happened. Implementation is the hardest step, so it is imperative that everyone is clear about his or her duties and responsibilities for implementing the plan (Crone & Horner, 2000; Rosenfield, 2008; Telzrow, 1995). The team needs to help the teacher and case manager determine two ways that the efficacy of the plan will be determined. Possible sources of evaluation information include:

- Subjective perceptions of teacher, parent, or student (are things better, the same, or worse?)

- Rating scale by teacher (e.g., one to five)

- Work products (assignments done, grades, tests, quality of work)

- Self-monitoring forms from student

- Systematic observations

- Data from reinforcement system (points earned)

> Implementation is the hardest step, so it is imperative that everyone is clear about his or her duties.

Next, identify what team members can do to help the teacher implement the plan. For example, if a self-monitoring form will be used, can one of the team members provide a sample for the teacher or develop a first draft of such a form? Can one of the team members meet with the student to teach expectations?

Finally, create a plan summary with clear specifications for who is going to do what and by when.

- Who will talk to the student and when?

- Who will teach/model positive behaviors to the student?

- When can the plan reasonably start?

- If parents aren't present, how and when will the plan be shared with them?

- Decide if a substitute teacher will be asked to implement the plan—how will this be communicated?

- Decide whether the plan needs to be shared with any other staff members who work with the student.

- Give a written copy of the plan to teacher and team.

 Case Study Continued (Wrap Up Final Details) »

Case Manager: (Ms. Trent)	I'm very pleased. I think we have a great plan. We have three minutes left to wrap up, so I want to be sure that we are all very clear about what we will be doing and when. Mr. Ingram, you will give Mr. Winfrey a copy of the self-monitoring intervention booklet. Do we want to get any other staff members or people outside of school involved?
Teacher:	I'm going to make a point to acknowledge Charlie in non-contingent ways in class. I think it would help if we got the office staff and Charlie's other primary teachers to do the same. It shouldn't be hard. She's very likable.
Case Manager:	Great. Charlie's goal will be to manage her workspace and time. To help her reach her goal, we will train the other students to ignore her if she is cruising around the room during independent work times. I'll come in to teach the other students how to ignore Charlie's behavior when she is off-task. Mr. Winfrey, would Tuesday at 9 o'clock work?

Teacher: (Mr. Winfrey)	Yes.
Parent: (Mrs. Metzger)	Is Charlie going to feel OK about this?
Case Manager: (Ms. Trent)	We will discuss all of this with Charlie ahead of time. She is a bright girl, and we can explain that we all have things we need to work on. We will let the other kids know we are doing this because Charlie is our friend. Then everyone will need to be extra supportive of Charlie for the next several weeks.
Parent:	I can see how this will help her. I just get worried.
Teacher:	I understand, Mrs. Metzger. I'll do everything I can to help everyone understand that this is part of our class effort to function as a learning community—by supporting and helping each other.
Case Manager:	Let's get a date down to talk this through with Charlie. Mr. Winfrey, can you meet with Charlie and me for lunch on Monday? That way I can fill you both in on the self-monitoring system.
Teacher:	Sounds great. Then Charlie and I can go to the room and set up her office. I think that will be fun. I'll hold off on the bulletin board until next week. That will give me another special time with her, maybe the following Monday. That would get these next two weeks off to a nice start. Mrs. Metzger, could I keep Charlie after school for 20 minutes a week from Monday so she could help me with the new bulletin board? Of course we will do this only if Charlie would like to do this.
Parent:	I think she will be thrilled. I'll arrange to pick her up.
Interventionist: (Mr. Ingram)	Good. Let's return for a minute to setting up the office. Mr. Winfrey, once it's set up, it would be helpful if you can demonstrate to Charlie all of the ways she could work appropriately in her office. Maybe do some role playing.
Case Manager:	I will make it a point to check in with Mr. Winfrey about the intervention at staff meetings. I'll keep records so we can monitor how things are going. Let's see, we also want to focus on positive interactions when Charlie is working appropriately in her office. This means trying to be conscious of when she is being responsible for herself.

Interventionist: One way to keep track of your interactions is to keep 10 popsicle sticks in a box. Every time you interact positively with Charlie, take one stick out. The box is your reminder. Or just make it a point to notice Charlie between every transition. When you finish answering a student's question or helping a student, you can monitor. When you finish working with a small group, monitor.

Teacher: I actually think the popsicle stick thing might work. Let me think that one over. You know, we didn't decide what to do if Charlie doesn't get her work done. I don't like keeping her in from recess.

Case Manager: Let's try this for two weeks and see if work completion increases without consequences. We can tell Charlie during the conference that we want to help her monitor her own work and let her enjoy the time at recess with her friends.

Teacher: I like that. It gives her some nice confidence to begin with.

Case Manager: I think that does it. Oops, Mrs. Metzger, you also wanted to do some home reading. You and I will set up a time to discuss helping Charlie with her homework. Now, one last detail: When should we have our first follow-up meeting?

Schedule a follow-up meeting. Schedule time for a follow-up meeting before ending the conference. If possible, the interventionist should check in with the referring teacher within a day or two of implementation. During the implementation phase, plans frequently need adjustment and fine-tuning. Occasionally, teachers need assistance implementing unfamiliar procedures. Once the plan is running smoothly, follow-ups can be scheduled less frequently.

 *Case Study Continued (Plan a Follow-Up)* »

Case Manager: Mr. Winfrey, do you have time to arrange a follow-up? I'd like to set a date for two weeks. We can always cancel if the time isn't needed.

Teacher: Sure.

Parent: I'd like to come to the follow-up too. Could you also keep me informed before that?

Case Manager: (Ms. Trent)	Absolutely. How about if you call me on Wednesdays? Let's set up a follow-up meeting for Friday, December 9 at 3 p.m. Is that OK? I'd like to thank both of you for coming today. I'm very pleased with this plan. There is a lot to it, but it's supportive and proactive, and once it's set up, it will be manageable. I believe Charlie will benefit from this. We'll make sure that everything is summarized in writing, and I'll get you each a copy by tomorrow.

CONCLUDE THE MEETING

Conclude the meeting with words of encouragement. However, warn the teacher that the misbehavior may actually increase for one or two days following initial intervention implementation, but the key to success is to be relentless in implementing the plan every day for at least two weeks.

To complete the process, the interventionist should give each participant a summary of the plan, outlining responsibilities and timelines in writing. Good intentions and the best-laid plans can easily become lost in the normal demands of daily activities.

CONCLUSION

The 25-minute planning process provides a structured, step-by-step, timed process for intervention planning teams to use to guide their problem analysis and intervention design. By combining the expertise of a group of professionals, a broader perspective and range of expertise is gained. The timed and structured agenda reduces the chance that meetings will be too long, off task, or negative in tone. When intervention planning teams function well, they can quickly and efficiently design interventions that have a high probability of helping the student in ways that earlier-stage interventions did not.

Reproducible Materials

Copies of the following reproducible materials appear on the CD. Permission is given for individual teachers, administrators, or other school personnel to reproduce these forms for in-district use.

Reproducible Form 8.1: 25-Minute Planning Process Worksheet

Reproducible Form 8.2: Implementing Corrective Consequences

CHAPTER 9

Multidisciplinary Team Approach

Using the Intervention Decision Guide

The Intervention Decision Guide: Multidisciplinary Team (IDG: MDT) process is intended to guide a multidisciplinary team in bringing the most resources to the table when addressing a student's behavior problem after earlier interventions at Tier 1 and Tier 2 have proven to be ineffective. Because the multidisciplinary team is composed of highly trained and experienced staff members such as the school counselor, school psychologist, school social worker, special education teacher, behavior specialist, school nurse, and administrator, the IDG: MDT process is likely to be the most time- and labor-intensive process that occurs on the B-RTI intervention continuum before a student enters into the phase of establishing eligibility for special education. The goal is to develop and implement a comprehensive intervention plan that reflects the best of what the school and district have to offer the student and the classroom teacher. This chapter describes how to implement the process outlined on the Intervention Decision Guide: Multidisciplinary Team (Reproducible Form 9.1, which appears on pp. 218–222 and on the CD that accompanies this book).

MULTIDISCIPLINARY OVERVIEW

The problem-solving process followed during the IDG: MDT is the same process used by the interventionist and/or intervention planning team at the earlier Tier 1 and Tier 2 stages of the B-RTI continuum. The key substantive difference is that the multidisciplinary team will devote more time and resources to a problem-solving process to develop comprehensive and appropriate interventions for high-risk students. However, for the IDG: MDT process to be effective and efficient, it is essential that earlier components on the B-RTI continuum are effective and successful in addressing the majority of students with behavioral difficulties. Otherwise, the number of referrals to the IDG: MDT process can easily overwhelm the multidisciplinary team and make it very difficult for the team to be effective and efficient (Bradley, Danielson, & Doolittle, 2005; Sugai et al., 2000, 2002; Walker et al., 1996).

The IDG: MDT process follows a standard problem-solving procedure. The multidisciplinary team's initial responsibility is to review previously collected information about the student's background, including interventions that have already been attempted. Next, the team determines what additional data needs to be collected, including multiple observations and interviews. The team analyzes all of the collected information and data to identify the function(s) of the student's misbehavior and options for possible intervention strategies. The teacher and multidisciplinary team then develop a comprehensive intervention plan. In the final stage of the process, the multidisciplinary team provides follow-up services that include evaluating the effectiveness of the plan, supporting the teacher, and recommending the best course to follow for continuing, adapting, and fading the intervention plan. It is likely that the multidisciplinary team will conduct at least three meetings to complete the IDG: MDT process. As in other phases of the B-RTI continuum, it is essential that the student's classroom teacher be an active participant in the IDG: MDT process, including collaborating with the team in the development and implementation of any intervention plan. Establishing and nurturing a collaborative relationship with the classroom teacher will enable the multidisciplinary team to provide the crucial support needed for the teacher to faithfully implement the developed intervention plan (Bergan & Kratochwill, 1990; Creed & Kendall, 2005; McGivern, Ray-Subramanian, & Auster, 2008; Noell et al., 2005).

In practice, the IDG: MDT process can serve two purposes:

Purpose 1. The main purpose is to stand as the final process within the Tier 2 interventions, in which the team collaborates with the referring teacher to create and implement a comprehensive intervention plan. The process is initiated after the 25-minute planning meeting has been completed and/or after the teacher has worked collaboratively with an assigned interventionist who completed the Intervention Decision Guide: Teacher Interview (IDG: TI).

Purpose 2. The process can also serve as a vehicle for completing the comprehensive functional behavior analysis (FBA) at Tier 3 if some members of the team meet the training qualifications needed to conduct a comprehensive FBA. At Tier 3, the multidisciplinary team could use or modify the IDG: MDT form to carefully document its completion of the FBA along with reporting all interventions developed and implemented during Tier 1 and Tier 2. Note that this description of the IDG: MDT is not intended to serve as the steps required to conduct the FBA that is needed to help establish potential eligibility for special education. The multidisciplinary team may also determine that additional interventions should be attempted, in which case the team would lead the process by completing Stages 3 and 4 of the IDG: MDT process.

The multidisciplinary team's initial responsibility is to review previously collected information about the student's background.

The multidisciplinary team may already have an established protocol that it follows. In that case, the multidisciplinary team can adopt or modify the IDG: MDT process and/or form to meet its needs. Consider printing the five-page Reproducible Form 9.1 from the CD and keeping the copy near you as read this chapter. When printed on the front and back of 11" x 17" paper, this form will guide the interviews with the teacher and other selected persons as well as provide a place to make notes. Our goal is that this form will be a useful tool as the case manager and multidisciplinary team work with teachers to develop interventions to help students improve behavior. The top of the form includes basic information about the student and the names of the multidisciplinary team members and teacher(s). Be sure to include whatever information may be needed later to demonstrate how this intervention interview fits as part of a comprehensive file—especially the date and the participants involved in the IDG: MDT process.

IDG: MDT FUNDAMENTALS—MAKING THE PROCESS WORK

Establishing an effective and efficient multidisciplinary team and using case management are two fundamental components that enable the IDG:MDT process to work.

TEAM MEMBERSHIP

Your school may already have a functioning multidisciplinary team, but if it does not, we recommend establishing one. Such teams are usually comprised of school-based and itinerant staff members representing different disciplines in the school and district, such as school counselor, school psychologist, school social worker, school nurse, special education personnel (e.g., behavior specialist and speech/language specialist), curriculum specialist (e.g., reading teacher and instructional coach), and administrator. In some cases, a general education teacher may also serve on the team (Burns, Wiley, & Viglietta, 2008; Scott & Nelson, 1999).

Because the student has already gone through several phases of the B-RTI continuum, one or more of the team members may have already been part of the service delivery for this student and may have served as the interventionist or worked with an intervention planning team. If this is the case, the multidisciplinary team's work is enhanced by this existing knowledge of the student's needs and the teacher's efforts to intervene.

It is essential that team members are trained and experienced in behavioral consultation and the entire range of behavioral intervention strategies available in the district (Benazzi et al., 2006; Forman & Burke, 2008). One set of strategies might include early-stage and highly structured interventions from *Interventions: Evidence-Based Behavioral Strategies for Individual Students*. Similar evidence-based interventions from other authors or resources may be appropriate as well. Training team members in how to use *The Teacher's Encyclopedia of Behavior Management* would also be helpful.

The ideal size of the multidisciplinary team is four to seven permanent members, with each member adding to the balance of expertise and experience. The team has the option of adding adjunct members for a referred student based on the student's unique needs and characteristics. For example, it would be appropriate to invite a speech/language specialist to join the team if the referred student has or is suspected to have a severe communication disorder.

TEAM ROLES

To be effective and efficient, the multidisciplinary team should create the following permanent team roles:

Team leader or coordinator. The responsibilities of this role include receiving referrals, developing the meeting agenda, assigning case managers, keeping the team focused on the agenda during meetings, keeping all participants engaged during meetings, and maintaining a file of completed forms and meeting notes for every student referred to the team. Some teams find it helpful to have co-leaders or co-coordinators because splitting the varied responsibilities between two members keeps one person from being overwhelmed. Having a co-leader also allows one leader to conduct a meeting if the other leader happens to be a case manager for the student or cannot attend a meeting.

Timekeeper. The responsibility of this role is to use a watch, kitchen timer, or computer timer to remind team members of how much time is left in a specific part of the meeting (e.g., brainstorming). The timekeeper's role is critical in ensuring that the meeting moves from step to step in an efficient manner.

Recorder. The recorder takes minutes on all parts of the team discussion and completes the team's official copy of the Intervention Decision Guide: MDT form. The recorder may want to consider using a laptop computer for keeping minutes and completing the form. The recorder could also write down the list of brainstorming ideas during Stage 3, unless the team decides it would be more efficient to appoint another member to do this job. If the recorder is the case manager for a referred student, another team member should be asked to serve as the recorder during any meetings about that student.

Once the team has been established, the first order of business is to set rules for the conduct of the meeting and the brainstorming sessions. See Chapter 8, pp. 188–189, for sample meeting rules and pp. 203–204 for a list of brainstorming guidelines.

LENGTH AND FREQUENCY OF TEAM MEETINGS

Given the demanding schedules of its members, we recommend that the team establish a schedule of regular meetings for the semester or (preferably) for the entire school year. It is easier to cancel a meeting if there isn't a referred case than to try to find a convenient time to meet on short notice. The team should also establish broad guidelines for how long each stage of the IDG: MDT process should last, including setting a target date for when Stage 4 will be completed. In addition, the team should establish suggested time parameters for how long meetings should last at Stages 2, 3, and 4 to keep the meetings focused and productive. For example:

First meeting, 15–20 minutes. The team convenes to discuss Stage 2: Collecting Other Essential Information. This involves reviewing the background of the case and setting up a plan for who, what, where, and when regarding observations, interviews, and records reviews.

Second meeting, 30 minutes. After collecting essential information, the team reconvenes to discuss Stage 3: Intervention Design. Using all the information collected, the team and the teacher design the next intervention to be implemented.

Third meeting, 10–15 minutes. The team reconvenes to discuss Stage 4: Follow-Up Meeting and determine if the intervention should be modified, maintained, or faded, depending on the progress of the student.

The multidisciplinary team should make sure the room in which it meets provides privacy, a table of appropriate size for everyone to sit around, enough comfortable chairs, and a clock. We also recommend that the case manager sit next to the referring teacher at the meetings, which may facilitate the joint sharing of information about the student.

The school or school district needs to determine how a teacher will request help from the multidisciplinary team. Because the student's behavioral problems have reached this final phase of Tier 2 or are starting Tier 3, it is a good idea for the referring teacher or staff member to complete a formal written referral. Although documenting requests and supports at this phase is important, it is also necessary to keep the referral form as simple as possible. Attaching copies of any already completed B-RTI intervention forms (25-Minute Planning Meeting or the IDG: TI) will eliminate the need for the referring staff member to record extensive background information. The formal referral should be given to the leader or coordinator of the multidisciplinary team.

CASE MANAGEMENT RESPONSIBILITIES

Like the case manager in the 25-minute planning meeting process, a case manager in the IDG: MDT process acts as a main liaison between the referring teacher and the multidisciplinary team. Furthermore, the case manager continues to handle the referral and work with the teacher until the multidisciplinary team closes the referral. We recommend that the multidisciplinary team have at least three or four members who serve as case managers. The team leader or coordinator should assign a case manager within two or three work days of receiving the referral. A quick assignment communicates to the referring teacher that the referral is important and services are forthcoming. When assigning the case manager, the team leader or coordinator should consider factors such as the referring teacher's relationship with potential case managers, the number of active cases the case manager has, and the age and presenting problems of the student. The team leader/coordinator should notify the team member of her appointment as case manager before informing the teacher.

Once the case manager is assigned, it is important that she contact the referring teacher within two to three work days to set up the initial interview in the IDG: MDT process. To avoid taking valuable team meeting time to collect and discuss background information, the case manager should gather background information from the teacher before the multidisciplinary team formally meets about the student. If Stage 1 of the Intervention Decision Guide: Teacher Interview (IDG: TI) has already been completed, the case manager can review that information. The case manager may also want to observe the student before meeting with the teacher.

The case manager and classroom teacher need to determine whether the parent has been informed of the student's problem. Often by this phase of the B-RTI process, signed parental consent has already been obtained. If not, it is recommended that signed consent from the parent be obtained as soon as possible. Depending on the team's protocol, the case manager and teacher will decide if the parent and/or the student need to receive an invitation to attend any meetings with the multidisciplinary team. The other responsibilities of the case manager are described in detail in the following sections that describe the four stages of the IDG: MDT process.

Stage 1: Background from IDG: Teacher Interview

Even if Stage 1 of the IDG: Teacher Interview was previously completed, it is still important that the case manager meet with the teacher. This allows the case manager to update the information collected earlier and to start establishing a collaborative relationship with the teacher. If possible, arrange to conduct this initial meeting in the teacher's room when students are not there. Meeting in the teacher's room will increase the teacher's comfort level and allow easy access to records and work samples. This initial meeting will likely last up to 30 minutes.

When meeting with the teacher, the case manager should make sure the seating arrangement is comfortable and allows the teacher to see the IDG: MDT form as it is being completed. Given the likelihood that the teacher is frustrated by the student's continued disruptiveness and resistance to change—despite previous intervention efforts—the case manager will need to practice good listening and communication skills to establish rapport and trust with the teacher (Lambert, 2004; McGivern et al., 2008; Norcross & Lambert, 2006; Rosenfield, 1987, 2004). For example, the case manager should face the teacher, maintain good eye contact, use a quiet/calm voice, nod her head, talk less and listen more, and let the teacher see what she is writing as she takes notes. The following items should be addressed by the case manager and teacher during Stage 1, with the case manager recording information and data on pages one and two of the IDG: MDT form (See sample Reproducible Form 9.1 on the following pages).

STEP 1 Introduce the Process

The case manager should start the meeting by stating the goal: "Today we are meeting so we can support the student's behavioral needs by evaluating the information and data already collected and by working together to develop a comprehensive intervention plan." The teacher should be given a blank copy of the IDG: MDT form so that she can see what will be used to guide and document the process. The case manager should also describe the following to the teacher:

- How the IDG: MDT process works

- The emphasis on collaboration between the teacher and the multidisciplinary team

- The importance of creating an intervention plan that the teacher selects and develops with guidance and help from the multidisciplinary team

- How the shared information will be considered confidential, including the IDG: MDT form

- The role of the parents during the IDG: MDT

- How other staff members may be asked to assist

- The approximate timelines for completing the stages of the IDG: MDT process

STEP 2 Confirm Parental Notification

The case manager should confirm that the parents have been informed of the student's problems. The case manager and teacher should discuss how the parents responded and whether or not the parents were involved with any previously attempted interventions. The case manager should make sure the parents have given signed consent for developing interventions to address the student's problems.

STEP 3 Review Reasons for Referral

Next, the case manager should review the teacher's reason(s) for referring the student. The case manager needs to hear the teacher's concerns, impressions, and frustrations.

Continued on p. 223

Reproducible Form 9.1 (p. 1 of 5)

INTERVENTION DECISION GUIDE: MULTIDISCIPLINARY TEAM (IDG:MDT)

Student _____ Age _____ Grade _____ Beginning Date _____

Referring Teacher _____ Team Member(s) _____

Stage 1: Background from IDG: Teacher Interview

1. Reason for referral and description of the problem:

   > **Code Red:** Are plans in place or needed? **Y N**   If yes, describe the plans:

2. What goal (target behavior) has been previously established? Is this still the teacher's main priority? If not, what is?

3. What data has been collected on this goal?

4. Describe below any academic or behavior interventions implemented within the past six months. See Intervention to Consider from the IDG: Teacher Interview.

Target Behavior	Intervention	When	Outcomes (Effectiveness & Fidelity)

5. What was the previous hypothesis regarding function? Did interventions confirm or contract that hypothesis? (Or does lack of implementation fidelity keep this question open?)

6. How has the teacher corrected the student's misbehavior? Has this been effective?

7. Describe any proactive strategies used by the teacher. Have they been effective?

8. Should the existing goal be maintained? **Y N**   If no, describe new goal and decide if any additional data should be collected:

Reproducible Form 9.1 (p. 2 of 5)   *IDG: MDT (continued)*

Stage 2: Collect Other Essential Information

Direct Observation

1. Identify behaviors to observe:

2. Set a schedule of observations for the classroom: Who? When (date & time)?

3. Other settings in which to observe behavior: Where? When (date & time)?

School Staff to Interview

1. Identify other staff members who interact with the student regularly or who knew the student in previous years:

    Who   Interviewed by   Questions to ask

Student Interview

1. When and by whom was the student informed of the problem and the goal? If not done yet, when and by whom can the student be interviewed?

2. Is the student motivated to improve?

3. Does the student have other goals or objectives?

4. Other relevant information or questions to ask:

Parent/Guardian Interview

1. When and by whom were the parents informed of the problem and the goal? If not done yet, when and by whom can the parent be interviewed?

2. Is the parent or guardian supportive of this goal?

3. Does the parent or guardian have other goals or objectives?

4. Other relevant information or questions to ask:

Reproducible Form 9.1 (p. 3 of 5)

Pertinent Information from School Records Review

Student:	School:	Date:

CONFIDENTIAL INFORMATION (To Be Kept in a Secure Location)

Area	Important Information and Notes
Medical History	Any diagnosed illnesses or diseases? **Y N** If yes, disease and impact on student: Significant birth and/or developmental history: Mother's age when child was born: _____ History of medications? **Y N** If yes, which one(s) and any known side effects? Wears glasses? **Y N** Hearing loss? **Y N**
Family History	With whom does the student live? Birth parents? ❑ Step family? ❑ Single-parent home? ❑ Dual custody? ❑ Sibling(s)? **Y N** Ages and gender: Education level and job (Mom):_____ (Dad): _____ Has a parent died? If yes, any details such as when, who, and how? Any seriously ill parent, grandparent, or sibling? If yes, describe the situation. Any agency involvement (mental health, DSS, private psychologist, etc.)?
School History	Is or was student served by special education? **Y N** If so, which classification, how long, and level of service? How many school changes/moves? Where: History of absenteeism: few vs. excessive (>20 a year): Which years were excessive? Any retentions? When? Summary of the history of report card grades: Identify strong and weak subjects from report cards: Describe any negative conduct ratings and comments from report cards:
Test Data	Summarize results from standardized/state accountability testing within the past 3 years: Has there been a psychological evaluation? **Y N** If yes, when given? Describe overall results.

Reproducible Materials Blank copies of the forms are provided on the CD. Permission is given for individual teachers, administrators, or other school personnel to reproduce any form labeled "Reproducible Form" for in-district use.

Reproducible Form 9.1 (p. 4 of 5)   *IDG: MDT (continued)*

Stage 3: Intervention Design

Date:_____   Members present:_____

_____

_____

1. Develop hypotheses: What is the function of the problem behavior? What seems to be maintaining or reinforcing the student's misbehavior?

   ❏ Ability   ❏ Awareness   ❏ Adult attention   ❏ Peer attention
   ❏ Power or control   ❏ Escape or avoidance   ❏ Competing reinforcers   ❏ Other _____
                          (task difficulty/discomfort)   _____

2. Brainstorm possible interventions:

3. Design and describe a comprehensive intervention plan, including what will be done when by whom:

4. Select and describe at least two methods for evaluating the intervention plan during first two weeks, including how and by whom the data will be collected:

5. Select a follow-up meeting date and time to discuss the intervention plan after two weeks:

6. Outcomes and recommendations (including the follow-up meeting) have been shared with:

   Classroom teacher? **Y N**   Date: _____   By whom: _____

   Parent/student? **Y N**   Date: _____   By whom: _____

Reproducible Materials Blank copies of the forms are provided on the CD. Permission is given for individual teachers, administrators, or other school personnel to reproduce any form labeled "Reproducible Form" for in-district use.

Reproducible Form 9.1 (p. 5 of 5)

Stage 4: Follow-Up Meeting

Date:_____   Members present:_____

_____

Data Collection

1. After two weeks, report all available data to the team (e.g., frequency count from the teacher, self-monitoring form from the student, and results of third-party observation).

2. Summary of the teacher(s)' perception of how well the plan has addressed the target behavior:

Team Actions

1. Team recommendations:
   - ❏ Continue implementation as is.
   - ❏ Continue plan as is, but adjust actual implementation.
   - ❏ Revise plan to address identified weaknesses.
   - ❏ Amend the plan to address other target behaviors.
   - ❏ Refer to special education.
   - ❏ Begin to phase out plan due to successful intervention.
   - ❏ Discontinue plan, as universal supports should be enough to maintain success.
   - ❏ Other:

2. Brief explanation for the team's recommendations and who will be responsible for the follow-up:

3. Outcomes and recommendations (including the follow-up meeting) have been shared with:

   Classroom teacher? **Y N**   Date: _____   By whom: _____

   Parent/student? **Y N**   Date: _____   By whom: _____

At this stage, the case manager needs to talk less and listen more. Doing lots of listening is likely to help the teacher believe that the case manager is interested in her perspective and feelings (Erchul, 2003; Lambert, 2004; Kratochwill, 2008; Rosenfield, 2008). Once the teacher's previous and current concerns are confirmed, the teacher needs to identify which behaviors are of the greatest concern at the current time.

STEP 4 Assess Need for Code-Red Plan

The case manager should determine if any emergency/code-red plans have been or need to be implemented to respond to dangerous behaviors by the student. If such plans were put in place, the case manager should have the teacher describe what was done and the outcomes. If emergency/code-red plans are currently needed, the case manager should immediately start to implement the district's protocol for such situations or employ the steps outlined in "Intervention G: Managing Physically Dangerous Behavior" or "Intervention H: Managing Severely Disruptive Behavior" from *Interventions: Evidence-Based Behavioral Strategies for Individual Students*.

STEP 5 Set a Goal for the Intervention

The case manager should have the teacher describe what goals (target behaviors) were established in previous interventions to determine if the initial goal is still the teacher's main priority. If not, the case manager should work with the teacher to establish the new goal to be addressed in the new intervention plan. Guide the teacher to identify a positive goal by stating what is expected of the student (instead of what she doesn't want the student to do), which will help the student feel proud of any accomplishments. For example, "learning to be respectful" is perceived better by a student than "learning how to not talk back to the teacher." The goal should be stated in clear, observable terms. "Increase respect in the classroom" is not as strong or as specific as "respond to teacher instructions in a respectful tone of voice or with no verbal reply." Effective goal statements comprise four parts:

1. Student
2. Target behavior
3. Time frame
4. Improvement metric

To illustrate, here are some sample goal statements:

- Within four weeks, the student will complete at least 80% of her classwork.

> At this stage, the case manager needs to talk less and listen more.

- Within two weeks, the number of disruptive acts will be reduced by 50%; within two months, the disruptive acts will have an 80% reduction.

- The student will learn to stay calm and manage his anger without screaming, hitting, or engaging in aggressive acts. The number of disruptive incidents for the month (or week) will be less than for the previous month (or week).

STEP 6   Detail Previous Interventions

The case manager needs to ask the teacher to describe in detail any academic or behavioral interventions implemented during the school year. Have the teacher describe the goals (target behaviors), intervention plans, when they were implemented and for how long, what data was collected to evaluate the plans, and what the outcomes were in terms of effectiveness and fidelity of implementation. Assuming that the intervention plans were not effective, the case manager can explicitly point out that some behavior problems require multiple plans and extra supports to be resolved, which will remove blame from the teacher. The case manager will need to obtain copies of any written plans or forms completed as part of these previous interventions.

STEP 7   Identify Student Strengths

The case manager needs to have the teacher identify at least three of the student's strengths (e.g., sense of humor, artistic, likes math, gets along with others, athletic, enjoys music). Strengths can be revisited as building blocks for the development of supports for the student. Ask the teacher to describe if and how any previous interventions attempted to capitalize on those strengths, including how effective the attempts were. In addition, you may want to ask the teacher about strengths of previous interventions. This information may also be useful for developing future supports.

> Strengths can be revisited as building blocks for the development of supports for the student.

STEP 8   Revisit the Function Hypothesis

A critical task during Stage 1 is to identify the previous hypothesis about the function (reasons) for the student's misbehavior. This hypothesis was generated either during the 25-minute planning meeting or with the interventionist during the IDG: TI process. The hypothesis will likely fall into one of the following categories:

- Ability

- Awareness

- Adult attention

- Peer attention

- Power or control

- Escape or avoidance (task difficulty or discomfort)

- Competing reinforcers

- Other

For detailed information about each function, see Chapter 7, pp. 151–154. The case manager and teacher should determine whether the previous interventions confirmed or contradicted the hypothesis. It is also important to identify any variables that the teacher believes made it difficult for her to fully implement the previous interventions. For example, the consequences provided the student with too much attention, which reinforced the misbehavior. Identifying any key variables that affected the fidelity of the previous interventions will enable the case manager and teacher to ensure that similar variables are accounted for in future interventions.

STEP 9   Identify Strategies Used Previously

The purpose of this task is to determine previously used preventive strategies as well as those for responding to appropriate and problem behavior. The case manager can help the teacher identify how she corrected the student's misbehavior during previous interventions by asking these questions:

- What consequences were used (e.g., verbal reprimand, time owed, timeout, points lost) and for what misbehavior?

- Were any misbehaviors purposely ignored by using planned ignoring? If yes, what were the outcomes?

- How consistent was the teacher in delivering the consequence every time?

- How did the student respond to the consequences? Did she try to argue with the teacher and create power struggles? If so, what happened then?

- How effective where these consequences? Were any consequences more effective?

- Was there a time or day of the week when consequences seemed more effective? When were consequences less effective?

- How often did the teacher refer the student to the office and for what behavior?

Have the teacher describe all proactive strategies used as part of the previous intervention by asking these questions:

- Which positive strategies were used? Examples include noncontingent attention, positive feedback, intermittent celebrations (including concrete rewards, celebrations, and meaningful work), boosting the ratio of positive interactions to at least three to one, and/or providing an incentive plan.

- Which positive strategies were most effective? How did the teacher know?

- What behaviors earned intermittent celebrations and incentives?

- How often did the student earn incentives? Which incentives appeared to be more powerful and effective with this student?

- Which positive strategies and incentives were not effective?

- Were any positive strategies or incentives delivered by the parents? If yes, how consistent were the parents? How effective were the home incentives?

STEP 10 **Determine Goal for the Current Intervention**

By the end of the Stage 1 meeting, the case manager and teacher will be in a good position to determine whether the existing goal (target behavior) should be maintained. If not, they should then identify the new goal. The case manager should make certain the teacher has input into the goal selection and feels comfortable with it (Rosenfield, 2008; Sheridan et al., 2004; Tryon & Winograd, 2002; Watson & Sterling-Turner, 2008). The case manager and teacher should also decide if additional data needs to be collected and how that might be done before proceeding to Stage 2.

Stage 2: Collect Other Essential Information

For Stage 2, the objectives are to collect additional data by conducting observations and interviews as well as by reviewing the student's school records. Given the amount of work required, we recommend that the case manager and teacher meet with the multidisciplinary team to share the essential information from Stage 1 and to identify what additional data needs to be collected by whom. The following actions should be addressed during Stage 2.

STEP 1 Introduce the Purpose of the Meeting

This will likely be the first meeting of the multidisciplinary team regarding this student, so it will be important for the team leader or coordinator to welcome everyone and explain that the purpose of the meeting is to share some background information and identify what additional information is needed before the team develops a comprehensive intervention plan. If there are people present who aren't standing members of the multidisciplinary team, the team leader/coordinator should make introductions and review basic ground rules.

STEP 2 Report Data

The team leader or coordinator should allocate 10–15 minutes for the case manager and teacher to summarize the collected information and data reported on the Stage 1 section of the IDG: MDT form. It might be helpful and more efficient for the case manager to give each team member a copy of the completed first two pages of the form.

STEP 3 Identify Any Needed Observations

The multidisciplinary team and teacher need to decide what direct observations need to be conducted by addressing the following:

Related behaviors. Identify which behaviors related to the goal (target behavior) should be observed for the purpose of collecting more detailed information to help understand the function of the misbehavior and to develop a more focused intervention.

Classroom observation. A crucial aspect of understanding the student's problem is to conduct a third-party observation of the student in the classroom. The multidisciplinary team should establish a schedule of observations in the classroom by determining the crucial times of the day to observe. (Are any specific days of the week or times of day more problematic for the student?) The multidisciplinary team should determine who will observe at what times on which date. The team should also identify what type of observational data is needed: frequency data, duration, latency, and/or intensity. The team should consider conducting at least two structured observations of the student in the key settings where the behavior has the greatest impact.

> A crucial aspect of understanding the student's problem is to conduct a third-party observation of the student in the classroom.

Range of settings. Another crucial aspect is to understand the range of locations and times of day that are related to the student's misbehavior. The multidisciplinary team should determine if the target behavior is problematic in other school settings for which observational data would be helpful. Options include other teachers' classrooms, cafeteria, playground, class change, and arrival/dismissal areas. If observations are needed in other school settings, the multidisciplinary team should identify who will observe, at what times, and on which date. The multidisciplinary team should also identify what type of observational data is needed here as well.

Summarize and share. The team leader or coordinator should ask all observers to briefly summarize their observations on one page or in a chart or table so that the data can be shared with the team at the Stage 3 meeting.

STEP 4   Arrange Interviews

Interviewing key people who have worked with or are working with the student can be another important source of information. The multidisciplinary team and teacher need to decide who needs to be interviewed for the purpose of collecting more background information about the student. Some options to consider are:

Other staff members. Decide if there are any other staff members who interact regularly with the student or who knew him in previous years, then determine who will conduct those interviews, when they'll take place, and what specific questions will be asked. Ask each interviewer to briefly summarize the information learned from the staff interviews in one page or less so it can be shared with the team at the Stage 3 meeting.

The student. Interviewing the student can yield important insights. The multidisciplinary team needs to determine if the student has been already interviewed and if these questions were asked:

- How much is the student aware of the problem?

- How motivated is the student to improve?

- What other goals or objectives does the student want to address?

- What types of things (e.g., rewards, celebrations, attention) would the student like to work for?

- Was there any other relevant information learned from the interview?

If the student was interviewed and the previous questions were asked, document when was this done and by whom. The team should decide whether another interview would be helpful. If the student has not been interviewed, the multidisciplinary team needs to identify who can interview the student and by what date. Have the interviewer ask the previous set of questions as well as any other questions deemed relevant by the team. Ask the interviewer to briefly summarize the information from the student interview in one page or less so it can be shared with the team at the Stage 3 meeting.

Parents/guardian. Insights from a parent or guardian can help the multidisciplinary team understand the student and develop an appropriate plan (Burns et al., 2008; Miller & Kraft, 2008; Rones & Hoagwood, 2000), so the multidisciplinary team and teacher should discuss the extent of parent involvement up to this point. The team should also document when the parent was informed of the problem and the goal that was established. If the parent has not been interviewed, the multidisciplinary team should assign the team member with the best rapport with the parents to conduct an interview. Questions that need to be answered include:

- Is the parent supportive of the identified goal? If not, to what do they object?

- What other goals or objectives does the parent have?

- Is there other relevant information or circumstances that may be contributing to the student's behavioral problems at school (e.g., history of the student receiving help, counseling from resources outside the school, any relevant medical or developmental history, family assets and resources, significant family crises within the past six months).

Ask the interviewer to summarize the information learned from the parent or guardian interview in one page or less so that it can be shared with the team at the Stage 3 meeting. The information learned from the interview with the parent should be considered confidential, meaning that the information should be shared with only those staff members who have a legitimate reason to know.

STEP 5 **Review Student's School Records**

The student's school records need to be thoroughly reviewed for the purpose of summarizing the relevant information. Too often, highly relevant information in the student's school records goes unaccounted for when the multidisciplinary team is attempting to understand the function of the student's misbehavior and develop an intervention plan. The multidisciplinary team should identify who will conduct this review. The review needs to identify if there is any documentation of concerns or issues in the following categories:

- Medical or physical problems (e.g., needs prescription glasses, taking medication for diabetes or asthma)

- Involvement of outside agency (e.g., mental health counselor, DSS worker, physician)

- Family history (e.g., deceased parent, ten siblings, parent in prison)

- Mobility patterns (e.g., changed schools and/or districts five times within the past three years)

- Retentions or classes/subjects failed

- Reports or teacher comments about conduct

- Results from any formal evaluations by school personnel, such as a school psychologist, school social worker, or speech/language specialist

To assist the person conducting the review, the portion of the IDG: MDT labeled Review of School Records is designed to provide a one-page quick summary for recording relevant information in the categories of medical history, family history, school history, and test data. This form, along with any written notes by the reviewer, should be treated as confidential. After the review is completed, the person conducting the records review should briefly summarize the information learned from the review in one page or less so it can be shared with the team at the Stage 3 meeting.

STEP 6   **Schedule the Next Team Meeting**

At the end of the Stage 2 meeting, the multidisciplinary team should schedule the next meeting to share the data and information collected from the observations, interviews, and records review and to complete Stages 3 and 4. Depending on the number of observations and interviews that need to be completed, the meeting should be scheduled for one or two weeks after the Stage 2 meeting.

Stage 3: Intervention Design

The main goal for Stage 3 is to design an in-depth intervention plan. This meeting will likely require 30 minutes, although it could be longer if the case is complicated or if the parent/guardian attends. It will be important that the student's teacher attend the meeting so that she will have input into the development of the intervention plan. Following are the main actions addressed by the multidisciplinary team during Stage 3.

STEP 1   **Make Introductions and Review Background Information**

Welcome. The team leader/coordinator should welcome everyone and create a positive, collaborative atmosphere dedicated to helping the student and the teacher. If the teacher or parent/guardian did not attend the Stage 2 meeting, be sure that all meeting participants introduce themselves and identify their roles at the school or their relationship with the student.

Overview. The team leader/coordinator should also describe the different actions that will be completed during Stage 3, what has already been done, the confidential nature of the information, team roles, and any time limits (including any use of a timer and/or bell). It might be helpful to provide each person with a copy of the IDG: MDT form.

Information review. Once the introductions and overview are completed, the team leader/coordinator can distribute copies of the summaries from the additional observations, interviews, and record review completed during Stage 2. Each person responsible for writing a summary should provide the team with a brief one- or two-minute review of the key findings. This sharing could take anywhere from five to ten minutes, depending on the number of observations and interviews to be shared. To avoid devoting more than 20–30 minutes to sharing the information, the team leader/coordinator and timekeeper needs to remind each person to be concise and brief, then give reminders about the time.

STEP 2   **Confirm the Goal and Develop Hypotheses About Function**

The multidisciplinary team and teacher should confirm that the identified goal from Stage 1 continues to be the primary goal for the intervention plan based on information and data collected and shared during Stage 2. The team also needs to identify possible hypotheses about the function (i.e., reason) for the student's misbehavior related to the goal (target behavior) (Alberto & Troutman, 2006; O'Neill et al., 1997; Scheuermann & Hall, 2008). To generate hypotheses, the team should consider the information and data collected during Stages 1 and 2 when looking for trends and insights. Try to identify the *when*, *where*, *how*, and *what* variables that appear connected to the misbehavior. The following types of questions should generate helpful information and assist in designing the intervention.

Does the data and/or information identify any triggers that set off the problem behavior? What occurs beforehand? Was the student frustrated with work, teased by a classmate, or finished with the assignment and had nothing else to do? This information is crucial in determining the function and developing an intervention to prevent and intervene with the problem behavior. For example, a low tolerance for frustration when working with math might lead to an intervention in which the teacher provides individual guided practice, check-ins every three or four minutes, and incentives for the student to attempt every problem.

> Try to identify the *when, where, how,* and *what* variables that appear connected to the misbehavior.

Where do the problems tend to occur? (Examples include getting off the bus in the morning, during math, at lunch, and at recess.) Does the problem occur in multiple settings or in just one place? Is there something in the setting that triggers the behavior? By determining if the problem behavior is pervasive across all settings, the multidisciplinary team can determine whether the behavior is habitual or whether the student doesn't have the appropriate behavior in his repertoire. The intervention could then include teaching the expected behavior to the student and implementing an incentive plan to reward the student for demonstrating the new behavior in a variety of settings. If the problem behavior occurs in only one or two settings, the team might be able to identify a trigger (e.g., having to dress out for P.E. when the student is being teased) that results in the problem behavior.

When does the problem occur? Is it throughout the day or at specific times? For example, does it happen mostly on Mondays after the student is at home for the weekend, or during reading time because the student doesn't like to read? Identifying when the behavior occurs can reveal proactive and preventive steps to include in the intervention plan. For example, it may become apparent that the student has significantly more problems after lunch each day, in part because the student goes to specialists (art, music, and P.E.) where there is less structure. Therefore, the intervention plan may attempt to provide additional structured activities during the specialist times to decrease the likelihood that problem behavior will occur in those settings.

How often does the misbehavior occur and how long does it last? Knowing that a student impulsively gets out of his seat eight times during reading could generate different intervention strategies than those for a student who gets out of his seat only once but wanders around the room for 20 minutes.

Does the student have a physical or neurological problem that affects his or her behavior? (Examples include ADHD, traumatic brain injury, significant communication disabilities, Tourette syndrome, Asperger syndrome, and fetal alcohol syndrome.) Knowing which behaviors can be reasonably expected to improve versus those that are stable due to the nature of the disorder (e.g., tics) will allow the multidisciplinary team to design accommodations in how the intervention will address what the student does and how the teacher responds. For example, it might be appropriate to establish and teach specific expectations for how a student should look and sound when doing independent work in light of his ADHD characteristics, while it would be appropriate to consider accommodations to support a student who has seizures because of a neurological condition.

Is the student aware of the problem behavior? Is the student's behavior functional or appropriate in some settings but not in other school settings? The teacher's perception and the interview with the student will provide insights when answering these questions, which in turn can influence the selection of interventions. For example, it might be appropriate to use self-monitoring or self-evaluation tools to help the student become aware of how often she engages in a behavior that annoys and distracts the teacher.

What does the student say about the misbehavior? Does the student want to change and improve his behavior? When a student is not motivated to change, the intervention may need to provide more extrinsic rewards through an incentive plan.

What appears to be maintaining or reinforcing the student's behavior? Is the student seeking attention from other students or adults, gaining power, escaping something aversive (reading in front of the class), trying to hide a perceived weakness (hates to write), dealing with competing reinforcers (loves to draw), or venting frustration or anger? What does the student gain from the behavior? Does the student benefit from being allowed to make choices or avoid commitments because he doesn't trust adults? How does the student handle frustration and/or anger?

Answering the previous questions will yield valuable insights that should help the multidisciplinary team determine possible functions of the problem behaviors. Identifying a hypothesis about the function helps the team link intervention strategies to that function. The list of possible functions is identical to those shared during the earlier B-RTI phases (STOIC analysis and intervention, 25-minute planning meeting, and IDG: Teacher Interview). The multidisciplinary team should consider the descriptions of each possible function when considering whether that function is contributing to the problem behavior. See the box "Functions to Consider" on the next page and Chapter 7, pp. 151–154, for detailed information about functions.

STEP 3 **Brainstorm Interventions**

After the multidisciplinary team identifies hypotheses for the function(s) of the misbehavior, the next step is to brainstorm possible interventions. Given that it is important for the intervention plan to include prevention, corrective consequences, and positive reinforcement strategies, the team should consider conducting two separate brainstorming sessions: the first to generate options for corrective consequences and the second to generate options for positive (prevention and reinforcer) strategies.

Each brainstorming session should last three to five minutes. We recommend that the first brainstorming session focus on options for consequences, followed by a session on possible positive strategies. The team's brainstorming rules should be shared before starting, in case some of the participants aren't familiar with how to conduct effective and efficient brainstorming. It is important that the ideas and strategies are recorded in a way that all members of the multidisciplinary team can see them. The visual display will help generate other ideas and provide an easy format to later discuss ideas and begin designing the intervention plan.

Whether brainstorming corrective consequences or positives strategies, the multidisciplinary team should consider ideas and strategies that are viewed as evidence-based interventions (Forman & Burke, 2008; IDEA 2004; Kratochwill & Shernoff, 2003; NCLB 2001, Roach & Elliott, 2008; Ysseldyke et al., 1996). One excellent resource is *Interventions: Evidence-Based Behavioral Strategies for Individual Students*, which includes both early-stage and highly structured interventions. Evidence-based interventions from other authors and resources should also be considered. Another excellent resource is *The Teacher's Encyclopedia of Behavior Management*.

❧ FUNCTIONS TO CONSIDER

Ability. Sometimes a behavior occurs because the student does not have the neurological or physiological ability to behave the way the teacher would like. Examples include ADHD, traumatic brain injury, significant communication disabilities, Tourette syndrome, Asperger syndrome, and fetal alcohol syndrome.

Awareness. Students may exhibit patterns of behavior about which they are almost completely unaware. Bringing the student to a conscious awareness of the problem behavior will make the intervention much more successful.

Adult attention. To get attention from an adult, some students may seek that attention in inappropriate ways. Interventions will involve giving far less attention to the misbehavior while increasing the attention the student receives for positive and appropriate behavior.

Peer attention. Some students misbehave to seek attention from peers—playing the class clown, showing off, arguing, bullying, or being annoying. Interventions will involve increasing the amount of attention the student receives in prosocial ways.

Power or control. Some students seek power or control by eliciting emotional reactions from teachers. Interventions involve giving the student control over certain aspects when she exhibits positive behaviors and avoids power struggles and arguments.

Escape or avoidance (task difficulty or discomfort). Typically, the student is trying to avoid or escape something. One example is avoiding work that is too difficult. Or a student may prefer to be sent to the office rather than participate in an activity that is uncomfortable.

Competing reinforcers. The student engages in misbehavior because he would rather do something other than the assigned task or activity. Interventions can tap into that preference by allowing the student to read a novel (or draw) after completing assigned work.

Other. Although these functions are the most common, other possibilities exist. For example, the student may exhibit emotional outbursts on Monday not because of what happens in school, but rather as a way to express frustration and anger over things that occurred at home on the weekend.

When brainstorming is completed, the team leader/coordinator should allow two or three minutes for any team member to ask questions about specific suggestions. It is important to encourage the teacher to ask questions if she is unfamiliar with any of the suggested strategies.

STEP 4   Design and Develop the Intervention Plan

In this part of Stage 3, the multidisciplinary team and teacher begin designing and planning the intervention. The team needs to be careful about advocating a specific intervention. The degree of teacher buy-in, effort, and fidelity of the intervention plan can be easily compromised if the teacher feels that she had little or no input into what was selected. This is especially crucial because it is likely that some, if not many, components of the plan will address classroom behavior by having the teacher change her behavior. On the other hand, this stage of the B-RTI continuum is specifically designed to involve the highest level of expertise and experience in developing a comprehensive intervention plan. This means the teacher will have more outside assistance to help than she did previously. In addition, more complex intervention options will be available for the teacher to select.

Therefore, the multidisciplinary team members should have more input into the design and development of the intervention plan than they did in the earlier phases of the B-RTI continuum, when the teacher was working with an interventionist or the intervention planning team. To achieve a balance between teacher input and team recommendations, the multidisciplinary team needs to actively seek and embrace teacher input in selecting corrective consequences and positive strategies while also providing guidance and input on how to proceed (Creed & Kendall, 2005; Elliott, 1988; Kratochwill & Stoiber, 2000; Roach & Elliott, 2008). Have the teacher consider the following variables when selecting consequences and positive strategies:

- The amount of time and effort required of the teacher to implement the corrective consequence or positive strategy is critical. Strategies that require extensive effort from a frustrated teacher who feels overwhelmed may need to be avoided.

- The amount of support available to help the teacher is relevant, especially if a highly structured intervention is selected. In this case, the teacher will need extensive help from the case manager, another member of the multidisciplinary team, or another staff member to successfully implement the intervention.

- The degree of student responsibility and motivation to change will affect which strategies are most likely to be successful.

> The degree of teacher buy-in, effort, and fidelity of the intervention plan can be easily compromised if the teacher feels that she had little or no input into what was selected.

Corrective consequences are typically a key part of the intervention plan. At best, a consequence will stop misbehavior from reoccurring, but it won't encourage or teach a more appropriate behavior (Bambara & Kern, 2005; Gresham, 2002; Scheuermann & Hall, 2008). Therefore, it is especially important that consequence strategies are used in conjunction with prevention and skill-building strategies.

When reviewing the range of consequences identified during brainstorming, the multidisciplinary team and teacher should consider the following suggestions in selecting consequences for the intervention plan.

Identify behaviors. Describe the inappropriate behaviors to be reduced or eliminated. Team members should ask questions or give scenarios to help the teacher get a clear picture of which behaviors to discourage or ignore and which behaviors trigger a corrective consequence. For example, what should the teacher do if the student shrugs his shoulders in reply when asked to do something? Is that respectful or disrespectful behavior? The multidisciplinary team needs to help the teacher be specific and objective when describing behaviors that will receive consequences. These descriptions of behaviors need to pass the "stranger" test, which means that two adults will easily agree that a specific type of behavior has occurred. It is important to consider the range of behaviors that constitute examples and nonexamples of an occurrence and attempt to find the minimal difference between appropriate and unacceptable behavior.

Be respectful. It is essential that selected consequences never embarrass or belittle the student.

Be logical. Logical and natural consequences work best because they teach a student that certain actions consistently lead to a specific consequence.

Be mild. Mild consequences are usually more effective because the teacher and other staff members are more likely to consistently deliver a mild consequence every time the misbehavior occurs. On the other hand, a teacher or other staff member is more likely to give threats or warnings in place of a severe consequence because he doesn't want to deliver the severe consequence for a variety of reasons (e.g., it takes too much time to document, it is toward the end of the school day, the misbehavior doesn't seem to warrant a severe consequence). When the consequence is not consistently delivered, the student realizes the predetermined plan to deliver consequences is actually negotiable. Such a realization can be reinforcing for a student, especially one who has a history of inappropriate behavior. The multidisciplinary team needs to help the teacher understand that it is the certainty and consistency of a consequence—not the severity—that stops misbehavior from reoccurring.

Be calm. The teacher and staff members need to deliver consequences without showing anger. If the adult is obviously angry, the student could easily perceive the consequence as tied to the adult's anger instead of to the student's misbehavior. In addition,

> It is essential that selected consequences never embarrass or belittle the student.

some problem behaviors that are maintained by adult attention may be inadvertently reinforced when adults become emotional and provide intensive attention during the corrective consequence delivery.

Create a ladder. If there is a cluster of different misbehaviors associated with the goal, the multidisciplinary team might consider identifying a consequence *ladder*. This is a process in which the teacher and team identify specific mild misbehaviors that should be ignored, misbehaviors that earn a mild in-class consequence (e.g., time owed or verbal reprimand), and misbehaviors that receive a moderate to severe out-of-class consequence (e.g., timeout in another classroom, office referral, or detention).

Link to function. The multidisciplinary team and teacher need to link the consequences to the function of the misbehavior:

- Use gentle verbal reprimands when the student doesn't know the behavior is unacceptable (ability function) or isn't aware that he is engaging in inappropriate behavior (awareness function).

- Whenever possible, ignore a student's misbehavior when she is seeking attention.

- Consider mild consequences when a student needs to stop a bad habit or needs to learn that there will be a consistent consequence. Some options include verbal reprimand, time owed, restitution, timeout, points lost, being sent to another class, parent contact, and filling out a behavior improvement form.

Positive strategies are the essential part of any intervention plan designed to change a student's behavior. An intervention plan comprised only of corrective consequences or punitive strategies is much less likely to succeed than one that is comprehensive and includes preventive strategies (Carr, Robinson, Taylor, & Carlson, 1990; O'Neill et al., 1997; Sugai et al., 2000, 2002). When reviewing the range of positive strategies identified during brainstorming, the multidisciplinary team and teacher should consider the following suggestions in selecting consequences for the intervention plan.

Replacement behaviors. The goal of the positive strategies should focus on teaching, encouraging, and reinforcing the student to display identified replacement behaviors. By using positive strategies, the teacher and other staff members teach the student that displaying the responsible behaviors will help meet her needs in appropriate ways while also fulfilling the established goal.

Desired behaviors/student strengths. The intervention plan needs to include a description of both the desired responsible behaviors (i.e., replacement behaviors) and the student's strengths that need to be encouraged and reinforced by using positive strategies. These behaviors are already in the student's repertoire or need to be directly modeled and taught (e.g., how to appropriately respond to an adult reprimand).

Guide selection. The multidisciplinary team needs to make sure that at least one to three positive strategies are selected to encourage the replacement behaviors. To increase teacher buy-in and create more integrity in the intervention, the multidisciplinary team and case manager should carefully guide and encourage the teacher to select those positive strategies that have a good chance to be effective considering the student's background and previous interventions.

Consider all options. Options for positive strategies include giving the student plenty of daily noncontingent attention, providing positive feedback on challenging academic and behavioral efforts, providing positive feedback on the strengths identified by the teacher, providing intermittent celebrations (including concrete rewards, celebrations, and meaningful work) when the desired behavior is demonstrated, boosting the teacher's ratio of positive interactions with the student to at least three to one, and designing an incentive or reinforcement plan.

STEP 5 **Finalize the Intervention**

Once the corrective consequences and positive strategies are identified, the next step requires nailing down all the details of the intervention. No matter how powerful the consequences and positive strategies, the success of the intervention plan depends on developing and documenting details. The multidisciplinary team needs to write down the various logistical details of the plan (i.e., who, what, where, and when) on p. 4 of the IDG: MDT form. Be sure to identify what resources the teacher needs (e.g., modeling, coaching, observations, forms, materials).

The multidisciplinary team also needs to address two key actions and reminders when developing and implementing the intervention plan. First, the multidisciplinary team should alert the teacher that the misbehavior might initially increase when the plan is implemented. It is essential that the teacher be relentless in implementing the plan every day for at least two weeks if the plan is to have any chance of success. Second, the multidisciplinary team and teacher should decide how the student will be told of the intervention plan by determining the following:

How to tell the student. By whom and when will the student be told of the plan and its details? Typically, this is done by the classroom teacher. If for some reason the teacher and multidisciplinary team feel that the student's relationship with the teacher might jeopardize the student's buy-in, the team should identify another staff member with whom the student has a more positive relationship to meet with the student. In this situation, consider having the teacher attend but allow the other staff member to lead the meeting and do most of the talking. When the student is told, it should be done in private and at a neutral time when the student has not recently misbehaved. Select a location where there won't be any interruptions or other students watching or listening.

> No matter how powerful the consequences and positive strategies, the success of the intervention plan depends on developing and documenting details.

What to tell the student. Whoever is talking with the student needs to plan ahead to determine what will be shared with the student. If two adults will be explaining the plan to the student, decide who would be best to describe what parts of the plan.

Student input. During the Stage 3 meeting, the multidisciplinary team and teacher should decide if the student will be given the opportunity for input on rewards and other details of the plan. If so, make sure the student understands that the teacher will have the final say in how the plan looks.

Plan for student feedback. The multidisciplinary team and teacher should decide when and how the student can talk with the teacher about an earlier delivered consequence, because the teacher should not allow the student to engage in such questioning and discussion when the consequence is being delivered. We recommend that you consider a time later that morning or afternoon when the teacher and student are calm and the discussion won't disrupt the instructional process.

Give the student details. Be sure to tell the student how the plan will be evaluated and what data will be collected before the intervention is actually implemented. Preferably, meet with the student one or two days before the intervention is scheduled to start. If the intervention plan requires the student to keep self-evaluation or self-monitoring charts, take the time to explain and teach the process, show the form to the student, and do some guided practice. Also tell the student that the data will be shared with him at the end of each week so that he and the teacher can assess how the intervention is working.

Be positive. It is essential that the teacher convey positive expectations about how the intervention will help the student. This is best done by having the teacher express confidence and enthusiasm when describing the intervention and telling the student that she and the school will continue working with the student until the problem is solved, even if it takes until the end of the school year.

Following are other crucial details and decisions that the multidisciplinary team and teacher should address when designing and implementing the intervention plan:

Choose a start date. Determine a reasonable day to start the plan within the next five work days. Delaying any longer than that could diminish both the teacher's enthusiasm for the intervention and her recollection of what needs to be done. We recommend that you do not start the intervention on Thursday or Friday. Starting at the beginning of the week gives the student four or five consecutive days of working on the intervention.

Who to include. The multidisciplinary team and teacher need to decide if the plan needs to be shared with any other staff members who are working with the student (e.g., the other teachers on a middle school team, the P.E. teacher, the reading teacher).

The multidisciplinary team and teacher should also determine what, if any, role the other staff members will play in implementing the intervention plan. Identify who is the best person to explain the intervention and what their responsibilities will be to any additional staff members who will be involved. Make sure this sharing occurs before the intervention is implemented.

Substitute teacher involvement. An important decision for the multidisciplinary team and teacher is whether a substitute teacher will be asked to implement the intervention plan. If the components of the intervention plan are fairly simple and/or can be delivered by another staff member (e.g., the school counselor), it may be appropriate to ask the substitute teacher to participate, especially if she is experienced, has effectively worked at the school before (preferably in this classroom), and relates well to students. The multidisciplinary team and teacher should identify when, how, and by whom the substitute teacher will be informed about the plan and her role in it. If the regular teacher will be absent for more than a couple of days, the multidisciplinary team should decide whether the intervention plan should be revised to reflect the presence of a substitute teacher. Before the plan is implemented, the team and teacher should also decide what to tell the student about the plan in regard to a substitute teacher. Will the interventions continue to be used? What is the student expected to do? It would be beneficial for the multidisciplinary team and teacher to identify who at the school will remind the student of the expectations whenever the teacher is absent.

Inform administrator(s). Given that we are nearing or entering Tier 3 on the B-RTI continuum, we recommend that the intervention plan be shared with the administrator and school counselor if they are not members of the multidisciplinary team. This is important regardless of whether they are participating in any way with the interventions, because they might be contacted by the parents or by another staff member about the student's behavior. In a school with more than one administrator or counselor, it would wise to inform any assistant principals or school counselors who might interact with the student. The multidisciplinary team should identify who will inform the administrator(s) and counselor(s) and when.

Parent contact. The multidisciplinary team and teacher must decide how and when the intervention plan will be shared with the parents/guardians if they were not present at the multidisciplinary team meeting. Having the teacher make this contact is appropriate unless there is some reason for another staff member with better rapport to make the contact. It is important to share the broad details of the plan (including the goal, consequences, and positive strategies) and how and when the parents will be updated about the status of the intervention.

Should the class be told? If the multidisciplinary team or teacher believes it is important to explain the interventions to other students in the class, decide what to share, including how they are expected to behave and how they should respond to certain misbehaviors by the student. The classroom teacher is the natural choice to explain the interventions to the class before implementing the plan. The multidisciplinary team can help the teacher by identifying what needs to be shared and how best to do it.

Once the Stage 3 part of the IDG: MDT process is completed, the case manager needs to make sure the teacher receives a written copy of the completed IDG: MDT form and intervention plan. The case manager and team coordinator will also need copies of the forms.

STEP 6 Evaluate the Plan and Follow Up

Before the Stage 3 meeting ends, the multidisciplinary team and teacher should identify methods that can be used to evaluate the effect of the intervention plan on the student's target behavior(s) during the first two weeks of implementation. The monitoring system needs to assess the frequency, duration, and intensity of the target behaviors as well as any triggers and functions of the behavior. Two independent means of evaluating progress should be selected, with at least one of the methods generating systematic, objective data.

Although your main focus at this time is on the first two weeks, it is important to consider whether the two-week monitoring plan will be appropriate to continue throughout the intervention or whether a modified outcomes-data collection system should be established. In addition to collecting data on student outcomes, a plan for monitoring teacher fidelity of implementation should be established. The classroom teacher will be an integral part of assessing fidelity because the intervention will likely have a major focus in the classroom. The case manager can talk with the teacher about the challenges of implementing the preventive strategies, positive consequences, and negative consequences.

Other intervention variables for the case manager and teacher to assess are collecting data, debriefing the student on a regular basis, responding to unique situations (e.g., a substitute teacher in the room, student absences or tardies, changes in the student's regular schedule). Besides talking to the teacher about fidelity, the case manager will likely have other opportunities to assess fidelity by talking with the student, observing in the classroom, or talking with other staff members who are working with the student. See Chapter 7, pp. 159–162, for detailed information about methods and data sources the multidisciplinary team and teacher can consider.

Following are a few other details and issues to consider when evaluating and following up on an intervention plan.

- The case manager or another team member should select a way to visually display the data on one page. Consider whether a table, bar graph, pie chart, or scatterplot will make trends and patterns apparent to the teacher, team, student, and parents.

- The team needs to identify a date and time to meet two weeks after the plan is implemented to discuss how it is working.

- It is essential that the case manager provide daily encouragement and support, especially during the first couple of days of implementing the intervention plan. The case manager could talk to the teacher in the morning before school starts, leave a positive note, and/or send a positive or encouraging e-mail message. This contact could also give the teacher and case manager time to resolve any minor glitches that develop.

- Whatever formal support or resources are promised to the teacher, the case manager needs to make sure they are delivered as planned!

- The case manager needs to remind the teacher to calmly and immediately deliver the identified consequences each and every time the misbehavior occurs. Remind the teacher not to threaten, lecture, or cajole—because the goal is to avoid power struggles with the student. Also remind the teacher to give warnings only if they are part of the plan.

- The case manager needs to remind the teacher to deliver the positive strategies (e.g., noncontingent attention, verbal feedback, rewards) that were identified as part of the intervention plan. The student must earn the attention, positive feedback, and rewards from the incentive plan if behavior is going to change. If the student is not earning the rewards, the case manager should work with the teacher to reduce the criteria for earning them so that the student can experience some early success.

See the opposite page for types of data that can be used to evaluate the efficacy of an intervention. Detailed information on data collection methods appears in Chapter 5.

> Whatever formal support or resources are promised to the teacher, the case manager needs to make sure they are delivered as planned.

Stage 4: Follow-Up Meeting(s)

The initial follow-up meeting is held two weeks after the intervention plan is first implemented. This meeting will typically be short (10–15 minutes) unless the circumstances of the student's situation require additional time. It is important that the teacher and case manager attend the meeting. At the meeting, the multidisciplinary team conducts the following actions:

❖ STUDENT OUTCOME ASSESSMENT DATA

Quality ratings. These provide valuable information about student behavior. Rating scales are usually accompanied by criteria for judging student behavior.

Work products. The data used may include the percentage of assignments completed, test scores, grades, and number of written words in a journal.

Self-monitoring data. This type of data requires a student to record, for example, the number of times he raises his hand and the number of times he blurts out in class without raising his hand.

Data from a reinforcement system. This data provides information about the effectiveness of the intervention by recording the number of times a student earns a reinforcer.

PLAN IMPLEMENTATION ASSESSMENT DATA

Frequency data. During observation, a count can be taken whenever the student engages in a particular behavior (e.g., the number of times the student gets out of his seat in a day or the number of times the student interacts disrespectfully with the teacher).

Duration data. Evaluation information might also include the amount of time a student engages in a particular behavior. ("Joey had three tantrums today for a total of 58 minutes.")

Latency data. This data notes how much time it takes for a particular behavior to begin after a stimulus occurs.

Audio or video records. Recordings are made both before the intervention is implemented and then at periodic intervals to document changes in student behavior. Frequency, duration, and latency data can be obtained from recordings.

Third-party observations. These can yield frequency, duration, and latency data about a behavior. To determine progress, observations should be scheduled to take place before the intervention begins and then periodically after its implementation.

STEP 1 Review Data

Review all the collected data from the two weeks of the intervention plan by discussing the visual display(s) of the data (e.g., tables, charts, or scatterplot).

STEP 2 Share the Teacher's Perspective

Share with the team the teacher's perceptions of how well the plan is addressing the goal (target behavior). These perceptions can be derived from subjective ratings, or the case manager could help the teacher summarize her thoughts before attending the meeting.

STEP 3 Evaluate and Adjust the Intervention Plan if Needed

Decide how to proceed with the referral from this point. The team can choose from the following options for how to proceed:

- If the interventions are working, continue their implementation. The team needs to encourage the teacher to celebrate the improvements and to provide the student and parents with positive feedback about the interventions.

- Continue the interventions as designed, but adjust the implementation to ensure that they are implemented with greater fidelity. Notify any staff member who will be affected by the adjustments. Inform the student and parents of the changes.

- Revise the interventions to make necessary modifications to address weaknesses or gaps. Decide how to inform the student of any changes and decide when to start implementing those changes. Implement the revised interventions for another two weeks and continue to collect data. Inform the parents of the current outcomes and modifications.

- Amend the interventions to address other target behaviors. Inform the student, parents, and any participating staff members of the changes. Implement the revised interventions for two weeks and continue to collect data.

- Refer the student to special education and/or other appropriate school or district services or programs. Inform the student and parents of this recommendation.

- Begin to phase out the intervention plan as a result of its successful effect on the target behavior. Set a gradual phaseout schedule. Inform the student and any participating staff members of the phaseout. Be sure to celebrate the student's success and inform the parents. Decide when to meet next to discuss the disposition of the phaseout.

- Once the phaseout is completed, discontinue the intervention plan and connect the student to any universal supports in the school that can meet the student's needs and help him or her have a successful adjustment. Inform the student and parents and be sure to celebrate. This fading is unlikely to occur until an intervention has successfully maintained the goal behavior over a period of a couple of months.

STEP 4 Summarize the Team's Recommendations

Once the multidisciplinary team makes its recommendations, a written explanation or rationale for the recommendation should be documented on p. 5 of the IDG: MDT form, including what will be done, by whom, and when.

STEP 5 Plan Further Follow-Up if Needed

The multidisciplinary team needs to decide if and when any additional follow-up meetings are needed. Identify what questions or issues need to be addressed at the follow-up meeting. When the meeting is held, be sure to document the outcomes and any recommendations by using the last page of the IDG: MDT form or adding another page to the form. The multidisciplinary team members should consider the recommendations previously listed for the first meeting during Stage 4 and provide the rationale for their decision.

STEP 6 Document Outcome

Once the referral is closed, the multidisciplinary team needs to carefully document its recommendations and findings on the IDG: MDT form and attach copies of relevant forms, collected data, and charts. This documentation should be kept in a confidential location that ensures appropriate access for involved staff members. Follow district policy on whether the IDG: MDT and related documentation should be placed in the student's official school records.

CONCLUSION

Although the problem-solving process implemented by the multidisciplinary team is very similar to that of both the IDG: Teacher Interview and the 25-Minute Planning Process, it differs in scope. The process involves more skilled professionals to create a greater breadth of perspective and includes the collection of much more information in the form of observations, interviews, and records review to ensure that all the available information is brought to bear in designing a comprehensive intervention. As has been stated many times, B-RTI is about matching the intensity of problem-solving and intervention to the needs of the student. This multidisciplinary process is occurring only because less intense processes have failed to yield a successful intervention. At this stage, every effort must be made to find something that will help the student succeed.

 Reproducible Materials

A copy of the following reproducible material appears on the CD. Permission is given for individual teachers, administrators, or other school personnel to reproduce this form for in-district use.

> Reproducible Form 9.1: Intervention Decision Guide:
> Multidisciplinary Team

CHAPTER 10

Connections

A Schoolwide Check-and-Connect Plan

Our experiences as parents and teachers have taught us that children have a better chance of succeeding when they receive consistent and supportive feedback. Connections is a schoolwide check-and-connect plan that builds on this basic truth with a formalized, easy-to-follow program.

Designed to meet the needs of academically and behaviorally challenged students, Connections uses a team approach—parents, students, teachers, and other staff members work together to help students improve their behavior and experience academic success (Neyhart & Garrison, 1992). It is a powerful student monitoring and feedback program that has demonstrated success in meeting a host of student challenges.

Unlike many other programs with similar goals, Connections does not require significant investment in technology or staffing. The program effectively accesses the resources currently present in your school, building, or district to develop the adult-student relationships that can effect positive behavior change. This chapter outlines how to set up and implement a Connections program in your school.

STRUCTURE OVERVIEW

Connections began in a low-income elementary school in rural Douglas County, Oregon, in the 1980s. Teacher Stefanie Neyhart, frustrated by the increasing number of young children experiencing behavioral difficulties in school, began studying strategies for student success. "One thing I absolutely knew without a doubt," she recalls, "is that more interaction and communication with adults always equaled more success for the students."

Armed with that belief, Neyhart and administrator Mickey Garrison developed a program based on frequent monitoring and feedback. The concept was simple: Students who were having difficulty would carry a card with them throughout the day. The card identified specific behavioral goals and awarded points for meeting those goals. Teachers and other staff members would make comments and award points on the card at frequent intervals throughout the day, and parents would examine the card and its comments at home and provide their input as well. Students would then be frequently rewarded for their successes in meeting the specified goals (Neyhart & Garrison, 1992).

Over the next several years, the Connections program was refined in that elementary school and several others. The program also proved successful at the middle school level and eventually was rolled out to schools nationwide.

Connections is not a radically new program, nor does it introduce a lot of new concepts. Rather, it integrates several successful tried-and-true techniques into one comprehensive strategy. One feature that makes Connections different from other daily report card programs is that it evaluates behavior at frequent intervals throughout the day instead of assigning an overall assessment for the entire day. Therefore, if a student has a single bad hour during the day, it doesn't negate the positive behavior that he or she may have exhibited in other settings or at other times. The program emphasizes positive behavior with immediate feedback and reinforcement.

THEORY OF SUCCESSIVE APPROXIMATION

The program works on the theory of successive approximation, or gradually molding correct behavior by positively reinforcing student responses that come close to the desired action. As the student progresses in the program, the behavior goals become more challenging, but the behavior, through practice, becomes easier. Garrison likens the process to an experience she had on vacation not too long ago: A sea kayaking adventure involved paddling into a series of caves through entry points that grew progressively more dark and difficult. But the experience of successfully navigating each entry acclimated the kayakers, so by the end of the day, they were able to pass through a channel with very little space or light and enter a stunning underwater cave—a place unlike anything they had ever experienced. The Connections program is a similar experience for students, gradually taking them through increasing challenges to a level of success that otherwise would not have seemed possible.

As the student progresses in the program, the behavior goals become more challenging, but the behavior, through practice, becomes easier.

CONNECTIONS COMPONENTS

Although the program is simple, it requires teachers' time and support and the dedication of an individual coordinator within the school or building. The leadership team will need to establish the program at the beginning of the school year and train all staff in how it works. The coordinator can be any instructional staff member—assistant principal, school counselor, teacher, or instructional assistant—but ideally should be a behavior specialist, if your school has the resources. To increase the potential success of the program, consider using people in your building who are especially well liked by students. For a truly sustainable program, a school should consider assigning a person full time or part time as the Connections coordinator.

REFERRALS

The process begins when a teacher refers the student to the program through the Connections coordinator. Referrals are simple and require no paperwork. Any teacher who has a concern about a student's behavior or academic performance and believes the student will benefit from the program can simply meet with the coordinator and request that the student be added.

In a training session at the beginning of the year, school staff learn about the program, the process for referring students, and what their role will be in providing feedback to students who are in their class and are part of the Connections program. In addition, teachers should be encouraged to use the program in the fairly early stages of a problem and not wait until a student has established a firmly ingrained pattern of misbehavior or missed assignments.

MEETINGS AND GOALS

Next, the coordinator arranges a meeting that includes herself, the referring teacher, the principal, and the student's parents or guardian. At this meeting, the parents are given an overview of the program and have an opportunity to share their goals for their child. At this point, parents are asked to give written permission for the intervention. The referring teacher also shares his or her goals for the student, and the group collaboratively outlines a set of progressively challenging daily goals. Some schools use their schoolwide Guidelines for Success or their schoolwide rules as the goals that will be rated on the carry cards. This creates a standardization that makes filling out the cards easy for staff because all students are being rated on the same three behavioral categories—for example, respect, responsibility, and safety.

The roles and responsibilities of all participants are also discussed. Teachers are responsible for providing the student with honest, constructive, and skillful feedback. The student is responsible for taking the card to each school setting throughout the day, showing it to her parents every day, and taking it to the coordinator first thing every morning. Parents are responsible for reviewing the student's daily performance and for monitoring homework. Many schools send a carbon copy home to parents so if the student forgets to bring the card back, there isn't a big problem. Some schools build in extra rewards for getting the card back to school, which can enhance communication between home and school and increase the chance the program will help a student.

Near the end of the meeting, the student is called in. The coordinator explains how the program works and shares the parent-teacher goals. With the student's collaboration, the group establishes a set of progressively challenging daily goals and the rewards that the student would like to work toward by being successful in the program.

Initial goals should be simple and easily achievable. The first goal may simply be "stay in my seat during class" or "turn in all assigned work." Once the student learns the procedure and has experienced initial success, the coordinator encourages the student to set new, more challenging goals. Ultimately, though, the coordinator is responsible for writing the student's daily goal on the card and ensuring that the student has a new goal when he has met the previous one with a 90% success rate for five consecutive days.

THE CARRY CARD

At the heart of the program is the Daily Progress Monitor, the card that the student carries to every educational setting throughout the school day. The most flexible aspect of this program is the structure of the card. We have provided examples (Reproducible Forms 10.1 and 10.2 shown on p. 253), but your school or building can design the card in a way that is appropriate for your student needs and available resources.

We recommend starting simple, either by having the same set of goal behaviors schoolwide, as mentioned earlier, or with all the teachers at a particular grade level agreeing on a set menu of behaviors to evaluate. All the teachers for that grade level can collaborate to design the card and choose the behaviors they would like to see addressed. A group of first-grade teachers might choose:

- Hands and feet to self

- Staying in chair

- Listening

Third-grade teachers might want to evaluate:

- Focuses and completes work in class

- Follows directions first time given

- Hands, feet, and objects to self

Initial goals should be simple and easily achievable.

Standardizing the behaviors to evaluate makes the program easier for teachers to implement, especially if they have several students who need cards evaluated and signed for every instructional period.

Student's role. The student is responsible for picking up a new card every morning, having it signed throughout the day, sharing it with his or her parents in the evening, and returning it to the Connections coordinator each morning. It is also the student's job to write down specific homework and missing work assignments on the new carry card if a teacher has checked "yes" to either MW (missing work) or HW (homework) on the card from the day before.

Parents' role. Parents need to ask for the card every day after school and discuss the student's day with him. (See "Using the Daily Progress Monitor" on the next page for more details.) Parents are encouraged to keep a tally of points at home and to help the student work toward meeting a home goal such as working on homework for an hour each night. This goal is different from the student's daily goals and is family specific. Some parents will be proactive about this goal and others will not. If the parents are unwilling or unable to participate, an adult in the school can act as a stand-in. In that case, the student would, at the end of the school day, take the card to the stand-in—say, the assistant principal—who would discuss the day's results with the student and sign where the parents would typically sign.

Parents should have a plan in place for when the student reaches goals or if the student does not follow through with the plan. Students who find themselves with no privileges before starting the program can create a plan with their parents to earn them back. After the student completes any homework, she shows it to a parent. The parent initials the carry card, confirming that the homework was completed. Students who have no homework are encouraged to read and/or study for an hour at night. In primary grades, this time period should be much shorter.

Staff members' role. Staff members need to give students consistent, constructive, specific, and honest feedback each time they sign the carry card. It is important that staff understand the importance of interacting positively with the student while providing feedback, as lack of positive interaction can be a common pitfall of the program. They need to help make the card important to the student by taking it seriously and having a system that helps the student know how and when to get the card signed in each particular classroom. When a student will not carry the card, the homeroom teacher assumes responsibility for collecting and returning that student's card to the coordinator.

> Staff members need to give students consistent, constructive, specific, and honest feedback each time they sign the carry card.

Coordinator's role. In the morning before school, the coordinator meets briefly with every student in the program, collects cards from the day before, writes each student's daily goal on her new card, and gives the card to the student. It is important that

Continued on p. 254

☞ *USING THE DAILY PROGRESS MONITOR*

The elementary monitoring card and the secondary monitoring card are essentially identical except for the schedule section. This section lists instructional intervals, with the reporting time at the end of the interval. On the elementary card, the intervals are sectioned by time. On the secondary card, the intervals should be indicated by first period, second period, etc. The intervals do not need to be the same length— for example, if a student has a homeroom period from 8:45 to 9:00 a.m., the end of that interval (9:00) is the first reporting time on the card. Then the student has a written language and reading period that ends at 10:15. The next reporting time is thus 10:15.

At the end of each period, the teacher rates the student using the scale (0 = No, 1 = OK, 2 = Yes) at the top of the rating card. The student is rated on three criteria:

- On Task
- Prepared
- Respects Others

In addition, the teacher indicates whether the student has homework (HW) or any missing work (MW) that needs to be completed for that class period. The teacher circles a Y for yes to indicate that there is homework or missing work.

The teacher can either quickly debrief with the student about the rating or simply hand the student the card. The teacher must use a pen to initial the card in the T.I. column. The teacher returns the card to the student, who reviews the teacher rating and initials the S.I. column if he or she agrees with the teacher. If the student disagrees, he or she places an X in the S.I. column. The Connections coordinator follows up on any Xs. The follow-up helps the student better understand what the teacher expects and why he or she received a particular rating. The follow-up also promptly addresses disagreements, thus minimizing student resentment.

The Teacher Comments column allows the teacher to highlight accomplishments, express concerns, and report on academic progress or upcoming projects (e.g., oral report due Friday, in-class quiz 87%).

The parent reviews the student's school performance. Parents are encouraged to be matter-of-fact about low ratings and to spend little time discussing the student's day. Parents are provided with one-liners for responding to low scores and with statements for future encouragement. For example, the parent might say, "You made inappropriate choices during period 3. Do a better job tomorrow."

Parents are encouraged to walk away from the student and allow 15–20 minutes to pass before they interact with the student again. When students receive high scores, parents are encouraged to spend as much time as possible with the student. Parents are also encouraged to bestow privileges when the student makes appropriate choices. The student can earn a total of 22 points at home for completing homework and getting the card signed. Ask parents to initial next to each homework assignment when it's completed. Reading is a homework substitute when there is no assigned homework. The Parent Comments section provides school staff with useful information (e.g., joys and concerns). The Connections coordinator will communicate parent comments to the appropriate teacher.

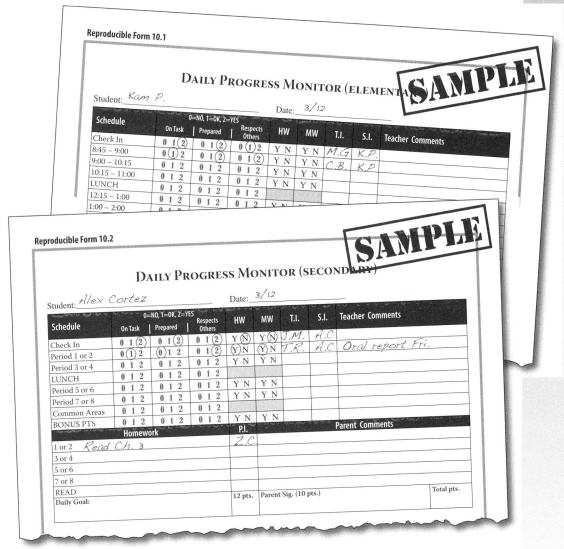

Reproducible Form 10.1

SAMPLE

DAILY PROGRESS MONITOR (ELEMENTARY)

Student: _Kam P._   Date: _3/12_

Schedule	On Task	Prepared	Respects Others	HW	MW	T.I.	S.I.	Teacher Comments
	0=NO, 1=OK, 2=YES							
Check In	0 1 (2)	0 1 (2)	0 (1) 2					
8:45 – 9:00	0 (1) 2	0 1 (2)	0 1 (2)	Y N	Y N	M.G	K.P.	
9:00 – 10:15	0 1 2	0 1 2	0 1 2	Y N	Y N	C.B.	K.P	
10:15 – 11:00	0 1 2	0 1 2	0 1 2	Y N	Y N			
LUNCH	0 1 2	0 1 2	0 1 2	Y N	Y N			
12:15 – 1:00	0 1 2	0 1 2	0 1 2					
1:00 – 2:00	0 1 2			Y N				

Reproducible Form 10.2

SAMPLE

DAILY PROGRESS MONITOR (SECONDARY)

Student: _Alex Cortez_   Date: _3/12_

Schedule	On Task	Prepared	Respects Others	HW	MW	T.I.	S.I.	Teacher Comments
	0=NO, 1=OK, 2=YES							
Check In	0 1 (2)	0 1 (2)	0 1 (2)	Y (N)	Y (N)	J.M.	A.C	
Period 1 or 2	0 (1) 2	(0) 1 2	0 1 (2)	(Y) N	(Y) N	T.R.	A.C	Oral report Fri.
Period 3 or 4	0 1 2	0 1 2	0 1 2	Y N	Y N			
LUNCH	0 1 2	0 1 2	0 1 2					
Period 5 or 6	0 1 2	0 1 2	0 1 2	Y N	Y N			
Period 7 or 8	0 1 2	0 1 2	0 1 2	Y N	Y N			
Common Areas	0 1 2	0 1 2	0 1 2					
BONUS PTS	0 1 2	0 1 2	0 1 2	Y N	Y N			

Homework		P.I.	Parent Comments
1 or 2	_Read Ch. 3_	Z.C	
3 or 4			
5 or 6			
7 or 8			
READ		12 pts.	Parent Sig. (10 pts.)	Total pts.
Daily Goal:			

Reproducible Materials Full-page blank copies of forms are provided on the CD. Permission is given for individual teachers, administrators, or other school personnel to reproduce any form labeled "Reproducible Form" for in-district use.

this interaction is positive and meaningful for the student. The check-in can serve as a proactive intervention because it can neutralize any difficulties the student may experience before arriving at school. In addition, the coordinator can precorrect the student based on previous struggles. ("Remember, as soon as you get to class, check in with Mrs. Atwood and get your homework assignment. That way you will have already met that goal for today. I know you can do it.") The coordinator will also be responsible for producing the cards, recording the student's points each day, and keeping a running total.

The coordinator should print out simple graphs every two to three days so the student can monitor his own progress (see the "Graphs and Charts" box for tips). Some students may even enjoy entering their points each day and reviewing the graph at that time. Spreadsheets can also help coordinators and students easily see where problem areas occur. Posting progress graphs on the classroom wall can offer students immediate and constant reinforcement. Graphing progress also provides data points that can be used for assessment purposes and data analysis. For example, a graph can show that a student is meeting the standardized evaluative expectations for every period but one. Once that problem time period is identified, the coordinator can arrange for the student to be observed during that time period, which can lead to identifying and correcting the problem.

SCHOOLWIDE PARTICIPATION

All adults in the school or building should be well versed in the Connections program so they can be effective participants. The program's success depends on adults in the school being willing to perform spot checks of the cards carried by participating students. Adults in the school also need to find opportunities to add points to a student's card. For example, lunchroom and recess monitors can and should add bonus points to a student's card when they notice good behavior. Catching students in good behavior and rewarding them for it is a very effective motivator. The Connections program is based on frequent positive feedback—on a schoolwide basis—for students who need it most.

Give careful thought to how all staff will be trained in their role in the program. The training should include classroom teachers, supervisors for playgrounds and cafeterias, security officers, and classroom-based paraprofessionals. In addition, the Connections coordinator should put together a one-page description of the program for guest teachers.

CELEBRATIONS

Once a month, the coordinator holds an awards ceremony for all students new to the program and for those who have met the point goal (for example, 1,000 points) for the previous month. In some ways, the celebrations are the most important part of the Connections program. They are an opportunity for students to receive public and

Posting progress graphs on the classroom wall can offer students immediate and constant reinforcement.

👁 GRAPHS AND CHARTS

Every few days, the Connections coordinator should create and print simple graphs so that students can monitor their own progress. Entering data from the carry cards into a spreadsheet program makes it easy to generate the following types of charts.

Individual student graph shows the student's daily progress over a specified period of time. It compares daily points and reveals trends and patterns. The information can be used when designing an intervention plan. It may also be helpful for the student, staff, parents, and support services, including physicians.

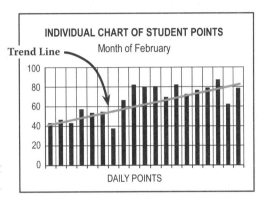

A chart of group points earned by a given date needs to be posted two to three times a week so students can see their point totals. Divide the chart into 1,000-point increments so students can compete against themselves at each level (if the chart runs from 0 to 8,000 points, students just starting will always feel left behind). When students check in, ask them to find and report to you their total number of points.

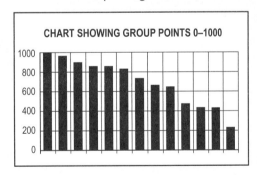

Custom comparison charts can be used in numerous ways. For example, you can compare student progress in a small skills group or compare the number of points acquired on different days of the week (e.g., Mondays and Fridays versus other days). You could also compare success by grade level. Often, students like to compete as a group against other grade levels to earn the most points in a month.

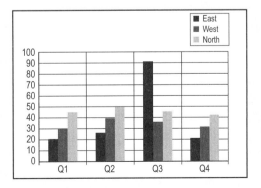

positive reinforcement for meeting their goals. Consider inviting parents and teachers to join these celebrations when possible.

Many young people have never received public praise; many have never given it to their peers. Celebrations allow this to happen.

Reward celebrations based on points earned and goals met need to be consistent, scheduled regularly, and fun. The Connections coordinator collects the data for each student in the program and records it in a computer spreadsheet program. The coordinator sets a point goal for each month. A reasonable goal is to add up what a perfect two weeks would equal in points, then make that total the goal for the month. A 50% success rate is a good way to start in order to get students excited about participating and experiencing success. A Connections Celebration is then held for all students who meet the point goal

At the awards ceremonies, students receive recognition for different categories. Examples include:

- Most total points

- Most homework completed on time

- Most cards turned in

- 100% attendance

- Greatest improvement in daily average points

- Highest daily average

- Most points accumulated since the last celebration

- No office referrals

- Academic successes

- Most points earned in the month

The coordinator usually picks three students in each award category. A celebration should include certificates, verbal praise, and concrete rewards. For elementary students, rewards could be lunch with a teacher, extra recess for the class, and school or art supplies. For older students, suggestions include varsity sports tickets, gift cards, and homework passes. All students who reach milestones such as 1,000 points, 2,000 points, and so on receive certificates.

Students who have previously received little recognition at other reward ceremonies need to be honored in this group as being successful. They need to practice success

Reward celebrations based on points earned and goals met need to be consistent, scheduled regularly, and fun.

and take pride in meeting their goals. These are often students who have never received any awards at the school awards ceremony. Having this opportunity to have their personal successes validated and celebrated is a new and important experience for them.

After the awards ceremony, the group spends the remaining time involved in a group game. This is another opportunity to teach and/or re-teach the skills needed to be successful in group activities.

In the elementary setting, students will often invite a parent to the celebration. In middle school, there is a specially designed formal celebration that parents are invited to once or twice a year.

OUTCOMES

The Connections program offers a host of advantages for many different areas of the school. For the student, the program provides accountability, incentives, immediate feedback, daily goal setting, and positive adult attention. Connections also serves as an important vehicle of communication for the adults involved in the students' lives, especially between home and school.

The success rate for a typical Connections program is about 75%, although the program has been as successful as 95% (Neyhart & Garrison, 1992). That is, 95% of the students in the program met their goals and earned enough points for celebrations. We find that success rate extremely encouraging, especially considering that students in the program are typically at-risk kids. Another benefit is that parents may become more involved in their child's daily goals and progress. Many parents comment on how much more in touch they feel with their child's daily activities.

In addition, student attendance often improves as participants begin to take pride in earning points on their card. Student self-esteem greatly improves because frequent positive attention from adults replaces negative interactions. Students' study skills, organizational abilities, and academic performance show measurable results. Office referrals decrease.

The staff benefits as well. They become more involved with these students in a supportive way and typically report that classroom disruptions decrease. When a student has been successful in the program for a period of months, consider gradually fading the student off the system. This can be done by removing check-in periods, then taking away the card, then taking away the teacher checks altogether while having the student serve as a helper or mentor for other Connections students. Some schools have graduation parties for students who are successfully weaned from this support system.

> Student self-esteem greatly improves because frequent positive attention from adults replaces negative interactions.

CONCLUSION

The program works by proactively addressing chronic social behavioral problems that can serve as barriers to learning. As a technique, the card-carry program works better and is less staff intensive than dealing with the fallout of failing to handle these problems early on. Connections begins by focusing on achievable baby steps. As students gain confidence in their success, accountability is increased according to individual needs and goals. Children must demonstrate the fundamental desired behaviors before participating in rewards.

What makes the program work? The same things that make the difference for students:

- Adults who demonstrate caring above and beyond their normal educational duties

- Skillful and intentional feedback and monitoring

- Specific, age-appropriate, and easily understood strategies for kids

- Effective strategies for adults that are easily incorporated in their busy days

- Parents who care about their kids

Although parental involvement enhances success, Connections-type programs have been demonstrated to be effective even if parents cannot or will not be active supporters.

There are no silver bullets for student success, but Connections offers a solid foundation for building a program that actually helps students learn to manage their behavior and academic performance—all while building self-esteem.

 **Reproducible Materials**

Copies of the following reproducible materials appear on the CD. Permission is given for individual teachers, administrators, or other school personnel to reproduce these forms for in-district use.

Reproducible Form 10.1: Daily Progress Monitor (Elementary)

Reproducible Form 10.2: Daily Progress Monitor (Secondary)

CHAPTER 11

Other Targeted Interventions

Mentoring and Other Ready-to-Implement Programs

When in the act of problem-solving, teachers, interventionists, and problem-solving teams need a broad range of interventions (things to do!) to select from as they build behavior improvement plans for individual students. Some of these interventions will involve the design and implementation of an evidence-based strategy such as a structured reinforcement system. The advantage of such an intervention is that the interventionist and teacher can apply what they know about effective structured reinforcement systems to design a plan that is tailored to meet the needs of a particular student and situation. The *Interventions* companion to this book (or a district-based protocol of interventions) provides a range of these tailored-to-fit strategies. However, that tailoring takes time and expertise. When you establish a buffet of group-based, ready-to-implement programs as part of the problem-solving process, a student whose needs might be met by one of these programs can simply be plugged into the program.

Connections, the program we highlighted in Chapter 10, is one important example of a program that can be pre-established and ready to implement whenever there is a student who may benefit (Neyhart & Garrison, 1992). There could be anywhere from three to fifty students involved in a Connections program.

This chapter contains descriptions of other group-based programs that you can set up as part of your B-RTI framework to increase the number and range of strategies for meeting the needs of individual students. Use this chapter to identify things that might work in your school. Let the ideas provided here also get your creative juices flowing about other types of programs that your school might benefit from. Then work through your school's behavioral leadership team to design, implement, and evaluate the efficacy of those programs.

MENTORING

Mentoring programs are elegant in their simplicity and powerful in their effect. Because lack of school connectedness is one factor that has been correlated with high school dropouts and drug/alcohol abuse (Bonny et al., 2000; Glover et al., 1998; McNeely & Falci, 2004; Resnick et al., 1997; Sprick, Garrison, et al., 2002; Yan et al., 2008), it is important that each student feels linked to school. Many students establish this link through their involvement with sports or arts activities. Another way for a student to build this connection is to establish a friendship with an adult who is involved in the school community.

Schools are full of students who desperately need an adult in their lives who they can talk to and get support from, someone who will ask on a weekly basis: How is your week going? Do you have any questions? Can I help you in any way? The effect of such interactions may not always be immediate or measurable, but our experience has taught us that the long-term payoff is profound. Mentorship programs can make use of business partnerships, Big Brother/Big Sister-type programs, partnerships with nearby retirement centers, or staff members. Following is a description of how you might use staff volunteers to set up a simple and easy-to-manage plan to provide mentorship support to students who may benefit from a bit of extra adult support.

STEP 1   Recruit Volunteers

The first step in setting up a mentoring program is to ask the entire staff—custodians, cooks, and administrative personnel as well as teachers—to volunteer. There should be no pressure to do so; teachers are incredibly busy people with plenty of personal responsibilities. Yet, they will volunteer. In the first Oregon school where we started a mentoring program, about half of the staff offered to meet with an at-risk student once a week.

> Mentoring programs are elegant in their simplicity and powerful in their effect.

STEP 2   Identify Students for Involvement

Next, identify students who would benefit from the program. Following are the guidelines we used:

- Chronic absenteeism
- Excess of disciplinary referrals
- Failing grades/behind in academic credits

Your school can be more inclusive, but our experience indicates that you will not lack for students in need of this program. In fact, in that first Oregon school, the list of qualifying students was three times as long as the list of volunteers. Rather than overburden the staff with multiple students, we elected to narrow the program and focus only on freshmen. This is just one option. Your school or district can construct a mentoring program that best meets the needs of your students.

STEP 3   Match Students With Staff

Next, staff volunteers meet and review the list of students. Some finesse is required to match students with volunteers. Teachers (and other volunteers) should be given an opportunity to identify students they know and may already have a relationship with. Yet we caution that students will be better served if their mentor is not their home-room teacher. A certain level of objectivity is required, and the homeroom teacher may be tempted to spend the meeting time talking about grades or assignments.

STEP 4   Get Students and Staff Together

The mentors approach the students they have been paired with and offer their support, making it clear that the mentor meetings are completely voluntary. They can say something like this: "Our staff has started a mentoring program to offer support to students, and I'd like to be your mentor. What that means is we would meet once a week for ten or fifteen minutes, giving you an opportunity to ask questions and get any help you need. We're doing this because we recognize that high school can be overwhelming, and we want to make sure that you have a good experience here. The program is voluntary. We'd like you to participate, but it's entirely your choice."

STEP 5   Give it Time to Work

Be patient, and the results will follow. One teacher in the Oregon school expressed concern that the program wasn't working. Her student showed up every week but didn't have anything to say. She described the meetings as painful. The key factor was that the student showed up every week—voluntarily. Clearly, he benefited from the meetings in some way, and so he kept coming and eventually opened up. In the school where we focused the program on freshmen, four years later many of the student participants reported that the support of their mentor was the main reason they graduated.

> Many of the student participants reported that the support of their mentor was the main reason they graduated.

During the problem-solving and intervention design process, teachers and interventionists can connect a student who needs additional adult attention and support with a mentor who is on the list of potential mentors. Having the program pre-established and a set of potential mentors on deck eliminates any delays between identifying mentorship as a potential intervention and getting the relationship started.

MEANINGFUL WORK

Providing a student with a specific and meaningful job within the school can be a great way to meet a student's basic needs, whether it is a need for attention, for purpose and belonging, or simply to get to school on time. This approach was first developed by two principals, B.J. Wise and Kim Marcum, and a school counselor, Mike Haykin. Later, it became a published program with 100 different job descriptions, application forms for students to apply for jobs they wanted, guidance for staff in how to train and supervise students on their jobs, and suggestions for making the whole operation run smoothly. (See *Administrator's Desk Reference of Behavioral Management, Volume III* by Randy Sprick and co-authors). Following is a description of how B.J. Wise came up the original idea for this program.

Christopher, the first-grade student who inspired the program, was sent to administrators with the warning that he was a problem. His teacher said that Christopher was behind academically. He was cruel and hurtful to other students, and he rarely completed schoolwork. The teacher had used assertive discipline with him, but the phone calls home resulted only in rancor between teacher and parent and had little or no effect on Christopher's behavior. Visits to the principal's office were equally ineffective. Administrators soon discovered that Christopher would push children down, pull chairs out from under them, and take anything he wanted from them by force. During independent work times, he tried to engage others in play and, when rebuffed, would hurt them. He very seldom completed an independent task and, when doing group work, often hindered the success of others. As his previous teacher had suggested, punishment only escalated Christopher's behavior.

The administrators called a staffing meeting to brainstorm a different system for dealing with his behavior. When listing his strengths and weaknesses, Christopher's teacher noted that the only time he displayed responsible behavior was when he was given a job to do that had some prestige with the rest of the class (e.g., passing out papers, cleaning erasers, or taking a message to the office). At those times, he was reasonable and could be dealt with pleasantly. The administrators decided to use the strategy of having him earn a job by displaying desirable behaviors. They coupled that with immediate timeout for hurtful behaviors.

They decided Christopher's job needed high visibility so adults throughout the school could compliment him on a job well done. It also had to be available on a daily basis so that when he earned the privilege, the job was immediately accessible. They selected distributing the lunch tickets to classrooms as the ideal job. It required that he visit every classroom in the school, it originated in the office so that he could have at least one positive contact with office personnel each day, and, if he failed to earn the job, he would have to observe someone else carrying out his duties.

> Providing a student with a specific and meaningful job within the school can be a great way to meet a student's basic needs.

They then discussed which of his inappropriate behaviors were the most critical to modify so that a behavior management sheet could be designed. Christopher's teacher chose 1) staying on task, 2) following directions, and 3) not hurting others as the three behaviors to monitor. These behaviors were entered on a behavior management sheet (Reproducible Form 11.1 on the next page) that was used to monitor when and how often the behaviors occurred. The teacher used this information to track progress and identify areas where trouble was most likely to occur. This information was also useful to Christopher, teaching him to monitor his own behavior, making the decision to behave or misbehave more of a conscious choice. On the management sheet, Christopher's day was broken down into subject areas and recess. Christopher earned a point for each time period for remaining within acceptable boundaries (no more than two warnings) for each of the three behaviors (on task, following directions, and not hurting others).

Christopher needed to earn 80% of his 15 possible points (three points for each of five subject areas) to earn job privileges. Hurting others resulted in an immediate timeout, as did getting two or more warnings for being off-task or failing to follow directions during any one subject area.

Next, they called Christopher into the office and told him they needed someone who was responsible to do the important job of delivering lunch envelopes to every classroom each day. His response was enthusiastic. They explained that as an employee, he would need to meet some requirements first—his teachers had some behaviors that he needed to work on. They explained the point system and how it would be used to calculate whether he would work each day. Christopher agreed that he understood and that it seemed reasonable.

Christopher's reaction to earning a job each day exceeded the administrators' greatest expectations. His hurtful behaviors decreased immediately and were extinguished within a month. Staying on task and following directions were more difficult, but Christopher consistently managed to stay under his two-warning limit and was able to earn his job on a regular basis. With improved reliability in following directions and staying on task came better assignment completion, which in turn increased academic achievement. Also, with improved behavior came the opportunity to call his mother and give her good news about her son. Soon, Christopher and his mother started attending school events, and the adults in his life cooperated with one another in his best interest. Eventually, the administrators expanded the use of meaningful work, and it continues to be one of the most effective ways to turn student behavior around and forge strong ties between students and the school.

Reproducible Form 11.1

SAMPLE

BEHAVIOR MANAGEMENT SHEET

Christopher	1	Ms. Reed	11/14
Student	Grade/Class	Teacher	Date

READING

	Warnings		Over the Limit
Remained on task	1	(2)	3
Followed directions	1	2	(3)
Avoided hurting others	1	2	3

I earned: 1   (2)   3   points

MATH

	Warnings		Over the Limit
Remained on task	(1)	2	3
Followed directions	1	2	(3)
Avoided hurting others	1	2	3

I earned: 1   (2)   3   points

RECESS

	Warnings		Over the Limit
Remained on task	(1)	2	3
Followed directions	1	2	3
Avoided hurting others	1	2	3

I earned: 1   2   (3)   points

SCIENCE/SOCIAL STUDIES

	Warnings		Over the Limit
Remained on task	1	(2)	3
Followed directions	1	2	(3)
Avoided hurting others	1	2	3

I earned: 1   (2)   3   points

SPELLING/HANDWRITING

	Warnings		Over the Limit
Remained on task	1	2	3
Followed directions	1	2	3
Avoided hurting others	1	2	3

I earned: 1   2   3   points

My goal is to earn 12 points. Today I earned _____ points.

Reproducible Materials Blank copies of the forms are provided on the CD. Permission is given for individual teachers, administrators, or other school personnel to reproduce any form labeled "Reproducible Form" for in-district use.

STEP 1   Identify Candidates for Jobs

Having a range of jobs available to plug students into can facilitate problem-solving. However, there are additional ways to use these meaningful jobs to get ahead of situations before they can turn in to problems. Some students are obvious candidates for inclusion in a meaningful work program, while others are less apparent. It is very important to have a cross section of the student population participating in the program. This is important for many reasons. First, you want to avoid having the jobs program become stigmatized as something only for problem children. If this happens, the effectiveness of the program can be lost. Second, the high-achieving student workers provide appropriate modeling of desired student behaviors. Including a variety of students not only provides social desirability but also promotes a positive learning environment. Lastly, high-achieving students may also have unmet needs. It is possible that a quiet, compliant student is hiding serious problems by blending into his surroundings. A job can fulfill many basic needs for this child just as it does for children with overt social or behavioral difficulties.

Teachers nominate both regular and at-risk students as potential workers. Students who are not at-risk may be picked because they are average students who seldom get individualized recognition. Generally, staff members nominate at-risk students because of concerns about social withdrawal or isolation, poor social skills, or recurrent behavior problems. Students experiencing the absence or loss of a parent or students who are either academically deficient or gifted may also benefit from the special attention this program offers. Basically, any life issue that suggests the student needs more attention or nurturing than is provided in a typical classroom can be an indicator for possible work placement.

Another way that students are referred to jobs is through the teacher assistance team or through a system that red flags certain students as needing individualized intervention plans (see Chapter 4, "Develop a Process"). Paired with assistance for academic deficiencies, a job can begin to transform a student into a successful member of the school community. Finally, parents can be an important referral source for including their children in a meaningful work program. Often parents will come to school with concerns about their child's emotional well-being. The student many have recently lost a grandparent, moved away from friends or family, or be in the midst of disturbing family problems. When a parent shares these concerns, it is important to ensure extra attention for the student through a high-visibility job that will guarantee more adult contact and a high rate of positive feedback. Giving special attention during times of high stress can help a child through difficult periods.

Any life issue that suggests the student needs more attention or nurturing than is provided in a typical classroom can be an indicator for possible work placement.

STEP 2   **Create Rewarding Jobs**

Identify a wide range of tasks that could potentially serve as meaningful jobs within the school. See the following Table 11.1 for some sample jobs.

Table 11.1

Perfect Jobs for At-Risk Students

Job	Why It Works
Video Editor	High prestige because of apparent difficulty level
Digital Picture Editor	High visibility, appears very technical, high prestige with others
Computer Repair	High visibility, appears difficult, high prestige with peers
Office Mail Sorter	High contact with office, strong reinforcement, appears official
Office Receptionist	High visibility, contact with mentoring adults, highly stimulating
Calendar Printer	High rate of positive contact with principal, high prestige with peers
Playground Equipment Manager	High visibility, image of power with peers, appears official
Tour Guide for Visitors	High prestige because representing the school

Another option is to develop school businesses as a way to provide student jobs while contributing to the student body fund and meeting a perceived need in the building. These businesses could include a school store, a book-trading company, a savings bank co-sponsored by a local bank, or a latte business that sells special coffees to teachers and parents each day. With the exception of the savings bank and book-trading company, these businesses can be open just before school starts each day. The trading company can be open every day during noon recess, and the school bank can be open once or twice a week for one hour during the school day. These businesses can employ many students, and we have found it necessary to have parents supervise these activities during these busy times of the school day.

STEP 3 — Match the Job to the Needs of the Student

The pairing of students to jobs is an important task that should be undertaken thoughtfully. The characteristics of each student may make him or her perfect for some jobs and a potential disaster for others. Students' talents, interests, and personalities come into play and need to be considered as you suggest jobs they might enjoy. Although a student who is very talented in art might enjoy making cards and posters, another child who has difficulty staying on task or who has difficulty with fine motor skills might find that job boring or too challenging. A student who is outgoing may be perfect to work in a first-grade classroom as a tutor or as a kindergarten bus greeter, while a student who is withdrawn and shy may find these situations stressful. This matching process requires more common sense than careful analysis, but these issues must be considered to increase the likelihood that students will enjoy and succeed in their job placements.

In addition to considering talents, interests, and personalities when assigning a job for a student, consider the needs of the student. That is, consider the difficulty a child is experiencing and try to find a job that addresses this concern. For example, a student who has an attendance problem may benefit from an early morning job such as flag raising, whereas a student who tends to lose it in the afternoons may benefit more from a job that takes place at that time of day. A student who constantly attempts to gain recognition though negative acting-out behavior might gain needed recognition as a building tour guide, and the student who is noncompliant and manipulative may respond well to the challenge and respect that naturally come with the job of computer repair helper. Other examples of matching students with jobs are:

- A student who is generally negative toward peers might be assigned a reinforcement activity such as popcorn crew.

- A student who has academic weaknesses that make her feel stupid might make an excellent tutor for a younger student.

- A student who has been abandoned by a parent may build strong ties and a sense of being needed by helping an instructional assistant.

- A student with poor social skills may benefit from working in a group situation.

- A student who is rejected by peers might be paired with student workers who are generally regarded as socially desirable.

When assigning jobs, be sure to consider the student's age and the amount of supervision the student may need. Simple tasks such as recycling go well with younger students' skills. More complex tasks (e.g., tour guide or computer repair person) are appropriate for older students. Pairing younger students with older students is often

> The characteristics of each student may make him or her perfect for some jobs and a potential disaster for others.

useful. Be practical in assessing a student's ability to perform tasks, although it may be useful to challenge students whenever possible so that they meet higher expectations and can take pride in their accomplishments. It is our experience that students will rise to the occasion when presented with high expectations.

STEP 4 **Select and Train Supervisors for Each Job**

For a meaningful work program to be successful, the responsibility for supervising student workers must be shared by a variety of adults; it cannot fall on the shoulders of just one person. The importance of having consistent supervisors who take the time to build relationships with students cannot be overstated. Supervisors may be school custodians, workroom assistants, principals, school counselors, or reliable parents and community members. When you brainstorm for supervisors, look for someone who knows the job to be accomplished and who will be consistently available to give the student feedback and reinforcement (see Table 11.2 for a list of supervisor duties). It is important to work with potential supervisors to make sure they are willing to be involved in building a relationship with the student(s) and overseeing the work.

Table 11.2

Responsibilities for Meaningful Work Supervisors

- Teach all skills and tasks related to the student's job.

- Monitor attendance.

- Monitor job performance.

- Communicate with the classroom teacher.

- Listen to staff concerns regarding student performance.

- Keep staff supervisors informed about skills and behaviors that need to improve.

- Maintain a record of the times and dates that different students work.

In some cases, you may want to select potential supervisors first and then work with them to develop jobs that work with their regular roles in the building. By carefully selecting supervisors, you may increase the overall success of the program. (After all, it's about more than putting students to work!) For example, if you ask the secretary to supervise a student sorting school mail, she may be resistant because she likes to see what mail comes into the building each day. If, however, you asked her to help brainstorm some areas of her job that could be assisted by students, she is more likely to be agreeable to accepting student help. Initially, you may need to twist a few arms to get people to supervise but, believe it or not, you will get volunteers after a couple of months. In fact, many teachers and staff become interested in being supervisors after they see the utility of having students perform tasks and the growth that the students make as workers.

Develop a relationship. The first and most important job of the supervisor is to develop a nurturing relationship with the student. Supervisors can accomplish this by greeting students with enthusiasm, showing interest in their day, and acknowledging not just their work but their other accomplishments as well. Treating students respectfully as co-workers is also very important. By recognizing birthdays and other life events, a supervisor can be an important link for the at-risk child—helping teachers, administrators, and other staff to identify and acknowledge student accomplishments.

Have consistent contact. One warning about assigning supervisors is to make sure that they have consistent contact with their worker(s). Some schools with whom we have worked have made the commitment that every adult in the school will supervise a student. Although this is a great goal, it may not be realistic unless structured very carefully. Some teachers can supervise older students who are tutoring, doing paper correcting, or materials preparation. Teachers of younger students may have difficulty finding classroom work that is not too taxing for younger or academically challenged students and may wish to supervise students before or after school when they can give more personalized attention to teaching work tasks.

Parent volunteers can be excellent supervisors if they will consistently come to school and treat the commitment as they would a job. We have had great success with parents as supervisors, but we have also learned a great deal in the process. For example, we have found that parents and community members tend to be leery of open-ended commitments. If these people wanted full-time jobs, they would probably already have them. So you must remember to fit the job to the volunteer's schedule and be very specific when you ask for a time commitment. Use a specific statement such as, "Mrs. Harvey, we would love to have you here working with some of our needy students. I was wondering if you would be interested in volunteering for half an hour twice a week. We could work around your schedule." This gives the volunteer a very clear idea of how much time is involved in the job.

Put a parent in charge. It is especially effective to have one parent supervise the scheduling of other parents so that there is always a supervisor attending students as they complete their duties. You can ask one parent to be in charge of scheduling volunteers and to recruit four or five other parents to commit to 45 minutes of supervision one day each week. The parent in charge also calls for substitutes when other parents cannot meet their commitment. This strategy has been highly effective because many parents are willing to help but can make only a small time commitment once a week The parent who does the scheduling does not even need to be at the school, so it can be done by someone who is housebound or has a job during the day.

> The first and most important job of the supervisor is to develop a nurturing relationship with the student.

Train, support, and acknowledge parent volunteers*.* Parent volunteers always need some training so that they understand what you are hoping to achieve with the meaningful work program. They need to understand that having the students do the work themselves is more important than having a perfect product. You'll also want to teach parents how to give students constructive but positive feedback. Also remind them about the importance of providing student workers with compliments and positive comments on a daily basis.

Parents need feedback just as students do*.* If you use parent volunteers to supervise meaningful work jobs, be sure to build in some opportunities to let them know how much you appreciate them. One way to accomplish this is to have a group of student workers create thank-you cards for the parents and plan supervisor appreciation events during the school year.

For more detailed information about using school-based jobs as a targeted intervention strategy, see the section on meaningful work in *Administrator's Desk Reference of Behavioral Management, Volume III*. This resource includes 100 job descriptions, job application forms, information on training supervisors, and everything needed to create a comprehensive meaningful work program in your school.

PASS PROGRAM

In this program, there is a classroom within the school run by a skilled teacher with knowledge of behavioral issues. This class serves as the home base for at-risk students when needed, but for the most part, these students are in a general education classroom with support from the PASS teacher. See the box on the next page for a description of this program, which was developed by Jim Poole and Dr. Hope Caperton Brown (in press).

HOMEWORK ROOMS

> Going to the homework room should always be entirely voluntary—no adult, not even the principal, can make a student go there.

Homework rooms, where students can get help with homework during lunch and before and after school, can be effective in pumping up academic performance. This concept is not the same as a detention-type setting that students can be assigned to attend. In fact, for this to work well, going to the homework room should always be entirely voluntary—no adult, not even the principal, can make a student go there. The key to making homework rooms successful is to have enough academically competent people available to provide immediate help when a student needs it.

In addition, it helps to have as many resources as possible (e.g., supplies, textbooks) available for students to use during their homework room time. In our experience, students who most benefit from resources such as a homework room may not be the most organized and so often arrive in the homework room without the right book

☀ PASS PROGRAM

PASS was founded on the belief that many behaviorally at-risk students and those identified with serious emotional or behavioral disabilities benefit behaviorally and academically when their educational placement is in mainstream settings rather than in self-contained/segregated programs. Designed by a behavior specialist and a licensed psychologist who together have more than 40 years of educational experience, PASS was developed to provide these hard-to-manage students with individualized programming that incorporates a positive behavioral approach with empirically based intervention strategies. Program methodology focuses on:

- Teaching replacement behaviors in a non-levels PASS classroom

- Coaching replacement behaviors in mainstream settings

- Analyzing behavioral progress in target areas using functional behavior analysis supported by PASS behavior analysis software

- Strategically moving students toward independence and self-regulation

PASS is implemented in four phases: 1) pre-placement, 2) orientation, 3) maintenance and inclusion, and 4) aftercare.

Pre-placement. This phase incorporates planning activities prior to PASS placement, such as developing a behavior intervention plan and ensuring that less intensive and restrictive interventions have occurred.

Orientation. In phase 2, the primary PASS focus is on instruction. In an expedited manner, the student is provided instruction in:

- PASS classroom expectations

- PASS program practices, including the monitoring and reinforcement systems

- Individualized social skills instruction in the area(s) targeted by the student's behavior plan

Maintenance and inclusion. Phase 3 moves the student from the PASS classroom into general education or resource settings. Monitoring of target behaviors by PASS personnel occurs on an individualized schedule that varies according to the frequency with which misbehavior is manifested in different educational settings. Behavior coaching is delivered when monitored behavior in targeted areas is inappropriate and follows a cognitive-behavioral approach of identification of:

1. Triggers that elicit the inappropriate behavior

2. Rehearsal of the replacement behavior

3. Problem-solving regarding potential consequences of different behavior choices made by the student

Reinforcement of behavioral success is a key component of this phase. After a period of behavioral success with PASS personnel providing monitoring, students move on to self-monitoring.

Aftercare. In phase 4, the aftercare component, students who have been successful in self-monitoring act as sponsors for students in earlier program phases.

Movement by students through the second and third phases of PASS is not unidirectional; rather, the level of services a student receives is fluid and dependent on his or her current behavioral needs. Students may, therefore, move from PASS monitoring back to the PASS classroom for a period of redirection and/or from PASS monitoring to self-monitoring. Analysis of PASS monitoring data informs the level of service provided throughout these phases.

Theoretical support for placing behaviorally disordered students in inclusive environments derives from the work of the social learning theory of Albert Bandura (1977) and the social-ecological theory of Urie Bronfenbrenner (1979). Specifically, these theories emphasize the effect of environments (including peer groups) on behavior. Additionally, the program's practice of placing students in inclusive settings is influenced by research (Dishion et al., 1996) that indicates the presence of an iatrogenic effect or contagion of placing students with antisocial behaviors together in segregated settings.

or supplies to complete the task. Although it is certainly possible to run an effective homework room without extra supplies, having these resources available is an added bonus for students who need support.

One middle school in an at-risk community established a homework room staffed by nearby high school students. High school students who wanted to participate were able to sign up for a class (called Pre-Teaching Experience) that was a full elective credit. Students were told that if they thought they might want to be teacher someday, they could learn if they liked the process and gain an educational credit on their high school transcript that showed their early interest in becoming a teacher. To apply, they were required to be juniors or seniors and have B averages or better. The job of these pre-teachers was to be in the homework room for 50 minutes each day to assist middle school students who came to the room and wanted help on their homework. The pre-teachers were given some basic instruction on how to be positive, how to guide students and not just provide answers, and how to correct errors in encouraging ways.

There was so much interest from high school students that 45 students were identified—15 were at the middle school for 50 minutes (the length of their high school's classes) before school began, 15 were in the homework room during lunch (with this time period cutting across the last half of the middle school's two lunch shifts), and 15 students were there for 50 minutes after school. The middle school saw a dramatic increase in students' academic performance. One caution is that these programs will not be effective if the room is staffed by only one teaching assistant. If a student has to wait 10 minutes to get her question answered while the assistant works patiently with another student, she won't likely come back.

Once the homework room is set up, teachers should bring their classes down to show students the room, introduce them to some of the high school students, and encourage students to voluntarily use the room. A teacher or interventionist should never make a student go to the homework room. However, if a student might benefit, part of the student's intervention for increasing work completion could include taking her to the room, introducing her to some of the pre-teachers, and encouraging her to go there. One or more of the pre-teachers could even be coached in advanced about how to be inviting to the student, encouraging her to just stop in and say hello whether she wanted to work on her homework or not.

STRUCTURED RECESS/STRUCTURED LUNCH

Designed for elementary and middle schools, this program is a recess 101 for children who "do not play well with others." In many ways, it's similar to driving school for adults. When a student misbehaves on the playground, or during lunch break in the case of middle school or high school, the student is assigned to three days of structured, or staff-supervised, recess (or lunch) to learn or relearn the "rules of the road." Structured recess (or lunch) functions as a punitive consequence, but the student does not lose the opportunity to play, just the opportunity for free play. The program can be most effective if a school counselor or behavior specialist provides the structured play and teaches social skills at the same time. Some days there may just be one student assigned to structured recess; other days there may be 10 or 12. The school counselor should not make the recess feel punitive, but she is there to correct students if they play unfairly or make inappropriate comments. Research literature indicates that people can learn social skills in a lesson setting, but they may not generalize

> Structured recess (or lunch) functions as a punitive consequence, but the student does not lose the opportunity to play, just the opportunity for free play.

those skills to real life (Chen & Bullock, 2004; Forness & Kavale, 1996; Gresham, 2002; Lewis, 1994; Sugai & Lewis, 1996). Structured play or a structured setting at lunch provides an excellent opportunity to teach social skills in a setting that the student may have already demonstrated is problematic.

If a school has either structured recess or structured lunch as an established program, a student who has major trouble with unstructured settings can be assigned to be part of the structured recess with the school counselor until such time that the student demonstrates he is ready for less-structured play. This program does not need to be only for students who exhibit externalizing behaviors such as aggression. It can also be used as an intervention for shy internalizing students who have not learned skills for making friends.

SOCIAL SKILLS TRAINING CLASSES

Each school or district must look at this issue and decide whether enough students in its care lack basic social skills to warrant setting up and implementing a social skills training program. These programs can take time away from academic instruction, but if lack of social skills is a big enough problem that it interferes with students' ability to learn, then such a curriculum may be beneficial and actually enhance academic success. An excellent program for teaching social skills is *The Strong Kids Programs: Social and Emotional Learning Curricula*. Dr. Ken Merrell and colleagues developed the Strong Kids programs to teach social and emotional skills, promote resilience, and increase the coping skills of children and adolescents. The series includes four components: *Strong Start* (for children in kindergarten through second grade), *Strong Kids—Grades 3–5*, *Strong Kids—Grades 6–8*, and *Strong Teens* (for students in grades 9–12). The Strong Kids programs are intended to be used for prevention and early intervention of mental health problems.

These programs do not specifically address antisocial behavior or school violence, but instead focus primarily on internalizing problems and promoting resilience. They specifically target emotional education, anger management, identifying thinking errors and how to change them, positive thinking, dealing with interpersonal conflict, reducing stress, and setting and attaining goals. The lessons are scripted and designed to be easy to use within the time frame of one 45–55 minute class period over the course of 12 weeks (one lesson per week). They have been used successfully with high- and typical-functioning youth as well as at-risk youth and those who have already developed significant behavioral and emotional disorders. Successful group leaders have been general and special education teachers, school counselors, school psychologists, and other mental health professionals. These lessons have been developed to complement academic skills such as critical thinking, analysis skills, and literacy. Many schools have integrated the lessons into the course of a typical language arts, health, or social studies curriculum. Several strategies have helped to successfully implement the social skills lessons. These include:

- Keep the pace brisk.

- Provide immediate feedback and opportunities to respond.

- Maintain a high positive-to-negative ratio of reinforcement.

- Maintain high student expectations.

- Ensure student participation.

- Consider using frequent rewards for participation.

- Consider small groups for activities.

- Incorporate schoolwide behavior supports.

Following are two other effective social skills programs.

Cool Kids. A proactive approach to social responsibility (Fister, Conrad, & Kemp, 1998). This is a proactive social skills curriculum that helps teachers deal with the increasing number of students who are deficient in social skills and who lack social responsibility. The Cool Kids philosophy is that social problems are the result of skill deficits rather than performance or motivational problems. The curriculum teaches social skills to all students by introducing concepts, demonstrating examples and nonexamples, and providing opportunities for practice and feedback. Thirty-six social skills are covered in Levels I and II of the Cool Kids program. Level I is geared toward preschool and early elementary students with 16 basic skills such as listening, waiting, working together, and following instructions. Level II is more appropriate for intermediate, middle, and high school students. Typical Level II skills include joining in, expressing yourself, making a request, reporting behavior, and resolving a disagreement. Although the focus of Cool Kids is on prevention, it also presents approaches for reacting to inappropriate behavior in a respectful manner. The Cool Kids lessons can be used by an individual teacher, a group of teachers, or an entire school staff.

The Tough Kid Social Skills Book. This program is designed to help teachers, school psychologists, school counselors, school social workers, and other school support staff implement social skills programs for tough kids. Tough kids are students who display excesses in noncompliance and aggression and deficits in self-management, academic, and social skills. The book targets the key deficit area of social skills, which are defined as learned behaviors needed to get along successfully in most social situations. *The Tough Kid Social Skills Book* discusses how to identify those tough kids in need of direct, structured social skills training and provides procedures and tools for leading social skills programs for small groups, classrooms, and schools. Specific tools covered include group discussion, modeling, role-playing, providing feedback, establishing contracts, and homework. The book also features training session outlines that provide flexible 60-minute lessons for use with groups of all sizes. The outlines cover skills needed for social entry, maintaining interactions, and solving problems.

If it is determined that teaching social skills is not appropriate for the entire student body, social skills can be taught in targeted group lessons. This may be done in a context such as structured recess or as a semester- or even year-long elective class in middle school or high school. When a student indicates a need for social skills training, the student can be encouraged, or in some cases even required, to sign up for the social skills class the following semester.

In one high school, the school counselor offered a course each semester called Leadership. Toward the end of a semester, the faculty spent a few minutes nominating students who were tending to fade into the woodwork, that is, those average students who never cause problems but are not a part of any club, sport, or other major school activity. Twenty of those students were then invited to participate in the elective credit, in which the school counselor taught social skills such as how to make friends, assertiveness, and conflict resolution. The students also conducted a major community service project and organized a school dance. The school counselor reported that by the end of the class, at least 90% of the students had also joined a club or started participating in a school sport.

BULLYING PREVENTION PROGRAMS

Bullying, or harassment, is a very common problem that may require schoolwide and targeted intervention. Many states have recently passed statutes that require all schools to address the problem. This may include lessons for all students, with targeted lessons for students who have demonstrated a propensity to be either bullies or victims.

One excellent program is *Bully Blockers* (Bowen, Ashcraft, Jenson, & Rhode 2008). Given evidence that early, mild forms of aggression can lead to more serious violence in later years, this program is designed for grades 1–6 to provide early intervention and training to students during their elementary years.

The program is intended to help school staff track the problems and types of bullying that are specific to your school or classroom. The Bully Blockers program targets all forms of bullying, from gossiping and exclusion to physical aggression to increasingly prevalent cyberbullying. It also teaches students about respecting differences, building confidence and friendships, acceptable and unacceptable behavior, and effective tools to consistently stop bullying where it's most likely to occur.

> Bullying, or harassment, is a very common problem that may require schoolwide and targeted intervention.

Considering that research indicates that schools where students resolve conflicts cooperatively and peacefully have higher levels of student achievement, we recommend that schools or districts add some type of bullying prevention program to their B-RTI framework.

☀ *Teaching Study Skills*

Consider also setting up schoolwide or targeted group lessons for students who lack organizational or other basic study skills. *Note:* If your school does not have a study skills curriculum, you might want to suggest that your staff consider *Advanced Skills for School Success* by Anita Archer and Mary Gleason, published by Curriculum Associates and *REWARDS* (Reading Excellence: Word Attack and Rate Development Strategies) by Anita Archer, Mary Gleason, and Vicky Vachon, published by Sopris West. These excellent curricula teach strategies for organization and studying that will enhance the academic achievement of students who are struggling to succeed.

FIRST STEP TO SUCCESS

First Step to Success (Walker et al., 1998) is a standardized, packaged intervention that allows interventionists to organize and implement the intervention with little or no outside support. First Step to Success is designed for children who begin school exhibiting signs of antisocial behavior. It is considered a packaged intervention because it consists of multiple components implemented in a standard format for all participating students. Research has documented that First Step to Success is well liked by teachers and parents and that it is effective in improving academic engagement and decreasing antisocial behavior in young students (Golly, Stiller, & Walker, 1998; Walker et al., 2001).

Although the program fits in the group intervention category because it can be made available for students to enter at any time, it is intended to be implemented with only one student per classroom at a time. One teacher may implement the intervention with several students over the course of the year; however, implementation with a new student does not begin until the intervention is faded for the previous student. First Step to Success targets kindergarten to second-grade students who are at risk for social or academic failure. It does so through the use of universal screening; consultant-based school intervention involving teacher(s), peers, and the child; and parent/caregiver training to support school adjustment. The primary outcomes of the program are improvement in the child's ability to get along with teachers and peers, an increase in the child's successful engagement in academic activities, and a diversion from antisocial behavior patterns (Walker et al., 1998).

Screening for students who may benefit from the First Step program occurs by having teachers evaluate each child in relation to behavioral risk factors. The school intervention module (CLASS) is a consultant-based intervention that attempts to decrease problem behavior and increase positive academic and social behaviors. It requires successful completion of 30 program days across consultant, teacher, and maintenance phases. Each day has a built-in criterion that must be met before the student can progress to the next day. Most students on the program need to occasionally repeat a day before moving on.

The first phase of the school intervention is the consultant, or coach, phase. In this phase, a trained First Step coach or interventionist works one-on-one with the student to teach appropriate academic and social behaviors. The coach wears a card (red on one side, green on the other) and turns the card to signal the student when she or he is behaving appropriately or inappropriately. Time spent engaging in appropriate behavior leads to rewards (points), and inappropriate behavior does not. The coach also informs the class that the target student has agreed to participate in a game in which the student will earn a classwide social reward (e.g., Simon Says, story time, special snack) with everyone's help (e.g., ignoring inappropriate behavior). The goal of this phase is to increase the student's success in the classroom by teaching the student to engage in appropriate behaviors using the red/green card.

As the student is successful in this phase (typically five to seven school days), the coach gradually transfers implementation to the teacher, and the program is systematically faded until the student is responding to the same contingencies that maintain other students' appropriate behavior (e.g., teacher praise, peer friendships). The parent component, HomeBase, is implemented by the coach in conjunction with the CLASS program at school. HomeBase includes a one-hour weekly training for six weeks that encourages parents to help students share their school experiences, set limits, clearly define expectations, and encourage appropriate academic and social behaviors (Golly et al., 1998; Walker et al., 1997, 1998, 2001).

STUDENTS TARGETED FOR SPECIAL ATTENTION

A middle school teacher who instructs a class of emotionally disturbed children developed this program, but it can be applied to any students who need extra attention. The program recognizes that, with some students, maintaining at least a three-to-one ratio of positive to negative interactions is challenging. So the basic idea is to single out students who desperately need positive attention and engage the entire staff to give them that attention.

The teacher who developed the program realized that his students thrived on attention. When he and his assistant maintained ratios of interactions skewed heavily to positive attention, it helped maintain mostly responsible behavior from the students. He recognized that when students were in his room, there were a maximum of 12 students with two adults (the teacher and his assistant), thus making it relatively easy to catch students behaving appropriately and to give them attention. He further recognized that when his students were out in general education classes, no classroom teacher—no

With some students, maintaining at least a three-to-one ratio of positive to negative interactions is challenging.

matter how skilled, compassionate, and positive—could give the same frequency of feedback with only one teacher and 33 students. So he decided to try an experiment.

He took pictures of his students, had them enlarged, and showed them at a staff meeting. He introduced the students by name and asked the staff to make a special point to say hello or interact with the students whenever they saw them in the hallway, cafeteria, or wherever. The effect was amazing. The teachers' interaction with the needy students served as a model, and soon other students were making a point to say hello as well. The emotionally at-risk students received lots of attention as they walked down the hall. This improved their in-class behavior in the general education rooms where the teachers could not provide as much attention as the students might need.

Any time a teacher or interventionist thinks a student could benefit from increased frequency of adult attention, they can get on the agenda of a staff meeting to show the student's picture, briefly describe some interests or other unique features of the student, and then encourage all staff to interact with the student whenever they see him. This can also extend to bus drivers by meeting with the student's driver and discussing the form and type of positive attention that this particular student is likely to enjoy.

CONCLUSION

Group-based interventions have the advantage of being pre-established and ready to implement whenever there is a student who might benefit. It is important to remember that targeted interventions do not necessarily involve groups of students but are readily accessible by any student when needed. When an individual teacher, interventionist, or problem-solving team is designing an intervention for an individual student, they can look first to the buffet of group-based programs already in existence and choose from those that might be applicable. For example, if a student needs lots of attention, plugging this student into a mentorship and targeting the student for special attention might help meet this student's needs. If a student needs to improve motivation at school, she might be encouraged to use the homework room to get encouragement from the high school pre-teachers and to take the elective Leadership class. By meeting students' needs in positive ways, problem behaviors often fade away from the students' behavioral repertoire.

Reproducible Materials

A copy of the following reproducible material appears on the CD.

Reproducible Form 11.1: Behavior Management Sheet

CHAPTER 12

Gang Prevention and Intervention

A B-RTI Approach to Youth Gang Issues

by Eleazar Ramirez, Ph.D.,
Vittorio T. Puente, Ph.D., and Alfonso Herrera

Eleazar Ramirez, Ph.D., is program manager in the Department of Safe and Civil Schools, Dallas Independent School District.

Vittorio T. Puente, Ph.D., is chief executive officer of Program Evaluation & Educational Research Solutions (PEERS).

Alfonso Herrera is chief executive officer, Herrera & Associates Gang Prevention and Intervention Services.

A typical day for school administrators, teachers, school counselors, mental health professionals, and other support personnel has changed dramatically in the last 20 years. School violence, drug abuse, and delinquency have taken a prominent role in our nation's psyche. The media constantly bombard the community with information about school shootings, student victimization, teenage pregnancy, and drug abuse. Yet the focus on school violence has primarily concentrated on individual students who are bullied, socially withdrawn, or emotionally unstable and has ignored precipitants to gang violence. The issue of prevention and intervention efforts with gang-affiliated youth in our schools has remained on the periphery despite its growing impact on the school day.

The effect of youth gangs is widespread. Youth gang membership has increased since the 1980s (Howell, Egley, & Gleason, 2002). According to a report by the National Youth Gang Center (Egley & Ritz, 2006), all states and all large cities have reported major concerns with youth gangs. The social impact and financial costs of youth gang-related activities in public schools are substantial and affect communities of all sizes. Youth gang members are responsible for a wide range of crimes against persons and property, including murder, aggravated assaults, and the sale and distribution of weapons and illegal drugs. A study by Chandler and colleagues (1998) found that guns and drugs are more likely to be in schools when there is a gang presence.

This chapter describes how the components used in B-RTI align with the Dallas Independent School District (ISD) initiative to reduce the gang presence by incorporating anti-gang strategies recommended by the Office of Juvenile Justice and Delinquency Prevention (OJJDP). To illustrate this alignment, we summarize the philosophy, process, and procedures of the Gang Response Program of the Dallas ISD in terms of the specific themes outlined in this book. In addition, this chapter provides lessons learned from the struggles and successes in moving from theory of change to effective practice.

CONTINUUM OF BEHAVIORAL SUPPORT

Chapter 1 describes B-RTI as a problem-solving process that consists of a full continuum of behavioral support procedures throughout all levels of a school. These procedures help educators reduce inappropriate behavior and increase student behavioral and academic success. Similarly, the literature on youth gangs maintains that a continuum of behavioral support assists interventionists in providing services for at-risk or gang-involved students and families. The Dallas ISD initiatives closely adhere to the notion of a continuum of behavioral support for identified students. The continuum is based on a two-tiered structure as recommended by the Office of Juvenile Justice and Delinquency Prevention. The first tier is a three-pronged anti-gang approach that comprises prevention, intervention, and enforcement strategies. The second tier is the processes and procedures that support coordination across agencies. This section of the chapter discusses the first-tier efforts by the Dallas ISD. The second-tier strategy is discussed in a subsequent section called "Linking Needs to Available Resources."

Historically, enforcement strategies have been the predominant approach to dealing with gang issues. However, time has revealed that although enforcement efforts are necessary, they are not sufficient to prevent and reduce gang-related activities. Collectively, a three-pronged approach that consists of prevention, intervention, and enforcement has proven effective in reducing gang-related activities in schools and communities (Howell, 1998). Moreover, the incorporation of these three strategies enhances a school district's efficiency and effectiveness in promoting the education of children in a safe and civil environment.

> The social impact and financial costs of youth gang-related activities in public schools are substantial and affect communities of all sizes.

PREVENTION EFFORTS

The effectiveness of prevention efforts is difficult to document and harder to support. However, disengaging youth from gangs is a far more difficult and complex task. It is far easier and more economical to prevent than to rehabilitate. Accordingly, the Dallas ISD adheres to the commonplace wisdom that "an ounce of prevention is worth a pound of cure." Gottfredson and Gottfredson (2001) describe a gang prevention effort as one that aims to reduce or deter gang involvement. Preventing children and adolescents from joining gangs appears to be the most cost-effective long-term strategy.

Prevention efforts employ strategies that target youth before they become involved in gangs. These efforts involve programs and services intended for youth who have already displayed early signs of problem behaviors or who are exposed to multiple risk factors for gang activity. Prevention efforts focus on creating personal, social, and environmental obstacles to gang involvement. For example, a prevention effort may include an afterschool program that addresses a student's social need to belong. These efforts typically include some form of individual risk assessment and often focus on youth ages 7–14 and their families. Younger siblings and family members of gang-involved youth are particularly suitable for these services.

The Dallas ISD is cognizant of using research-based activities that include teaching social competence, taking responsibility for personal actions, and facilitating academic performance. Some approaches to increase the value of non-gang activities may include introducing recreational programs for youth to combat boredom and alienation, fostering peer support, and cultivating a sense of belonging. Furthermore, the district employs workshops on gang demystification, life skills, problem-solving skills, and assertiveness skills to buffer the allure of a gang lifestyle. Finally, cultural programs and activities in the community (e.g., recording and transmitting the traditions of elders, ceremonial feasts) help students feel welcome and valued in their school community.

INTERVENTION EFFORTS

Without an appropriate conceptualization of the targeted population, the problem, and the processes involved in change, intervention efforts can be misguided. The direction is simple; the process is challenging. Gottfredson and Gottfredson (2001) define a gang intervention effort as programs or activities directed at youth who are involved with gangs or at risk for gang involvement. Intervention efforts typically address key activities and behaviors that help reduce gang-related violence in school communities. Change is conceptualized through intervention efforts that endorse asocial abstinence for the gang-involved student and that similarly act to prevent relapse into gang activity. In this model, change is supported by schools and surrounding communities that implement gang intervention measures before, during, and after school hours as a way to help prevent and reduce gang recruitment activities, delinquency, intimidation, and violence in school environments.

> Disengaging youth from gangs is a far more difficult and complex task. It is far easier and more economical to prevent than to rehabilitate.

Additionally, intervention efforts are supported by personnel dedicated to the reduction of gang activity. The Dallas ISD contracts with consulting firms that provide gang intervention services throughout the academic school year. To provide intervention services successfully, it is imperative to accurately and appropriately identify a gang-involved youth. Identification of such youth requires interviews and reconnaissance by skilled gang consultants. Gang consultants attend to early warning signs of potential gang involvement (e.g., gang symbols, attire, tattoos, graffiti, mannerisms, language), which are often carefully masked from people not affiliated with gangs. Once a student is identified, his or her needs are assessed and an individualized plan of services is created to adequately address the student's unique situation.

After identification and assessment, intervention efforts consist of gang consultants and dedicated school personnel coordinating wraparound services for a student already involved in gangs and for students who are at high risk for gang involvement. The intervention strategies used by the Dallas ISD are consistent with OJJDP recommendations. Intervention efforts include emerging community-based programs, such as the Positive Passages Program, that balance the delivery of services through educational, recreational, and employment opportunities with effective supervision and accountability. These forms of intervention services typically involve outreach to youth and families, individual risk/needs assessment, case management, home visits, gang rumor control, crisis response services, gang intelligence, service referrals, coordinated service delivery, and supervision. In addition to these wraparound services, students receive mentoring and the opportunity to establish meaningful relationships with caring adults who serve as positive role models.

ENFORCEMENT/SUPPRESSION EFFORTS

Political agendas tend to support harsher enforcement and penalties. However, enforcement efforts alone have had little long-term positive effects on reducing gang membership (Howell, 1998). The Dallas ISD conceptualizes the role of enforcement as a way to increase the value of the prevention and intervention efforts through activities that reduce the attraction of gang membership. Coordination between interventionists and enforcement personnel is vital because the information helps determine current and subsequent interventions in terms of level of need and type of intervention. Moreover, enforcement efforts involve community- and problem-oriented policing strategies that focus on gang activity. Included in these policing efforts are collaborative enforcement strategies that involve probation officers focusing on prosecution in areas with a high rate of gang offenders, gang leaders, and serious violent offenders.

Law enforcement is one essential element in the broad tapestry of suppression efforts. To address some gang concerns, law enforcement personnel are used for surveillance investigations, deterrence, suppression, arrest, prosecution, and detention/incarceration. In addition to providing the basic services associated with law enforcement, law

> Enforcement efforts alone have had little long-term positive effects on reducing gang membership.

enforcement personnel also provide information to school officials about major gang-related activities in sectors of the city with the highest gang presence. Information is used to provide additional patrols or presence in those sectors to deter violence and asocial behavior. Police alone are not expected to provide suppressive efforts. Probation/parole officers are also important because they enforce the conditions of probation/parole and report violations to the juvenile courts.

To provide schools and faculty support for violence prevention and gang intervention, the Dallas ISD Police and Security Department coordinates services with the City of Dallas Police Department and the Dallas County Juvenile Department. Additional partners include the North District of Texas U.S. Attorney's Office, Texas Youth Commission, Dallas County Prosecutor's Office, and Dallas Area Rapid Transit Police and Security Department. Moreover, the Dallas ISD participates in two federal initiatives, Project Safe Neighborhood and Weed and Seed, which address violence and gun control. Additional enforcement responses to gangs include:

- Consistent enforcement of the student code of conduct

- Districtwide anti-gang campaigns at the local and community level

- Introduction of a dress code and student uniforms

Crises involving gang-affiliated youth can be especially daunting to administration and staff. The Dallas ISD addresses crises that purportedly involve gang members by using information from the site of the crisis to determine immediate and sustained police presence. Based on this information, specific law enforcement agents are dispatched to provide a presence or to intervene in possible gang activity. In addition to the school campus, geographic areas are taken into consideration in determining enforcement issues.

Gang interventionists are positioned in several schools in the district. One important function they provide is to gather intelligence and intervene in situations that involve gang members. In the event of a crisis, a team of gang interventionists is dispatched to the school community where the situation occurred. They interview known gang members in an attempt to minimize the possibility of retaliation by another gang. Collectively, enforcement efforts serve to maximize prevention and intervention efforts.

THE ROLE OF A DISTRICT-BASED LEADERSHIP TEAM

Chapter 2 describes the importance of establishing a school-based leadership team to design and manage the B-RTI process. This section discusses the Dallas ISD's effort to establish a leadership team at the district and community level to address the complexities associated with adequately implementing prevention, intervention, and enforcement strategies.

The OJJDP suggests that school settings in cities with chronic and emerging gang issues will benefit from special anti-gang programs in their district. In light of this suggestion, the Dallas ISD created a Gang Response Program that incorporates the suggestions articulated by Arciaga (2007) for developing a multidisciplinary leadership team. The first consideration in developing a team is choosing the right members. The selection of team members is critical to the long-term success of the anti-gang initiative. It is important to choose members who have previous experience working with youth who are already gang involved or at high risk for gang involvement. Team members should also have knowledge of navigating through various systems that affect youth and families (e.g., educational, juvenile justice, mental health).

It is essential that team members understand the purpose of the anti-gang program and respect the skills and knowledge that each partner brings to the team. Consistent with Arciaga's (2007) recommendations, team members should be familiar with the urban landscape, targeted schools, and neighborhood hot spots. Given the diversity in many communities and the preponderance of ethnic minorities in gangs, team members must also be culturally and linguistically responsive. A final essential element is for team members to be generous, yet professional, when sharing information with interested stakeholders. The OJJDP emphasizes the need to protect the confidentiality of certain youth information because it may include critical identifying information such as special education status or social security numbers. School administrators, school psychologists, social workers, community liaisons, and police officers are typically well suited to be team members.

PARTNERSHIPS AND COLLABORATIVE EFFORTS

Collaboration, collaboration, collaboration! This point cannot be emphasized enough. Active collaboration serves to empower a community to address its specific issues and take ownership of its problems and opportunities. Methods in creating partnerships and collaborative efforts vary. Some communities are implementing multidisciplinary teams that provide a venue to share information and resources across professional boundaries, thereby increasing efficiency of action. A significant component of the Dallas ISD Gang Response Program is the Gang Task Force. The Gang Task Force was formed as a collaborative, cross-functional effort that emphasizes community partnership. It is a multiagency, coordinated committee of professionals with a goal to serve as a network of resources. It also functions as a referral mechanism for social service agencies.

> Active collaboration serves to empower a community to address its specific issues and take ownership of its problems and opportunities.

The Gang Task Force collaborates with partners to coordinate resources for prevention, intervention, and enforcement strategies. The task force ensures that collaboration occurs between school officials, law enforcement personnel, and other gang experts to provide preventive, standardized training on gang activities to school personnel, community residents, parents, and agency staff and administrative personnel who can help counter gang influence. Comprehensive planning among all agencies that provide services to children and families is imperative to maximize the effectiveness of interventions. Collaboration ensures that gang-involved youth are not disappearing through the wasteland of disorganization and, conversely, that they receive appropriate assistance. In the event that an identified youth is arrested, the task force's multiagency team can better facilitate communication among local and state law enforcement, corrections, parole and probation, and prosecutors to reassess the limitations of previous intervention efforts.

Structurally, the Dallas ISD Gang Task Force brings together representatives with the goal of weaving together a strong, sustained, collaborative partnership capable of producing positive outcomes. Table 12.1 below provides a concise overview of current participants in the Gang Task Force.

Table 12.1
Gang Task Force Partners

Internal to Dallas ISD	External to Dallas ISD
▸ Department of Safe & Civil Schools • Schoolwide Positive Behavior Supports (e.g., *Foundations* and *START! on Time*) • Classroom management (e.g., *CHAMPs*) • Gang Response program ▸ Department of Police and Security ▸ Educators ▸ Department of Psychological and Social Service ▸ Department of Special Education Services ▸ Department of Parent Services ▸ Department of Alternative Programs ▸ Department of Student Support Teams ▸ Department of Safe and Drug-Free Schools Program ▸ Truancy Department	▸ Dallas Police Department ▸ Probation officers ▸ Court officials (juvenile & family) ▸ Prosecutors ▸ Social service agencies ▸ Youth-serving agencies ▸ Grassroots community agencies ▸ Faith-based organizations ▸ Outreach workers ▸ Texas Youth Commission ▸ Sheriff's Department ▸ Dallas Area Rapid Transit (DART) officers ▸ Substance Abuse (Phoenix House) ▸ Project Safe Neighborhood ▸ Herrera & Associates ▸ Vision Regeneration ▸ U.S. Attorney General's Office North Texas Crime Commission

THE GANG TASK FORCE

As mentioned previously, the Gang Task Force provides collaborative and coordinated services to gang-affiliated and at-risk youth. The purpose of the Dallas ISD Gang Task Force is to enhance the safety and welfare of students and school staff in learning communities through multifaceted, proactive efforts. The Gang Task Force meets weekly to exchange information about youth gangs from various geographic regions of the district, to identify and disseminate information about criminal and delinquent gang activities, and to identify areas of the district where additional assistance is needed to immediately respond to significant increases in gang violence. Information shared at meetings has prevented violent situations from escalating and, on occasion, has led to arrests.

One major objective of the Gang Task Force is to coordinate services between agencies through activities such as gang safety briefings, gang intervention debriefing, and crisis deployment, all of which identify the campuses with the highest priority. Information is shared within the task force for specific reasons. Identification of hot spots and data trends/patterns allows resource allocation to be based on information collected in weekly meetings. Task force members (e.g., gang prevention and intervention specialists, law enforcement officers) are dispatched to provide a presence or to intervene in possible gang activity. During these meetings, participants also discuss debriefings, review success stories, develop action plans to serve targeted youth, prioritize subsequent activities, and determine areas for improvement.

Task force members are trained at the beginning of each year on reporting issues specific to federal, state, and local mandates. One topic of training emphasizes that the group's efforts are to help clients. Information is shared not to penalize or find reason to expel or exclude a student from school but to find appropriate supports and interventions. The development of a consensus around a set of priorities is vital to the long-term success of gang prevention and reduction efforts. Solutions typically need continuous and concerted efforts over a long period, and a stable vision backed by widespread agreement is critical to success. Furthermore, membership is open to any organization, agency, or individual committed to the mission and vision of the Gang Task Force.

> The development of a consensus around a set of priorities is vital to the long-term success of gang prevention and reduction efforts.

The strength of the Gang Task Force is its diversity of perspectives represented by its members as well as its dedication to improvements across the school community. By identifying and providing concentrated services to those within the gang culture, the team seeks to improve the quality of life for all residents of the community, thus reducing gang crime and improving community safety.

Roles and responsibilities. Four positions are essential to operate the Dallas ISD Gang Task Force. Each position carries independent responsibilities that function to support the overall goals of the program. Core positions contribute specific skills, provide access to information, supply resources for clients, and bring other professional attributes to a multidisciplinary team (Arciaga, 2007). The four key positions at the Dallas ISD Gang Task Force are gang presvention and intervention specialists, gang intelligence specialists, gang consultants, and law enforcement personnel.

Gang prevention and intervention specialist. The duties and responsibilities of this specialist position include presenting workshops on gang awareness, prevention, and intervention to school staff, students, parents, and other interested stakeholders. These members provide technical assistance in designing strategies on how to prevent and deter gang development and/or gang involvement as well as assist in the identification of risk factors that may play a role in deciding whether or not to join a gang. In addition, specialists customize services that address the unique situation of each campus. Finally, and most important, specialists develop case management plans for students served and provide feedback on progress to Gang Task Force members.

Gang intelligence specialist. This position is responsible for collecting and analyzing data related to gang activities. This data helps develop trends and patterns of criminal and delinquent behavior that have the most significant effect on the safety of school communities. This specialist also conducts gang-related needs assessment for each campus to help identify which campuses need immediate services and also disseminates gang intelligence to appropriate responders in a timely manner. In addition, the gang intelligence specialist works closely with other gang prevention and intervention specialists to identify timely topics for gang workshops.

Gang consultant. At the Dallas ISD, gang consultants function similarly to outreach workers. They regularly meet with gang-involved youth and their families to help establish contingencies that facilitate change in a student's gang-affiliated lifestyle. Consultants follow three primary objectives that align with the educational obligation of the Dallas ISD:

- Increase academic achievement
- Increase school attendance
- Decrease discipline referrals

In addition, consultants work with school personnel to support a student's social needs.

Gang consultants serve several functions. They are positioned in schools throughout the district and provide intelligence to the Gang Task Force and intervene in situations involving gang members. In the event of a gang crisis (e.g., major fight, riot, walkout, neighborhood shooting involving identified gang members), a team of gang consultants is dispatched to the school community where the situation occurred. Team members talk with known core gang members and their associates and attempt to conclude the violence and minimize the possibility of retaliation by another gang.

Consultants also function as educators through classroom-by-classroom presentations to demystify the gang lifestyle. For school staff, consultants present workshops on how to identify students who are involved with gangs or at risk for gang involvement (e.g., behaviors, graffiti, gang attire, signs, and symbols) and, most importantly, how to help these students.

Law enforcement personnel. The Dallas ISD uses internal and external law enforcement officers to support anti-gang initiatives. Officers provide an array of services such as campus surveillance, criminal and delinquency investigations, security for extracurricular events, and transports for arrests. In terms of their participation in the Gang Task Force, law enforcement officers provide information to school officials about major gang-related activities in various sectors of the city. Information is used to provide additional patrols or presence in those sectors in the effort to deter violence and asocial behavior.

CREATING A CULTURE AND PROCESS OF DATA-DRIVEN DECISIONS

A central tenet of a B-RTI approach is that objective data is the only legitimate way to determine the effectiveness and efficiency of interventions. Chapter 5 in this book discusses the importance of collecting, analyzing, and using data to address students' needs—which aligns with the Dallas ISD anti-gang initiatives. The literature on youth gangs supports the notion that creating a culture and process of data-driven decisions is critical to the success of programs. Researchers recommend that schools and communities conduct a thorough assessment as a first step in developing a clearer understanding of the nature, scope, and dynamics of their gang problem (Arciaga, 2007; Goldstein & Kodluby, 1998; Howell, 2006; National Youth Gang Center, 2002). Assessing the nature and magnitude of the youth gang problem in a school community is difficult but well worth the effort. Gottfredson and Gottfredson (2001) hold that programs developed from assessments are implemented more effectively than those not based on data. The authors continue by stating that "programs guided by assessments are of higher quality, of longer duration, make more use of best practices with respect to the methods employed, involve a larger proportion of students, and achieve a higher level of use by school personnel." Regardless of population size, any community that senses that it is experiencing a youth gang problem needs to undertake a thorough, objective, and comprehensive assessment (Howell, 2006). The National Youth Gang Center (2002) asserts that a properly conducted assessment of the gang problem will help do the following:

- Identify the most serious and prevalent gang-related problems.
- Determine potential factors contributing to gang problems.
- Identify target group(s) for prevention, intervention, and enforcement efforts.

Any community that senses that it is experiencing a youth gang problem needs to undertake a thorough, objective, and comprehensive assessment.

Data-driven assessment. The Dallas ISD conducts school community assessments to determine the extent and effect of gangs in the various communities of the school district. To obtain an accurate picture of how gang activities affect schoolchildren, the Dallas ISD collects information about gang-related activities before, during, and after school. For example, gang consultants collect data trends one hour before school and one hour after school on various travel routes to school to ascertain hot spots. By collecting and analyzing data, school districts are in a better position to plan and allocate resources (e.g., availability of personnel, cell phones, two-way radios, megaphones) in a deliberate manner.

Surveys and interviews of school staff, students, parents, and Gang Task Force members are major components of the school community assessment. For the past 15 years, the Dallas ISD has contracted with Herrera & Associates, a gang prevention and intervention consulting firm, to conduct all of the school district's community assessments. The assessments provide a global school community picture that draws from external and internal sources of data. The assessment begins with an external data collection effort and concludes with an internal examination of school dynamics. On the following page, Table 12.2 provides a brief glimpse of the types of data collected and analyzed. External data sources deal with groups, and internal data sources deal with both groups and individuals.

Findings from the assessment often positively affect the community's impression of the gang issues, largely because they help clarify the number and types of gangs in the school community and the types of criminal and delinquent activities occurring. In addition, the assessment presents a more realistic picture of the challenges and struggles within the school community.

When a school has been thoroughly assessed based on the data mentioned previously, a gang prevention and intervention specialist may be deployed to the school to provide training for the staff, consult with administrators, and/or determine the need for specialized services from a gang consultant. The gang consultant has several roles. Based on need, the consultant may be asked to work with specific youth who are deeply involved in the gang culture or in a position to be affected by the gang culture. The consultant draws on much of the data from his or her work to connect with the at-risk or gang-affiliated youth from within the youth's beliefs system and through meetings with the parents/guardians.

Similar to the B-RTI use of the upside-down triangle to conceptualize students' level of need, the Gang Task Force uses consultants from Herrera & Associates to ascertain the degree and potential impact of the student's involvement in the gang culture. Herrera & Associates propose a three-tier system: entrenched, central, and peripheral. The use of resources and personnel is determined by a descending hierarchy of need that is based on an addiction model for behavioral intervention.

By collecting and analyzing data, school districts are in a better position to plan and allocate resources in a deliberate manner.

Table 12.2

Data Sources for School Community Gang Assessment

External to School Building	Internal to School Building
▸ State Juvenile Justice data and trends (10 years)	▸ Re-entry information from State Youth Commission to school district
▸ State Halfway House data and trends (10 years)	▸ Re-entry information from Juvenile Department to school district
▸ County Juvenile Justice data and trends (10 years)	▸ Juvenile Justice Alternative Education Placement data and trends
▸ City Gang Unit data and trends (10 years)	▸ School District data and trends • School administrators • Probation/Parole officers
▸ Community geographic boundary • Graffiti • Apparel/clothing/jewelry • Colors • Posturing/mannerism/hand symbols • Tattoos	▸ School Police Dept. (if available) or Security Dept.
▸ School travel routes • Walking • Buses	▸ School geographic boundary • Graffiti • Apparel/clothing/jewelry • Colors • Posturing/mannerism/hand symbols • Tattoos
▸ Park and recreation centers	▸ Passing/Transition period routes • Hallways • Stairways • Portables • Arrival • Dismissal
▸ Businesses (e.g., malls, movie theaters)	▸ Common areas • Cafeteria • Courtyards • Auditorium • Gymnasium
▸ Interviews and surveys • Parent/guardians • Businesses • Church/faith-based organizations • Community members/activities • Community organizations/agencies	▸ Examination of school building and furniture
	▸ Interviews and surveys (school climate) • Students • School staff • Parents/guardians • Alumni

Entrenched. At the most severe level of involvement, the Dallas ISD Gang Response Program defines the entrenched gang member as one who:

- Exhibits extensive police contacts
- Has multiple placements in the juvenile justice system
- Is 14–16 years old
- Has one or more family members in a gang
- Has multiple tattoos representing gang membership
- Is an overage student for grade level
- Has a history of violence

Central. The next tier, the central member, tends to have better responses to intervention. The central member has:

- A few police contacts
- A short placement at a juvenile facility
- Only a sibling in a gang
- Academic difficulties
- A history of fighting

Peripheral. The peripheral gang member is most common and most amenable to moderately intensive interventions. These students typically:

- Wear colors of a gang
- Claim to participate in gang activity
- Have minor incidents in school requiring a police contact
- Are in middle school
- Have no family in a gang
- Have problems in some classes
- Have some disciplinary issues related to oppositional behavior in school

Herrera & Associates conducts school community gang interventions for the Dallas ISD and tailors services to respond effectively to the unique needs of a particular campus. The central and entrenched students are targeted for the most intense services, which involve coordination between law enforcement and community service providers as well as active involvement from a parent or guardian and school mental health staff. Students receive mentoring and the opportunity to establish meaningful relationships with caring adults who serve as positive role models.

Law enforcement departments differ in their roles in the assessment process. Law enforcement personnel react toward the student based on the crime, if any, that is committed. They mobilize patrols based on internal information related to crime. With their participation, the data provided to staff is conveyed in a manner that maintains the confidentiality of specific police initiatives. Law enforcement officers meet with community leaders to review the tactics to be deployed, but most significantly, they meet with gang members to lay out in concrete terms the intensive police attention they are about to experience until the violence stops.

As part of a comprehensive assessment, it is important to identify a youth's specific goals in order to provide individualized services that address the youth's unique needs. These goals are reviewed periodically with interested stakeholders, especially with the parent/guardian, to determine the degree of improvement. The results are cross-referenced with system data on school community gang activity, which includes delinquent and criminal acts, to determine the extent of broader, community-wide benefits. In the event that little or no progress is noted, the Gang Task Force efforts are reevaluated to determine the allocation of resources. Thus, it is imperative that law enforcement agencies continually update staff training and monitor specific gang culture in their own jurisdictions. In addressing gang problems, interventionists should keep in mind that no single response will work universally.

Data-based obstacles to overcome. With this in mind, a couple of obstacles need to be addressed before such a program can be successfully implemented. One major obstacle is the assumption that data from one geographic community is relevant and reflective of another community based on some similar demographic information. What is effective in one area of the community may have little effect in another (Howell et al., 2002). Given the likely diversity of community issues, the Dallas ISD emphasizes realistic and accurate applications of resources, along with periodic reviews of success. For example, misreading a gang's enterprise as selling illegal drugs rather than coordinated home invasions could make intervention efforts useless. Because the characteristics of local gangs and their criminal involvement may differ from the features of gangs in distant cities, different strategies may be required to effectively address the local gang problem.

A second major obstacle to a data-driven approach to sustainable programming is the threat of reactionary tactics to gang problems. Starbuck and colleagues (2002) stress the importance of understanding the continual changes in the dynamics of youth gangs. The Dallas ISD officials realize the utility of using data proactively instead of reacting to events. All too often, critical incidents (e.g., a shooting on or near campus) drive resource allocation, instead of careful and ongoing collection and analysis of basic incident data that facilitates rational decision-making. Fashioning responses based on data analysis may prevent, or at least reduce, the frequency of future incidents and allow more appropriate resource allocation.

> Gang programs should collect data and base decisions on the evidence that supports effectiveness.

Gang programs should collect data and base decisions on the evidence that supports effectiveness. The combination of this structure and the focus on data collection and analysis creates a process in which decisions are made based on what will be most effective rather than on political considerations. The efforts by the Dallas ISD Gang Response Program have shown increasing success in implementation and increasing recognition of Dallas County as a model process for systematic work with gang-affiliated youth.

LINKING NEEDS TO AVAILABLE RESOURCES

Chapter 4 describes the B-RTI problem-solving process of identifying students' needs and linking students and families to available resources that will address identified needs. An important point of the process is to identify and design effective, efficient, and timely interventions. A consistent challenge in designing a plan of action for identified youth gang members is that they often receive overlapping services from multiple agencies. Information sharing, collaboration, and coordination among agencies can reduce the unnecessary depletion of finite resources (Arciaga, 2007). To accomplish this effort, the Dallas ISD follows the second-tier recommendations offered by the OJJDP—the coordination of efforts across agencies.

Youth affiliated with gangs often have multiple social, academic, and behavioral needs that are not addressed through typical school-based student support efforts. For instance, a gang-affiliated youth who is failing half his classes, chronically truant, on probation for assault, and experimenting with illegal substances requires coordinated efforts from multiple agencies to ensure systematic and professional response to identified problems. An important function of the Gang Task Force is to link individuals from various professional systems (e.g., juvenile justice, substance abuse, truancy, mental health, special education) to work as partners for the benefit of gang-affiliated or at-risk youth and families. Using current data and knowledge of student development, the Gang Task Force identifies needs and designs strategies for gang prevention, intervention, and enforcement activities as well as for other factors that impede learning. Following recommendations offered by the OJJDP, resources are coordinated across agencies to maximize efforts and reduce duplication of services.

Another important function that the Gang Task Force partners provide is to serve as a consultation group that considers options and provides recommendations for individual students who have received a variety of services and have been referred to resources and community professionals within the district, but still require further assistance or alternatives to experience academic success.

CONCLUSION

Youth gangs have been a significant part of the American culture since the dawn of the industrial revolution, and it is not likely that our communities will return to a time without gangs. We can reasonably expect, however, that the violence and criminal activity associated with youth gangs can be moderately curtailed in our school communities. Through collaboration and coordination of the services of stakeholders, this

> Youth affiliated with gangs often have multiple social, academic, and behavioral needs that are not addressed through typical school-based student support efforts.

expectation is reasonable and attainable, although creative and concerted efforts are needed to facilitate its realization.

Undoubtedly, the presence of youth gangs in a school community adversely affects learning environments by posing a threat to safety and civility. By designing anti-gang strategies based on the extensive literature of positive behavioral supports, criminology, sociology, and other fields in the social sciences, school communities can prevent and reduce gang-related problems and enhance the productivity, safety, and well-being of all citizens.

REFERENCES

Adelman, H. S., & Taylor, L. (1997). Toward a scale-up model for replicating new approaches to schooling. *Journal of Educational and Psychological Consultation, 8,* 197–230.

Alber, S. R., Heward, W. L., & Hippler, B. J. (1999). Teaching middle school students with learning disabilities to recruit positive teacher attention. *Exceptional Children, 65,* 253–270.

Alberto, P., & Troutman, A. (2006). *Applied behavior analysis for teachers* (7th ed.). Upper Saddle River, NJ: Merrill/Prentice-Hall.

Alexander, K. L., Entwisle, D. R., & Kabbani, N. S. (2001). The dropout process in life course perspective: Early risk factors at home and school. *Teachers College Record, 103,* 760–823.

Algozzine, B., Ysseldyke, J., & Elliot, J. (1997). *Strategies and tactics for effective instruction.* Longmont, CO: Sopris West.

Allen, S., & Graden, J. (2002). Best practice in collaborative problem solving for intervention design. In A. Thomas & J. Grimes (Eds.), *Best practices in school psychology IV* (pp. 565–582). Washington, DC: National Association of School Psychologists.

Alvero. A. M., Bucklin, B. R., & Austin. J. (2001). An objective review of the effectiveness and essential characteristics of performance feedback in organizational *settings. Journal of Organizational Behavior Management, 21,* 3–29.

Angle, H., Hay, L., Hay, W., & Ellinwood, E. (1977). Computer-assisted behavior assessment. In J. D. Cone & R. P. Hawkins (Eds.), *Behavioral assessment: New directions in clinical psychology* (pp. 14–75). New York: Guilford Press.

Archer, A., & Gleason, M. (1989). *Skills for school success.* North Billerica, MA: Curriculum Associates.

Archer, A., & Gleason, M. (2002). *Advanced skills for school success.* North Billerica, MA: Curriculum Associates.

Archer, A., Gleason, M. M., Vachon, V., & Isaacson, S. (2000). *REWARDS.* Longmont, CO: Sopris West.

Arciaga, M. (2007). Multidisciplinary gang intervention teams. *National Youth Gang Center Bulletin.* Washington, DC: U.S. Department of Justice, Office of Justice Programs, Office of Juvenile Justice and Delinquency Prevention.

Ardoin, S. P., Martens, B. K., & Wolfe, L. A. (1999). Using high-probability instruction sequences with fading to increase student compliance during transition. *Journal of Applied Behavior Analysis, 32,* 339–351.

Arra, C., & Bahr, M. (2005). Teachers' and students' preferences for mathematics interventions: Implications for teacher acceptability in consultation. *Journal of Educational & Psychological Consultation, 16*(3), 157–174.

Auster, E. A., Feeney-Kettler, K. A., & Kratochwill, T. R. (2006). Conjoint behavioral consultation: Application to the school-based treatment of anxiety disorders. *Education and Treatment of Children, 29*(2), 243–256.

Baer, D.M., Wolf, M.M., & Risley, T.R. (1968). Some current dimensions of applied behavior analysis. *Journal of Applied Behavior Analysis, 1*(1), 91–97.

Bambara, L.M., & Kern, L. (2005). *Individualized supports for students with problem behaviors.* New York: Guilford Press.

Bandura, A. (1977). *Social learning theory.* Oxford, England: Prentice-Hall.

Bandura, A. (1986). *Social foundations of thought and action: A social cognitive theory.* Englewood Cliffs, NJ: Prentice Hall.

Barnhill, G. P. (2005). Functional behavioral assessment in schools. *Intervention in School and Clinic, 40*(3), 131–143.

Batsche, G., Elliott, J., Graden, J., Grimes, J., Kovaleski, J., Prasse, D., et al. (2005). *Response to intervention: Policy considerations and implementation.* Alexandria, VA: National Association of State Directors of Special Education.

Belfiore, P., Basile, S., & Lee, D. (2008). Using a high probability command sequence to increase classroom compliance: The role of behavioral momentum. *Journal of Behavioral Education, 17*(2), 160–171.

Benazzi, L., Horner, R. H., & Good, R. H. (2006). The effects of behavior support team composition on the technical adequacy and contextual fit of behavior support plans. *Journal of Special Education, 40*(3), 160–170.

Bergan, J.R., & Kratochwill, T. R. (1990). *Behavioral consultation in applied settings.* New York: Plenum.

Beutler, L., Moleiro, C., & Talebi, H. (2002). Resistance. In J. C. Norcross (Ed.), *Psychotherapy relationships that work: Therapist contributions and responsiveness to patients* (pp. 129–143). New York: Oxford University Press.

Bonny, A. E., Britto, M. T., Klostermann, B. K., Hornung, R. W., & Slap, G. B. (2000). School disconnectedness: Identifying adolescents at risk. *Pediatrics, 106,* 1017–1021.

Boscardin, M. L. (2005). Promoting effective educational outcomes for all students: Administrative considerations for school psychology trainers. *Trainer's Forum, 25*(1), 20–26.

Bowen, J., Ashcraft, P., Jenson, W.R., & Rhode, G. (2008). *The tough kid bully blockers book.* Eugene, OR: Pacific Northwest Publishing.

Bradley, R., Danielson, L., & Doolittle, J. (2005). Response to intervention. *Journal of Learning Disabilities, 38*(6), 485–486.

Bridgeland, J. M., DiIulio, J. J., & Morrison, K. B. (2006). *The silent epidemic: Perspectives of high school dropouts.* Washington, DC: Civic Enterprises and Peter D. Hart Research Associates for the Bill & Melinda Gates Foundation.

Brophy, J. (1986). Teacher influences on student achievement. *American Psychologist, 41,* 1069–1077.

Brophy, J. E., & Good, T. L. (1986). Teacher behavior and student achievement. In M.C. Wittrock (Ed.), *Handbook of research on teaching* (3rd ed., pp. 328–375). NY: MacMillan Publishing.

Bronfenbrenner, U. (1979). *The ecology of human development: Experiments by nature and design* (pp. 16–42). Cambridge, MA: Harvard University Press.

Broughton, S. F., & Lahey, B. B. (1978). Direct and collateral effects of positive reinforcement, response cost, and mixed contingencies for academic performance. *Journal of School Psychology, 16,* 126–136.

Brown, D., Pryzwansky, W. B., & Schulte, A. (2000). *Psychological consultation: Introduction to theory and practice* (5th ed.). Boston: Allyn & Bacon.

Brown-Chidsey, R., & Steege, M. W. (2005). *Response to intervention: Principles and strategies for effective practice.* New York: Guilford Press.

Burnett, P. C. (1994). Self-talk in upper elementary school children: Its relationship with irrational beliefs, self-esteem, and depression. *Journal of Rational-Emotive & Cognitive Behavior Therapy, 12*(3), 181–188.

Burnett, P. C., & McCrindle, A. R. (1999). The relationship between significant others' positive and negative statements, self-talk, and self-esteem. *Child Study Journal, 29,* 39–48.

Burns, M., Wiley, H., & Viglietta, E. (2008). Best practices in implementing effective problem solving teams. In A. Thomas & J. Grimes (Eds.), *Best practices in school psychology V* (pp. 1633–1644). Washington, DC: National Association of School Psychologists.

Carr, E. G., Dunlap, G., Horner, R. H., Koegel, R. L., Turnbull, A. P., Sailor, W., et al. (2002). Positive behavior support: Evolution of an applied science. *Journal of Positive Behavior Interventions, 4,* 4–16.

Carr, E. G., & Durand, V. (1985). Reducing behavior problems through functional communication training. *Journal of Applied Behavior Analysis, 18,* 111–126.

Carr, E. G., Robinson, S., Taylor, J. C., & Carlson, J. I. (1990). *Positive approaches to the treatment of severe behavior problems in persons with developmental disabilities: A review and analysis of reinforcement and stimulus-based procedures.* Seattle: The Association for Persons with Severe Handicaps.

Carr, J. E., Nicolson, A. C., & Higbee, T. S. (2000). Evaluation of a brief multiple-stimulus preference assessment in a naturalistic context. *Journal of Applied Behavior Analysis, 33,* 353–357.

Carter, D. R., & Horner, R.H. (2007). Adding functional behavioral assessment to first step to success: A case study. *Journal of Positive Behavior Interventions, 9,* 229–238.

Casey, A., Skiba, R., & Algozzine, B. (1988). Developing effective behavioral interventions. In J. L. Graden, J. E. Zins, & M. J. Curtis (Eds.), *Alternative educational delivery systems: Enhancing instructional options for all students* (pp. 413–430). Washington, DC: National Association of School Psychologists.

Cashwell, T. H., Skinner, C. H., & Smith, E. S. (2001). Increasing second-grade students' reports of peers' prosocial behaviors via direct instruction, group reinforcement, and progress feedback: A replication and extension. *Education and Treatment of Children, 24*(2), 161–175.

Chalfant, J., Psyh, M., & Moultrie, R. (1979). Teacher assistance teams: A model for within building problem solving. *Learning Disability Quarterly, 2,* 85–96.

Chandler, K.A., Chapman, C.D., Rand, M.R., & Taylor, B.M. (1998). *Students' reports of school crime: 1989 and 1995.* Washington, DC: U.S. Department of Education and U.S. Department of Justice.

Chen, K., & Bullock, L. M. (2004). Social skills intervention for students with emotional/behavioral disorders aged six through 12 years. *Emotional & Behavioral Difficulties, 9,* 223–238.

Christle, C. A., Jolivette, K., & Nelson, M. (2007). School characteristics related to high school dropout rates. *Remedial and Special Education, 28*(6), 325–339.

Codding, R. S., Feinberg, A. B., Dunn, E. K., & Pace, G. M. (2005). Effects of immediate performance feedback on implementation of behavior support plans. *Journal of Applied Behavior Analysis, 38,* 205–219.

Colton, D., & Sheridan, S. (1998). Conjoint behavioral consultation and social skills training: Enhancing the play behaviors of boys with attention deficit hyperactivity disorder. *Journal of Educational and Psychological Consultation, 9,* 3–28.

Colvin, G., & Fernandez, E. (2000). Sustaining effective behavior support systems in an elementary school. *Journal of Positive Behavior Interventions, 2,* 251–253.

Colvin, G., Kame'enui, E., & Sugai, G. (1993). School-wide and classroom management: Reconceptualizing the integration and management of students with behavior problems in general education. *Education and Treatment of Children, 16,* 361–381.

Colvin, G., & Sprick, R.S. (1999). Providing administrative leadership for effective behavior support: Ten strategies for principals. *Effective School Practices, 17*(4), 65–71.

Colvin, G., Sugai, G., & Patching, B. (1993). Precorrection: An instructional approach for managing predictable problem behaviors. *Intervention in School and Clinic, 28,* 143–150.

Comer, J. P., & Haynes, N. M. (1991). Parents' involvement in schools: An ecological approach. *Elementary School Journal, 91,* 271–277.

Commission on Chronic Illness (1957). *Chronic illness in the United States.* Cambridge, MA: Harvard University Press.

Conroy, M., Asmus, J., Sellers, J., & Ladwig, C. (2005). The use of an antecedent-based intervention to decrease stereotypic behavior in a general education classroom: A case study. *Focus on Autism & Other Developmental Disabilities, 20,* 223–230.

Conte, K. L., & Hintze, J. M. (2000). The effects of performance feedback and goal setting on oral reading fluency within curriculum-based measurement. *Diagnostique, 25,* 85–98.

Cook, B. G., Landrum, T. J., Tankersley, M., & Kauffman, J. M. (2003). Brining research to bear on practice: Effecting evidence-based instruction for students with emotional behavioral disorders. *Education and Treatment of Children, 26,* 345–361.

Cooper, J.O. (2007). Schedules of reinforcement. In J. O. Cooper, T. E. Heron, & W. L. Heward, *Applied behavior analysis* (2nd ed., pp. 304–323). Columbus, OH: Merrill.

Cooper, J. O., Heron, T. E., & Heward, W. L. (2007). Improving and assessing the quality of behavior management. In J. O. Cooper, T. E. Heron, & W. L. Heward, *Applied behavior analysis* (2nd ed, pp. 102–124). Upper Saddle River, NJ: Pearson.

Copeland, S. R., & Hughes, C. (2002). Effects of goal setting on task performance of persons with mental retardation. *Education and Training in Mental Retardation and Developmental Disabilities, 37,* 40–54.

Cormier, S., & Nurius, P. (2003). *Intervening and change strategies for helpers: Fundamental skills and cognitive-behavior interventions* (5th ed.). Pacific Grove, CA: Brooks/Cole.

COSMOS Corporation. (2007). National Evaluation of the Gang-Free Schools Initiative. Unpublished draft report submitted to the Office of Juvenile Justice and Delinquency Prevention, as quoted in *Best practices to address community gang problems: OJJDP's comprehensive gang model.* Bethesda, MD: COSMOS Corporation.

Creed, T., & Kendall, P. (2005). Therapist alliance-building behavior within a cognitive-behavioral treatment for anxiety in youth. *Journal of Consulting and Clinical Psychology, 73,* 498–505.

Crone, D., & Horner, R. (2000). Contextual, conceptual, and empirical foundations of functional behavioral assessment in schools. *Exceptionality, 8,* 161–172.

Crosbie, J. (1998). Negative reinforcement and punishment. In K. A. Lattal & M. Perone (Eds.), *Handbook of research methods in human operant behavior (*pp. 163–189). New York: Plenum.

Cruz, L., & Cullinan, D. (2001). Awarding points, using levels to help children improve behavior. *Teaching Exceptional Children, 33*(3), 16–23.

Curtis, M. J., & Stollar, S. A. (2002). Best practices in system-level change. In A. Thomas & J. Grimes (Eds.) *Best practices in school psychology IV* (pp. 223–234). Washington, DC: National Association of School Psychologists.

Daly, P. M., & Ranalli, P. (2003). Using countoons to teach self-monitoring skills. *Teaching Exceptional Children, 35*(5), 30–35.

Deno, S. (1985). Curriculum-based measurement: The emerging alternative. *Exceptional Children, 52,* 219–232.

Deno, S. (2002). Problem solving as "best practice." In A. Thomas & J. Grimes (Eds.), *Best practices in school psychology IV* (pp. 37–56). Washington, DC: National Association of School Psychologists.

Denton, D. (2003). *Reading first: Lessons from successful state reading initiatives.* Atlanta, GA: Southern Regional Education Board.

DePlantry, J., Coulter-Kern, R., & Duchane, K. (2007). Perceptions of parent involvement in academic achievement. *Journal of Educational Research, 100,* 361–368.

Desimone, L. (1999). Linking parent involvement with student achievement: Do race and income matter? *The Journal of Educational Research, 93,* 11–30.

DiGennaro, F. D., Martens, B. K., & McIntyre, L. L. (2005). Increasing treatment integrity through negative reinforcement: Effects on teacher and student behavior. *School Psychology Review, 34,* 220–331.

Dishion, T. J., & Andrews, D. W. (1995). Preventing escalation in problem behaviors with high-risk young adolescents: Immediate and 1-year outcomes. *Journal of Consulting and Clinical Psychology, 63,* 538–548.

Dishion, T. J., Spracklen, K. M., Andrews, D., & Patterson, G. R. Deviancy training in male adolescent friendships. *Behavior Therapy, 27*(3), 373–390.

Dishion, T. J., & Stormshak, E. (2007). *Intervening in children's lives: An ecological, family-centered approach to mental health care.* Washington, DC: APA.

Duchnowski, A., Kutash, K., Sheffield, S., & Vaughn, B. (2006). Increasing the use of evidence-based practices by special education teachers: A collaborative approach. *Teaching and Teacher Education, 22,* 838–847.

Duhamel, F., & Talbot, L. R. (2004). A constructivist evaluation of family systems nursing interventions with families experiencing cardiovascular and cerebrovascular illness. *Journal of Family Nursing, 10,* 12–32.

Dunlap, G., Hieneman, M., Knoster, T., Fox, L., Anderson, J., & Albin, R. W. (2000). Essential components of inservice training in positive behavior support. *Journal of Positive Behavior Interventions, 2,* 23–32.

Egley, A., Jr., & Ritz, C. E. (2006). *Highlights of the 2004 national youth gang survey (OJJDP Fact Sheet, April 2006–01).* Washington, DC: U.S. Department of Justice, Office of Juvenile Justice and Delinquency Prevention.

Elliott, S.N. (1988). Acceptability of behavioral treatments: Review of variables that influence treatment selection. *Professional Psychology: Research and Practice, 19,* 68–80.

Elliott, S. N., Witt, J. C., & Kratochwill, T. R. (1991). Selecting, implementing, and evaluating classroom interventions. In G. Stoner, M. R. Shinn, & H. M. Walker (Eds.), *Interventions for achievement and behavior problems* (pp. 99–136). Silver Spring, MD: National Association of School Psychologists.

Elliott, S. N., Witt, J., C., Kratochwill, T. R., & Callan-Stoiber, K. (2002). Selecting and evaluating classroom interventions. In M. R. Shinn, H. M. Walker, & G. Stoner (Eds.), *Interventions for academic and behavior problems II: Preventative and remedial approaches* (pp. 243–294). Bethesda, MD: National Association of School Psychologists.

Erchul, W. P. (2003). Communication and interpersonal processes in consultation: Guest editor's comments. *Journal of Educational and Psychological Consultation, 14*, 105–107.

Ervin, R. A., Schaughency, E., Goodman, S., McGlinchey, M., & Matthews, A. (2006). Merging research and practice agendas to address reading and behavior school-wide. *School Psychology Review, 35*, 198–223.

Feldman, E. S., & Kratochwill, T. R. (2003). Problem solving consultation in schools: Past, present, and future directions. *The Behavior Analyst Today, 4*(3), 48–58.

Filter, K., McKenna, M., Benedict, E., Horner, R., Todd, A., & Watson, J. (2007). Check in/check out: A post-hoc evaluation of an efficient, secondary-level targeted intervention for reducing problem behavior in schools. *Education & Treatment of Children, 30*(1), 69–84.

Finn, C.A., & Sladeczek, I.E. (2001). Assessing the social validity of behavioral interventions: A review of treatment acceptability measures. *School Psychology Quarterly, 16(2), 176–206.*

Fisher, D., Frey, N., & Thousand, J. (2003). What do special educators need to know and be prepared to do for inclusive schooling to work? *Teacher Education and Special Education, 26*(1), 42-50.

Forman, S., & Burke, C. (2008). Best practices in selecting and implementing evidence-based school interventions. In A. Thomas & J. Grimes (Eds.), *Best practices in*

school psychology V (pp. 799–811). Bethesda, MD: National Association of School Psychologists.

Forness, S. R., & Kavale, K. A. (1996). Treating social skills deficits in children with learning disabilities: A meta-analysis of the research. *Learning Disability Quarterly, 19*, 2–13.

Fox, J., & Gable, R. A. (2004). Functional behavioral assessment. In R. B. Rutherford, M. M. Quinn, & S. R. Mathur (Eds.), *Handbook of research in emotional and behavioral disorders* (pp. 143–162). New York: Guilford Press.

Freer, P., & Watson, T.S. (1999). A comparison of parent and teacher acceptability ratings of behavioral and conjoint behavioral consultation. *School Psychology Review, 28*, 672–684.

Friman, P. (2000). "Transitional objects" as establishing operations for thumb sucking. *Journal of Applied Behavior Analysis, 33*, 507–509.

Fuchs, L. S. (1995). Best practices in defining student goals and outcomes. In A. Thomas & J. Grimes (Eds.), *Best practices in school psychology III* (pp. 539–546). Washington, DC: National Association of School Psychologists.

Fuchs. L. S., & Fuchs. D. (1986). Effects of systematic formative evaluation: A meta-analysis. *Exceptional Children. 53*, 199–208.

Fuchs, L. S., & Fuchs, D. (2007). The role of assessment in the three-tier approach to reading instruction. In D. Haager, J. Klinger, & S. Vaughn (Eds.), *Evidence-based reading practices for response to intervention.* Baltimore: Brookes.

Gable, R. A., Hendrickson, J. M., & Van Acker, R. (2001). Maintaining the integrity of FBA-based interventions in schools. *Education and Treatment of Children, 24*(3), 248–260.

Galloway, J., & Sheridan, S.M. (1994). Implementing scientific practices through case studies: Examples using home-school interventions and consultation. *Journal of School Psychology, 32,* 385–413.

George, H. P., Harrower, J. K., & Knoster, T. (2003). School-wide prevention and early intervention: A process for establishing a system of school-wide behavior support. *Preventing School Failure, 47,* 170–176.

George, H. P., & Kincaid, D. K. (2008). Building district-level capacity for positive behavior support. *Journal of Positive Behavior Interventions, 10,* 20–32.

Gingiss, P. L. (1992). Enhancing program implementation and maintenance through a multiphase approach to peer-based staff-development. *Journal of School Health, 62(5),* 161–166.

Glover, S., Burns, J., Butler, H., & Patton, G. (1998). Social environments and the emotional well-being of young people. *Family Matters, 49,* 11–16.

Goldstein, A. P., & Kodluboy, D. W. (1998). *Gangs in schools: Signs, symbols, and solutions.* Champaign, IL: Research Press.

Golly, A. M., Stiller, B., & Walker, H. M. (1998). First step to success: Replication and social validation of an early intervention program. *Journal of Emotional and Behavioral Disorders, 6,* 243–250.

Good, R. H., & Kaminski, R. A. (Eds.). (2002). *Dynamic indicators of basic early literacy skills* (6th ed.). Eugene, OR: Institute for the Development of Education Achievement. Available from: http://dibels.uoregon.edu.

Good, R. H., Simmons, D. C., & Kame'enui, E. J. (2001). The importance and decision-making utility of a continuum of fluency-based indicators of foundational reading skills for third-grade high stakes outcomes. *Scientific Studies of Reading, 5,* 257–288.

Gordon, R. S. (1983). An operational classification of disease prevention. *Public Health Reports, 98,* 107–109.

Gortmaker, V., Warnes, E. D., & Sheridan, S. M. (2004). Conjoint behavioral consultation: Involving parents and teachers in the treatment of a child with selective mutism. *Proven Practice, 5,* 66–72.

Gottfredson, G. D., & Gottfredson, D. C. (2001). *Gang problem and gangs in a national sample of schools.* Ellicott City, MD: Gottfredson Associates, Inc. (ERIC Document Reproduction Service No. ED 459408)

Gravois, T. A., Knotek, S., & Babinski, L. (2001). Educating practitioners as instructional consultants: Development and implementation of the IC team consortium. *Journal of Educational and Psychological Consultation, 13,* 113–132.

Gravois, T. A., & Rosenfield, S. A. (2002). A multi-dimensional framework for evaluation of instructional consultation teams. *Journal of Applied School Psychology, 19,* 5–29.

Greene, M. B. (2005). Reducing violence and aggression in schools. *Trauma, Violence, & Abuse, 6,* 236–253.

Gresham, F. M. (1985). Conceptual issues in the assessment of social competence in children. In P. S. Strain, M. J. Guralnick, & H. M. Walker (Eds.), *Children's social behavior: Development, assessment, and modification* (pp. 143–213). New York: Academic Press.

Gresham, F. M. (1989). Assessment of treatment integrity in school consultation and prereferral intervention. *School Psychology Review, 18,* 37–50.

Gresham, F. M. (2002). Teaching social skills to high-risk children and youth: Preventive and remedial strategies. In M. R. Shinn, H. M. Walker, & G. Stoner (Eds.*), Interventions for academic and behavior problems II: Preventive and remedial approaches* (pp. 403–432). Bethesda: National Association of School Psychologists.

Gresham, F. M. (2004). Current status and future directions of school-based behavior interventions. *School Psychology Review, 33,* 326–343.

Gresham, F. M. (2005). Response to intervention: An alternative means of identifying students as emotionally disturbed. *Education and Treatment of Children, 28*(4), 328–344.

Gresham, F. M., MacMillan, D., Beebe-Frankenberger, M., & Bocian, K. (2000). Treatment integrity in learning disabilities research: Do we really know how treatments are implemented? *Learning Disabilities Research & Practice, 15*(4), 198–205.

Griffin, B. W. (2002). Academic disidentification, race, and high school dropouts. *High School Journal, 85*(4), 71–81.

Grimes, J., Kurns, S., & Tilly, W. D., III (2006). Sustainability: An enduring commitment to success. *School Psychology Review, 35,* 224–244.

Grimes, J., & Tilly, W. D., III (1996). Policy and process: Means to lasting educational change. *School Psychology Review, 4,* 464–475.

Gunter, P., & Denny, K. (1996). Research issues and needs regarding teacher use of classroom management strategies. *Behavioral Disorders, 22,* 15–20.

Gunter, P. L., & Jack, S. L. (1993). Lag sequential analysis as a tool for functional analysis of student disruptive behavior in classrooms. *Journal of Emotional and Behavioral Disorders, 1,* 138–149.

Guskey, T. R. (1994, April). *Professional development in education: In search of the optimal mix.* Paper presented at the Annual meeting of the American Educational Research Association, New Orleans, LA.

Guskey, T. R. (1999). Apply time with wisdom. *Journal of Staff Development, 20*(2), 10–15.

Gutkin, T. B., & Curtis, M. J. (1999). School-based consultation theory and practice: The art and science of indirect service delivery. In C. R. Reynolds & T. B. Gutkin (Eds.), *The handbook of school psychology* (pp. 598–637). New York: John Wiley.

Haager, D., & Mahdavi, J. (2007). Teacher roles in implementing intervention. In D. Haager, J. Klinger, & S. Vaughn (Eds.), *Evidence-based reading practices for response to intervention* (pp. 245–263). Baltimore: Brookes.

Hagopian, L. P., Fisher, W. W., Sullivan, M. T., Acquisto, J., & LeBlanc, L. A. (1998). Effectiveness of functional communication training with and without extinction and punishment: A summary of 21 inpatient cases. *Journal of Applied Behavior Analysis, 31*, 211–235.

Hanley, G., Piazza, C., Fisher, W., & Maglieri, K. (2005). On the assessment of and preference for punishment and extinction components of function-based interventions. *Journal of Applied Behavior Analysis, 38*, 51–65.

Harn, B., Kame'enui, E., & Simmons, D. (2007). The nature and role of the third tier in a prevention model for kindergarten students. In D. Haager, J. Klinger, & S. Vaughn (Eds.), *Evidence-based reading practices for response to intervention* (pp. 161–184). Baltimore: Brookes.

Harrower, J. K., & Dunlap, G. (2001). Including children with autism in general education classrooms: A review of effective strategies. *Behavior Modification, 25*, 762–784.

Hawken, L. S., & Horner, R. H. (2003). Evaluation of a targeted intervention within a schoolwide system of behavior support. *Journal of Behavioral Education, 12*(3), 225–240.

Hawken, L. S., MacLeod, K. S., & Rawlings, L. (2007). Effects of the behavior education program (BEP) on the office discipline referrals of elementary school students. *Journal of Positive Behavior Interventions, 9*(2), 94–101.

Hawkins, R. P. (1986). Selection of target behaviors. In R. O. Nelson & S. C. Hayes (Eds.), *Conceptual foundations of behavioral assessment* (pp. 331–385). New York: Guilford Press.

Henderson, A. T., & Mapp, K. L. (2002). *A new wave of evidence: The impact of school, parent, and community connections on student achievement.* Austin, TX: Southwest Educational Development Laboratory.

Henderson, A. T., Marburger, C. L., & Ooms, T. (1986). *Beyond the bake sale: An educator's guide to working with parents.* Columbia, MD: National Committee for Citizens in Education.

Heward, W. L. (2005). Reasons applied behavior analysis is good for education and why those reasons have been insufficient. In W. L. Heward, T. E. Heron, N. A. Neef, S. M. Peterson, D. M. Sainato, G. Cartledge, R. Gardner, L. D. Peterson, S. B. Hersh, & J. C. Dardig (Eds.), *Focus on behavior analysis in education: Achievements, challenges, and opportunities* (pp. 316–348). Upper Saddle River, NJ: Pearson Press.

Hieneman, M., Dunlap, G., & Kincaid, D. (2005). Positive behavior support strategies for students with behavior disorders in general education settings. *Psychology in the Schools, 42*, 779–794.

Hilty, E. B. (1998). The professionally challenged teacher: Teachers talk about school failure. In D. Franklin (Ed.), *When children don't learn: Student failure and the culture of teaching* (pp. 134–159). New York: Teachers College, Columbia University.

Hintze, J., Volpe, R., & Shapiro, E. (2008). Best practices in the systematic direct observation of student behavior. In A. Thomas & J. Grimes (Eds.). *Best practices in school psychology V* (pp. 319–335). Bethesda, MD: National Association of School Psychologists.

Horner, R. H. (2002). On the status of using punishment: A commentary. *Journal of Applied Behavior Analysis, 35*(4), 465–467.

Horner, R. H., Dunlap, G., Koegel, R. L., Carr, E. G., Sailor, W., Anderson, J., et al. (1990). Toward a technology of "nonaversive" behavior support. *Journal of the Association for Persons with Severe Handicaps, 15,* 125–132.

Horner, R. H., Sugai, G., & Todd, A. W. (2001). Data need not be a four-letter word: Using data to improve school-wide discipline. *Beyond Behavior, Fall,* 20–23.

Horner, R. H., Sugai, G., Todd, A. W., & Lewis-Palmer, T. (1990). Elements of behavior support plans: A technical brief. *Exceptionality, 8,* 205–215.

Horner, R. H., Sugai, G., Todd, A. W., & Lewis-Palmer, T. (2005). Schoolwide positive behavior support. In L. M. Bambara & L. Kern (Eds.), *Individualized supports for students with problem behaviors: Designing positive behavior plans* (pp. 359–390). New York: Guilford Press.

Howell, J.C. (1997). *Youth gangs* (OJJDP Fact Sheet, December 1997–72). Washington, DC: U.S. Department of Justice, Office of Juvenile Justice and Delinquency Prevention.

Howell, J.C. (1998). *Youth gangs: An overview* (Juvenile Justice Bulletin, Youth Gang Series). Washington, DC: U.S. Department of Justice, Office of Justice Programs, Office of Juvenile Justice and Delinquency Prevention.

Howell, J.C. (2006). *The impact of gangs on communities* (National Youth Gang Center Bulletin). Washington, DC: U.S. Department of Justice, Office of Justice Programs, Office of Juvenile Justice and Delinquency Prevention.

Howell, J.C., Egley, A., & Gleason, D. K. (2002). *Modern-day youth gangs* (Juvenile Justice Bulletin, Youth Gang Series). Washington, DC: U.S. Department of Justice, Office of Justice Programs, Office of Juvenile Justice and Delinquency Prevention.

Howell, J.C., & Lynch, J. (2000). *Youth gangs in schools* (Juvenile Justice Bulletin, Youth Gang Series). Washington, DC: U.S. Department of Justice, Office of Justice Programs, Office of Juvenile Justice and Delinquency Prevention.

Howell, K. W., & Nolet, V. (2000). *Curriculum-based evaluation: Teaching and decision making.* Belmont, CA: Wadsworth/Thomason Learning.

Individuals with Disabilities Education Improvement Act, P.L. 108-446 § 20 U.S.C. § 1400 (2004).

Ingram, K., Lewis-Palmer, T., & Sugai, G. (2005). Function-based intervention planning: Comparing the effectiveness of FBA indicated and contra-indicated intervention plans. *Journal of Positive Behavior Interventions, 7*, 224–236.

Irvin, L. K., Tobin, T. J., Sprague, J. R., Sugai, G., & Vincent, C. G. (2004). Validity of office discipline referral measures as indices of school-wide behavioral status and effects of school-wide behavioral interventions. *Journal of Positive Behavior Interventions, 6*, 131–147.

Jacob, S., & Hartshorne, T. (2007). *Ethics and law for school psychologists* (5th ed.). Hoboken, NJ: John Wiley & Sons.

Jimerson, S. R., & Furlong, M. J. (Eds.). (2006). *Handbook of school violence and school safety: From research to practice.* Mahwah, NJ: Erlbaum.

Joyce, B., & Showers, B. (2002). *Student achievement through staff development* (3rd ed.). Alexandria, VA: Association for Supervision and Curriculum Development.

Kame'enui, E., Good, R., & Harn, B. (2005). Beginning reading failure and the quantification of risk: Reading behavior as the supreme index. In W. Heward, T. Heron, N. Neef, S. Peterson, D. Sainato, G. Cartledge, R. Gardner, L. Peterson, S. Hersh, & J. Dardig (Eds.) *Focus on behavior analysis in education: Achievements, challenges, and opportunities* (pp. 69–89). Upper Saddle River, NJ: Pearson Press.

Kaminski, R. A., & Good, R. H. (1996). Toward a technology for assessing basic early literacy skills. *School Psychology Review, 25*, 215–227.

Karwoski, L., Garratt, G. M., & Ilardi, S. S. (2006). On the integration of cognitive-behavioral therapy for depression and positive psychology. *Journal of Cognitive Psychotherapy: An International Quarterly, 20*, 159–170.

Kellam, S., & Anthony, J. C. (1998). Targeting early adolescents to prevent tobacco smoking: Findings from an epidemiologically based randomized field trial. *American Journal of Public Health, 88*(10), 1490–1495.

Kerkorian, D., McKay, M., & Bannon, W. (2006). Seeking help a second time: Parents'/caregivers' characterizations of previous experiences with mental health services for their children and perceptions of barriers to future use. *American Journal of Orthopsychiatry, 76*, 161–166.

Kern, L., & Clemens, N. H. (2007). Antecedent strategies to promote appropriate classroom behavior. *Psychology in the Schools, 44*, 65–75.

Kincaid, D., Childs, K., Blasé, K. A., & Wallace, F. (2007). Identifying barriers and facilitators in implementing schoolwide positive behavior support. *Journal of Positive Behavior Interventions, 9*, 174–184.

Knoff, H. (1996). The interface of school, community, and health care reform: Organizational directions toward effective services for children and youth. *School Psychology Review, 25*, 446–465.

Knoff, H. (2002). Best practices in facilitating school reform, organizational change, and strategic planning. In A. Thomas & J. Grimes (Eds.), *Best practices in school psychology IV* (pp. 235–253). Washington, DC: National Association of School Psychologists.

Knoff, H. (2008). Best practices in implementing statewide positive behavioral support systems. In A. Thomas & J. Grimes (Eds.), *Best practices in school psychology V* (pp. 749–762). Bethesda, MD: National Association of School Psychologists.

Koegel, L. K., Koegel, R. L., & Dunlap, G. (1996). *Positive behavioral support.* Baltimore: Brookes.

Kratochwill, T. R. (2008). Best practices in school-based problem-solving consultation: Applications in prevention and intervention systems. In A. Thomas & J. Grimes (Eds.), *Best practices in school psychology V* (pp. 1673–1688). Bethesda, MD: National Association of School Psychologists.

Kratochwill, T. R., Elliott, S. N. & Callan-Stoiber, K. (2002). Best practices in school-based problem-solving consultation. In A. Thomas & J. Grimes (Eds.), *Best practices in school psychology IV* (pp. 3–20). Washington, DC: National Association of School Psychologists.

Kratochwill, T.R., & Pittman, P.H. (2002). Expanding problem-solving consultation training: Prospects and frameworks. *Journal of Educational & Psychological Consultation, 13*(1), 69–95.

Kratochwill, T. R., & Shernoff, E. S. (2003). Evidence-based practice: Promoting evidence-based intervention in school psychology. *School Psychology Quarterly, 15*, 233–253.

Kratochwill, T. R., & Stoiber, K. C. (2000). Empirically supported interventions and school psychology: Rational and methodological issues, Part II. *School Psychology Quarterly, 15*, 233–252.

Kratochwill, T. R., & Stoiber, K. C. (2002). Evidence-based interventions in school psychology: Conceptual foundations of the procedural and coding manual of Division 16 and the Society for the Study of School Psychology Task Force. *School Psychology Quarterly, 17*(4), 341–389.

Kratochwill, T. R., Volpiansky, P., Clements, M., & Ball, C. (2007). Professional development in implementing and sustaining multitier prevention models: Implications for response to intervention. *School Psychology Review, 36*(4), 618–631.

Lambert, N. (2004). Consultee-centered consultation: An international perspective on goals, process, and theory. In N. Lambert, I. Hylander, & J. Sandoval (Eds.), *Consultee-centered consultation: Improving the quality of professional services in schools and community organizations* (pp. 3–19). Mahwah, NJ: Erlbaum.

Landsberger, H. A. (1958). *Hawthorne revisited.* Ithaca, NY: Lenox Library Association.

Lane, K. L., Beebe-Frankenberger, M. E., Lambros, K. L., & Pierson, M. E. (2001). Designing effective interventions for children at-risk for antisocial behavior: An integrated model of components necessary for making valid inferences. *Psychology in the Schools, 38*, 365–379.

Lasky, S. (2000). The cultural and emotional politics of teacher–parent interactions. *Teacher and Teacher Education, 16*, 843–860.

Lerman, D., Iwata, B., & Wallace, M. (1999). Side effects of extinction: Prevalence of bursting and aggression during the treatment of self-injurious behavior. *Journal of Applied Behavioral Analysis, 29,* 345–382.

Lerman, D., & Vorndran, C. (2002). On the status of knowledge for using punishment: Implications for treating behavior disorders. *Journal of Applied Behavior Analysis, 35*(4), 431–464.

Lewis, T. J. (1994). A comparative analysis of the effects of social skills training and teacher directed contingencies on the generalized social behavior of pre-school children with disabilities. *Journal of Behavioral Education, 4,* 267–281.

Lewis, T. J., Colvin, G., & Sugai, G. (2000). The effects of pre-correction and active supervision on the recess behavior of elementary students. *Education and Treatment of Children, 23,* 109–121.

Lewis, T. J., Hudson, S., Richter, M., & Johnson, N. (2004). Scientifically supported practices in emotional and behavioral disorders: A proposed approach and brief review of current practices. *Behavioral Disorders, 29*(3), 247–259.

Lewis, T. J., & Sugai, G. (1999). Effective behavior support: A systems approach to proactive school-wide management. *Focus on Exceptional Children, 31*(6), 1–24.

Lewis, T. J., Sugai, G., & Colvin, G. (1998). Reducing problem behavior through a school-wide system of effective behavioral support: Investigation of a school-wide social skills training program and contextual interventions. *School Psychology Review, 27,* 446–459.

Luborsky, L., McLellan, A. T., Woody, G. E., O'Brien, C. P., & Auerbach, A. (1985). Therapist success and its determinants. *Archives of General Psychiatry, 42,* 602–611.

Luiselli, J. K., & Cameron, M. J. (Eds.). (1998). *Antecedent control: Innovative approaches to behavioral support.* Baltimore: Brookes.

Mace, F., Hock, M., Lalli, J., West, B., Belfiore, P., Pinter, E., & Brown, K. (1988). Behavioral momentum in the treatment of noncompliance. *Journal of Applied Behavior Analysis, 21,* 123–142.

Mager, W., Milich, R., Harris, M. J., & Howard, A. (2005). Intervention groups for adolescents with conduct problems: Is aggregation harmful or helpful? *Journal of Abnormal Child Psychology, 33,* 349–362.

March, R. E., & Horner, R.H. (2002). Feasibility and contributions of functional behavioral assessment in schools. *Journal of Emotional and Behavioral Disorders, 10*(3), 158–170.

Martella, R. C., Nelson, J. R., & Marchand-Martella, N. E. (2003). *Managing disruptive behaviors in the schools.* Boston: Allyn & Bacon.

Massarella, J. A. (1980). Synthesis of research on staff development. *Educational Leadership, 38*(2), 182–185.

May, S., Ard, W., Todd, A. W., Horner, R. H., Glasgow, A., Sugai, G., & Sprague, J. (2003). *Schoolwide information system.* Eugene: Educational and Community Supports, University of Oregon.

Mayer, G. (1995). Preventing antisocial behavior in the schools. *Journal of Applied Behavior Analysis, 28,* 467–478.

McConnell, M. (1999). Self-monitoring, cueing, recording, and managing: Teaching students to manage their own behavior. *Teaching Exceptional Children, 32*(2), 14–21.

McDougal, J., Clonan, S. M., Martens, B., & Nastasi, B. (2000). Using organizational change procedures to promote the acceptability of prereferral intervention services: The school-based intervention team project. *School Psychology Quarterly, 15,* 149–171.

McEvoy, A., & Welker, R. (2000). Antisocial behavior, academic failure, and school climate: A critical review. *Journal of Emotional and Behavioral Disorders, 8*(3), 130–140.

McGivern, J. E., Ray-Subramanian, C. E., & Auster, E. R. (2008). Best practices in establishing effective helping relationships. In A. Thomas & J. Grimes (Eds.). *Best practices in school psychology V* (pp. 1613–1631). Bethesda, MD: National Association of School Psychologists.

McGoey, K., & DuPaul, G. (2000). Token reinforcement and response cost procedures: Reducing the disruptive behavior of preschool children with attention deficit/hyperactivity disorder. *School Psychology Quarterly, 15*(3), 330–343.

McIntyre, L. L., Gresham, F. M., DiGennaro, F. D., & Reed, D. D. (2007). Treatment integrity of school-based interventions with children in the Journal of Applied Behavior Analysis 1991–2005. *Journal of Applied Behavior Analysis, 40,* 659–672.

McNeely C., & Falci, C. (2004). School connectedness and the transition into and out of health-risk behavior among adolescents: A comparison of social belonging and teacher support. *Journal of School Health, 74*(7), 284–292.

Meichenbaum, D., & Goodman, J. (1971). Training impulsive children to talk to themselves: A means of developing self-control. *Journal of Consulting and Clinical Psychology, 40,* 148–154.

Merrell, K.M. (2003). *Behavioral, social, and emotional assessment of children and adolescents.* New Jersey: Lawrence Erlbaum Associates, Inc.

Merrell, K., & Buchanan, R. (2006). Intervention selection in school-based practice: Using public health models to enhance systems capacity of schools. *School Psychology Review, 35,* 167–180.

Miller, D., & Kelley, M. (1994). The use of goal setting and contingency contracting for improving children's homework performance. *Journal of Applied Behavior Analysis, 27*(1), 73–84.

Miller, D., & Kraft, N. P. (2008). Best practices in communicating with and involving parents. In A. Thomas & J. Grimes (Eds.). *Best practices in school psychology V* (pp. 937–951). Bethesda, MD: National Association of School Psychologists.

Miltenberger, R. G. (2004). *Behavior modification: Principles and procedures* (3rd ed.). Belmont, CA: Wadsworth.

Moncher, F. J., & Prinz, R. J. (1991). Treatment fidelity in outcome studies. *Clinical Psychology Review, 11,* 247–266.

Munk, D., & Karsh, K. G. (1999). Antecedent curriculum and instructional variables as classwide interventions for preventing or reducing problem behaviors. In A. C. Repp & R. H. Horner (Eds.), *Functional analysis of problem behavior: From effective assessment to effective support* (pp. 259–376). Belmont, CA: Wadsworth.

National Youth Gang Center (2002). *A guide to assessing your community's youth gang problem.* Tallahassee, FL: National Youth Gang Center. Retrieved October 28, 2008, from http://www.iir.com/nygc/acgp/assessment.htm.

Nelson, J. R. (1996). Designing schools to meet the needs of students who exhibit disruptive behavior. *Journal of Emotional and Behavioral Disorders, 4,* 147–161.

Nelson, J. R., Benner, G. J., & Mooney, P. (2008). *Instructional practices for students with behavioral disorders: Strategies for reading, writing, and math.* New York: Guilford Press.

Nelson, J. R., Martella, R. M., & Marchand-Martella, N. (2002). Maximizing student learning: The effects of a comprehensive school-based program for preventing problem behaviors. *Journal of Emotional and Behavioral Disorders, 10,* 136–148.

Nelson, J. R., Roberts, M. L., Mathur, S. R., & Rutherford, R. B., Jr. (1998). Has public policy exceeded our knowledge base? A review of the functional behavioral assessment literature. *Behavior Disorders, 24*(2), 169–179.

Nelson, R. O., & Hayes, S. C. (1979). Some current dimensions of behavioral assessment. *Behavioral Assessment 1,* 1–16.

Nersesian, M., Todd, A. W., Lehmann, J., & Watson, J. (2000). School-wide behavior support through district-level system change. *Journal of Positive Behavior Interventions, 2,* 244–247.

Newcomer, L., & Lewis, T. (2004). Functional behavioral assessment: An investigation of assessment reliability and effectiveness of function-based interventions. *Journal of Emotional and Behavioral Disorders, 12,* 168–181.

Neyhart, S., & Garrison, M. (1992). *Connections: A group-based behavior monitoring plan.* Unpublished implementation manual.

No Child Left Behind Act of 2001, PL 107-110 § 20 U.S.C. § 6301 et seq.

Noell, G. H., Gresham, F. M., & Gansle, K. A. (2002). Does treatment integrity matter? A preliminary investigation of instructional implementation and mathematics performance. *Journal of Behavioral Education, 11*(1), 51–67.

Noell, G. H., Witt, J. C., Slider, N. J., Connell, J. E., Gatti, S. L., Williams, K. L., et al. (2005). Treatment implementation following behavioral consultation in schools: A comparison of three follow-up strategies. *School Psychology Review, 34*(1), 87–106.

Norcross, J. C., & Lambert, M. J. (2006). The therapy relationship. In J. C. Norcross, L. E. Beutler, & R. F. Levant (Eds.), *Evidence-based practices in mental health: Debate and dialogue on the fundamental questions* (pp. 208–218). Washington, DC: American Psychological Association.

Nord, C. W., Brimhall, D., & West, U. (1997). *Fathers' involvement in children's schools* (Report ED 409 125). Washington, DC: U.S. Department of Education.

O'Neill, R. E., Horner, R. H., Albin, R. W., Sprague, J. R., Storey, K., & Newton, J. S. (1997). *Functional assessment and program development for problem behavior: A practical handbook.* Pacific Grove, CA: Brooks/Cole.

O'Shea, L., Algozzine, R., Hammittee, D., & O'Shea, D. (2000). *Families and teachers of individuals with disabilities: Collaborative orientations and responsive practices.* Boston: Allyn & Bacon.

Patterson, G. R., Reid, J. B., & Dishion, T. (1992). *Antisocial boys.* Eugene, OR: Castalia.

Pearce, C. L., & Herbick, P. A. (2004). Citizenship behavior at the team level of analysis: The effects of team leadership, team commitment, perceived team support, and team size. *Journal of Social Psychology, 144,* 293–310.

Perepletchikova, F., & Kazdin, A. (2005). Treatment integrity and therapeutic change: Issues and research recommendations. *Clinical Psychology: Science and Practice, 12,* 365–383.

Perez-Johnson, I., & Maynard, R. (2007). The case for early, targeted interventions to prevent academic failure. *Peabody Journal of Education, 82*(4), 587–616.

Peterson, C., & McConnell, S. (1996). Factors related to intervention integrity and child outcome in social skills interventions. *Journal of Early Intervention, 20,* 146–164.

Philpot, V. D., & Bamburg, J. W. (1996). Rehearsal of positive self-statements and restructured negative self-statements to increase self-esteem and decrease depression. *Psychological Reports, 79,* 83–91.

Piazza, C., Roane, H., Keeney, K., Boney, B., & Abt, K. (2002). Varying response effort in the treatment of pica maintained by automatic reinforcement. *Journal of Applied Behavior Analysis, 35*(3), 233–246.

Poole, J., & Caperton-Brown, H. (in press). *PASS: A positive approach to student success.* [Manual]. Eugene, OR: Pacific Northwest Publishing.

Poulin. F., Dishion, T. J., & Burraston, B. (2001). 3-year iatrogenic effects associated with aggregating high-risk adolescents in preventive interventions. *Applied Developmental Science, 5,* 214–224.

Power, T., Blom-Hoffman, J., Clarke, A., Riley-Tillman, T., Kelleher, C., & Manz, P. (2005). Reconceptualizing intervention integrity: A partnership-based framework for linking research with practice. *Psychology in the Schools, 42,* 495–507.

Quinn, M., Gable, R., Fox, J., Rutherford, R. V., Van Acker, R., & Conroy, M. (2001). Putting quality functional assessment into practice in schools: A research agenda on behalf of E/BD students. *Education and Treatment of Children, 24*(3), 261–275.

Reid, R. (1996). Research in self-monitoring with students with learning disabilities: The present, the prospects, and the pitfalls. *Journal of Learning Disabilities, 29,* 317–331.

Reinecke, D., Newman, B., & Meinberg, D. (1999). Self-management of sharing in three pre-schoolers with autism. *Education and Training in Mental Retardation and Developmental Disabilities, 34,* 312–317.

Repp, A. C. (1999). Naturalistic functional assessments in classroom settings. In A. C. Repp & R. H. Horner (Eds.), *Functional analysis of problem behavior* (pp. 238–258). Belmont, CA: Wadsworth.

Reschly, D. J., & Ysseldyke, J. (2002). Paradigm shift: The past is not the future. In A. Thomas & J. Grimes (Eds.), *Best practices in school psychology IV* (pp. 3–20). Washington, DC: National Association of School Psychologists.

Resnick, M. D., Bearman, P. S., Blum, R. W., Bauman, K. E., Harris, K. M., Jones, J., et al. (1997). Protecting adolescents from harm: Findings from the national longitudinal study on adolescent health. *Journal of the American Medical Association, 278,* 823–832.

Richmond, G., Mancil, M., Conroy, A., & Alter, J. (2006). Functional communication training in the natural environment: A pilot investigation with a young child with autism spectrum disorder. *Education and Treatment of Children, 29,* 615–633.

Richtig, R., & Hornak, N. J. (2003). 12 lessons from school crises. *Education Digest, 68*(5), 20–24.

Roach, A. T., & Elliott, S. N. (2008). Best practices in facilitating and evaluating intervention integrity. In A. Thomas & J. Grimes (Eds.), *Best practices in school psychology V* (pp. 195–208). Bethesda, MD: National Association of School Psychologists.

Rodriguez, B. J., Loman, S., & Horner, R. H. (2008). Improving the success of first step to success by focusing on implementation fidelity: The impact of coaching feedback. Manuscript in preparation. University of Oregon.

Rones, M., & Hoagwood, K. (2000). School-based mental health services: a research review. *Clinical Child and Family Psychology Review, 3*(4), 223–241.

Rosenfield, S. (1987). *Instructional consultation.* Hillsdale, NJ: Erlbaum.

Rosenfield, S. (2002). Best practices in instructional consultation. In A. Thomas & J. Grimes (Eds.), *Best practices in school psychology IV* (pp. 609–623). Washington, DC: National Association of School Psychologists.

Rosenfield, S. (2004). Consultation as dialogue: The right words at the right time. In N. M. Lambert, I. Hylander, & J. H. Sandoval (Eds.), *Consultee-centered consultation: Improving the quality of professional services in schools and community organizations* (pp. 337–347). New York: Erlbaum.

Rosenfield, S. (2008). Best practices in instructional consultation and instructional consultation teams. In A. Thomas & J. Grimes (Eds.). *Best practices in school psychology V* (pp. 1645–1659). Bethesda, MD: National Association of School Psychologists.

Rosenfield, S., & Gravois, T. (1996). *Instructional consultation teams: Collaborating for change.* New York: Guilford Press.

Rosenshine, B. (1971). *Teaching behaviours and student achievement.* London: National Foundation for Educational Research.

Ruth, W. J. (1996). Goal setting for students with emotional and behavioral difficulties: Analysis of daily, weekly, and total goal attainment. *Psychology in the Schools, 33,* 153–158.

Salvia, J., & Ysseldyke, J. (2004). *Assessment in special and inclusive education* (9th ed.). Princeton, NJ: Houghton Mifflin.

Sandoval, J. (Ed.) (2002). *Handbook of crisis counseling, intervention and prevention in the schools* (2nd ed.). Mahwah, N.J.: Lawrence Erlbaum Associates.

Scheuermann, B., & Hall, J. A. (2008). *Positive behavioral supports for the classroom.* Upper Saddle River, NJ: Pearson Education.

Scott, T. M., McIntyre, J., Liaupsin, C., Conroy, M., & Payne, L. D. (2005). An examination of the relation between functional behavior assessment and selected intervention strategies with school-based teams. *Journal of Positive Behavior Interventions, 7*(4), 205–215.

Scott, T. M., & Nelson, C. M. (1999). Universal school discipline strategies: Facilitating positive learning environments. *Effective School Practices, 17,* 54–64.

Seligman, M. E. P. (2002). Positive psychology, positive prevention and positive therapy. In C.R. Snyder & S.J. Lopez (Eds.), *Handbook of positive psychology.* New York: Oxford University Press.

Seligman, M. E. P., & Csikszentmihalyi, M. (2000). Positive psychology: An introduction. *American Psychologist, 55,* 5–14.

Sheridan, S. M., Erchul, W. P., Brown, M. S., Dowd, S. E., Warnes, E. D., Marti, D. C., et al. (2004). Perceptions of helpfulness in conjoint behavioral consultation: Congruence and agreement between teachers and parents. *School Psychology Quarterly, 19,* 121–140.

Sheridan, S.M., & Kratochwill, T.R. (1992). Behavioral parent-teacher consultation: conceptual and research considerations. *Journal of School Psychology 30, 117–139.*

Sheridan, S. M., Kratochwill, T. R., & Bergan, J. R. (1996). *Conjoint behavioral consultation: A procedural manual.* New York: Plenum Press.

Shinn, M. R. (1989). *Curriculum-based measurement: Assessing special children.* New York: Guilford Press.

Shinn, M.R., & Bamonto, S. (1998). Advanced applications of curriculum-based measurement: "Big ideas" and avoiding confusion. In M.R. Shinn (Ed.), *Advanced applications of curriculum-based measurement* (pp. 1–31). New York: Guilford Press.

Skiba, R., Deno, S., Marston, D., & Casey, A. (1989). Influence of trend estimation and subject familiarity on practitioners' judgment of intervention effectiveness. *Journal of Special Education, 22,* 433–446.

Skiba, R., & Peterson, R. (2000). School discipline at a crossroads: From zero tolerance to early response. *Exceptional Children, 66*(3), 335–346.

Sprague, J. R. & Golly, A. (2004). Best behavior: Building positive behavior support in schools. Longmont , CO: Sopris West Educational Services.

Sprick, R. S. (2003). *START on time! Safe transitions and reduced tardies.* Eugene, OR: Pacific Northwest Publishing.

Sprick, R. S. (2006). *Discipline in the secondary classroom: A positive approach to behavior management* (2nd ed). San Francisco: Jossey-Bass.

Sprick, R. S., & Booher, M. (2006). Behavior support and response to intervention: a systematic approach to meeting the social/emotional needs of students. *Communique, 35*(4), 34–36.

Sprick, R. S. Borgmeier, C., & Nolet, V. W. (2002). Intervention for prevention and management of secondary level behavior problems. In G. Stoner, M. R. Shinn, & H. Walker (Eds.), *Interventions: School psychologists in the schools.* Washington, DC: National Association of School Psychologists.

Sprick, R. S., & Garrison, M. (2001). Make your school's hallways safe and secure: Part 1. *Inside School Safety, 5*(11), 9–11.

Sprick, R. S., & Garrison, M. (2008). *Interventions: Evidence-based behavior strategies for individual students.* Eugene, OR: Pacific Northwest Publishing.

Sprick, R. S., Garrison, M., & Howard, L. (1998). *CHAMPs: A proactive and positive approach to classroom management.* Eugene, OR: Pacific Northwest Publishing.

Sprick, R. S., Garrison, M., & Howard, L. (2002). *Foundations: Establishing positive discipline and school wide behavior support* (2nd ed.). Eugene, OR: Pacific Northwest Publishing.

Sprick, R. S., Howard, L., Wise, B.J., Marcum, K., & Haykin, M. (1998*). Administrator's desk reference of behavior management* (Vols. 1–3). Eugene, OR: Pacific Northwest Publishing.

Sprick, R. S., Knight, J., Reinke, W., & McKale, T. (2007). *Coaching classroom management: Strategies and tools for administrators and coaches.* Eugene, OR: Pacific Northwest Publishing.

Sprick, R. S., Sprick, M., & Garrison, M. (1992). *Foundations: Developing positive schoolwide discipline policies.* Longmont, CO: Sopris West

Sprick, R. S., Swartz, L., & Glang, A. (2005). *On the playground: A guide to playground management.* Eugene, OR: Pacific Northwest Publishing and Oregon Center for Applied Sciences.

Sprick, R. S., Swartz, L., & Glang, A. (2007*). In the driver's seat: A roadmap to managing student behavior on the bus.* Eugene, OR: Pacific Northwest Publishing and Oregon Center for Applied Sciences.

Stager, G. S. (1995). Laptop schools lead the way in professional development. *Educational Leadership, 53*(2), 78–81.

Sterling-Turner, H. E., Watson, T. S., & Moore, J. W. (2002). The effects of direct training and treatment integrity on treatment outcomes in school consultation. *School Psychology Quarterly, 17,* 47–77.

Stewart, R. M., Benner, G., Martella, R., & Marchand-Martella, N. (2007). Three-tier models of reading and behavior: A research review. *Journal of Positive Behavior Interventions, 9,* 239–253.

Stokes, T. F., & Baer, D. M. (1977). An implicit technology of generalization. *Journal of Applied Behavior Analysis, 19,* 349–367.

Strain, P., Guralnick, M., & Walker, H. (1986). *Children's social behavior: Development, assessment and modification (*Chapter 4). Orlando, FL: Academic Press.

Sugai, G., & Horner, R. H. (2002). The evolution of discipline practices: School-wide positive behavior supports. *Child and Family Behavior Therapy, 24,* 23–50.

Sugai, G., & Horner, R. H. (2006). A promising approach for expanding and sustaining school-wide positive behavior support. *School Psychology Review, 35,* 245–259.

Sugai, G., Horner, R. H., Dunlap, G., Hieneman, M., Lewis, T., Nelson, C. M., et al. (2000). Applying positive behavior support and functional behavioral assessment in schools. *Journal of Positive Behavioral Interventions, 2,* 131–143.

Sugai, G., Horner, R. H., & Gresham, F. M. (2002). Behaviorally effective school environments. In M. Shinn, H. Walker, & G. Stoner (Eds.), *Interventions for academic and behavior problems II* (pp. 315–350). Bethesda, MD: National Association of School Psychologists.

Sugai, G., Horner, R. H., & McIntosh, K. (2008). Best practices in developing a broad scale system of school-wide positive behavior support. In A. Thomas & J. Grimes (Eds.), *Best practices in school psychology V* (pp. 765–780). Bethesda, MD: National Association of School Psychologists.

Sugai, G., & Lewis, T. J. (1996). Preferred and promising practices for social skills instruction. *Focus on Exceptional Children, 29,* 1–6.

Sugai, G., & Lewis, T. J. (2004). Social skills instruction in the classroom. In C. Darch & E. J. Kame'enui (Eds.), *Instructional classroom management: A proactive approach to behavior management* (2nd ed.). Upper Saddle River, NJ: Pearson/ Prentice Hall.

Sugai, G., Sprague, J., Horner, R., & Walker, H. (2000). Preventing school violence: The use of office referral to assess and monitor school-wide discipline interventions. *Journal of Emotional and Behavioral Disorders, 8,* 94–101.

Sugai, G., & Tindal, G. (1993). *Effective school consultation: An interactive approach.* Pacific Grove, CA: Brooks/Cole.

Sulzer-Azaroff, B., & Mayer, G. (1991). *Behavior analysis for lasting change.* Chicago: Holt, Rinehart, & Winston.

Sutherland, K. S., Wehby, J., & Copeland, S. (2000). Effect of varying rates of behavior-specific praise on the on-task behavior of students with EBD. *Journal of Applied Behavior Analysis, 8,* 2–8.

Task Force on Promotion and Dissemination of Psychological Procedures (1995). Training in and dissemination of empirically-validated psychological treatments. *The Clinical Psychologist, 48,* 3–23.

Taylor-Greene, S., Brown, D., Nelson, L., Longton, J., Gassman, T., Cohen, J., et al. (1997). School-wide behavioral support: Starting the year off right. *Journal of Behavioral Education, 7,* 99–112.

Tedeschi, R. G., & Kilmer, R. P. (2005). Assessing strengths, resilience, and growth to guide clinical interventions. *Professional Psychology: Research and Practice, 36,* 230–237.

Telzrow, C. F. (1995). Best practices in facilitating intervention adherence. In A. Thomas & J. Grimes (Eds.), *Best practices in school psychology III* (pp. 501–518). Washington, DC: National Association of School Psychologists.

Terpstra, J. E., & Tamura, R. (2008). Effective social interaction strategies for inclusive settings. *Journal of Early Childhood Education, 35,* 405–411.

Tharp, R. G., & Wetzel, R. J. (1969). *Behavior modification in the natural environment.* New York: Academic Press.

Thompson, T., Symon, F.J., & Felce, D. (2000). Principles of behavioral observation: Assumptions and strategies. In Thomson, T., Felce, D., & Symons, F.J. (Eds.). *Behavioral observation: Technology and applications in developmental disabilities* (pp. 3–16). Baltimore: Brookes.

Tombari, M. L., & Bergan, J. R. (1978). Consultant cues and teacher verbalizations, judgments, and expectancies concerning children's adjustment problems. *Journal of School Psychology, 16,* 212–219.

Tryon, G., & Winograd, G. (2002). Goal consensus and collaboration. In J. C. Norcross (Ed.), *Psychotherapy relationships that work: Therapist contributions and responsiveness to patients* (pp. 109–125). New York: Oxford University Press.

Upah, K. (2008). Best practices in designing, implementing, and evaluating quality interventions. In A. Thomas & J. Grimes (Eds.), *Best practices in school psychology V* (pp. 209–223). Bethesda, MD: National Association of School Psychologists.

U.S. General Accounting Office. (2002). *School dropouts: Education could play a stronger role in identifying and disseminating promising prevention strategies* (GAO-02-240). Washington, DC: Author.

Van Leuvan, P., & Wang, M. C. (1997). An analysis of students' self-monitoring in first- and second-grade classrooms. *Journal of Educational Research, 90*(3), 132–143.

Walker, H. M. (1995). *The acting out child: Coping with classroom disruption* (2nd ed.). Longmont, CO: Sopris West.

Walker, H. M. (2004). Commentary: Use of evidence-based interventions in schools: Where we've been, where we are, and where we need to go. *School Psychology Review, 33,* 398–497.

Walker, H. M., & Fabre, T. R. (1987). Assessment of behavior disorders in the school setting: Issues, problems, and strategies revisited. In N. G. Haring (Ed.), *Measuring and managing behavior disorders* (pp. 198–243). Seattle, WA: University of Washington Press.

Walker, H. M., Horner, R. H., Sugai, G., Bullis, M., Sprague, J. R., Bricker, D., & Kaufman. M. J. (1996). Integrated approaches to preventing antisocial behavior patterns among school-age youth. *Journal of Emotional and Behavioral Disorders, 4*, 193–256.

Walker, H. M., Kavanagh, K., Stiller, B., Golly, A., Severson, H. H., & Feil, E. G. (2001). First step to success: An early intervention approach for preventing school antisocial behavior. In H.M. Walker & M.H. Epstein (Eds.), *Making schools safer and violence free: Critical issues, solutions, and recommended practices* (pp. 73–87). Austin, TX: Pro-Ed.

Walker, H. M., Ramsey, E., & Gresham, F. M. (2004). *Antisocial behavior in schools: Evidence-based practices* (2nd ed.). Belmont, CA: Wadsworth.

Walker, H. M., Severson, H. H., Feil, E. G., Stiller, B., & Golly, A. (1998). First step to success: intervention at the point of school entry to prevent antisocial behavior patterns. *Psychology in the Schools, 35*, 259–269.

Walker, H. M., & Shinn, M. R. (2002). Structuring school-based interventions to achieve integrated primary, secondary, and tertiary prevention goals for safe and effective schools. In M. R. Shinn, G. Stoner, & H. M. Walker (Eds.), *Interventions for academic and behavior problems: Preventive and remedial approaches* (pp. 1–26). Silver Spring, MD: National Association of School Psychologists.

Walker, H. M., & Sprague, J. (2006). Early, evidence-based intervention with school-related behavior disorders: Key issues, continuing challenges, and promising practices. In J. B. Crockett, M.M. Gerber, & T. J. Landrum (Eds.), *Achieving the radical reform of special education: Essays in honor of James M. Kauffman.* Lawrence Erlbaum Associates.

Walker, H. M., Stiller, B., Golly, A., Kavanagh, K., Severson, H. H., & Feil, E. G. (1997). *First step to success: Helping children overcome antisocial behavior: Implementation guide.* Longmont, CO: Sopris West.

Warberg, A., George, N., Brown, D., Churan, K., & Taylor-Greene, S. (1995). *Behavior education plan handbook.* Elmira, Oregon: Fern Ridge Middle School.

Warger, C. (1999). *Positive behavior support and functional assessment* (ERIC/OSEP Digest E580). Reston, VA: ERIC Clearinghouse on Disabilities and Gifted Education. (ERIC Document Reproduction Service No. ED434437)

Watson, L. S. (1967). Application of operant conditioning techniques to institutionalized severely and profoundly retarded children. *Mental Retardation Abstracts, 4*, 1–18.

Watson, T., & Sterling-Turner, H. (2008). Best practices in direct behavioral consultation. In A. Thomas & J. Grimes (Eds.), *Best practices in school psychology V* (pp. 1661–1672). Bethesda, MD: National Association of School Psychologists.

Weissberg, R. P., & Gesten, E. L. (1982). Considerations for developing effective school-based social problem-solving (SPS) training programs. *School Psychology Review, 11,* 56–63.

Whelan, R. J. (2005). Personal reflections. In J. M. Kauffman (Ed.), *Characteristics of emotional and behavioral disorders of children and youth* (8th ed., pp. 66–70). Upper Saddle River, NJ: Merrill/Prentice Hall.

White, J., & Mullis, F. (1998). A systems approach to school counselor consultation. *Education, 119,* 242–253.

White, M., & Epston, D. (1990). *Narrative means to a therapeutic ends.* New York: Norton.

Wickstrom, K. F., & Witt, J. C. (1993). Assessment in behavioral consultation: The initial interview. *School Psychology Review, 12,* 42–49.

Witt, J. C., VanDerHeyden, A. M., & Gilbertson, D. (2004). Troubleshooting behavioral interventions: A systematic process for finding and eliminating problems. *School Psychology Review, 33*(3), 363–383.

Wood, B. K., Umbreit, J., Liaupsin, C. J., & Gresham, F. M. (2007). A treatment integrity analysis of function-based intervention. *Education and Treatment of Children, 30*(4), 105–120.

Yan, F., Beck, K., Howard, D., Shattuck, T., & Kerr, M. (2008). A structural model of alcohol use pathways among Latino youth. *American Journal of Health Behavior, 32,* 209–219.

Ysseldyke, J., Murns, M., Dawson, P., Kelley, B., Morrison, D., Ortiz, S., et al. (2006). *School psychology: A blueprint for training and practice III.* Bethesda, MD: National Association of School Psychologists.

Yu, M., Darch, C., & Rabren, K. (2002). Use of precorrection strategies to enhance reading performance of students with learning and behavior problems. *Journal of Instructional Psychology, 29,* 162–174.

Zins, J., & Erchul, W. (2002). Best practices in school consultation. In A. Thomas & J. Grimes (Eds.), *Best practices in school psychology IV* (pp. 625–643). Washington, DC: National Association of School Psychologists.